WINTER HARVEST

WINTER HARVEST:

JEWISH WRITING IN ST. LOUIS, 2006-2011

Edited by Howard Schwartz
and Barbara Raznick

The Brodsky Library Press

St. Louis

2011

Cover art © 2011 by Tsila Schwartz

This book was brought to publication with
generous assistance from the following
Benefactors
Marian and Maurice Hirsch
Martha B. and Robert E. Kohn
Anne H. Bader
Jerry and Rosalie Brasch
Rabbi James Stone Goodman
The Sachs Fund

Contributors
Anna Navarro and Harriet Blickenstaff
Inda Shaenen and Michael Dee
Carmie and Shelly Fredman
Bob and Millie Kaufman
Susan Feigenbaum and Jay Pepose
Carol M. Portman
Lawrence and Miriam Raskin
Robert and Martha Senior
Larry and Lisa Orden Zarin

Typesetting and Layout by Jeff Hirsch

Winter Harvest: Jewish Writing in St. Louis, 2006-2011

ISBN 0-9657880-2-4

The Saul Brodsky Jewish Community Library is a beneficiary agency
of the Jewish Federation of St. Louis

Visit the Saul Brodsky Jewish Community Library online at
www.brodskylibrary.org

and the Jewish Federation gateway to the Jewish community
of St. Louis at **www.jewishinstlouis.org**

Special thanks to Lorraine Landy and Miriam Roth.

Contents

Howard Schwartz & Barbara Raznick   *xiii*   Introduction

I POETRY

Elaine Alexander	3	Elegy for Isaac
Gloria Attoun	6	Cycle
	6	Heartbeat (a song)
Leah Silberman Bernstein	8	Before Creation
	8	Sagging Flabby
	9	Timeless and Ageless
L.D. Brodsky	12	Rainbow
	12	Superjew
	14	Magical Alphabet
Jan Castro	16	Beginning is the End
	16	Upon Approaching Man en Vrouw, 1964, by E. Dodergne (b. 1923)
	17	La Velata, Pitti Palace
Michael Castro	18	Contraction
	19	Stella's Story
	21	The Knots
	22	Undergrowth
Jack Cohen	25	It was the Law
Allison Creighton	26	The Nameless Sea
	27	Iowa
	27	Bed of Thorns
	27	On a Night Too Hot for a Sheet
Helen Eisen	29	Tikkun
	29	Illumination
	30	Afterwards
	31	Undressed
Merle Fishlowitz	32	Megiddo
Ronnie Fredman	33	Moses Climbed Mount Sinai
	33	I Met Confucius
	34	Jerusalem--Yerushalayim
Jeff Friedman	36	The Golem in the Suburbs
	36	Blessing for the Hats
	37	Night of the Rabbi
	39	Noah Looks Back
	40	Jacob and the Angel
	41	Burial at the River
James Stone Goodman	43	Jeremiah's Plan for Peace

	45	To David a Song
	46	Yehudah HaLevi Meets Shlomo Ibn Gavirol
	47	O Heavens O Earth
	48	The Prince and the Prophetess
	49	The Prince Wants
	50	The Prince and the Healing
Suzanne Greenwald	51	The Warning
Maurice Hirsch	52	Choosing Burial Plots
	52	Building Blocks
	54	Camp Nebagamon
	55	Sparta, Illinois – 1963
	55	Foment
	56	October Night on the Huzzah
Jane Ellen Ibur	57	Mrs. Noah's Seduction
	58	Mrs. Noah's Sing-a-Long
	60	Third Year
Bob Karsh	62	The Only President: FDR in memoriam
Lynn Levin	63	Azazel
	64	Eve and Lilith Back at the Garden
Morton Levy	66	An American Survivor
	67	The Auctioneer's Window
	68	The Avenger
Marvin Marcus	70	My Life in Architecture
	72	My Life in Hebrew
	75	The Holocaust, Uncle Shmuel, and I
Steven Moskowitz	80	A Modern Rendition of Psalm 150
Nikki Nymark	81	Angels
	82	Her Hands, Her Hair
	83	When They Ask Us Who We Are
Jerry Perkoff	85	Dante's Dream
	85	Chrysalis
	86	I Am A Jew
Nancy Powers Prichard	88	Thou Shalt Not Covet
	88	Evening at Home
Marilyn Probe	90	My Beginnings, Scraps of Memory
	91	The Little Jewish Girl in Iowa, 1901-1903

	92	When I looked Out Our Window
	92	My Brother Ben and I Were Pals
	93	During the 1904 World's Fair
	94	The Nights Were Quiet
	94	We Liverd by the Water Tower
	96	Tikkun Olam
	96	Windy City of My Yiddish Past
Carol Rose	97	Lodged in the Heart
	97	Lunar Plexus
	98	Keep the Nightmares from Her Sleep
	99	Rabin Square
	100	When They Bowed Their Heads
Ann Leslie Rosen	101	God's House
	101	Blessing
	102	Fourth Grade
Jane Schapiro	103	Coming Upon My Old Diary
Amy Scharff	104	Letting Go
Jackie Schechter	106	Cardinals
	107	Reading in the Dark
Lon Schneider	108	Kafka
Steven Schreiner	109	Even in a Dream the Dead are like the Photograph Still Inside the Camera
	111	Heartless
	112	Barren
Henry I. Schvey	115	Sleepaway Camp
Howard Schwartz	116	Breathing in the Dark
	117	A Portrait of My Son
	117	Spirit Guide
	118	Feathers
	119	Escape Artist
Shira Schwartz	121	Soul Journey
	121	Water Poem
Nathan Simon	123	Cartography
	124	From the Autobiography of Benvenutto Cellini
	124	To Sari at Forty
Pat Lorraine Simons	126	At the Holocaust Museum in Washington, D.C.
Jason Sommer	127	Film Clips of Munkacs, 1933
	130	What Old David Felt

	130	Sons of Adam
Judith Stix	131	The Holocaust Memorial, Washington, D.C.
	132	Two Enchantments
Maria Szapszewicz	133	I Promise I Will Tell the World
	134	Today Never Tomorrow
Jane O. Wayne	135	Seven Years Later
	136	The Portrait
	137	Visits
	138	A Quick Lesson
	139	A Distant Cello Plays (November 10, 1938)
Sharon Weissman	140	In Loving Memory of Cantor Edward Fogel
	141	My Rabbi's Hands
Renee Winter	142	To Stephanie Ruth
	143	With Benefit of Kaddish

II FICTION

Lane Barnholtz	147	Pavel Spits on Stalin
Laurie Bennett	163	You're Welcome
Denise Bogard	166	The Song at the Sea
Edward Farber	173	Papa's House
Jeff Friedman	180	Family
Michael Getty	182	The Tower
Andrea Jackson	185	Second Thoughts
Natasha Kaminsky	186	Jerusalem Stone
Bob Karsh	193	Compensatory Advantage
Susan Koppelman	199	Her Mother's Chicken Soup
Robert M. Levin	203	A Brief History of Howard
Stacey Levine	208	The Day of Silver Candlesticks
Charlotte Mielziner	211	The Secret
Barry Nove	216	Isaac in a Bind, Again
Howard Schwartz	225	The Celestial Orchestra
Joe Schwartz	230	King of Hearts
Rachel Schwartz	238	Leaving Anatevka
Pat Lorraine Simons	248	Snippet
Pamela Singer	252	Letter to Frieda in Antwerp

III LIFE STORIES

Beth Arky	259	Hello Muddah, Hello Faddah, Sure Did Love It, at Camp Sabra
Abby Bader	261	Bubby

Debra Solomon Baker	263	Plenty of Wednesdays
	265	To Piwniczna
Diann Joy Bank	267	My Bubbela
Henry Berger	269	How I Came to My Jewish Identity and Did It Matter
Saramina Berman	278	B'sharet
Ben Fixman	282	My Mother
Harris Frank	285	Whatever Happened to the Sunday Family Dinner?
Shelly R. Fredman	287	Writing Towards Home
Yonason Goldson	290	Shylock in Jerusalem
James Stone Goodman	303	Jackie
Felicia Graber	307	The Old Woman
Rita Horwitz	310	Childhood Memories of the World War II Years
Sharon Katz-Weintraub	313	An Eternal Flame
	313	Around the Corner
Cissy Lacks	315	From Miriam's Way (chapter four)
	321	Llama lo arba?
Morton Levy	323	The Saturday Debating Society
Bobbi Linkemer	326	Unconditional Love
Liz Lippa	329	My Jewish Identity
Gerry Mandel	333	Under the Red Goose Sign
Maryellen McSweeney	336	Mrs. Rubenstein
Miriam Friedman Morris	338	In the Aftermath of the Holocaust, St. Louis was Home
Steven Moskowitz	355	Funeral Blues
Jordan Oakes	357	The Jews of Rolla
Miriam Spiegel Raskin	360	Bedtime Stories
	365	Questions Without Answers
Warren Rosenbloom	368	Philosemitism: A Berlin Story
Leah Rubin	372	Millicent's Journey
Margaret R. Ruhe-Spencer	382	Daddy's Story
Amy Scharff	387	The Lost Spirit of Micah
Howard Schwartz	395	Close Calls
Miriam Schwartz	397	An Israeli Flightmare
Bettina Schwarzman	404	Seders in the Basement and Story Time at the Brodsky Library
Ronit Sherwin	407	Painted Toe Nails
Nathan M. Simon	409	Halitzah: The Unloosing

IV ESSAYS

Laurie Bennett	423	Our Daughters

Robert A. Cohn   425   Papa Portnoy Revisited: Philip
                            Roth as a Stepfather
Marty Ehrlich   442   Words on Music
Shelly R. Fredman 444   With a Prayer
Daniel Kohn   446   The Times—They Have a'
                            Changed! Thoughts on the
                            Relationship between Diaspora
                            Jewry and the State of Israel
Robert E. Kohn   456   The Jewess in Kate Chopin's *The
                            Awakening*
Pier Marton   459   Beyond Belief
Howard Schwartz   469   Gathering the Sparks
Susan Talve   471   Synagogue: Breaking the Color
                            Barrier
Randy Zimring   477   If I Close My Eyes

                     481   Notes on the Contributors

Introduction

With the publication of *Winter Harvest,* the Jewish community in St. Louis has continued the tradition established in 1997 and in 2005 with the publication of the two previous anthologies of Jewish writing in St. Louis, *First Harvest* and *New Harvest.* This has now become an historic tradition, in that St. Louis is still the only city in the world whose Jewish community has produced such anthologies of its Jewish writers. This collection could not exist without the support of local writers who continued to encourage the editors, and we are especially grateful to Maurice Hirsch and Robert Kohn for their exceptional support. We are also grateful to the generous contributors who made this publication possible. We fully believe that these anthologies offer a vivid and accurate portrait of the rich literary life found among the Jewish writers of St. Louis. For the editors, it is especially interesting to note the rise of a new generation of talented writers, as well as the exceptionally rich and beautiful writing found among the older, established writers.

We have focused on four important categories of writing, Poetry, Fiction, Life Stories, and Essays. We know from past experience that the life stories are the most popular among readers, and we know our readers will enjoy the wide range of stories recounted here. Those who read the sections of poetry and fiction will be greatly rewarded, as our writers have shared their finest work. And those who read the section of essays will find much food for thought.

The publication of these anthologies has also been accompanied by very well attended readings, in which the writers represented came together to share from their works. We are planning such a reading for this publication as well, and we hope that you, our readers, will join us.

Howard Schwartz
and Barbara Raznick

I
Poetry

Elaine Alexander
Elegy for Isaac

You were a small, saline pool,
Split from the sea.
And the sun was searing.
Dispassionate.
Its rays: prick, prick, prick.

You were parched.
Entirely alone.
You thought: surely
I will perish of thirst.

Prick, prick, prick.
You began rising
Out of yourself.
Molecule by molecule,

Prick, prick, prick.
You left yourself behind,
Bit by bit.
You hung in the air.
You were scattered.

Prick, prick, prick.
You watched yourself from above
Turning to a crust of salt.
You were past caring,
Dry and numb.

Then, the sky grew dark.
It wasn't night, but the sun was gone.
And—the booming.
It went all through you.
From one end to the other.
Your knees were as water.
You were that frightened.
But nobody saw.

Not even in the quick, jagged light.
And that's when you dared to cry.

First, only silent weeping.
But then your grief gathered.
It sucked all the sound
You had ever known
Into itself,
It became you,
You became it:
A ravenous screaming.

And when you lay
Hoarse and spent,
It began to rain.

With your mouth to the sky,
Drop by drop,
The crust dissolved.
You were restored to yourself.
Larger than ever before.
And you slipped
Into a deep, dreamless slumber.

Before too long,
Again the dispassionate sun.
But—the very, next day
And part of the day
After that was grey
And misted.
And instead of the sun,
A benevolent bier.
Or... No. No. Not a bier.
A canopy of water and air,
To keep you safe and deep.
A reprieve.
A gift from the universe to you.

But too late.
Already the monster had sprung
From your own silvery throat.

Gloria Attoun
Cycle

I am awakened by
heat
after cool.
Aroused by the tightness
in my scored, splitting shell.
I call to you
my mate of memory
in the lush haze of our summered frenzy
when days last always a lifetime.
We will sourround the trees,
the sky,
the others
and hold them prisoner
in a cage of sound
until the cool, night air
tightens our breath to nothing.
Like unwanted fruit,
we will litter the paths
until we are only
one slow tired ticking.

When the days become too short for songs,
the purpose of our frantic yearning
lies beneath the frozen ground--
waiting
for their own urgent calling.

Heartbeat (a song)

My beginning
comes from air
Somewhere out there, but I'm not sure where.
Maybe from the hum
Or a beat of a drum
Or from a ring that goes ding

Or a voice that says
"Come".

    When did I start? Will I ever be done?
    Questions can be answered if you ask the right ones.
    What makes a heartbeat?
    What keeps it going?
    It could stop like that without anybody knowing.

Will the time come when I've learned life's dance?
The first hint of green
I've got another chance
The drone of the grass and the wave of a tree
Open up the window
Hear a symphony.

    When did I start? Will I ever be done?
    Questions can be answered if you ask the right ones.
    What makes a heartbeat?
    What keeps it going?
    It could stop like that without anybody knowing.

Rain.
Each drop is a word
I can pick and I can choose any word that is heard
Warm, wet words fall down at my feet
And they turn into a puddle that's giving and sweet.

    When did I start?
    Will I ever be done?
    Questions can be answered if you ask the right ones.
    What makes a heart beat?
    What keeps it going?
    It could stop like that without anybody knowing.

Leah Silberman-Bernstein
Before Creation

God
Close Your eyes
And see Within
A swirling spectrum upon
stars shooting stars
Dream of the surreal
the *not yets*
the *weres*
whirring by instants
hints of
openings winding and crowning
through the soul potent pot
imagination envisioning a rainbow
"Let there be
Light," and there
was light.

Sagging Flabby

I am witness
to my body
what were once
tight closeknit curves
are becoming
stretched
marked
rounded
oblonged
swollen then deflated
then swollen again
with milk to nourish
to nurse
to mother.

I pray that my child
will always know
will always feel
that the sagging flabby
which grew as she grew
inside me
softened me, loosened me,
spiraled me curvier and more wonder full
to be
there to hug and hold on
outside me
that the sagging flabby is
a post-Renaissance painter's model
softer to hug and hold onto
to be
a foundation of her spirit
so that when I become just
a spirit,
my child will
know in the deepest depths
of the support and spiritlove
that guides
and sighs with pride
and
loooooooooove

Timeless and Ageless

Daughters of God,
At once, we know we are women
our power, our beauty, timeless and ageless.
internally, we move through life with our secrets, hidden
delicate existences tight as a rope walk through time
if they knew, if we told the untellable stories
our tales of war, of woe

Three Daughters of Israel
Of Hannah[1] who watched her seven sons

[1] The First Book of the Maccabees, Apocrypha Literature.

one by one, make the choice, of her tutelage
to die rather than worship their idol god.
Her pride, her terror, her future
beheaded blunt and abrupt.

Of Judith[2],
slowly, she peeled off her shroud of mourning
for the love of her life, each layer of sack cloth
the last symbol of her true love. "people die in war"
they told her, as if that cold fact
could remove the pain buried in the dark cave
of her soul, naked
her skin shone radiantly glowing
reborn with a mission, which Judith wore
as she exited the besieged gate of Jerusalem –
Into the wilderness, at night
Judith arrived at his tent
soldiers let her pass, they saw vulnerability.
what could she be carrying in her bag?
Surely, some bits of fun and games
to accessorize her flowing, diaphanous gown.
a floating goddess, ethereal Aphrodite
come to earth for a spell with Holofernes.
With her slender finger and bared arm,
she opened her bag to offer him cheeses
and yet another goblet of wine,
to quench his thirst
"Your days at battle must be so hard
It is night now, a dark starless night
Rest, in peace, my sleepy dear."
As Judith moved through the soldiers' tents,
toward *her* city gate
the soldiers saw only her curves,
they failed to recognize the familiar look in her eye
of a battle won, a victorious soldier.
the soldiers did notice her weightier bag
which she tried not to struggle to carry.
Given only to the choicest prostitutes
must be a gift from Holofernes.

---

[2] The Book of Judith, Apocrypha Literature.

Nameless[3], our last heroine remains
maybe making her story the most important to recount
so unknown, her tale is barely a *midrash* of *Chanukah*.
it is best that we do not know her name.
how does a mother burden an innocent newborn
with such an unbearable load?
As her father gave her away on her wedding day
more beautiful she never looked, they all said
the fire burning her cheeks rosy, her lips crimson
had its source with the uniformed man beyond the crowd
waiting with a tightly smirked mouth
for her, *jus prima noctis*
this first night would be his,
as joyous guests danced around her and her *chatan*.
She saw the married women whose destinies would be
her rite of passage into the hushed talks.
Inside, screaming and shouting, leaping onto the table
as she stripped off her clothes
furiously until there was nothing left
but the embarrassment of her brothers
Judah, Jonathan, Simon, John, Eleazar
each of her *Maccabee* brothers lurching toward her,
and her father, Mattathias
whose expression startled her back
At once, she realized that her internal fear and fury had found its release,
quite publicly.
But as she stood above the crowd of guests,
the uniformed man was smiling broadly now
tonight's romp would be more intriguing with this one.
She lifted her strong arm and pointed at him.
Her brothers immediately understood this look
in her eye and gave that look
the power to kill.

Timeless and Ageless
our beauty, *our stories* of war
our power, in the darkness, to ignite a candle,
to light.

---

[3] Mimekor Yisrael: Classical Jewish Folktales, Volume 1, collected by Micha Joseph Bin Gorion. (Late 19th Century). Edited by Emanuel bin Gorion. Translated by I.M. Lask. Indiana University Press, Bloomington and London.

L.D. Brodsky
Rainbow

Now, Mount Ararat fades
Like a graveside face
Shrinking back into a shroud.

My weathered vessel
Slides further away from shore,
With the tidal sway.

The past has trapped me below deck,
In its cargo hold —
Just another chunk of ballast.

Adrift, perpetually lost
In miasmic waters,
I attempt to stave off desperation

By counting the rats
Scurrying through my hallucinations,
Gnawing at my paranoia,

And hope, one day, perhaps,
By gratuitous accident,
I might awaken to discover myself

Becalmed, content, permanently anchored
At the base of a rainbow,
Free to begin dismantling my ark.

Superjew

He's a kibitzing kibbutz-rube in the big city,
A mild-mannered cub reporter
For the *Jerusalem Daily Planet*,
Who operates out of the men's room at the King David Hotel,
Assigned, by day, to interview Palestinian suicide bombers

And, by night, to work the Dung Gate/Aish HaTorah beat.
He's a seasoned vet of a dozen Armageddons
(Including the Six-Day and Yom Kippur wars),
Poised to locate, at the drop of a yarmulke,
An empty phone booth, doff his suit,
Perforated captoes, horn-rimmed glasses, club tie,
Streimel, payess, phylacteries, tallis, and beard,
Fly into the sky, in his cape, tights, blue-and-white tutu,
And make a spectacle of himself,
Zooming through a multitude of aahs, oohs, and oy veys,
Tying up Yassir Arafat, Lex Luthor,
And their main squeeze, Miss Abdullah Teschmacher,
As she flaunts her Monica Lewinsky designer bra and thong.
He's a skyscraper-leaping Messiah come in the flesh,
To save the Promised Land of Matzopolis from itself.

He cuts a certifiably meshuga figure,
For a latter-day planetary saint on the run,
A loose cannon on the deck of Ben-Gurion's *Pequod*,
That desert vessel out of the ancient seaport of Jaffa,
On the bum, on the skids, down on its luck,
A ghost ship without a home port, in a storm,
A three-master with cruciform rigging,

Sporting, on its sails, a skull-and-crossbones swastika
Inside a Mogen David.
He's Clark Kent, Benyamin Netanyahu, and Golda Meir
All rolled up into one Hasbro action figure.
He's archetypal, surreal — a mensch,
Savior of Holocaust victims, Ethiopians, Russians,
Brooklynites making frequent-flier-mile aliyahs,
And other wandering putzes.
But where are the omniscient Adonai, Perry White
(To help Superjew keep the Sabbath holy, keep kosher),
And that all-American *shiksa*, Lois Lane
(To relieve his bodacious case of lover's nuts)?
They're in the kitchen, frying kryptonite bacon.

Magical Alphabet

The alphabet he employs, today,
Is of the same posthieroglyphic script
Egyptians were using in 1900 B.C.,
To communicate, with symbols of sounds,
Their deepest feelings, visions, fears,
Noble philosophies, proud histories, theologies,
And most capacious meditations on timelessness and life.

He knows those strokes cold,
Recognizes those letters that form his words
As having had their beginnings many long generations ago,
Earlier, by millenniums,
Than when he learned to compose poems.
He has no doubts about this,
This exquisite curse that's haunted him since his birth.

But before he ever lays down a line of verse,
He turns heavenward, closes his eyes,
And finds himself inside ancient minds,
He, like them, inspired by the divine in mankind,
Moved to unite all the past with the future,
Despite the ineluctable unknown,
Its reluctance to disclose its holy design.

Once contemplating his mortal possibilities,
He settles in for an exuberant spell of internal rhyming,
With a passion to create something beautiful and new,
Something few have dared to bring into being:

Decoded genome, nuclear fission, Cubistic guitar,
Reconfiguration of a Ptolemaic universe,
Movable type, gunpowder, Earth.

But in the final analysis, as in the first,
It's the gift of this magic alphabet
That allows him to map his soul's Promised Land,
Every wadi and desert, garden, oasis, and grotto.

It's his vast vocabulary that frees him from the quotidian,
Sanctifies his permission to wander alone
And scribble on cliffs and stones and tablets,

Inscribe, on papyrus, with his mystical reed-pen,
Spiritual lyrics his ancestors whispered and sang,
Whether Sumerians, Egyptians, or Judeans,
Recording them for a posterity he's terrified won't exist
When it comes time for his writings to be excavated
From their cave-preserved clay pots —
Dead Sea Scroll–poems he conceives in his dreams.

Jan Garden Castro
Beginning is the End
After Michelangelo, Sistine Chapel

You take my hand. We are not lovers but
the original makers of love – the
pulse and heart of skin stretched taut
around the globe, skin variously humped
with cities made and unmade by man: once
mountains and rivers fed each other,
forests thick with trees made their own rain…

Can a man be known for his crimes the way you are
known for taking back your hand? Who knows
where this skin of ours stretches or if
the message in our bloods unites us the instant before
our fingers draw apart?

Upon Approaching Man en Vrouw, 1964, by E. Dodergne
(b. 1923)

I entered the garden
wthout a map, the way
one enters one's mind
lost in sleep.

          And here they were,
in stone, a manandwoman
connected by the crude
diagonals of chisels,
by the outjuttings of bodily parts, by
proximity. The hands that
made them together also
kept them apart.
          Her face was split
and his, unbridled,
had indifferent eyes
and no mouth.

They were of the same place and time
yet had not yet
the gift (or the
curse) of speech.

Kröller-Müller Museum, Otterlo, The Netherlands

La Velata, Pitti Palace[1]

You paint your love *only:*
the mudbrown background softens beside
the undecorated gauze veil over hair and shoulders,
the white dress, revealing bodice, empire sleeves,
bellowing gold cording <the copyist has it bronze>,
her peerless skin <the copyist is not getting
the tone, making it olive rather than fawn>,
the jewel in her hair <he has it too white>.

Her hand embracing book to breast --
a large gesture, relaxed and confident
<he has her fingers further apart>.
Her face! <He has not the *bowl* of it!>
Ovaline circle filled with small lips,
relaxed <not so red> peach,
nose simple and straight <too much shadow!>

Eyes pure and brown
echo the background,
form the center <you have them too dark>.
And last, the variegated amber beads
circling her neck, a wide neck,
one you loved.

[1] The Veiled Lady, Raphael's Fornarina, lifelong love, model for Madonna of San Sisto.

Michael Castro
Contraction

Something in me wants to resist,
to pull back from full participation
in the creation of the moment.

Kabbalah describes a resistance
like this that existed within God himself—
a part of "Ein Sof" held back
in the initial contraction--
a part apart, did not open out, did not beam,
held back from the subsequent creation.

Kabbalists related this resistance
to the origins of evil.

I wear a black baseball cap
with "OM" stenciled in white Sanskrit letters
above the brim.

I beam the unity of consciousness
out to an unconscious world.

I pour more
than myself into the poem.
Can I love, holding back?
Can I make light?

These are the struggles
of a poet, of a lover, of a man.

After God's contraction
something held back--
the radiant vessels shattered.

I walk searching
out the sparks,
amidst shards & shells
in a broken world.

Stella's Story

First they round us up
in the town square, on Rhodes, then ship
us like freight to Greece--
the lucky ones they drown--
unloaded ashore, shifted
from one darkness to another--
packed in boxcars, bouncing
& lurching, miles upon miles,
smothering in the terror--
where are we going?
                will we ever return?--
din of the engines
& the grinding wheels,
days on end in the August heat,
stench of sweat & piss & fear,
sickness & suicides, & wild
 (though in retrospect tame) rumors--
looks in eyes I'd never seen.

The doors open, we're herded out
into the clear Greek light,
suddenly tinged with an unspeakable evil.
We're in an open area, a sort of corral
adjoining the tracks, left to bake
& air out, while men with guarded eyes
service the train.
German guards issue numbers
& arrange us, behind their
uniforms, their rifles,
into small groups.
"Processing," they explain.
Officers move through
           to inspect the shipment--us.
One strides toward our group, he is very tall,
he has a riding crop--
This is Waldhiem.

How do I know?

Her eyes close. She points with her finger
to the bridge of her nose
& traces a straight line down.
His nose, she says, he had a large nose,
he was very tall, & those thin lips,
his voice . . .
Her eyes open.   I know him
a long time.
I watch him.
I see him
approach
my father. He is
shouting something in German.
We don't understand the language.
The words sound like growling and barking.
Waldhiem strikes my father with his crop, once, twice.
Father staggers backwards & falls.
Waldheim shouts at him again, raises his crop again,
my father is on the ground, inching backwards,
his hand raised to ward off the blow,
Waldhiem strikes again. Someone yells
a translation: *Take off your shoes.*
He thinks you're hiding gold.
Gold? In his shoes? Trembling,
Father pulls them off. All he has
to reveal are his feet & socks.
Waldheim looks away, inhales tightlipped rage
& looks around at us, at my mother
at the gold wedding ring he notices on her finger.
He erupts,
an explosion of abuse.
She understands, & yet she doesn't.
She pulls,
but mama's fingers are swollen & moist,
& the ring won't budge.
Waldhiem is screaming at her & at the guards. *Will he*
cut off her hand, her finger, kill her

My sister & I instinctively fly toward Mama.
We pull at the ring, crying. We pray & squeeze, push,   force it
off--thank God,
                    God!--
            & without a thought
throw the ring at Waldheim
as a thing
despised.

A subordinate goes down on his knees to retrieve it;
& Waldheim nods,
            & walks away with what
kind of expression
or feeling
I cannot say. He walks away
to his fate & fame
& leaves us, sends us   knowingly,
            to ours.

This was but a minor incident,
a few moments in a pitstop
en route to Auschwitz.
My family's last moments
together, in Greece

The Knots

To untie the knots sealing the soul's light
from the dream of life—
a slow unraveling, a slow climb.
Each unraveled seal, a labyrinth revealing
a rung on a rope ladder we ascend upon,
newly illuminated, toward the next seal.
The light must be rationed in bearable doses.

At new levels of illumination, perspective shifts:
white spaces on the page brim with deep meanings,
while the printed black letters recede

into obtuse obscurity.
God's secrets are etched
in white flame on black flame.

Undergrowth

Train tracks overgrown with wild grass.
Roads to death overgrown with life.
Insistent life asserts identity
pushily, through the earth, needing

no classification, no numeration, no objectifying.
Whitman saw the grass's meaning
as "there is no death" --
in absolute terms; & maybe
he's right, in absolute terms,
but here, by these tracks,
we deal with relatives.

Memory likes the grass to grow
likes the new to blur, & cover, & bury,
prefers the smell of dewy grass & spring's promises
to that of mass graves at the end of the line.

& so we survive, overgrowing, overgrown,
pushing forward life
& would, if we could, ignore
who we are
in a deep & rooted sense,
letting life's grassy fragrances
prevail.
But we can't quite forget.

The anguished ghosts are sometimes insistent
as the grass covering the tracks, haunting
like mist over the field
or a veil-like aura around us.
the places where they arrived
places in Europe

& in us.

The whispers of the ghosts are persistent, pushy,
they make us uncomfortable, for they are sounds of those
whose tongues were severed from the world,
whose names were denied,
whose souls & divinity
brutalized, unrecognized--
& they whisper horrors,
in a soundless language,
of what was done to them,
of what can be done to us too,
for we bear
their imprint,
their names,
their blood
We too
are pushy with life.

And these voices within us
whisper & warn,
if you really listen,
in the pride of your identity,
in the pride of your assumed victimhood,
they tell of what you can become
on either side
of the awful human equation.

Enough of that.
We don't want to hear it.

But dealing with absolute facts,
relatively,

there are almost no Jews left living
in Greece now, where once, vaguely within memory,
there were many.
Silent voices,
speaking ghostly Ladino,

swell with the wind,
from time to time,
in Salonika, Jannina, Corfu.
The temples are desolate, decaying,
awesomely silent,
scrawled & slurred with grafitti.

And the tracks that
the people--
men, women, children,
they *were* people,
humans,
rode away on,
packed like freight,
the tracks
are covered with wild grass
a dark wind whispers through.

The wind moves
pushily
through the high grass
of the graves of Europe.

Jack Cohen
It Was the Law

All the Jews, near and far
Were forced to wear a yellow star,
It was the law.

And when the mobs hurled stones
And when they broke Jewish bones,
It was the law.

The Nazis passed their laws with skill
Making it legal for them to kill,
It was the law.

Yes, there were a few
Who tried to help a Jew,
But, that was against the law.

Allison Creighton
The Nameless Sea

We'd been sailing all morning
some distance from the shore
when we stopped to watch the tide
lunging and receding—
lunging, then receding
into the sapphire water.

Your arms encircled me from behind
as waves crashed all around,
carrying echoes of your name to me
and then back out to sea.

We looked from the water
to the blue above
and saw no beginning—
we saw no end—
only scenes from our youth, playing
in the center of the sky.
We were laughing and running together
over an endless sea of sand.
But when we reached the water's edge
you didn't run into the water,
you ran into the sky.

I could feel you letting go—
your arms sliding away from mine,
your hands slipping from my skin.

Then echoes of my name
called from high winds
and gathered overhead
like the first peals of thunder.

I looked from the sky
to the tide,
lunging and receding—
lunging, then receding
into the sapphire water.

Iowa

I'd been alone for hours in the clear blue expanse
where the weeds, the rake, and the scarecrow
had fallen miles away. The wheels I'd seen
spinning for days, slipped over a gray horizon.

I heard footsteps—
but when I turned, no one was there,
just a heavy clothesline strung across a field
where the door of a vacant home had blown open.

Gathering clouds made the morning unclear,
and all I could feel was this vast distance—
flying forever ahead of me
and reaching for miles behind,
the past and future colliding
at the point where I stood.

Bed of Thorns

In late May you lay your body near a rose bed, blooming.
At your side lies a white-haired boy with eyes like the sea.

He says you're not alone each day you're growing older.
He pleads at last into your ear, *Break yourself in me.*

You wonder what these words mean. At night
moonlight lies upon your twisted bodies.

The wind crouches low beside you,
breathing of the blood a single thorn can bring.

On a Night Too Hot for a Sheet

Now that you have entered
the space that surrounds me,

we shall be as one.
I will pull you inside
with such a touch
that the finest light will waver.
Your lips are bittersweet
as the root of love itself.

One by one I hand you my secrets.
My fear of the color orange
and all its bright laughter.
A secret buried in a wild garden
where no one ever goes.
How I tried for decades
to tie two distant souls together.
Each way I struggled
to force another to speak.
The stark summer night
when childhood vanished
in an instant.
Days my tires spun
in lost rotations
down a country road far from home.
The shrinking black-out windows.
Shadows of my phantom's figure.
The thorn in his beard.

A tremor shifts across my body
as I start to tell the secret
too scared to breathe.
Your eyes, unblinking,
hover above me.
You wait and wait.
You press your body
hard against me,
a ghost.

Helen Eisen
Tikkun

Light is the needle
Darkness the thread

Rents in the sky
Are patched

With stars

And wind's breath
Polishes each stitch

Illumination

> *What is to give light must endure burning.* –Victor Frankl

As the rains roar, and lightning
finds another tree
I wonder if I, so near,
am struck as well
and suffer
as you did, and do

Were I seared and felled
might I yet endure—
(could I bear)
steadfast in the flame's
extinguishing light—
the burning

Am I, even now, breathing
white flame
cleaving to its will
or away, seeking in its sway
The way beyond
The way

Afterwards

I knew her father had been a tailor. I knew
in Vlotzlovik her home had been filled

with fabric, cut spare, worked on the kitchen table;
and I knew, here in America, everywhere I looked

were worn scraps, parts—of sheets, towels
pillowcases, socks—mended and re-mended—

to be ordered in drawers like little folded flags
or the shelved spines of books. In this new country

libraries of remnants—biography, adventure, anecdotes,
riddles, translated and un-translated, read and unread—

remnants of remnants my mother saved—bags of rags
in corners, under counters resting in assorted containments

of paper and plastic. Later with money came suede
or felt, drawstring bags kept for our leftover bits and pieces.

No longer holding elegant shoes, they lay plumped
or crumpled, dimpled with ears, tails, noses, shadow

kangaroos and bears, wild horses.   I imagined.
In my twenties, I addressed my mother in a poem.

I am not a right or wrong remnant of your self / pleat
and curl / placed /just so/ against the pattern.

I did not know then the Yiddish term for survivors: sheyes-hapleyte,
from the Hebrew she'arit hapleitah, literally the escaped remnant.

My language had been taken -- our language, our words covered
in shame. Children of survivor groups were still in the making,

Schindler's List for a while longer, unfilmed. I was a child of two
survivors. Books were stone and brick, barracks and wire and
thread.

We were thought of as lambs, sheared and led to slaughter.
Yet the masses of wool, scattered and gathered, somehow,

warmed a part of my home when I wrote to the mother
in my mind; even then, when I did not want to be

one of the remnants saved.

Undressed

There is nothing as naked as a naked body that is dead.
All the mystery there is in the world is contained under
skin that cools like wax – the wick is there, but there is
no movement, no warmth, no light. An absence I cannot
hear, that will not listen, enters a room, and disappears.
The match to light the wick will not light. It will not.

Merle Fischlowitz
Megiddo

Gathered stones mark the paths
where tourists walk
to view remains
of twenty civilizations.

Each painted sign explains
what men lived, fought,
and worshiped here.

"Warning! Danger of Collapse!"
guides us away from aged precipice,
as the roar of Phantoms,
flung Pharaoh-ward,
fills the valley, overwhelming
the sound of grass
covering the hill again.

Ronnie Fredman
Moses Climbed Mount Sinai

Moses climbed Mount Sinai
with an orange in his knapsack.

The orange was perfect in the presence of God.
In the presence of one million angels singing
In the presence of one thousand scribes
copying the word of God onto papyrus
In the presence of a prophet, a songwriter,
a poet asking the children of Israel
bittersweet with freedom
asking them to give ear,
to give a listen

and one billion ears gave a listen
and a symphony was born
amongst thorn bushes, cacti,
and sand

still
the orange was perfect

I Met Confucius

I met Confucius
through a darkened glass
whose silver skin was sloughing
part a mirror
part a mere window
gazing upon an odd shape shepherd
disparate

Here was Confucius
there was a tree
alive with the first buds of spring
trailing into the wisps of his beard

Here was Confucius
grasping the knob of his cane
which branched into the muddy stream
Here was the hem of his garment
embroidered with calligraphy
and footprints of the robin
hopping through
Here his eyes narrow
pupils glinting in the sunlight
like sparks off flint
waves dancing like lovers

Jerusalem—Yerushalayim
December 27, 2005

Jerusalem is no exception.
Pious with walls rebuilt
overturned again;
with gates opened
and welded shut.

The rain is closer to my skin here,
Everything about me tears easier,
my eyes and my mourning cloak.
Even the morning's mist
seems to drift with a million prayers,
melting from the lips up.

The shawl upon the mountain
lifts and folds upon itself.
The roads like phylacteries
cut into the arm
closest to the heart.

The fog returns each night
to remind me of the morning's temper.
I awoke wrapped in swaddling clouds.
I drifted to sleep with milky lips.

Everything was judged in one light
as it should be
without exception.

Through ruins and reconstructions
my dreams wander
in the sun

in one
the sweet milk turns on my lips
waiting for the New Moon.

Jeff Friedman
The Golem in the Suburbs

Everything will be okay,
my father said, but he lied,
then plotted to kill me. He raised me
from the dust, from four letters
of the alphabet repeated in the right

sequence seven times,
from the secret names of God.
He was the last to go.
I squeezed the air from his windpipe
and threw him down, a breathless heap.

Now my killing binges have ended.
My skin turns blue.
I stumble through the suburbs, looking
for someone I can talk to, but no one
comes out of the silent wood houses.

The magic tablet melts
under my tongue. Flies thicken,
a loud humming in their dark brains.
Read the word on my forehead,
Truth or *Death*?

Appeared in *Black Threads*,
published by Carnegie Mellon University Press, 2007

Blessing for the Hats

Say a blessing for the hats
that waltz over the hard floors,
that bob on the ocean of their own

making with their memories intact.
Say a blessing for the sweaters

that gave too much of themselves,

clinging relentlessly, that unraveled
or stretched until their fibers
snapped. Say a blessing

for the fossils humming in your nails
and teeth, for the kisses that remember
your lips. Say a blessing for

the bones that gave in to love,
putting on their bodies and walking out
at daybreak. Say a blessing for the

body with its narrow caves,
for the clattering cups, the noisy
prayers, for the heat of the eyes,

the wild burning, the sweet
smell of flesh, the rain
ripping up the rusty river.

Appeared in *Black Threads*,
published by Carnegie Mellon University Press, 2007

Night of the Rabbi

"No son of mine is quitting
Hebrew school," my father declares,
pounds his fist on the table.
Judah trembles in the South
and glittery forks twirl
in air like 5-pointed stars,
and the rabbi closes his eyes
as he rocks in the squeaky chair.

While my sisters bow their heads
to their plates and the rabbi says a blessing

over the brisket, ruddy and tender,
my mother touches her index
finger to the spot between her eyes,
signaling I should adjust my glasses.
The windows steam up as the rabbi
raises his knife toward the ceiling
like Abraham hunching over his son.
"Where's the lamb?" I ask.

He chews and talks,
telling the story about the rabbi
who lost his sidelocks in Vegas,
the rabbi who forgot to kiss
the mezuzah and couldn't get a congregation
for five years, the rabbi
and the funeral of the Jewish hit man,
"The nicest guy on earth."
A light spreads over the table
as he recalls a thousand bar mitzvahs,
fortunes made in gifts,
and I imagine a room full of pen
and pencil sets, monogrammed
handkerchiefs, and tie clips.

Now the rabbi rasps
Yiddish folk songs,
clapping his hands and laughing.
"He gets a free meal
every night," I blurt out,
but my sisters sing along
and my father's face falls,
his snoring loud as a plague
of locusts, and my mother lights
a candle in the burning bush.

Appeared in *Black Threads*,
published by Carnegie Mellon University Press, 2007

Noah Looks Back

I remember the flood, the river
of ashes, the crushed stones,
the glinting ores. Families
vanished in a flash, but the cries
continued for centuries, oblivious
waves of sound shattering
against teeth. I remember the shells
whispering, the doves flying
out at dawn into the lush
foliage. The ark shipwrecked
on the tip of God's tongue.
I remember the unending vowels
echoing in the dark, the salt
crusted on my lips. Fish
swam in white sand.
Promises rained from the sky
into thorny beds
where lovers were knotted.

I remember the dense effluvia,
the faint ribs, the indistinct
lines, the hanging genitals
disappearing into rock, the lost
eons calling from the caves,
calling through brittle bones
blasted with gamma rays,
the black candles on the shore,
prophets buried in sand—
the carnage quiet
on their swollen blue lips.

Appeared in *Black Threads*,
published by Carnegie Mellon University Press, 2007

Jacob and the Angel

after Yehuda Amichai

She balanced on a ledge,
a stony lip
between desire and doubt,

between hope and anger,
her eyes scouring
my face as shadows

wavered at her feet.
"Come," I said.
"It's time to let go

of your fears," but she
flinched, wrapping
her arms around her breasts.

The moon spread
its silky sheet
over white sand.

If she had wings,
they quivered behind her
in the cool night air.

If she had blood
it pulled her downward
toward the restless waves,

toward the earth, waiting
for her return. When
she came to me at last,

the scent of persimmon,
almonds and figs
floated through the night

and a wind passed over my thighs,
and a slow heat rose
through the soles of my feet.

Then I knew her
name and cried out,
falling beneath her.

Appeared in *Black Threads*,
published by Carnegie Mellon University Press, 2007

Burial at the River

I plant my father, a white gravel,
in water. Nothing grows, but his will
to go on selling women's wear to strangers.
Old clothes wash up, a polyester blouse,
a pair of khaki slacks, a dress
made of rayon. Catfish skim
his remains from the bottom land. In the greenish
waters pioneers fill their bellies
with German sausages and watch
fireworks flare against the sky.
The misshapen coins I toss into the river,
wrought beneath the wheels of trains,
crack rocks. I find traces of my father
in the crevices of the wharf and dig them out
with a stick. His voice jackhammers
the Eads Bridge. When smokestacks puff out,
the toy factory on the hill fails again—
the smell of glue sticking in the wind.
The river becomes a small room. On the wharf
an old woman lops off fish heads
and prepares a stew in her iron kettle.
The lightkeeper ignites a flame
in the blue globes strung
from post to post. My father's fleshy
face blinks away pain.

He unfolds the damp dollar bills
crumpled in his pocket and lays them
on the radiator one by one.

Appeared in *Taking Down the Angel*,
published by Carnegie Mellon University Press, 2003

James Stone Goodman
Jeremiah's Plan for Peace
> *Behold, the days come*
> — Jeremiah 31:30 ff.

A new agreement
a starting over always
My teachings shall I place
in your kidneys --
in your hearts.

I will be God
you will be human beings
we will each live
up to our dream
of one another,

No one will blame
accuse or intimidate --
everyone will know Me,
from the littlest to the
highest
starting now.

The past –
entirely forgiven.
I have forgotten it
we will cease calling it
past.
it is now
        -- the future.

Who lights the fires of the future?
Who writes the stories?
The sun by day
The passing of the moon
the lights by night
who stirs up the Sea?

If you can measure heaven above
search out the earth below
-- just as likely
I will abandon you.

Never.

To David a Song

A northern wind blew on David's harp and it played. The northern wind is the hidden spirit
[the northern is lacking]. I will give you what your heart lacks.
Babylonian Talmud, Pesachim 117a, Berakhot 3b, Rebbe Nachman, Likkutei Moharan, #8, Psalms 20:6

Seven days
shall you keep
a feast because
God will bless
you in all your
increase, and
in all the work
of your hands,
and you will be
altogether
joyful.
Deuteronomy 16:15

"Then I
commended
joyfulness,"
Eccl. 8:15,
this is the joy
of the mitzvah.
. . the
Shekhinah rests
upon a person
not through
gloom. . .but
only through a
matter of joy.
Babylonian
Talmud,
Shabbat 30b

james stone goodman

To David a song.
First the *Shekhinah* came and
sat on his shoulder
then David played
flat out on that axe of his --

A song to David.
First David started to scat THEN
the *Shekhinah* came and kissed his face
so sweetly he sang the secret bird song
to his son King Solomon who KNEW
the *Shekhinah* would not descend where
there is laziness or sadness
silliness light talk but --

when there is joy the deep joy of the *mitzvah*
then WOW your mind Is BLOWN like
when the slow hand player came to play
the hand of God rested UPON him --

I heard this when the northern wind blew
through David's singing
harp in the palace
of the King.

Shekhinah: the inner presence
Mitzvah: the real deed

Shekinah:
the inner Presence
quiet, internal, you
wait and you wait
*what time is the
Shekhinah coming?*

We waited between
the suns
that's when we saw
her walking

we learned patience
the Shekhinah
would be
brought down by the
mitzvah:
which is
the real deed

the complete
gift.

The Shekhinah rests
only on a prepared
place.

The language in the superscription to the Psalms: *leDavid mizmor*, signifies To David a song –
the Shekhinah rested upon him and THEN he uttered the song. The language *mizmor leDavid*,
a song to David -- he lifted up his voice in song FIRST, then the Shekhinah
descended upon him afterwards. The Shekhinah rests upon a person when there is joy, as it is said,
*but now bring me a minstrel. And it came to pass, when the minstrel played,
the hand of God came upon him.* 2 Kings 3:15, Babylonian Talmud, Pesachim 117a.
Blue always quoted this teaching before he began to play.

Yehudah HaLevi Meets Shlomo Ibn Gavirol

It is enough that your teacher and your Creator
Know your excellence
-- Talmud Yerushalmi, Sanhedrin 1:2

The blind Rabbi Solomon
Munk cataloguing
manuscripts in the
Bibliotheque Nationale
mid 19th century
pieced together that the
poet/philosopher beloved
by the Franciscans
for almost ten centuries
as Avicebron
was the Jew
ibn Gavirol.

Shmuel David Luzzatto
working from a manuscript
found in Tunis
published the *diwan* [divan]
collection of sixty-six
poems by Yehudah HaLevi
in 1840, *Betulat bat
Yehudah.*

james stone goodman

Well educated I am
Yehudah ben Shmuel HaLevi
Born in the Christian north
I am drawn to the Sepharad of the south
To the music and the verse forms
Practiced there

I sought Moshe ibn [son of] Ezra

I never lost my yearning
Libi b'mizrach
My heart is in the East
I left for *Yerushalayim*
And somewhere near the holy city
I died

V'anochi b'sof ma'arav
At the edge of the West,
Ibn Ezra taught me
It is enough that your teacher
And your Creator
Know your excellence

Ibn Ezra praised me
after my death
Shlomo the son of Yehudah Ibn Gavirol
A generation earlier than you
Forgotten until
The blind rabbi
Repaired history
In my time I was the best
Of the Andalusians

I was taught
It's enough, that your teacher
And your Creator
Know your excellence

Ibn Gavirol
born in Malaga
c. 1021,
died c. 1058

He wrote
grammars in
verse
eulogies

Yehudah HaLevi
born in Toledo
c. 1085/6
died c. 1141

Moshe ibn Ezra
born c. 1070
died after 1138
praised both
poets

Ibn Gavirol for
his
philosophical
poetry

Yehudah HaLevi
for his
religious poetry

After the death of his wife, Yehudah HaLevi left to fulfill his yearning for
the Holy Land. Legend has him murdered approaching Jerusalem.

In a legend about Ibn Gavirol, he was murdered by a jealous poet and buried
under a fig tree. In coming years, the tree bore uncommonly fine fruit, and his
murderer brought to justice.

O Heavens O Earth

At the turning of   *TaSH-'A-A*   *Tih'ye SH'nat Ayin Alef*   The year of the *ayin alef*
the year of the eye   vision   mindfulness
and alef the silent unity   focus
the deep look   the year of 'Iyyun and alef

After some
efforts, failed
and successful,
the community
began to disperse.
We had diminished,
this we knew.
We felt the
necessity to do —
something.

We met together to
gather our
strength, to build
from what already
was in place and
reason together to
the next effort,
and the next, and
the next.

This first: We
took the
conversation to a
larger group.

We also intended
to fire up our
community
and to remind each
other that we need
our best efforts —

Now rather than
then.

Give ear O heavens
And I will speak   Deut. 32:1
Listen earth
To the words of my mouth

I stood on a rock
With You
You were wrapped   Ex. 33:21
In a *tallit* of light
And there I was given forgiveness
For all of us   RH 17b
When I came down the mountain
My face was fire
And on that fire
A mask

If we believe in justice   Ex. 34:33
It is a double course justice
If we believe compassion
There is no stranger
Or we are all strangers
Not just then
But always

If we believe in good
Then there is good
And only good   Deut. 16:20

If we choose life
We take each day   Deut. 29:10
With the intention of joy

You are endlessly forgiving
Compassionate
When will You abandon us –

Never

We were debating how to bring everyone into the camp
when Blue said, *there is no one outside the camp tonight,
there is no other, no them, only us — all of us — within.*

The Prince and the Prophetess

I lost my purpose for a few days, couldn't find it anywhere.
At the grocery store, I ran into the Prince,
I went up to him and asked
do you remember me?
Sure -- I remember you, said the Prince.
He was with another man
and a woman dressed in heavy boots, fleece jacket
signifying she had been to the peak.

How you doin? The Prince asked me.
I've been better. I lost my purpose.
How long?
Couple of days.
Couple of days is nothing.
I need a purpose.
There's your problem, said the Prince – need, your problem is need.

By then we were standing in the check out line.
Three kids came up and asked him for an autograph
he signed a cantaloupe and wrote this:
I love you with all my broken heart.
He introduced me to the woman with him.
Do you know who she is? he asked me.

No.

She's a prophetess, ask her what my purpose is.
So I asked her: the Prince – what's his purpose?
This is what she said:
He is a vessel.

The Prince Wants

Prince wants to do something right
thinking
maybe this can help me.
He wants to be filled up
Prince wants most
to be significant
he wants to be remembered as having
lived.

He sees someone bagging groceries at Schnuck's
one night
late
there is one happy man
thinks Prince.

He sees the grocery bagger another night
soon Prince goes back to the store
whenever he is thinking too much
Prince watches the man bag groceries.

One night he feels the opportunity
I am watching you, says Prince,
what makes you so happy?

I used to steal from this store
says the grocery bagger
now I work here
now I am giving something back.

There is nowhere
I would rather be right now
than here
says the grocery bagger.

He looks at Prince to see if he understands
thinking
You do, don't you.

The Prince and the Healing

A long time after his illness
I ran into Prince at Schnucks.

He was still recovering
But walking on his own now

I made a deal, he said to me, like conspirators
If I lived, I'd give my life over to God

We walked outside, I looked at him, both of us squinting into the sun
And if you would have died?

I'd have given my life over to God
He said.

Suzanne Greenwald
The Warning

Yesterday I turned 60 and married a man named Lance,
Yes, Lance! Not Max or Saul or Sidney or Sam.

When my father left the shtetl,
He heard the wind whisper a warning,
"There are strong forces," it said, "that will tempt you."

At 22, in America, he felt the forces;
he understood the warning and he resisted:
He married the rabbi's daughter
And he remembered the Sabbath to keep it holy.

At 40, my father, Frank, and his beautiful wife, Rachela
joined the Friday night poker club.
When they ordered Chinese take-out,
my father murmured that surely the
Torah allows egg rolls and chicken chow mein.

Their oldest, Gary, named after the rabbi, Gedalia,
graduated from Princeton,
Then joined an ashram.

The youngest, Malka,
tap danced her way to Broadway.
She lives with her partner, Chloe, in Chelsea.

I married the Jewish doctor
and when our children were grown,
He left me for the shiksa, Darlene.
She promised him blond-haired children.

Yesterday, I turned 60 and married a man named Lance.

Maurice Hirsch
Choosing Burial Plots

At New Mt. Sinai, the smartly-dressed,
over-perfumed saleswoman explains
Jewish society
in the nineteenth century. As she drones,
my eyelids close. Her raised voice
wakes me, her wine-red fingernail points
to possible sites on the wall map.
She speaks of their virtues
as if selling me a home.
Here's one near a prominent family.
Another is next to a road — on rainy days
there's no need to walk around other graves: just park and visit.
A third has a spigot nearby to water pots of geraniums,
an oak at its edge, is
across from the maintenance building,
the outer boundary chain-link fence and
the 1950s ranch house subdivision beyond.

Alone, I visit each site in order,
lying on my back
as if I'm testing mattresses,
close my eyes, listen.
The last is my favorite,
near men who will trim overhanging branches,
weed the perpetual-care ivy.
My hands behind my head,
I say to the breeze, *Perfect.*

Building Blocks

224 South 39th
1959

Ravel's *Bolero* blares
hour after hour, all night long.

In the basement hallway,
blindfolded, we pledges hold our knees
together, sit still, silent, scared.
Like prisoners waiting for judgment,
we lose all sense of time
as we listen to our hearts thump,
the thrum of the music, know
Bolero will always conjure this scene.

256 South 37ᵗʰ
1960

Four guys fall down the stairs
five minutes before eight.
We hurry across the street,
settle in for chalk on blackboard,
scribble notes, return to our second-floor apartment,
       pocked claw-foot bathtub,
       tattered red-fringed carpet,
       chipped wood-trimmed settee,
ignore mice in the oven,
garbage on the sidewalk,
smells from the first-floor deli
with its "C" health department rating.

3912 Pine
1961

In suit and tie/dress and stockings,
prenuptial hearts in our mouths,
palms sweaty,
we sit in the office
of to our soon-to-be
slum landlord,
eager to be found worthy
to rent his crumbling brick,
rats-in-the-alley,
third-floor walkup.

Camp Nebagamon

Age ten, in a huge screened cage,
hands protected by thick leather gloves,
I held a frightened chipmunk.
It squirmed. I squeezed
too tightly, then stuck it
into a pile of leaves
to hide its dead body
from the counselors. Discovered,
I was banned from the zoo. The shame
burned my cheeks.

Age eleven, issued
two safety matches, a menu,
ingredients, a reflector oven,
I made empty #10 cans
into pots, skillets. Dressed in white,
I represented my cabin
in the "Chef's Cap"
cooking contest, won
four years in a row.
          (Now it's All-Clad on a natural gas flame, an infrared broiler.)

Almost sixteen, my final year,
I volunteered to be chaplain
on the "See America First" bus tour,
put together eight
non-denominational services,
dittoed prayers and passages
from the Prophets and familiar liturgy.
The campers, Jews, denounced
my efforts as too Jewish. Someone else
was assigned my duties, my blue-on-white copies
tinder for the campfire as we tented in Zion.
All summer I took 35mm color slides,
now like fossils caught in amber.

Sparta, Illinois
1963

Like half the town
I work at "The Comic Book,"
where white men adjust
printing presses and bindery machines
that spew white heroes
Superman,
Archie,
Casper the Friendly Ghost,
while blacks wield brooms, load freight cars.

Six months pregnant
with our first child,
Marian walks to the plant,
our tiny black poodle,
Voodoo, on a leash.
As we stroll home for lunch,
she tells me the dog bit her hard.
We chat about baby names.

Later, I go to Rotary.
The minister sitting next to me says:
You're the first Jew I've ever talked to.

Foment

Three bucks for an inch
of espresso, tons of foam.
Grande, nonfat, extra dry
gives me a buzz to light up
midday. Not much to drink, it weighs
as much as a feather.
They know me at the local shops,
get my order brewing before
I reach the register, ask
if the resulting cardboard cup

is light enough. I sit and sip,
read *The Wall Street Journal*,
see which makes my heart
beat faster.

October Night on the Huzzah

Jim eases the johnboat off the bank.
Bib-overalled on the bow platform,
I lift a trident gig, and Clifton
attaches wires to a car battery.
Spotlights illuminate the creek
like an aquarium. I stab, hit nothing
but creek bottom—the fish
are not where they seem.
Like a marksman trying to sight in,
I adjust to the left, right, up, down.
It's not the weapon's fault.
Taking his turn, Clifton
fills the boat's floor with drum and carp.

We skid onto a gravel bar
next to three other boats. Wives
surround a bonfire, tend pots
of boiling lard, make hushpuppies
of cornmeal, eggs, and bacon grease.
The men gut and clean the fish,
throw heads and entrails into the weeds.
The women rinse bodies in the creek,
dredge them in paprika-and-pepper laden flour,
pop them in to fry until their bones melt,
their skins golden. Rough men and women
wolf hot fish and fixings, drink cheap beer,
laugh and chatter until nothing is left but embers.

Jane Ellen Ibur
Mrs. Noah's Seduction

Tonight, bake lasagna in a deep dish,
Sweep up your hair in a new French hairdo.
Do what you have never done, take a dare.
You can turn the clock where it was before.
Be interesting so he won't want to leave.
Does he still love you? On this you pray.

He's standing on the deck in a cold spray.
Invite him in; offer him a warm dish.
Make him remember to you he should cleave.
Don't give up with so many things to do.
Ask him to sit and talk about before.
Spend a little time sharing the same air.

Show him that through all of this you still care
About your relationship, you still pray.
You hint you have something special in store.
You are tonight's treat, his hot, spicy dish!
Get him turned on; he won't know what to do.
Build up pressure only you can relieve.

Prance and strip for him; start with your left sleeve.
He will be panting, sucking at hot air,
But you keep on dancing, don't be subdued.
Your trick is working, you hope and you pray.
The room is uncluttered, not one stray dish.
You yearn to discover you are adored.

Later you leave him to sleep and to snore.
He won't hear you as you get up to leave.
You go for the ice cream in a deep dish.
The chocolate sauce you don't try to spare.
You hunt for cherries; you'd think they were prey.
You deserve a treat; it's long overdue.

All that time on the deck, what does he do?
His faraway mind you want to explore.
You want your husband to return, you pray.
You're always wondering why does he leave
You out? It's cruel and it just isn't fair
And there's not even a girlfriend to dish

With. What can you do? You sure cannot leave.
Therefore, don't be sucked in by life's despair.
Continue to pray, then bake a new dish.

Mrs. Noah's Sing-a-Long

The ants go marching two by two, haroo, haroo,
buffalo running two by two, haroo, haroo
centaurs tiptoe two by two
and everyone halts to stare at you
as we all go marching down, in the hold, to get out, of the rain
boom boom boom

dragons breathe fire two by two, haroo, haroo
eagles soaring two by two, haroo, haroo
flies annoy me two by two
and everyone halts to stare at you
as we all go marching down, to the hold, to get out, of the rain
boom boom boom

grasshoppers hop on two by two, haroo, haroo
horses gallop two by two, haroo, haroo
insects enter two by two
and everyone halts to stare at you
as we all go marching down, to the hold, to get out, of the rain
boom boom boom

jaguars sprinting two by two, haroo, haroo
kangaroos bounding two by two, haroo, haroo
llamas huddle two by two
everyone halts to stare at you

as we all go marching down, to the hold, to get out, of the rain
boom boom boom

marsupials groggy come on board in twos, haroo
newts come slithering two by two, haroo, haroo
owls are swooping two by two
everyone halts to stare at you
as we all go marching down, in the hold, to get out, of the rain
boom boom boom

ponies trot in two by two, haroo, haroo
quail flutter two by two, haroo, haroo
rhinos charge in two by two,
everyone halts to stare at you
as we all go marching down, in the hold, to get out, of the rain
boom boom boom

seals come barking two by two, haroo, haroo
turtles inching come in twos, haroo haroo
ungulants trotting in by twos
everyone halts to stare at you
as we all go marching down, in the hold, to get out, of the rain
boom boom boom

vultures skulk in two by two, haroo, haroo
wolves come howling two by two, haroo, haroo
xerxes enter two by two
everyone halts to stare at you
as we all go marching down, in the hold, to get out, of the rain
boom boom boom

yaks come herded two by two, haroo, haroo
zebras canter two by two, haroo, haroo
Noah and I are the last ones through
and now we say goodbye to you
As we all go marching down, in the hold, to get out, of the rain
Boom boom boom
Boom boom boom
Boom boom boom
boom

Third Year

This year I sleep till 10 a.m.,
sleep right through the 5 a.m. call
of three years ago.
My heart pounding, I jump
from bed and grab clothes
waiting on a chair for five days:
five days of coma,
five days of fifteen-hour visitation,
five days of silence, watching
her chest rise and fall,
rise and fall, rise and fall,
counting each breath, waiting
for her to forgive me.

Sunday night till 2 a.m., I read aloud
psalm after psalm after psalm.
Mary loved it when I read the Psalms to her,
her tool for my benefit, my reprieve.

Grief, such a singular time,
undulates like waves,
expanding and contracting.

If I pulled on a T-shirt instead
of buttoning a blouse. If I wore
thongs instead of tying shoes.
If the pants had elastic instead
of zipper and snap.

No cars on Grand Avenue,
all the lights yellow,
I sped down that road,
parked illegally.
If I ran up the eight flights…
instead I raced down the hall,
entered the room too late.

A nurse on each side held

her useless hands.
Her open mouth
pardoned me.

Bob Karsh
The Only President: FDR in memoriam

The children, I think,
were his best friends.
I hope that all of them
asked the Lord that night
to stop awhile from His other duties
and guide their champion
through heaven.

He died at Warm Springs. Warm Springs,
the name was like honey on his lips.
In a one-story cabin, he died.
He died in the midst of friends,
friends for whom he worked,
friends for whom he died,
friends who will remember.

The rolling green valley is innocent,
and so are the country fiddlers.
The Brunswick stew is bubbling
and the artist sketching, even now,
as the blood vessel bursts,
and the tired pulse stops,
and the president dies.

His last years were one with their first, the children who cried at his death.
They were his generation;
he was their president.
And so they cried,
like children, they cried,
for the only president they ever knew.

Lynn Levin
Azazel

So it was by the luck of the draw
that he died to purify and I survived
as goatishly as I could
in the wilderness.
And which of us was better off was hard to say.
His blood became a kind of bleach or soap
and mine a species of dung.
Like the boy who did not break the pitcher
but was beaten for it anyway,

it was my lot to be blamed.
Therefore after a frolic
I often hung my head in self-pity
pretending to graze.
I did this so often the hart
accused me of being a glutton
for punishment.

Believe me: the first year was the worst
for I was alone and misery loves company.
But each year brought me another
innocent sister or brother,
and the gossip from town was rich.
We multiplied. We organized a herd.
Every morning we bleated
our thanks to God
who had not made us human.

This poem was previously published: Levin, Lynn. *Fair Creatures of an Hour*. Bemidji: Loonfeather Press, 2009

Eve and Lilith Back at the Garden

Eve and Lilith peered through
the padlocked gates of the garden
now a restricted community – *No Jews Allowed!*

Eve glared at Lilith, "You told me it was easier
to beg forgiveness than ask permission. Now look."
Lilith offered an apologetic shrug.

"That's what I always do," she said
aware that under the circumstances she sounded pretty lame.
"Plus," fumed Eve, "I think I'm pregnant."

"I told you to use protection," said Lilith.
"But Adam promised…"
Lilith rolled her eyes.

"Him and his teaspoon of joy," said Eve.
A fault line threatened her brow.
"Girlfriend," counseled Lilith,

"either change your life or accept your life
but don't go around mad.
Let that anger go," said Lilith. "Just let it go."

Eve hated it when her friend got preachy.
Anyhow when it came to holding onto anger
Eve was an Olympian, a gold medalist.

She clung to a grudge
like a shipwrecked sailor to a scrap of wood.
It had something to do

with her excellent memory.
As Eve sucked on the red lollipop of her hurt
the two women trudged back to Nod.

All of a sudden something dark waved in the grass.

"Eek!" shrieked Lilith. "A snake!"
She high–stepped in panic

then jumped into Eve's arms.
Oy, what a nelly, thought Eve.
She grabbed a Y-shaped stick

immobilized the critter's head
stared straight into its eyes.
The snake looked back at her with a *who me?* look.

"This one's harmless.
It's only a dumb animal," said Eve.
"Kill it! Kill it!" pleaded Lilith.

"Sorry," said her friend. "No can do."
Eve let the snake go.
She just let it go.

Morton Levy
An American Survivor

A wailing SS wagon
breaks the afternoon quiet
DaaDah, DaaDah, DaaDah.
Boots on the stairs,
door broken down,
Anne Frank will soon be
ashes darkening Europe's sky,
and I will head to a drive in
for a hamburger and a milk shake.

I loved the war.
Black market Double Bubble,
souvenirs from soldier cousins,
the thrill of the victories at sea,
on the atolls and in Europe.
I was safe in my bed,
assured by movies that I was protected
by John Wayne and William Bendix.
Yes, I loved the war. There was
no DaaDah, DaaDah, DaaDah for me.

After the Diary of Anne Frank,
over and over in my dreams
that harrowing sound appeared
serenading faces from Vishniac albums.
Faces of little boys no longer my age,
as they followed the path to the
transports, death, and incineration,
while I acquired adulthood
and reproduced.

Where was my face amongst them?
Images so much like mine.
What must I do with the life
I was given a chance to complete
by the fortunate migration of

grandparents to America.?

I too am a Holocaust Survivor,
without the suffering,
the humiliation, or the loss.
We all survivors of a sort,
sharing the guilt, the shame,
the remorse, and most of all
the obligation to those in ashes
not to be silent should anyone
try to repeat this horror.

The Auctioneer's Window

In the auction house window
sat a blue and white toy submarine
waiting to be reclaimed.

Years of fruitless searching
now accidentally rewarded
rekindled the childhood memories
of a six-year-old's joy.

Christmas was an opportunity
for my parents, to show
that although we were Jewish,
we could also be Americans.
So they decorated a tree,
ran a Lionel train around its base,
and gave me a wind-up submarine
which would even run underwater.

That World War II winter
I sank tons of Jap ships,
littering the bottom of my tub
with imaginary wrecks,
until we moved, then
somehow, somewhere

my submarine got lost.
After sixty-seven years
rust was here and there,
the wind-up handle was stuck
and the coning tower bent a little.
But, I still loved it, wanted it,
demanded it be mine,
'til someone bid three hundred
and I came to my senses.

I celebrate Chanukah now,
No longer need Christmas
to feel I'm an American,
the way my first-generation parents did.
But, I'll keep searching for another submarine
so I can reclaim the memories of my youth,
as I did the day I saw that one
in the auctioneer's window.
Morton Levy

The Avenger

Two souls bound together
not by fate, but by design,
cross paths on a Caribbean isle,
beside an azure lagoon
beneath serene sheltering palms.

Moonlight through the fronds casts
shadows upon pristine sand
as the wind moves them sending
a secret semaphore of death and life.

The old one's slow pace, a far cry
from the terrifying stomp of the guard
and his gaggle of goose stepping friends
in years past, is monitored by the stalker.
Around the old man hover ghostly faces
of the hunter's mother, father, grandparents.

They, along with those of his little sister,
his childhood friends look to him silently,
as if he alone can free them.

His mother says, "take him back
to face his accusers, his justice,"
 but the deafness of vengeance
muffles her plea.

Stepping from behind the palm, the hunter
slams his weapon upon the old man's head,
bending it down further with each s blow,
until he lies face down in crimson sand.

Using a stick as paintbrush, he dips it
into the boiling blood of the devil,
and on the sand writes,

 "Arbeit Macht Frei".

Marvin Marcus
My Life in Architecture

I stood with my sister on a ship
A ship with plumbing, electrical outlets,
With our sweat-shop Holocaust-
Survivor parents, standing on the deck of
This ship, a far cry from steerage, sure
But there it was, as we entered the harbor
Of New York, this great city, like so many
Before us— The Statue

Years later I designed a museum—
My first one
Anyone can *design* a museum
But you've got to *build* the damn thing
I design a lot of museums these days
Berlin, Denver, South America
It's all about memory
Memory and concrete

My father
His name was Nachman
My father used to haul paper
My brother worked downtown
But I went to Tunisia
To talk to boy scouts
In a basement in the capital
Where I saw a faded xerox
Of all the U.S. presidents
What a country, America, I thought

But the world is under pressure
As the Bible says
Everything, everything is contested
Every day every square inch
Everyone is different—
Which is what I said last week
To handicapped people in Switzerland

But here I am in this gorgeous space
With this beautiful organ
It sits in silence, I know,
But such music I hear
And let me tell you this—

Democracy will triumph
Mark my words
I know things viscerally
I touch things and know them

In the pit at Ground Zero
I touched the slurry wall—
This thing that refused to fall—
In the pit I had a naked emotion
And I decided to build it tall,
To make it soar
Because people told me to
And I trust the people
'Trust the invisible,' my father said
I trust that too

My father was a whistler, a good one
He whistled at some Communists
In 1928 and they threw him in jail
Where he lived like a herring
Sleeping on top of people
1928 it was, and he tapped on the wall
Tapped in code
Kept on tapping
And someone tapped back
The someone got out, got big,
And helped my wall-tapping father
Become a factory manager

But I became an architect
After years of tapping
On the walls of my mind
I design walls, and other things

I win design competitions
Berlin, Denver, South America
I am a lucky man
God bless America

Daniel Libeskind
Washington University
December 6, 2004

My Life in Hebrew

I was a baby
For eight terrible months
My parents never spoke Hebrew
They knew nothing
And so I became a Hebrew writer

I love Hebrew
Hebrew has wisdom, for example
The word for love—*ohev*
The word for enemy—*oyev*
So close, these two words
Just shift a single letter, and you
Move from love to hate
From hate back to love

But when we moved to B'nai B'rak
We were torn—*k'riya*—torn
Which is also what happened to me
On my wedding night
Torn, a tearing, a terrible tearing
And then the tearing of death
To be torn by death

I think of Stabat Mater,
The mother standing, watching
As her child is torn from her—
Akira, arika—an uprooting, a desertion

Just reverse the letters
A wise language, Hebrew

Back to B'nai B'rak—
I wanted to read books
To leaf through pages
With my mind, with my heart
I wanted to call out, to shout
To study these books
But such things could not be
Not in B'nai B'rak
With its shackled girls and women

I craved books, but they were forbidden
Dangerous, seductive
I will die without books I thought
The librarians
They took pity on me,
This rebellious girl
They gave me books
Books in paper bags

I married at eighteen
To a *yeshiva bocher*
He sat and studied, studied and sat
I took the early bus
Three buses, actually,
And went to teach,
To teach with my head scarf
The kids were wild
All day they ran around
I went home, collapsed on the bed
Cried, got up, made dinner
For the *yeshiva bocher* husband
Who went off to study somewhere
I went off to my room
Where else was there to go?

I had terrible thoughts

Why are women not allowed to learn?
Why am I so miserable all the time?
I burned inside—a feminist burning
But I didn't yet know the word
Then I got pregnant
And calmed down
Then the baby died and I was lost

One day I found a book
And opened my eyes
I cried out for this book
And it came to me
It spoke to me—in English
As it turns out

I gave birth nine times
Two died
Seven lived
Seven children
And I still wanted to study
The *yeshiva bocher* said no
No, he said
No, he said again

I rebelled
I started to write
I used a pen name
Nobody knew who this writer was
But the word got out

I was just a writer—
A writer
I took my children and left
One of them—the boy—
Wanted to study with the rabbis
Fine, I said
Study
The girls—they wanted a new life
I gave it to them

Seven children I took with me
Walked out
And got a divorce
I wrote fifty books
Ghost-written things at first
Biography, history

But now I write for myself
In my own name
At first I wanted to be Faulkner
I had to learn to be myself
I am still learning
I am still writing

Yehudit Rotem
Washington University
November 7, 2005

The Holocaust, Uncle Shmuel, and I

I am a private person
Not an expert
I wrote a book, true
But it was an accident
Everything is an accident
This one began in rooms
With old Jews—
Relatives who pinch your cheek
Then burst into tears—
Oy, like Shmuel you look
They'd say

Uncle Shmuel disappeared
Dead and gone
Not a trace
My grandfather, with his stories
All lies, but such stories
Yet not a single story about his brother—

My Uncle Shmuel
As fate would have it
I grew up on Long Island
Near a mall named for Walt Whitman
Things were quiet
Until grandfather showed up
With his stories
Because Florida was too hot

Stories of Poland, Ukraine, Austria,
Depending on point of view
Stories of the old town— Bolohov
And its cast of characters
There was an album of photos
Glued, reglued, unglued,
Titled, untitled
And three photos of Shmuel—
One younger, one older,
One with wife and children
All with the same caption—
'Killed by the Nazis'

Then my grandfather died
I went to Florida and heard stories
About his wives, his station wagon,
The canary named Shloime,
And his clothing—
The man was obsessed with clothing
Four outfits a day, laid out on the bed
And two wallets— always two wallets,
One ordinary, the other ostrich skin

So here is what happened
In the midst of the Florida rummaging
I come across the ostrich-skin wallet
I pick it up
And out fall some old letters—
Letters from Shmuel, from 1939
Begging for help

Get me out
Get me out of Poland

Here was the truth
The voice of Uncle Shmuel
And my grandfather's terrible guilt
And here was the book
Staring me in the face
But who could stroll into Poland
Through the Iron Curtain
And sniff around for a dead Jew?

Then Gorbachev
The walls came down
The internet went up
And missing persons could be searched
In archives, on websites
Family trees could grow branches
The dead could come to life

A guy named Alex got in touch
He could find things—
Or so the email said
Fine
Then nothing
Two years passed
And the doorman buzzes me—
You got a big box down here
I go down
Such a box— weird stamps,
Twine and wire, kicked and bruised
And inside, a treasure—
A hundred twenty documents
Papers from centuries past
The family sealed in this box

The door had opened
And I would walk through
Into the old country

To the town where the woodsman
Would come down on Yom Kippur
To stay with the Jews
For good luck, he said
Where Aunt Sylvia earned a reputation
As 'goddess of bitterness'
What was so bitter—
I had to find out

So we flew to Lvov
Then drove to Bolohov
Speeding down the cow paths
In search of this man
'Killed by the Nazis'

We spoke with many people
One, an old lady, outside the church,
Remembered Shmuel
Remembered him and his shop
Only the one lady—
Not enough for a New York Times piece
Another lady told of the shootings
The summer of 1943, when her mother
Had to run the sewing machine
To drown out the machine guns

But I needed more
Back to New York I go
And the phone rings
A Polish Jew calling about Shmuel
Calling from Australia
He heard from the grapevine
What grapevine might this be I thought
That I was looking for Bolohov Jews
He says come to Sydney
Five of us here—
We knew your Shmuel
We knew his family
As for me— I dated Shmuel's sister

Here was the book—
Pieced together from visits to Australia,
Then Stockholm, then Minsk
Twelve Bolohov Jews
Scattered across the globe
Who told stories
Stories of Shmuel, his family,
And my Aunt Esther
Esther, who had nice legs
As one of them recalled—
Legs retrieved from oblivion

Daniel Mendelsohn
Annual Holocaust Lecture
Washington University
November 12, 2008

POETRY

Steven Moskowitz
A Modern Rendition of Psalm 150

Praise God
Praise God in the sanctuary and
     In the vastness of nature
Praise God for goodness and compassion
     For blessings and wonders
Praise God with piano and song
     With guitar and cello
     With sax and drums
     With clarinet and violin
Praise God with an orchestra of sounds
     And a symphony of music
Let every soul praise God
Let every breath sing praises to the Lord.

Niki Nymark
Angels

Angels are here,
crushing and pressing
among us.
Their wings shudder,
to music
only they can hear.
Restless, itching,
they embrace us
in brass arms,
strike lightening,
sing out to G-d.
although their music
would sound to us
like screaming,
would deafen us
if we could hear it.
Their skin shines
like porcelain mirrors.
If we could see them,
we would burst
into flame,
burn to cinder.

Angels have great powers
and perfection,
but they envy us,
covet our ability
to choose, to fail,
to fall, to be
forgiven.

Her Hands, Her Hair

Your face
on the hard, white pillow
that last night when we
sat holding your hands
in the almost dark,
reading prayers aloud,
wondering if you could hear.
Your body a shadow under the sheet,
your face all bones,
an ivory carving
of someone hard at work dying.

Your hands no longer
holding mine,
the hands that held me up
for fifty years.
The nails you always tended
with such care
now yellowed, brittle, broken,
but your hair still lustrous,
thick and dark. Even in those final days
I loved to brush it,
wondered if you knew
who brushed your hair
or sang those silly songs
while she brushed.

You died without permission,
closing your soft, green eyes,
done with us before
we were done with you.
We held your hands,
told you it was alright
to go---begged you---
wanting the struggle, the harsh
breathing to stop.
When you died

we couldn't leave you.
We sat in the darkness
holding your hands.

When They Ask Us Who We Are

When Moses saw the golden calf,
he shattered the Commandments
into dust like desert sand,
gold and azure speckles
that spilled and filled
the peoples' eyes, and ears,
the corners of
their mouths and
the fringes of their garments.
Nobody knew what the
fragments said,
but everyone had a atom of
"I am," or "Thou shalt," or
"Father and Mother."
Everyone had a particle of
"lech lecha," or "if not now, when."

God didn't make it easy.
God said, "The first tablets, I created
 with gold and precious gems,
I signed My name in the corner,
"The Artist of the Heavenly Word".
This time you'll have to make them by hand.
I'm not even going to tell you what to say,
you have to remember that yourselves."

Moses kicked himself. The people
cried aloud,
but they felt the prickly shards
of Torah in their eyes,
they could taste them
in their mouths.

they itched with curiosity,
began to search for
the ten words, so elusive,
and all the meaning
folded within them.
We search for them still.
It takes a whole people to find
all the tiny letters,
no one can do it alone.
So, who are the Jews?
We are the people who feel the itch.
We are the people who search together.

Gerald Perkoff
Dante's Dream

What terrible dreams
Dante must have had,
to have known the
pathways through
Hell.

Or is it possible
he nearly died, and
saw in this sulfurous place
where the margin between
life and death is
greatly blurred,
a stimulus a great poet
could hardly resist.

He may even have
overstayed his welcome
to soak up the visions
laid out before him.

But in the end he returned,
to write it all down.
I too would turn away
from Virgil's beckoning finger
to transcribe this nightmare
on display in the nether-home
of Death.

Chrysalis

The old emerges slowly from sleep, like
butterflies from the chrysalis,
wings tentative, steps uncertain,
not quite ready to fly.

Does the butterfly ache, as I do,
as he moves from darkness to light?

Does he too begin his day
in an envelope of silence,
taking in the small sounds
that come from nearby hills
and restless waters?

And when he escapes
the earth and flies, does he
remember his earlier fragility?

Or does he do as the old
dream of doing,
fling caution to the winds
and ride the updrafts of his
all too brief time?

I Am a Jew

I am
a Jew. My middle European genes made me
five-foot-two, squat, bald, rounded. I look
a lot like those millions who were stripped
of hair, and teeth, and possessions, and
incinerated. I do not smell
of the ovens but I carry the ashes
of every victim on my shoulders,
the shochets and the peddlers,
the red-wigged wives and the little girls,
who played with dreidels on the floors
of the shacks and hovels of the Pale, and ran
from Cossack swords that seemed
to materialize from nowhere
in the dark night.

The weight
of all who died is on me, a past that
colors my thought and behavior,
no matter the fools who deny
the terrible acts of the past.

Yet, I have great gifts
non-Jews do not have, except for those
I have given them by inheritance,
than to the warrior kings of
paes-wearing fundamentalists,
the little people who gave me
the genes and the drive to rise
above the everyday to be
doctor, counselor, father, and then
Zayda to my five young people
entering the maelstrom of life as a Jew, whether
they like it or want it or acknowledge it.

Yes, I am a Jew.
I am filled with love of life,
grateful for family,
grateful for Torah,
needing at least another eighty years to understand
and apply the principles of the ages
in any meaningful way.

Why haven't I said
anything about God
in all this bragging, you ask?
God, that's a whole
other story.

Nancy Powers Pritchard
Thou Shalt Not Covet

Summer's riches riot; the neighbor's wife
planted red, pink, coral. From her sharp shears shorn
blooms tumbled among green leaves, saw-edged, rife
with chartreuse worms. Fierce scents drenched the morning
haze, fat caterpillars nibbled the cockscomb.

Your desire, brief as snow drops vanished, lure of home
faded. Something tedious caught your eye, a comb
tangled with hair that lost its luster, shoes, heels broken down.
Will you uproot a life that feels gnawed to the bone?

Go, then, but leave the garden where it was planted:
the lush loosestrife stolen from the neighbor's woods
that purpled the hill below the gate; where sunlight slanted
beneath the kitchen door yellow tansy and dogwood
also stay: they were chosen for this house, this life

Evening at Home

Galling as the scrape of a knife
on a plate, the sound of his voice
makes her flinch as if slapped.

Distant, she concentrates
on her food, gives him nothing
when he asks about her day.

He tries too hard and it's draining.
She has only two questions left
to ask: What is yours? What is mine?

While she washes the dishes
he waits at the table like a child
punished; *no dessert for you.*

Even though she ignores him
he comes close behind her,
his approach tentiative, unwelcome.

She scrubs at a speck of chicken
burned onto the broiler pan,
lets hot water gush over

her hands. Grease clings
to her reddened knuckles.
He rubs his hips against her,

nuzzles her damp neck.
She spreads the silverware
to dry, feels through

the murky water, pulls the plug,
watches the water vanish
down the dark, dark drain.

He says, *I love you*. She doesn't care.
He backs toward the stairs, beckoning.
She shrugs, dries her hands, surrenders,

stopping here to straighten
the sofa cushions, there
to untangle the rug's long fringe.

Marilyn Probe
In Her Own Words Edith Pearl Lena Harris Probe, 1897-1984

> *The following poems are based on my recorded interviews with Mother and stories she wrote in the archival journal I gave her.*

My Beginnings, Scraps of Memory

My earliest memory
is being run over by a street car
that caught me up in a wire-net-
like basket which saved me—
I was running away from a group
of older boys jumping rope
who scared me, screaming,
"The boogeyman is coming."

Some neighbor
with the door of her house
right next to the pavement
lifted me up
and called Mother.
I don't remember crying,
but it's funny, I remember
the candy she gave me,
a small tin frying pan
with pink candy—
How happy I was.

Next to that I remember
my brothers yelling out the window,
"Scabs, scabs!"
I think it was a streetcar strike.
For my father was a union man.
I remember him
talking with Samuel Gompers
in our living room.

The Little Jewish Girl in Iowa, 1901-1903

When I was about four we moved
to Burlington, Iowa—Papa bought
a department store with other men,
Mr. Joe Ritter and Dr. Moses DeVorkin.
I remember
we had a beautiful house,
with a horse and stable
and an apple and cherry tree
with bleeding hearts
along the walk.
When it rained, the wind blew
cherries off the tree. Once a horse
ran wild. My brother Ben hurt himself
jumping on a pitchfork.

It was so lovely there.
On Valentine's Day
all the children would go
to one another's homes,
leave a valentine and then run.
On Mayday we did the same thing
for our mothers, leave flowers,
ring the bell and run.
On July 4th all the neighbors
would have a big bonfire—
throw potatoes in and eat them—
it was so much fun,
the sweetest memory of my childhood.

We were the only Jews living there.
My oldest brother Harry brought me
to school one day and the teachers
took me to almost every room
and showed me off as the little
"Jewish" girl who is in our city.
My father couldn't make any money.
as the people wouldn't patronize

the "Jew" store. So, broke, Papa
had to move us back to St. Louis.

When I looked out our window

I saw a saloon on one corner
and a school on the other
at Ninth and Washington.
My brothers, Harry, Ben and I
all went to that Jefferson School.
There were all kinds of Irish there, then.
I remember I bought a new trunk,
just a foot and a half long
of red and blue cardboard. I put
all my valuables in it. Then McGillicutty
lit a firecracker under my brother
Harry's hand. He came home, got mad
at me and stuck his foot through
my new trunk. The next day I saw a fire
and I screamed all the way to school.
Why did I scream? Who was I fooling?
I screamed to get attention.

My brother Ben and I were pals

and he always took me with him,
even walking the trestle near Creve Coeur.
We landed at a farm house
where a Chinaman lived with his wife.
She gave us two baby ducks.
How thrilled we were!
We took them home and trained
our dog, "Lutzer" to walk with the ducks
on her back around the block—
the whole neighborhood children following—
how proud we were!

Ben used to make "Poppy Shows"—
a shoe box with a hole to look through
and three rooms with curtains
and homemade furniture—
he made the prettiest of all poppy shows.
We had a candle inside and would call out—
"A pin to see my Poppy Show,
a pin to see my Poppy Show."
We would be stopped and give anyone
a look for a pin—
Even a pin counted in those days.

During the 1904 World's Fair

we moved to 18th and O'Fallon,
a tough neighborhood.
It was a time when out-of-towners
found it hard to get rooms. So when
a teacher from Burlington came,
Mother let her stay with us.

I was around six
and my brother Ben nine.
My father sold popcorn and peanuts
at the Fair and he'd take us with him.
I had long black curls and he'd sit me
on the barrel of peanuts to call attention.
Down the street
was a "Hoochy Koochy Dancer"
and my brother Ben took me along.
We sneaked in and he saw naked dancers
emerge from colored water.
I don't remember the dancers,
but I remember the terrible beating
my brother got from Dad.
He was hard on Ben, my favorite

The nights were quiet

at 1836 O'Fallon. I never went
out alone in this Kerry Patch
where the sidewalks had no trees.
We played baseball in the street,
but we never went beyond the corner.
I was good at baseball. Once I hit
my sister Esther in the eyebrow
and she ran to our neighbor, Mr. Rugg,
a chess columnist for the St. Louis Globe
Democrat. He put witch-hazel and Kremoline
on the bump. To fight bedbugs we also
stuck the legs of our big brass beds
in Kremoline.

Our flat had a long narrow hall
and three bedrooms were in back.
Brothers Harry and Ben slept in one bed,
my sister Esther and I in the other.
Our windows faced the roof
and through the hall window
we could climb on to it,
but more often we danced
on our beds. The springs squeaked.
Once the Goldman girls came to sleep.
My brothers said, "Take off your night
gowns. We won't peek."

But from under the quilts, they did peek.
We were only eight years old.

We lived by the water tower

in 1906 on North Grand, near
the Jewish Old Folks Home
where my father was superintendent.
We were the only Jewish children there.

Across the street, I had a friend,
Jean Williams. When I'm friends
with someone, I adore them.
So I decided to give her a party. I was
an organizer, even at that young age.
Everyone was to bring something,
so my mother made mandel bread.
I was so proud of it and so was she.
As I served food, bringing it from one room
to another, I felt very important.
But I heard the girls whisper,
"Edith brought stale cake."
I let them know, "That cake's not stale.
That's the way it's supposed to be—
toasted like that."

Still, they didn't serve my cake.
But I didn't go home for that reason.
I left because they mistreated
Margaret McGernicle. She was so sweet
and truthful. I worshipped her. We were
playing musical chairs. Margaret McGernicle
sat on a chair and another girl's mother
pushed her off. I walked out,
but Margaret stayed.

Tikkun Olam

When our house is barren
of all but a clock,
we will weep into a white hand.

When even time is removed
we'll be stripped to bare ground,
drift to landscapes that soothe,

where rotting fences, stakes
of sovereign borders are supplanted
by gates of snowflakes
blanketing the hemispheres
in peace, bearing only an oblique
relevance to our former maps.

Windy City of My Yiddish Past

Eye level with the El in the morning, recalling my last
evening's tears to Myriam Fuks'Yiddish *Papierossen,* a brash
alto, an ageless singer, framed by steel wings that gleam to refract
rays of lambs in clouds, I emerge through Papa's strains of ashes,
peel off my lapses, my shame, my armor, release grief
barefoot before God in wrinkles, missteps. Into this sphere
I wriggle. Naked. Sabbath day is no honeymoon but a thief
if it robs me of my true voice. Not rolled rags of goodness, I fear
being judged from clods of dirt that slide off the past.
Call it a Mitzvah, slipping out from trashcans of the underbelly,
windy city sweeping out all static that catches in the blast
that sweeps Chicago--the city of Els, amphitheaters, Jewish delis,
Yiddish song, Gypsy violins, gladiolas--mine, a testament to the Torah,
a Chassidic descendant, stalking at midnight the ghosts of Gomorrah.

Carol Rose
lodged in the heart

behind iron bars, lodged in the heart of the old city
sits copenhagen's synagogue, its walls thick with history
its gates locked against visitors.   inside its courtyard
an elderly woman paces back & forth, she mutters
first in danish, then in german   *can not,*   she says
you can not   i don't have the right   can't let you in
come in the evening when the men come to pray.
i press my face between the metal slats, lean closer, ask
'do you take care of this synagogue'   *no*   she says   *i live here*
in back   in the garden   i come from poland   my grandfather
brought me   an old man   beloved   he came to this place
three times a day   i came with him   now i have no one
no mother   no father   no husband   no children   my
grandfather died   i live in the home behind the garden
i have a good life here   the danes never beat me.   i listen
carefully   try to understand   *the danes never beat me*
i have a good life here   why did you come   can you speak
hebrew   do you know the prayers   i have a good life here.
a nurse enters the courtyard, takes the woman out
of the sun, back to her home in the garden.   the old
woman turns to me, says   *it's good you know hebrew*
good that women still know   come back in the evening
come back with the men,   she whispers, *come back & pray.*

lunar plexus

i remember sitting with a remote
control, flipping channels
for news, clicking pictures
(of mothers, soldiers, children)
with a wireless box, linking
people unable to speak their pain,
face to face, on a night chosen to hide
weapons, from infrared missiles,
under shadows of a new desert moon.

i remember jerusalem
waiting for moonlight
women & men recalling a time
(measured in cycles) when
seasons brought new life, prized
above rubies or oil, when
children planted saplings
in forests, with songs
of shalom on their lips

keep the nightmares from her sleep
for adira

she runs home from school breathless
tells me about the tv crew, their cameras
& microphones ready to capture the news,
report the 'incident'. we watch anti-semitic
graffiti flash across our screen, see words of
hate, know this has happened many times
before, even in canada, hear the reporter say
 the jewish community is up in arms, wonder
what that means to folks listening to the news
over their six o'clock dinner, feel the fear.

after the news, she talks about the other children
how they tell her that if the bad people came
to their school they would take off everything
that made them look jewish, their stars,
their pendants, their head coverings, everything.
she seems puzzled, asks *how can they hide who they are?*
why should they, they didn't do anything wrong!   I hold her
tell her that she's right, hope that it's enough
to calm her, keep the nightmares from her sleep,
wonder if the viewers think about our children
as they surf the channels looking for entertainment.

rabin square

like layton i want to shout
israel   where are your prophets
your psalmists   your poets

on the streets of tel aviv
jewish students carry flowers
light candles   cry out for peace
their ankles ringed in blood
as they move past the
footprints of their elders

i want to shout
israel   learn from these young ones
see with their eyes   lidded with baby's
breath & sprigs of fresh green
your old hearts melting like candle wax
in the warmth of their vision

i want to shout
but remain silent
their vigil too holy for words

when they bowed their heads

she reads how beneath the sewers the earth sleeps & she imagines it
dreaming of earlier times, when trees filled the forests & flowers scented
the cloudless air. she thinks about her own life, about the way things
used to be, children running everywhere, four little boys clambering
for their place at the dinner table, each wanting to be served first, each
wanting to be heard, shouting as their exhausted parents tried to calm
them, give each his due, how they loved each other, the parents & the
children, how they fought too, mostly about toys & sports & how to pay
the bills, how they argued about child-rearing, wanted the best for their
kids, wanted to teach them to love each other, respect each other & the
world, how they hated arguing,
loved it when the tensions melted on a friday night or saturday,
melted
in their sabbath songs, their sabbath loaves, melted when they bowed
their heads & blessed each other, how they miss that now, miss the
pillows on the living room floor, the blankets, books & special toys, the
lego cities standing tall, full of love.

Ann Lesley Rosen
God's House
after Kenny, age 12

In Chicago, it's the 20th floor penthouse,
rising high over Lake Shore Drive,
floor-length windows all around,
sky so close, it's like flying,
lake on one side, city unfolding on the other.

In Chelsea, Oklahoma, lead-painted tricycles
rust in the front yard as weeds creep
over flat tires, through broken links
in the fence. Cobwebs dust the white siding,
cracked shingles cling to the roof,
a plastic sheet flaps in a broken window.

It's a two-storey in Yankton, South Dakota,
white with green trim, turret on top,
screen porch clustered by raspberry bushes.
On the street out front, people push strollers.

In Jerusalem, it's just a door frame,
a corner of chalky white stone,
somewhere in the Old City, beyond
black hats and long beards.
Maybe its floor is sand,
maybe stone.

Blessing

The way her fingers wrap
around mine, small nails
stinging in a grip strong
and soft. How her head
fits in the curve
of my chest, lost
puzzle pieces returned.

Tiny socks hiding
in the laundry. A bib
on the arm of the couch.
Pink washcloths
in the sink.

The way her eyes widen
when she sees me, kicks
her legs, smiles
at a mirror.

How something so small
can change the world,
fear so thick,
joy so full.

Fourth Grade

I imagined the rock, soft
with algae, shiny
in the brown lake water,
and his foot, light brown,
trapped despite the slickness
of the rock.

I didn't know what it meant
to die, just that he was a fifth grader,
who was too fat but smiled a lot
and had tight curls on his head.

It was Boy Scout camp
where he drowned, his father
was there but couldn't save him,
and I was never his friend,
a shy fourth grader awed
by the big kids
I didn't want to become.

Jane Schapiro
Coming Upon My Old Diary

One name and I'm back in my seventh grade gym,
standing in line for the trampoline.

Susan Donnelly and I'm in the air,
pumping my arms above my head.

If I beat her, I can make the East West Meet.
I just gotta make the East West Meet.

Over and over, the entries repeat,
just gotta make the East West Meet.

My daughters laugh at my junior high
thoughts circling the same pothole.

Knees to stomach to swivel hips.
I'd draw out each jump like a deep exhale,

try to add one final flip.
What if I don't make the East West Meet?

To my giggling daughters these are just words,
aged and shriveled like spent balloons.

Where will I sit if I don't make the team,
if no one waves me over to them?

That one sinking fear I didn't record. Even now.
I tell them how high I jumped,
over, above everyone else.

Amy Scharff
Letting Go

Morning frosted gloss shimmer on the lawn
long shadows from the east
a feast waiting
left in my garden.

Afternoon I claim my next harvest
unstake the vegetables
explore with open mind and find
what I did not plant.

Still in the sunshine the branches and brambles
radish and lettuce
none that I sowed
bent bean canopies shadowing fruits from the night frost.

Marigolds shout orange yellow reminiscent
summer splashed cool and mellow
Lush oranged cherries sour in the cold
unbelievably late but somehow still grow.

Two seeded turnips left to mature and
see what might happen
now stand old bitter proud
Despite the lost dill
still the sweet round fennel seeds
crown the ends of their stalks
full and loud young acolytes
sucking sunlight and faith from their surrounds.

And beneath the creeping runaway tomato and
brittle bristles of what was
a surprise vine climbs ripe with cucumber
melon-large and turgid
resting against the rocks
just outside the garden's line
I decide to leave it there

expectant in protected sun
to grow or grow old
cycling like the summer's seeds
will turn again to springtime.

Jackie Schechter
Cardinals

Times were best
when my mom could carry me,
into the ballpark,
draped across her shoulder
my arms clutch the back of her neck,
and my head buried in,
her soft shirt.
My dad would be right beside us,
carrying his orange bottle
of cold Hawaiian sunscreen.

They snuck me in,
pretended I was too young for my own seat,
and it worked if I hid my face,
and my coffee colored freckles.

I listened to the blur of noise,
 "Buuuuud Light!"
"McGwire! McGwire!"
"Booo"
and the scrape of light brown peanut shells under tennis shoes,
as I sat on my mom's strong freckled thighs,
and as the yellow sunlight
flooded my eyes.

My dad held my mom's peach colored hand,
and tossed me his cap.
I loved its golden world series,
Its silver all-star,
its cardinal pins,
and I loved how it slid over my face,
smelled of cherry cough drops,
and mint tooth picks,
and covered my eyes,
until all I could see was
red, red, red.

Reading in the Dark

It was worth staying up late
into the night,
running my eyes
over curved book pages,
herding them in and out of beautiful words,
that rest gently on the page.
I would press the book to my face,
breathe in the fibers
of the old old pages,
like the thin orange dust of a butterfly's wings.
I could sit by the cool,
wide window
that blew manes of wind through its cracks and corners
late in the spring night,
for hours,
and the blue moonlight would pour from the iced pitcher of the sky
to pool in puddles of light on my pages.
My eyes would run,
back and forth,
through the valleys of sweet images,
and metaphors,
through the chapters,
through the wide open fields of tall golden hay
until they lay down
quietly,
like sleepy stallions in the grass.

Lon Schneider
Kafka

The doctor is a violation of the body.
The body is a violation of the family.
The family is a violation of the corporation.
The corporation is a violation of the state.
The state is a violation of the law.
The law is a violation of logic.
Logic is a violation of the truth.
The truth is a violation of the absurd.

Steven Schreiner

Even in a Dream the Dead are like the Photograph Still Inside the Camera

Mother was pleased
by the small private collection
of Impressionists, including
the Christmas scene by Grandma
Moses. The blue sky!
That drew me. I was sad
the whole trip and not even
Chagall could enliven me
with his allure. His love for Bella
dispirited me. In this late painting
she has recently died
and his horse face is flayed.
The eyes are a conflagration.
He longed for her breasts
and had lavished his love
on their shape, youthful
and alike, the twin fauns
of Solomon's fruitful lust.

Lou, Mother's companion, a type
of late husband even at this
stage, shuffled agreeably
through one gallery into another.
To be with someone you've known
so briefly compared to your children
and grandsons, your departed, your
doctor—what is it but an aggravation
of daily proportion, epoch-less?

Yesterday at my nephew's party
after becoming a man,
we waited to celebrate, as if by custom
on the coast of California,
in the historic nautical museum.
As the sun crashed into the surf

we had our drinks on the deck
in the cool summer air.
Then we were steered into the reception
amid the chaos of the children.
No one looked
at the cases of antique diving equipment.
The great gold helmet
weathered in an airless exhibit
sitting on a seabed of sand.
The ghostly absent diver
could feel the cold coming
through the canvas suit,
seeping inside the stiffened gloves.

When the sound track began
to the video of my nephew's life
it ushered in the hush. Teens drummed
the floor beneath crossed legs
as he appeared, newborn, like the advent
of a prophet held in his mother's
unsuspecting arms. My sister radiated serenity
and satisfaction, yet she looked
airbrushed into pornography,
soft focus, bathrobe, shot
rays of window light, as if
the rapture of birth had taken place
under a sprinkler.
We followed the family snorkeling
in the blue waters of Baja,
enjoying Hawaii, and recently France
with its bilious Seine below
their houseboat. I began to begrudge
the unending movie of life with children.
When my turn came
to appear in the film
each frame showed me surrounded
by nieces and nephews, wives
edited out; in the more recent years
the children cluster around me

on the beach or in the lobby, while I smile
like I'm wincing from the glare.

Would it help if I imagined
that my father, standing behind his camera
at the beach, the sea so small
in fits inside the view,
watched over me with imperishable
pleasure? I was a boy
when he became a handful of sand.

Death is that day on which
it makes no difference what
you choose to imagine.

Heartless

In East Orange, just off the Parkway,
I couldn't pass the cemetery

without trying to hold my breath.
In the midst of life we are in death.

Today, I saw the widow's neck
bare as the glare on the glass. Check.

Remembered my mother, myself, my brother
driving through March snow together

first in a line behind the hearse.
I didn't think it was wrong to curse

now that you were dead, your face
enclosed in the dark, your thoughts erased

except for regret. I worried that
I'd see your Borsalino hat

in the hall closet when I was alone.
Would you know? Could you atone?

I passed the escort, the sound of a boat,
and the balaclava at his throat

solemnized his ivory Harley.
The grass of an office park waved like barley.

I remembered us gathered under a tent,
my mother in a chair, the way the casket leant

slightly lower on one end, slung
between straps and castors. Kaddish sung.

And then we turned around to greet
the faces. Goodbye. We drink, we eat.

Barren

I found a tick there
in the loose skin that hangs,
days after returning from the woods
of a state park in Missouri.
It was full summer, signs warned hikers
to stay away from the brush, wear
pants tucked into socks, and explore
the body you bathe when you return;
for even a speck of dirt
that you can't flick away
or even a freckle
can turn inward and grow.

Like the poppy-thin skin of a man's cheek
whose old body has puckered,
like the milky pod
that dangles from a sapless limb,

like the fig tree Jesus withered,
like seedfruit and breadfruit
but not a flower and not a fruit
the testicle deceives.
What purpose, what wisdom
and what end contained
in the sightless process
led us here, where our limits
come up like an empty net,
a purse seine drawn together
by our two boats
to be a sign of prosperity, to feed us
for our labors,
to close upon sea water.

I thought a miracle might happen.

Sarah must wait forever, it seems,
and learning she will bear a son
laughs and barely escapes
more wrath. Rebecca's womb
is closed for a time
though in a world where time
stretched on and on
it seemed forever
she was denied children
as numerous as the sand

or the stars that cover heaven
or the dust that spreads across
the dry and barren land.
Like Jacob I labored
to make someone mine.
For a time we believed
God would grant us children
if only I forgave. But
unlike Jacob I was mistaken.
The stone upon the well
was very heavy, and

she who married me waited
while I moved it aside, but
the well was dry. Dear
tick, hanging black as a seed,
suck deep, drink, grow fat
from me, be a life
that I have fed, that found
its way to my body,
then fall, be fruitful, and multiply.

Henry I. Schvey
Sleepaway Camp

When I was a little boy, each blade of grass
Was painted one particular shade of emerald.
I took the train all by myself
To sleepaway camp way up in Maine.

My mother's sad face squashed against the filmy window,
Blowing me desperate kisses. I don't care,
Why should I? I'm a big boy now,
And Camp Wildwood is magic:
I learn to swim in a lake teaming with shimmering fish,
Start a campfire without striking a single match
And on a rough trail covered with
Pinecones and needles, find somebody's prize
Arrowhead.
I tuck the treasure in my shorts,
Searching the sky to see if maybe God has witnessed my crime.
Only the fir trees are watching:
I figure they don't care.

Now I am in Poland at another camp.
It has trails strewn with pinecones
And grass painted one particular shade of emerald.
I come to a clearing,
Expecting to hear the fire crackle,
The sweet, teasing songs of summer,
And the joyous laughter of city boys
Devouring summer air.
Instead I see stones
Rising from the grass,
Pits where naked children
Are stacked head to toe
Like frying fish
Before they are burned to ash and blown into dust.
I search the sky to see
If God has witnessed the crime.
But only fir trees are watching:
I figure they don't care.

Howard Schwartz
Breathing in the Dark
    for Ava

So many months breathing in the dark—
the scent of underground springs
sustains you,
a hidden moon beckons you
to grow ripe.

While you sleep,
an angel whispers the secrets of creation,
showing you
every branch of the tree of life.
Someday
you will dimly recall
all that was revealed
of roots
and branches
and breath.

You wake,
a lilac
waiting for the wind,
a sensual stone,
a leaf
thirsty for a kiss.
From now on
you will wake with this thirst
every morning
and drink in
everything
until the crickets rub their wings together,
singing.

A Portrait of My Son

He has climbed high in the branches of almond trees
to shake them free of their fruit,
harvested holy weed,
braided challahs while it was still dark,
hawked warm loaves in the *shuk*.

He is full of contradictions:
a sniper with a conscience,
an impatient student who loves to read,
a would-be chef, tour guide, translator.
When here, he longs to be there;
when there, he longs to be here.

He ignores the wisdom of the Fathers
and the wisdom of his father,
preferring the mystery of being
with no questions asked.
What he loves
is to feel the wind in his face,
and to bask in the warmth of the sun.

Spirit Guide
for Miriam

One morning
Miriam woke up
holding her grandmother's hand.
Savta had come to her
from the spirit world
to reveal
that the souls of her children
have already chosen her,
and that in a past life
she and Savta
were sisters.

She tells
of traveling
with many spirit beings,
of being busy with old souls,
and with helping children
cross over.
She has brought Miriam three gifts
that need to be revealed:
a gold bracelet,
a blue shawl for protection,
and a white lily
for her heart.

Kissing her forehead,
touching her hair,
Savta stays close by.
*You're here
and I'm here,* she whispers,
but I will always be with you.
Among the secrets she reveals:
journey like a river,
sing like a sweet bird,
let the angels in.

Feathers

for Ruth Krasnoff

Before she died,
your mother promised to visit you,
and whenever she did,
she would leave a feather behind.
Ever since you have encountered,
in the most unlikely places,
a solitary feather.

If you pick up that feather
you might hear her whisper—

Listen,
if you only knew how easy it is
to glide away from this world,
all your fear
would vanish.

Somehow those feathers
fell through the cracks
between worlds,
to remind you
how much is hidden.

Escape Artist
for Tsila

My wife is an artist—
an escape artist.
You can find her in Prague,
Amsterdam,
Copenhagen,
or
Berlin.
Even Houdini would admire her sleight of hand—
now you see her,
now you don't.
Only Jerusalem can hold her back.

There
she wanders the streets of the old city
searching for her son,
our son,
who has also escaped.
But he knows
she will find him
no matter where he is hidden,
and that it is hopeless
to hide.

I wake here alone.
The walls are filled with her artwork,
but she is not here.
Jerusalem has prevailed
again.
And I know
that as soon as she gets back
she will be planning
her next escape.

Shira Schwartz
Soul Journey

You filled my heart with love
You healed so many years of hurt
With just one glance

When our eyes first met
I knew the day had come
I had found the one my soul had been
Waiting to reunite with

It is as if we have lived many lifetimes
Together
And yet I don't know your name
Until today

And finally we meet again
After so many lifetimes
The circle is complete

Destiny is already written
Just waiting to rediscover
The path our souls have travelled so far
Waiting to
Reunite

Water Poem

Dreaming in the daytime
Water rushing downward
Falling to her knees
She is in awe

Nobody can see her
But
          Angels
                    Alive
Watching

With open eyes

She feels their presence
She knows they are there

Nathan Simon
Cartography

Do I know this place?
Salt, flint and ashes
A cruel geography of crevassed
Deserts abandoned to blasts
Of firey and icey wind.

Cartographers of Hell have
Drawn on stories of survivors.
They do not come themselves
To take sightings, mark medians
And locate peaks and canyons.

But survivors' tales make poor maps.
Most come mindlessly, by accident
A few mad ones by a
Design that failed because
They blundered out again.

Survivors remember the mountains
Higher and the canyons deeper
Only the demons they encountered
Can you believe true.
The details defy imagining.

Through cracked lips they lie
To hide the secret of their
Escapes. Raspy stories of calming
Visions and guiding stars. Brilliant
Decisions grown of desperate logic.

Only to one another in
Whispers do they admit
They threw compasses, food and
Water away and gave themselves
Over to wild laughter.

From the Autobiography of Benvenutto Cellini

Their father saw the salamander
Dancing in the center of a winter's fire
He called the children from their bed
Pointed to the mystery in the flames
Boxed their ears, thrust pennies in their hands
So they would remember
And kissed them.

Head ringing, fingers clenched
Skin flushed and moist
The boy remembered and sought
The fire's image a thousand times.

I see that creature, flame defined,
Evoked in winter's dark smoky spaces
Of desire, lit by omnipotence.
Full of joy, I call you and point
"There! There it is! See it!"
I box your ears, thrust pennies in your hand
And kiss you
Cover you with loving kisses.

To Sari At Forty

When the woman customer complained
About growing older, I laughed and
Told her some things
Grow better with age.
The boss overheard and fired me
That ended my career in the grocery business.

I was fifteen. She was forty and
Stacked. I really liked her.
Forty sounded like such a funny
And improbable age.
You get to be 16 and drive,

18 and graduate or 21 and vote,
But forty? That was no where!

Sari! Sari! did you ever really believe
You would be forty. Not once in a
Million well modulated syllables
Inside and outside your head.
Some part of you ignoring time
Still stands knee deep in the new fallen
Snow believing it will never stop.

Pat Lorraine Simons
At the Holocaust Museum in Washington, D.C.

At the end of the tour, I enter the room
where signs say come in, reflect and be silent.
A spacious room, breathless and white,
light as a ghost, its dome lit clean by skylight and sunlight.
Here and there, survivors cluster,
bunched like bouquets of withering flowers,
their blue tattoo petals drinking the sunshine.
They cluster together ignoring the signs,
gesturing, joking and laughing out loud.
Why are you laughing, I whisper.
We've done all our crying, they say.

Jason Sommer
Film Clips of Munkacs, 1933

These bits of film are all the light
left to us of the tens of thousands
come to Munkacs for the Rebbe's
daughter's wedding,
                    reflecting like moons,
worlds, each of them. Jews
in sashes in bicycle parade
or massed, adrift, crossing the field
of view on foot: fedoras, shtreimels,
marriage wigs and kerchiefs, one white
babushka, long coats, dark coats, coats
of many colors in monochrome,
faces bespectacled or not
as can be seen, feet shod as can't—

all such as will be the harvest of
other light than this that fixes
them a solid phalanx framed
on screen awaiting the wedding party,
several thousand with their million
tiny movements like the blink
of leaves in the first hard scattering
of rain—small startlements
in the general sway of limb that presses
bodies against the straining line
of gendarmes, high helmets bobbing,
and the white babushka again, against
them down right, drawing the eye.

If it's true that light goes on forever,
could some of what these people reflect
pass by the sun it came from, continue
outward into the universe
to be received there just as we
here, looking on the countenance
of stars, receive the images

of icy calm or fierce last gasping
that traveled eons to us in silence?

It's sound that dies at the air's border.
His voice remains with us only,
the Munkatcher Rebbe, tightly ringed
in an eddy of crowd, speechifying
through microphones to America,
finger-wagging to remember
the Sabbath to keep it holy, which many
have not forgotten but do not keep,
cannot keep instead, of course,
much of these figures at the wedding:

a glimpse of the bride making her way
to the synagogue, but broad backs
of Hassids in their stripped black serge
and a flash photographer in the khaki
and cap of a soldier smother the chuppah
scene and therefore have become it.
Beyond them from a space at the center,
chanted blessings rise to disperse
in air like smoke.
                    We can't be sure
we've seen the groom whose history
is of the lesser agonies
even direct sun does little
to illuminate. He will survive
to renounce the post inherited
at the famous father-in-law's death.
He will accept, at least enough
to live in their state, the Zionists
he and his-father-in-law so
inveighed against,

                    these very ones
who dance—young men and women linking
hands to step the steps of hora
in two concentric circles, and one

smaller ring beside, round
and round as if for the Hassid wedding,
but if so it's so in counter joy
that the worlds might know another sort
than thou-shalt-not and next-world Hassids.
They sing and wheel, dancing to
the verses they sing over and over.

The song two-hundred-something children
sing once through in their filmed moments
is Hatikvah, which the old Rebbe would
have condemned—if not the *kinder* themselves,
then that desire the girls and boys
are taught to sing with the song, to have
the land before the Messiah comes.
Some few of them—star faces, faces
angled every phase of moon—
may have reached that land. The light could show.

What Old David Felt

"...but the King did not cohabit with her"—1 Kings 1

For one brief moment retrograde
as Abishag came to his bed
what flared inside the aged king
was anger borne of pride that such

a man for women as he'd been
should go so docilely to sleep
beside a lovely virgin for
the temperature, that the fire burned

so low by which he once could heat
himself and others also, still
he'd do such things—he knew just what
they were—and then he let it go.

Sons of Adam

It's certain Abel didn't live to breed,
while Cain wed one of those new women sprung
from nowhere. God's tattoo on him intrigued
her. So, bad-boy allure and *born to run*
assured his seed's continuance till Flood.
Then all aboard the ark were all God left,
and Noah's clan came from that later brood
of Eve and Adam, blank unstoried Seth—
from whom, then, us. His entry in the Bible,
obituarial; begotten, he begot;
named to replace his herder brother Abel;
departed aged nine-hundred; survived by Enosh.
A born forbear for us, no great repute
of either sort, sent in as substitute.

Judith Stix
The Holocaust Memorial, Washington, D.C.
September 16, 1993 · Rosh Hashanah, 5754

Walking this experience, this history
contemporaneous exactly with my own,
walking this spiral of enduring, spiral
that is the symbol of eternity in many
cultures, I see with eyes of darkness, speak
with my hand covering my mouth.

Kristallnacht, the Night of Broken Glass,
glitters. In my home place, Gemünden's
little synagogue was burned, just one
of many; but on the night before that
night, the fire was practiced with great
care — a cordial former soldier told me.

Color itself turns mute and silent here,
where shoes, gray shoes, shades of gray
shoes, hundreds and thousands of shoes,
march on together now in perfect stillness,
till shades themselves flare into shining.

Suitcases, pitiful suitcases, lie piled
below a boxcar as they fell, beside tracks
reaching to Heaven like a new Tower of Babel,
crying out for remedy, the angels weeping.

Tears on tears. Tears
for the victims. Tears
for the righteous helpers
who fought to save them. Tears
where the blood of Abel
speaks, a brother's blood
crying from the ground.
Tears on tears.

In the house where I am staying, a grave post
from Madagascar carries the stacked stars
on the head of a mourning woman, her eyes
just darkness, one hand covering her mouth.

Two Enchantments

I. A Story

There was a woman who lived a fairy tale,
who did and didn't want to look
into the mirror, and then, an old hag,
she looked and saw too late the beauty
she had had in youth. Now let the background
as she watches fill up with flowers, every
flower of spring, in a late burst of bloom.

II. Metamorphosis

What bird was I? Was I a goose? A swan?
A loon's voice broke from my startled throat,
and suddenly I dived into the sky-blue
of an icy lake, swimming a long way
and peering through clear waters, surfacing
at length into another sky, new-made.
I'm in my element. This is the day.

Maria Szapszewicz
I Promise I Will Tell the World

I speak about what happened to six million Jews
Babies, children, young and old.
But people turned so cold.

I heard it said so many times.
Forget about it.
That is the past.
You are here.....my dear.

But I spoke anyway.
Letting the world know.
Oh but they knew.
Not standing up for us.

It's so powerful,
The wounds never heal.
Nobody knows how we feel.

Now they are saying the survivors
Did not want to speak.
Maybe some did not.

But the rest of us rising from the ashes
Like the sphinx trying out our wings.
These survivors are my heroes
Who accomplished so very much.

They built new lives as they
Contributed to culture and civilization.
Building our own nation.

ERETZ ISRAEL

Oh G-d have mercy on us as
You watch us from above.

Today Never Tomorrow

When you have work to do
Don't wait; just do it now.
When you want to say something
Nice to a friend, say it now.
Don't wait for tomorrow.
Say it with love and compassion.
Today the sky is blue and bright
And there is so much light.
Tomorrow the sky might be dark,
And full of clouds.
If you are feeling blue and down,
Try to sing a song now.
Music will fill you heart
With love and compassion.

When you want to say
"I love you," to somebody,
Don't wait! Say it now.
Don't wait for tomorrow.
When you hurt someone,
Don't wait for fancy words to apologize.
Say "I'm sorry now.
We are not here forever.
When you want to say
A kind word to somebody,
Don't put it off and wait for tomorrow.
SAY IT NOW!!!
Tomorrow may never come.
We all can make a better world today.
Don't wait for tomorrow.

Jane O. Wayne
Seven Years Later
(*South of Zagreb*)

Nothing evident
                 except here and there
in poorer towns along the road,
the houses have white scars
             in the stucco, round as targets.

And further south
one small town keeps an outdoor museum
             where lights are strung
between tall poles
so wires zigzag over the collection—

             rust-bottomed tanks
in camouflage;
             and sculptural on a stand,
a fighter-jet, its fuselage lacerated
like an opened tin can.

             Whoever planned the layout
left a row of cannons
standing guard
outside a three-storey building
             that's already been bombed.

No roof, no window panes,
             most of the bricks flayed
from the pale stone skeleton
and the entry boarded up.
             A light rain starts. Stops.

Starts again
             until the grass is wet,
and the only other structure left
             doesn't shelter—
a few crumbling walls where we look

            out frameless windows
onto a stand of trees, fields,
                    hills in the distance—
        everything green again, as if the earth
forgave the fire.

First published by *Natural Bridge Magazine*

The Portrait

>   *...like trying to pick up the contents of a glass of water*
>   *without the glass.*
>   Robert Musil

Two dimensional. Only outlines.
        Oh, maybe a detail here
and there—
bifocals slipping down the nose,
                    or eye-brows arched in jest,
still it fails to breathe,
            lacks fire, bounce— and photographs
don't help—frozen moments
where nothing more can happen.
                    I could go on

about his leaving drawers
and closets open,
                    or how his shoulders shook
when he laughed, and keeping time
            to jazz, the way he bobbed
in place. You could even see
                    what he saw—
            the man seated at the end
of a bed in a self-portrait, the angularity
            of legs, one ankle rested

on the other knee as if tying a shoe;
                    and his clothes, the bed,

the walls—everything in blues
       and mauves, everything intentional,
but you wouldn't know him
any better than the peasant
                quietly climbing the hill,
a bundle of reeds on his back,
       in the Japanese print
on the other wall.

Published in *The Other Place You Live,* Jane O Wayne

Visits

In a burst
as when you lift a lid from boiling water
he comes back:
a penciled note tucked inside a book,
or a jar of salvaged varnish
crusted over, like a scab.
The house is mined.
A plate breaks; a kitchen chair
teeters on hind legs; even bread-crumbs
careless on a stick of butter can explode.
You've happened onto gloves
buried under papers,
or on the bottom of a drawer
a roll of film that's been exposed.
That's all it takes.
A room can give off sparks
the way a burning log does—
bright visits that you're never ready for.
When you tear a rag in two
it's not shredding you hear
but a dust-cloth reverting to a shirt.

Published in *From the Night Album,* Jane O. Wayne

A Quick Lesson

You might have left it out overnight,
the way it's lying in the shade near your swing,
its brindled fur smooth as a new toy animal's.

It lets you hunker down to get a closer look,
even lets you nudge it in the side—the same prod
you'd use to wake the cat

though this sleeper doesn't startle
toward the privet-hedge. Nothing happens
until you claim it with both hands,

then what was docile on the ground
takes on a cardboard-stiffness—
some stronger hold than yours already on it.

There's a moment—still cradling it—
when whatever stopped in the garden
makes you stop—and in the hush

though you're far too young
to ask if it weighs now what it did before,
if the life in it weighed nothing

you must be weighing
something in your mind
before you let it go: rabbit and all.

Published in *From the Night Album*, Jane O. Wayne

A Distant Cello Plays (November 10, 1938)
for Hedy Epstein

When she tells her tale, the group grows silent.
She's going back, leading the way by heart
over the broken glass, showing us the detour,
the same streets and alleyways
she took home from school that day.
We can see her climb the fence,
thief-like, into her own garden
and enter the back door too late – the house
still full of cooking odors, but empty.
She doesn't stay so we follow
along the narrow side streets, hiding with her
in an entryway, while nearby a crowd is jeering –
heaving bricks through the windows
of her uncle's hardware store, looting
in the broad daylight of the past.
We're breathless then, running until reach
her uncle's house where the women let us in
and bolt the door behind us. We climb the stairs
to watch the street from an upstairs balcony.
Men with luggage pass, a grim procession
toward the station – familiar faces,
neighbors, then her father.
He doesn't look up, and we don't call out.
We're closing the shutters, closing the wardrobe
behind us on the third floor, huddling
with them in the darkness: her aunt, her mother,
and the girl without whom
we'd never have found this hiding place.

Published in *The Other Place You Live*, Jane O. Wayne

Sharon Weissman
In Loving Memory of Cantor Edward Fogel

The songs
The jokes
The fun
we would have at choir practice
listening to stories of all the places
where he had sung

Making beautiful harmonies together
under his tutelage
and sharing this with the congregation

Listening to his Aveinu Malkenu

Memories of Ed officiating at my sons'
Bar Mitzvahs as well as my Bat Mitvach

The joy he brought others with his
wonderful voice and the joy
he received from music are his legacy

May the heavenly angels welcome him with song
and may he serenade G-d with the
glorious melodies of his soul

May his memory always be for a blessing

My Rabbi's Hands

The lovely hands
the long fingers
speaking their own language

Reaching, emphasizing,
expressive and elegant
"up, out, in"
leading the way
Opening, clenching,
circling thumb and forefinger,
hand to heart

Fingers together—joining
lyrical, demonstrating
always pointing the way

Lifting open hands to G!d

May I emulate the lessons her hands teach

Renee Winter
To Stephanie Ruth

In the beginning (of the Secular Year)
G-d Created her,
A vibrancy that jostled and expanded inside of me.
That caused me to laugh, to glow, to cry, to pray, to love
To wonder, imagine, marvel and fear
And to focus on the blossoming sphere that was a part of me.

A girl? A boy?
A name?
A child.
A miracle.
Erev ROSH HASHANAH her demands commenced,
Intensifying with a crescendo of pain
That ripped me open as she propelled forth at 12:57 a.m.,
Announcing her separateness.

In the beginning (of the Jewish Year)
She was born.
A daughter who grows and explores outside of me.
Who causes me to smile, to yell, to worry, to care, to hope.
To try, teach, encourage and influence
And to focus on a human being who is a part of and from me.

A baby.
A toddler.
A bat mitzvah.
A miracle.

Happy Birthday, my dear daughter.
Happy New Year.

G-d bless.

Without Benefit of Kaddish

He died when I was nine,
Or so I decided.
Without benefit of Kaddish
Mourning was stifled.

His remains, unburied, I sought in the shape of others I would love.

I resurrected him when I was thirty,
And so I questioned
Without benefit of funeral,
Why did you die?

His reasons I heard, yet still cried for one I had loved.

He left when he was angry.
For I remained silent.
Without benefit of usage,
"Father" could not survive.

He died when he was aged,
Or so I was told
Without benefit of my presence.
Now, do I pray?

"May G-d remember the soul of my father who has gone to his eternal rest. In remembrance of him, I shall perform acts of charity and goodness. May his soul be bound in the bond of eternal life, in the company of the immortal souls of Abraham, Isaac and Jacob, of Sarah, Rebecca, Rachel and Leah who have merited the bliss of immortality. Amen"★

From The Prayer Book by Bokser Bluzim

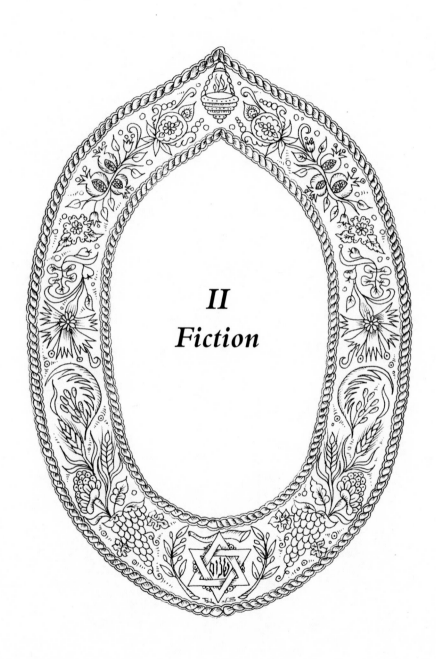

II
Fiction

Lane Barnholtz
Pavel Spits on Stalin

For a time, life had somewhat returned to normal. It was summer 1937. Two and a half years had passed since the assassination of Leningrad Party boss Sergei Kirov, when mass arrests followed—and I swear, at least one family on every floor of our apartment building had vanished.

Since that time I had climbed in the Red Army's Political Department to the rank of regimental military commissar, a more impressive sounding title than my responsibilities merited, since I rarely ventured into the field with troops. I spent the bulk of my time behind a desk in the divisional Political Section, editing pamphlets and writing propaganda leaflets, all the material composed in language rudimentary enough for common foot soldiers to understand. This innocuous activity and menial bureaucratic duties filled my uneventful days, which is how I liked it. All I wanted from life was the energy and peace of mind to enjoy time with my wife and daughter and to insulate them from the horrid possibilities of our time.

But then, things began to heat up again.

You must understand our time. It was a time when an unannounced visit by the NKVD meant a Siberian penal colony. A time when twenty minutes tardiness for a day's work on a collective farm, in a state factory or for any office job brought charges of economic sabotage— punishable by death. A time when grumbling about food shortages or unenthusiastic applause at a Party rally equaled anti-Soviet agitation— no maximum penalty specified by the Criminal Code. A time when children, indoctrinated with revolutionary zeal, informed on their parents; when the state enslaved entire villages because it needed their labor; when public worship of God exposed one as a political criminal when counterrevolutionary minorities, such as Jews, disappeared.

And I was part of this system. For if one was not of it, it consumed you. And if one was of it, it owned you. What began after the Revolution as a national endeavor to construct utopia in a generation, had corrupted into a bureaucratic hierarchy of paranoia sustained by labor camps, deportations, terror and murder.

A knock on your door at 3 a.m. Four NKVD agents ransack your home then haul you away in a steel-gray prison van—standing room only in the wagon. The villains toss you into a cell in Kresty Prison where a series of blue-capped NKVD interrogators beat a confession out of you in three days' time. And for what? Because the district NKVD has its production quota, too.

Next, the state prosecutor argues that you violated Article 58 of the Criminal Code, Section 6: dealing with crimes of espionage, suspicion of espionage, unproven espionage and contacts leading to suspicion of espionage. Remember Uncle Vanya's neighbor when you were a boy? He spoke German, didn't he? Consorting with a spy. The judges sentence you to ten years in Gulag, the collection of NKVD forced-labor camps and penal colonies scattered throughout Siberia and Central Asia.

Let us not forget, ten years without the right to correspond. But it makes no matter. Who will you correspond with? The following day NKVD operatives arrest your wife and children for infraction of Article 58, Section 12: failure to denounce an enemy of the people.

★ ★ ★

Pavel Vassilyevich Rozanov was an amiable fellow: mid-thirties, short, round, balding, clean shaven, a smile for most everyone. No one in our Political Section could say a terribly bad thing, or for that matter a wonderfully good thing about Pavel, except that he could always make you laugh. Poor fellow, though, allergies tormented him.

We worked late that summer evening near the end of Leningrad's famous white nights, the time between mid-June and early July when neither dusk nor dawn visits the city, and Leningrad knows only daylight. Pavel asked if I would like a rest from my duties and care to accompany him on a stroll.

"A break would be nice," I agreed with Pavel. "There's nothing I can work on tonight that won't be on my desk tomorrow morning."

"And what of my desk!" Pavel announced. "There are only so many pamphlets a man can edit and manuals he can revise before his brain boils."

"I wouldn't want your brain to boil."

"So why do we wait?"

We exited our office, two overworked political commissars clad in brown military uniforms. Our Political Section was located in a building facing Nevsky Prospect, the main thoroughfare of Leningrad, now sparsely populated due to a recently completed rain shower. A fresh film of water slicked over the boulevard's pavement. The liquid twinkled in the semi-twilight of the white night, like a just waxed Winter Palace hallway, and a humid mist hovered in the air.

I imagine that during the white nights Nevsky Prospect is not only the most breathtaking place in Russia, but the world. Italian and

French architects designed most of the structures along the Nevsky in the eighteenth and nineteenth centuries. Imposing classical facades alternate with baroque ornamentation. Gilded spires hang on the horizon, glistening in the ethereal light. Mist oozes off the River Neva and clings to cobblestone streets. Canals ripple underneath pedestrian bridges. And no building rises higher than the Winter Palace, the former royal domain, located adjacent to the western end of the boulevard.

Pavel and I walked past the Kazan Cathedral, the most majestic structure on Nevsky Prospect. Awe-inspiring statues of saints and Russian warriors adorned the niches in the cathedral's facade. A semicircular granite colonnade extended from the sanctuary and backed a square containing statues of two of Imperial Russia's greatest military commanders.

The shrine, modeled after St. Peter's Cathedral in Rome, the Party had converted into the Museum of the History of Religion and Atheism. Erected to be one of the world's greatest monuments to Orthodox Christianity, the house of worship the Party now dedicated to the infamy of God.

"Nikolai Ivanovich," Pavel spoke. "My allergies have been mild today. My wife says it is unwise to tempt luck, but I say we follow the Moika Canal to the Summer Garden."

"If you like," I assented. "But if your luck turns sour, don't complain to me."

"Of course, not. I'll complain to my wife."

We turned right at the Moika Canal. Above us, the orange-red sun bled across the sky. Below us, the channel water escorted us alongside its granite-lined embankment.

We then reached the Summer Garden, intended by Peter the Great to be Russia's equal to France's gardens of Versailles, for two centuries the park having served as the city's hub of social life and also the chosen spot for individuals seeking solitary renewal. A fragrant breeze drifted out the garden and rolled in our direction. Pavel breathed in deeply and slowly exhaled.

"Did you smell that?" Pavel alerted me in an excited state.

"The canal water?" I teased him. "It smells rancid."

"No, you fool. Lilacs. Linden trees. Can you believe it?"

"Why shouldn't I believe it?" I continued to play Pavel. "This is summer in Leningrad."

"Yes, and every summer I am nearly bedridden by allergies. But tonight, not even an itch." Pavel clasped his hands together and raised them over his head. "Finally, my years of drinking have cured me. The vodka has killed the allergies that torture me every summer."

"Bravo, comrade doctor," I congratulated Pavel. "But if you don't mind cutting short your celebration, I'd like to see the park this evening."

"Comrade doctor, hmm. I rather like that."

We walked alongside the Summer Garden's wrought-iron fence, approaching the park's entrance. Medallions decorated with Medusa heads, the mythological beast with a mane of serpents and whose gaze transformed beholders into stone, adorned the grille. We passed unscathed and entered the garden.

We followed the Main Alley, the park's central promenade, past a statue of Ceres, goddess of the harvest, and by marble embodiments of Truth, Plenty and Justice; and I laughed to myself, more in lament than amusement. I imagined the half-serpent Medusa was an NKVD agent assigned with petrifying mankind's highest ideals—Truth, Plenty and Justice victims of her glare.

As for Pavel: "I am so refreshed," he bubbled. "Jasmine. Cherry blossoms. And my allergies have not struck once. And look!" Pavel stepped onto a side path and pointed at a patch of scarlet roses alongside the base of a statue, ten or fifteen meters down the path. "Magnificent," he marveled.

The roses were handsome and as always the Summer Garden regal, but my thoughts had turned to Masha and Katya. "Yes, Pavel, the flowers are beautiful," I said. "But the truth is, Masha frets when I work late, and I'd like to go home and have time with Katya before she goes to bed."

"Just a few minutes longer," Pavel requested. He tilted back his head and sniffed the air. "Roses. I haven't smelt them for years."

Smelling roses may have been an event for Pavel, but it was no novelty for me. And besides, the scent of the flowers commingled with the stench of makhorka tobacco, the most common Soviet tobacco. Makhorka consisted of tobacco stems rather than leaves, the result being a particularly pungent odor. Two smokers sat on a bench across from the roses, eyeing Pavel and I while we spoke.

"Pavel, I cannot tell you how touched I am that you can enjoy the flora in the Summer Garden tonight," I humored him. "But since I am unable to express how I feel, I'm leaving. I want to see my wife and daughter."

"Wait just one more minute," Pavel appealed. "I want to smell a rose. It's been years. I won't be long."

Pavel did not wait for my decline. He turned onto the side path and briskly walked toward the patch of roses.

By now the burnt-orange sun half dipped below the horizon, refusing to fall any farther. A hazy pink sheen pulsed in its wake. Against this blurry gloss, Pavel's hurried form and the profiles of the two seated smokers whom Pavel neared all projected like black silhouettes against a vaporous pink backdrop.

Pavel came to the flowers and squatted. He bowed his face over the blooms and cradled a single rose between his palms, as if it were an injured butterfly. He dipped his neck and lowered his nose so to sample the flower's bouquet. Then, without warning, Pavel's allergies attacked. His eyes filled with tears and his face blushed blood red. A fit of sneezing and coughing gripped him. He hacked and wheezed with such force, it was as if a demon had entered his body and was jerking it to and fro. At one point, the seizure was so strong that Pavel lost his balance and fell over. After a minute or so the attack passed. Pavel pulled a kerchief from his back pocket, cleaned his face, spat and rose.

As it should happen, the pedestal that the patch of roses wrapped around supported a life-sized casting of Comrade Stalin. The two smokers on the bench threw their tobacco to the ground and approached Pavel.

"Excuse me, comrade," the taller of the two silhouettes confronted Pavel. "As a habit do you spit on the General Secretary of the Communist Party?"

Plain-clothed NKVD. Their moment of commune with nature and a cast-iron incarnation of their benefactor had been ruined by a pudgy, wheezing bureaucrat who had the audacity to spit at their lord's feet.

Pavel wiped his face again and straightened himself as tall as possible. "This is a terrible mistake," he stuttered. "You see, if I may explain, by the way, I am a Party member, but as I was saying—"

"Your identification," the shorter shadow demanded.

"But whatever for?" Pavel mumbled.

"It will only be worse for you if you stall us," the taller shadow threatened. "Don't force us to ask again."

I hid behind a hedge and observed, uncertain what to do, fearing for Pavel, but also afraid for myself. Had they seen me?

Pavel pleaded with them in a plaintive voice: "But, I've done nothing. I have allergies, you see. I only wanted to sniff a rose. Perhaps it was foolish of me. Ahh … no question. It was foolish of me. Yes, it was very—"

The taller shadow cocked back his right arm and punched Pavel square in the nose. I heard a hollow "Pop!" like a chicken bone snapping.

Pavel moaned, staggered and fell to one knee. Blood streamed out his nostrils, over his lips and onto his uniform. He looked up at his two interrogators. His expression in the pinkish light resembled that of a toddler who had touched fire for the first time, so astounded by the unexpected pain that he was unsure how to react.

The taller shadow seized Pavel by the scruff of the neck and forced Pavel into a kneel. He thrust Pavel's face into the bed of roses. Pavel's face descended below the roses' foliage into their thorny stems.

I wanted to run, but I knew better. A dash may have drawn attention, and the last thing I wanted was an NKVD escort to Kresty or Shpalerny prisons. I cautiously stepped backward away from the side path, minding to remain blocked from view by bushes or trees, and then I swiftly walked to the Summer Garden's exit with my head always over one shoulder, checking to be sure I had not been followed.

What else was there to do? Remain and attempt to extricate Pavel by explaining to the NKVD brutes that poor Pavel should be excused for spitting at Stalin's feet because he has allergies? Yes. And then they would arrest me for collaborating with an enemy of the people! I know of citizens executed for less. I know as a fact the NKVD exiled Natasha, the janitor in our Political Section, to Siberia because she swatted a fly that crawled across a portrait of General Secretary Stalin. How was Natasha to know that one of the informers in our office witnessed her innocent act and reported to the NKVD that she maliciously slapped Stalin's likeness with a dirty rag!

No. I am neither brave nor foolish. I backed away from the incident and hurried from the park.

★   ★   ★

I walked home in a daze. Leningrad's alleys and avenues felt like a labyrinth of caverns and caves. The deeper I penetrated her catacombs, the tighter they closed in around me. I arrived at my apartment building's courtyard and ascended the stairs to our second-floor flat, but each step up felt like a descent leading to an NKVD prison cell. I came to our door and opened it.

"Papa!" Katya shouted. She ran to embrace me. Her hug jolted me from my underworld spell. She squeezed me tightly and looked up at me with wide eyes.

"Papa," she stuttered, "Papa, I'm happy you're home. But Papa, I want—"

I lowered my right arm and stroked my hand through my five-year-old daughter's chocolate-colored, shoulder-length hair. Katya was too agitated to appreciate my affection.

"—Papa, my tummy says it's angry at you," she blurted out.

"Why is your tummy angry at me?" I addressed the fairy who had plucked me out of my trance.

"My tummy is angry, because my tummy says it's hungry." Katya released her embrace, placed both her hands over her stomach and rubbed.

I slid my hand out of her hair, squatted and patted her stomach.

"I'm sorry I'm late," I apologized to Katya's stomach. "You cannot imagine how sorry."

"How sorry?" Masha quipped as she approached and then crouched beside me. "And how late again?"

Masha was dressed casually, barefoot, wearing only a white cotton dressing gown, as was her habit before sitting to supper. Katya, as well, changed into a matching gown before most suppers. Katya tried in as many ways as possible to emulate her mother.

Both were unkempt with disheveled hair, as anyone would be this late in the evening. The never-ending stream of late evenings and worrisome days had just now begun to show on Masha's face. But tonight when I looked at her, I saw the teenage girl whom I had met beneath a Leningrad white night on Nevsky Prospect seven summers ago: round face and round features; straight auburn hair brushing against her shoulders; light-hazel eyes with deep, almost bushy eyebrows; slightly plump build, but not heavy; unusually clear skin—her finest feature—clearer than a tumbler full of vodka; the aroma of earth and birch in her hair.

True, Masha was a peasant girl. She lacked sophistication. Yet, in her simplicity, her consistency, lie her beauty and my joy. Masha was Masha—uncomplex, reliable, no deeper layers to explore, no motivations to question. What I saw was her, what she revealed was her. No secrecy, no pretense—just truth.

"Well, I don't want our daughter to suffer hunger any longer," Masha declared, "or for you to endure her stomach's anger. So then, let's sit to supper. But first ..." Masha nuzzled her nose against my cheek and kissed me. Then she whispered in my ear, "I hate it when you work late. I hope you have a good excuse. Otherwise, I'll name a punishment later tonight."

"Hey! No secrets," Katya objected. "Secrets aren't fair."

"You want me to tell you a secret?" Masha tempted Katya.

"Yeah!" Katya accepted without a second thought. Our daughter was not above invoking moral principles, but only for her benefit.

Masha leaned over to Katya's ear. Katya smiled wildly in anticipation, and Masha spoke in a voice loud enough for me to hear: "I told your Papa that I miss him when he's late and that I love him."

Katya looked at me, obviously disappointed with the lack of drama in Masha's secret. "That's no secret. Papa, is that all Mama said?"

"In so many words."

We sat to supper, three mismatched chairs around our unfinished pine table in our front room. The table was tiny, but no more so than our two-room flat. Our plain ceramic dishware barely fit on its surface.

Our flat originally had been part of a multistoried, private residence owned by a wealthy industrialist. We speculated that it and the other flats on the second floor had been servants quarters. However, after the Revolution the government confiscated the property, as it did all apartments and homes of enemies of the people, and partitioned the properties into flats that it then assigned to Leningrad citizens.

The flats were cramped and in disrepair, as were all living spaces in Leningrad, except those occupied by the Party elite. Our bed and bureau barely fit into our lone bedroom, leaving just enough space to walk around the bed. The front room had only enough space for our dinner table, which we had pushed against a wall in order to save space; a tea table with a samovar; and a lumpy, faded-pink sofa.

Still, Masha and I knew ourselves fortunate to have a home near the city center, just two blocks off Nevsky Prospect—an excellent location. Furthermore, Masha continually added touches to the flat to compensate for its dingy state. Over cracks in our grayish plaster walls Masha hung family portraits that she had drawn with charcoal and hand framed. She covered the majority of the scuffs in the front room's hardwood floor with a second-hand remnant of green-and-gold-checked carpeting, and she knitted a lace tablecloth that she spread over the tea table upon which stood our samovar.

That evening, Masha had prepared an exceptional meal, for it was summer in Leningrad and food was plentiful. A borscht of cabbage, onion, carrot, potato and beet, spiced with garlic, waited for me. A fresh round of black bread lay sliced on a plate, and we had enough butter to smear over each slice, if we chose, as well as sour cream to drop into our borscht. And for our entree, Masha had fried three beef cutlets with garlic and onion, still tender and warm.

I so appreciated that Masha consistently cooked delicious suppers for Katya and me. Although there is no question that cooking as well as she did required extra effort, not least of which was sharing the communal kitchen with the five other families on our floor, Masha enjoyed feeding us well.

And for my part, I always attempted as best I could to release the frictions of my day before sitting to dine with my girls, so as in no way to diminish the pleasure of our suppers together. Although initially it was difficult, hiding distress from Masha and Katya had become second nature. After nearly a decade employed in the Red Army's Political Department, I now instinctively masked anxiety. But Pavel would not leave my mind. I tried to forget, but thoughts of Pavel resurfaced and pounded against my brow. The stench of makhorka tobacco conjured in my nose and ruined my appetite. How to tell Masha of Pavel's arrest? How long till Pavel denounced me under torture and an NKVD prison van came for me? How could I face my daughter, knowing this likely the last she would ever see of me? As a grown woman would she remember me, or would Katya's memory of me be as ephemeral as autumn's first frost?

I forced myself to eat, so not to insult Masha. For comfort, I looked at my darling daughter. Katya ate ravenously. Even for her, she ate with exceptional zeal. She was small for her age, a half head shorter than the next smallest child in her class. Yet, she ate as much as Masha, if not more.

"Why is your tummy so hungry tonight?" I asked Katya, expecting that conversation with my daughter would lighten my mood. "Didn't you eat lunch?"

"We had fish. It smelt like dog." Katya burst into laughter. "Dogs stink."

Dogs terrified Katya. Masha and I were at a loss as to why. Katya loved cats. She attempted to pet every one she saw and never became discouraged, although almost without exception cats scampered away from our bold daughter.

But dogs Katya loathed. Furthermore, whenever Katya thought disparagingly of something—a person, a toy, clothing, food—she likened it to some aspect of a dog. Our neighbor's impulsive boy acted like a dog. A doll with frayed hair looked like a dog. Uncomfortable clothes scratched like a dog. Food Katya disliked smelt like a dog.

Katya's abhorrence of canines even infiltrated her dreams. She occasionally had nightmares in which hounds smashed down our door and dragged her away. Or perhaps, it once occurred to me, it was not her fear of dogs that intruded upon her slumber, but the terror of her dreams that impinged on her waking life.

Whichever, our daughter's was an odd obsession that we assured ourselves she would eventually outgrow. But at the time, Masha and I agreed not to overreact to Katya's bewildering remarks.

"This borscht is my favorite," Katya announced. "It doesn't smell like dog. Watch me. I can eat it all up. I ate three carrots. Two of these." She pointed at a slice of beet.

"Beets," I said.

"Yeah. Two in a row. And one potato in a row." Katya rocked back and forth in her chair and hummed while she ate. "I'm going to eat my borscht to the very last one," she declared.

"What did you do at kindergarten today?" I asked.

"Nothing."

"Nothing? But you were there all day."

"Ah . . ." Katya popped a chunk of beet into her mouth and spoke while chewing, "we sang."

"What did you sing?"

She dropped her spoon onto the table and contorted her face, as if to let me know I couldn't have asked a more ignorant question.

"We sang songs," she huffed, then picked up her spoon and resumed eating.

"I know you sang songs. Which songs?"

"Papa, I love you," Katya said to me while she investigated an oddly shaped section of carrot, attempting to deflect my question.

Masha smiled at me, then spoke to Katya. "Sunshine, sing Papa the song you learned today at school."

Katya held the bumpy section of carrot between her thumb and forefinger. "Mama, do I have to eat this?"

"No, you don't have to eat it," Masha bargained. "Now how about a song instead?"

"Can I have another bowl," Katya answered, ignoring our requests, then quickly added, "pleeease."

"Since you said *please* you can have another bowl. But first, sing your Papa a song."

"Do I have to?"

"An easy song"

Katya sighed, then began serenading the carrot gripped between her fingers:

    The moonlight, the bright moonlight
    White light of the moon
    Shows the way
    Shows me the way home.
    The moonlight—

Katya stopped in midverse. "I forgot the rest."

"That was beautiful, Katya," I praised her. "I will always remember it. Sunshine, is your tummy still angry at me?"

"Never," Katya replied as she ogled the bowl of borscht Masha was placing in front of her.

"What does your tummy say now?"

Katya looked at me. "My tummy says, 'Smile.'"

Soon after supper Katya became drowsy. As was our custom before our daughter's bedtime, either Masha or I read Katya a story. So for the fourth night in a row, Katya requested I read *Maria Morevna* to her, the story of how Ivan Czarevich liberates his kidnapped wife Maria Morevna from Koshchey the Deathless, the ancient wizard who would not die. With assistance from both a talking queen bee and a speaking lioness, as well as help from several magical birds, Ivan Czarevich not only defeats Koshchey the Deathless, but also outwits Baba Yaga, the sorceress who lives beyond the river of fire.

The story enthralled Katya, especially the wild animals that could speak. Katya recited sections of the story she had memorized, counted bees and lion cubs, and knew all the characters by name.

But as spellbound as Katya was by the story, I was even more enchanted with her. She was innocent. Perfect. Her world and life were good. She could fathom nothing else. She justified my existence.

I flitted my eyes between the text and glances at Katya's tiny features: a nose that turned slightly up, toes that curled under during dramatic moments in the story, dark hazel irises devoid of imperfections, gaps in her smile caused by missing teeth. I wondered how she would look in a year, if the next time I saw her she would be a grown woman. Would Katya forgive me for being absent from her childhood? Would Masha be forced to take domestic odd jobs in order to feed our daughter? Would the memories of this evening be enough to sustain me through ten years of forced labor in a Siberian salt mine? How long till Pavel denounced me? When would the NKVD arrive?

My good friend Yuri Kostin, also a Red Army political commissar, had confided to me that since the Kirov purges he had kept ready a bundle of personal effects and winter garments on his dresser, should an NKVD squad come for him at night. I knew this was a common practice among Leningrad Party members, but I did not want to worry Masha and Katya. I packed no traveling bag. Perhaps I should have, not only as a precaution but also as a contrivance to compel Masha and I to face the truth of our time. But no. I wanted my home to be a refuge from the insanity, even if the haven were erected upon delusions.

I picked up Katya off my lap and sat her on our pink sofa, which doubled as her bed.

"Good night, dear little one." I kissed her forehead. "I love you."

"I love you, Papa. You can read me the story tomorrow."

Masha approached with a pillow and bed linen folded in her arms. I retired to my and Masha's bedroom, and observed through the open bedroom door as Masha and Katya arranged the bedding on the sofa. Masha fluffed Katya's pillow, and then our little girl situated herself between a white cotton sheet and a hand-knitted red quilt.

I slipped off my boots and disrobed from my uniform down to my under garments. I watched Masha tuck Katya in under the quilt, and I savored the sight of them exchanging their goodnight affections. I felt like a fallen angel permitted a final glimpse of paradise.

Masha entered our bedroom and silently shut the door halfway. She retrieved her most recent knitting project from our closet, socks for her sister Valya. She joined me in bed, and as was our routine, Masha quietly knitted, waiting for Katya to fall asleep before initiating conversation with me.

I lay on my back staring at the ceiling, listening for any unusual activity in the street. I was distracted by the rubbing of Masha's knitting needles and the ruffling of Katya's bedding. But it was not long till our daughter settled into a comfortable position, and I heard the delicate breaths of her slumber.

I refocused my attention to outside. Silence. For now, the hounds of Katya's nightmares and the demons of state security were at bay.

Masha rose, closed the bedroom door, and returned to bed. "You are quiet tonight, my husband," she commented. "Is something troubling you?"

"No, nothing."

Masha put her needles aside. She laid her head on my right shoulder and tilted her neck, so to look upon my face.

"I don't believe you," she murmured.

I do not enjoy lying to Masha, not even white lies. And she would not ask unless she truly wanted to know. I knew that about her, sure enough. I looked over her full lips, curled into a contented smile, and her patient eyes, half concealed by her tired squint. I stroked her cheeks with my left forefinger and watched her skin fold in around my finger. I did not want to hurt her. But she needed to know. And better she heard it from me than from an NKVD officer demanding entry into our home.

"Masha, they've arrested Pavel."

"What!" she screamed.

I placed my left hand lightly over her mouth to muffle her cry, so not to chance waking Katya, and I repeated, "The NKVD took Pavel." I removed my hand.

"It's a mistake. Yes, tomorrow they'll release him and all will be as before. We have nothing to fear." Masha spoke in a constricted whisper, like air hissing from a punctured rubber ball. She tried to quell both her emotion and tone, but her panic streamed forth. I looked into her eyes. They pleaded for hope, but I knew of none to console them with.

"Masha, I wish it, but they won't release Pavel," I quietly told her. "We must face what is. They never release anyone."

"They do!" Masha contended in a barely audible whisper that filled our bedroom with fright. "I read in *Leningradskaya Pravda* that—"

"Lies," I cut her off.

"How do you know?" Masha demanded. "Did you see the arrest?"

My brow pounded. I ground my teeth, squeezed shut my eyes and furrowed my fingers into my forehead.

"Don't argue with me, wife!" I snapped. "I saw them arrest Pavel. I was with him. In the Summer Garden. Tonight."

"No, Kolya! You idiot!"

"Quiet. You'll wake Katya."

"Better me than the NKVD," Masha shot back. "I can't believe you are so stupid! What were you doing there?"

"Just walking. It was so innocent. Pavel has allergies. He sneezed and spat. Two bluecaps saw and thought he was spitting on the statue of Stalin."

"Pavel spit on Comrade Stalin!" Masha gasped.

"Just a statue. Not so loud."

"Just a statue! Pavel may just as well have kicked the devil in the face."

Masha rose to her feet and paced at the foot of our bed.

"Masha, what are you doing?"

"What were you doing, Kolya? What were you thinking?"

Masha stopped pacing and sat on the floor next to my side of the bed. She was attempting to get close to the earth, a habit from her peasant roots that comforted her when she became distressed.

She continued to harass me in a wheezing hiss: "Katya and I beg you to come home early every night. What will I do if they arrest you? What will become of us? No. This isn't happening. You are a good Communist. Not to us."

"Masha, I'm so sorry. It's not my fault."

"Don't talk to me, Kolya. I can't hear any more of this."

"Masha, we can't ignore this. Don't blame me."

Masha placed her right hand over her heart and extended her left hand to me.

"Kolya, come here and just hold me."

I came to the floor and held her, and she gripped me. I listened in the street for unfamiliar noises. I felt her silent tears saturate the shoulder of my undershirt. I reviewed the pained regrets of my life. If I only had acted differently at those times, perhaps I could have averted the series of events that had brought us to our impending ruin. I burrowed my face into Masha's hair, into which I had always found comfort, and I cried my first tears as a man.

"I love you, Kolya," Masha whispered as she sobbed onto my shoulder.

"Masha, its impossible to say how much I love you," I stuttered, unaccustomed to my own tears. "I tried to protect us. I tried so hard."

"Kolya, I don't blame you. I'm sorry if I said otherwise. What will we do?"

We huddled on the floor, believing this our last evening together. So much to say. Where to begin? But what we thought to be our final moments with each other were too precious to squander on belated apologies and sentimental revelations. I pressed my body against Masha's. This is all I wanted. All that mattered. To expend energy elsewhere would diminish our embrace.

We remained on the floor until Masha could cry no more and my few tears ceased any longer to provide solace. We returned to our bed, cuddled and waited.

As the night progressed and our initial hysteria subsided, my thoughts turned to tactics for safeguarding Masha and Katya from NKVD persecution. Together, Masha and I settled upon a strategy of whom among our family and friends to betray to false accusations when NKVD agents would demand denunciations from us and whom among our loved ones to defend. Though at some point while under arrest, we both acknowledged that I, and most likely Masha, would have to confess to crimes.

I explained to Masha the importance of when to confess and how many people to denounce at a time in order to limit suffering during interrogation. Too many confessions too quickly—your interrogator will believe he has a real patsy and torture you for more admissions: "Stand in that corner for three hours while I write your confession," your interrogator commands. "And if you should lean against a wall? Well, then we will see how long you can balance on your knees, feet off the floor, straight back. Now begin!"

Too few denunciations too late—your inquisitor casts you into an unheated punishment cell so cramped you cannot sit, let alone bend your knees more than a few centimeters. Twenty-four. Forty-eight. Seventy-two hours. It is your interrogator's whim. No food. No water. And sleep—not permitted!

Yes, minimizing one's pain and maximizing the interrogator's gratification was an art in itself.

And for the finishing touch, Masha and I accepted that if necessary, we should betray each other in order to lessen our suffering. However, we both swore to protect Katya.

So we waited.

They did not come. That night, the next night, the next, nor thereafter.

All that week I expected at any moment NKVD agents would barge into my Political Section and whisk me away. Fellow workers fretted over Pavel's unexplained absence. In spite of their best efforts to bury it, their dread surfaced onto their faces. But none dare gossip. All feared what I knew, that at that instant an NKVD interrogator was demanding that Pavel denounce the confederates of his spy ring. And how many would Pavel expose in order to end his misery? A single arrest never sated the NKVD. It craved batches. After all, logic dictates that for every admitted spy of the international bourgeoisie there must be ten at large. And who more culpable than the confessed criminal's family, friends and fellow workers? Rats run in packs, now don't they?

But the NKVD never came.

Did Pavel not denounce me? Unlikely. Pavel was the sort who dickered down the prices of family keepsakes that kopeckless widows peddled in open-air markets after NKVD executioners had plugged eight grams of lead into the heads of their husbands.

Were NKVD prisons full? Never too full. I heard rumors that in Shpalerny Prison guards locked forty prisoners into four-man cells, in Kresty Prison twelve prisoners into one-man cells.

Perhaps Pavel was the final arrest that fulfilled the district NKVD's quota? Or maybe Pavel's interrogator was himself arrested, thus, his future prey spared. Who knows by what fortune the NKVD did not come for me. By what whimsy of fate did my family and I survive? I fear the answer. For to have survived and to have risen in the ranks, as I, meant dozens of innocents fell to make my path. At times I even prayed to the bourgeois outlaw, God himself, for an answer. But no one must know this confession, not even Masha. Sharing religious thoughts brands one a socially dangerous element spreading counterrevolutionary propaganda—eight years in Gulag.

Laurie Bennett
You're Welcome

Thelma and Morris will be coming to visit from March 20th through April 4th. I have offered them your room. It's silly, I don't know why I should feel a little bit guilty about this, but I do. Anyway, we can't wait to see you.

I folded the letter from my mother-in-law. Well, you should feel guilty. Plenty guilty. My in-laws had set up the guestroom for us during our first year abroad. They had opened up the trundle bed and treated the two twin beds as one king. They had purchased a beautiful new comforter in geometric shades of brown and white and wall-papered one wall to complement the new comforter. There was a new lingerie chest with three drawers for me and three drawers for Steve. The guestroom was *our* room when we came home for the two month break between academic years. My husband Steve said we could stay at his sister Carol's.

I had mixed feelings about the upcoming trip home. I was looking forward to being back in the United States, of course. The weather in the Philippines was unrelentingly hot and humid, sapping us of all energy. The U.S. felt so breezy, so fresh, so *clean* after spending ten months in a tropical marine climate. The American wives I had met in the Philippines looked even prettier back home, without the thin film of oil on their faces, with their hair lustrous and shiny from the far lower humidity.

But in the Philippines, Steve and I had our own place. Steve was in his second year of Veterinary School at University of the Philippines. There were only seventeen veterinary schools in the entire United States and admission was tough. Steve had always wanted to be a vet and an education abroad provided him with a Plan B. We had a charming little one bedroom bungalow with a huge overhanging roof. We could watch the relentless rains of the typhoon season from under our roof, cozy and dry, gazing at the drenching the city was receiving from the security of our living room. Our furniture was sparse, inexpensive and second hand; even our linens were secondhand. We were on a student's budget. But house rules were my rules. I was at liberty to organize my Spartan abode any way I saw fit.

As much as we looked forward to visiting home and seeing our friends and the people whom we loved, there was no place for us at home. We were guests at either my parents' home or Steve's parents. We were beholden to others for transportation. We had no car in either the U.S.

or the Philippines, but in the Philippines, there was public transportation, never mind that it was excruciatingly slow. In suburban New York, you either drove or you stayed at home.

Morris and Thelma were the English cousins. There had been five siblings, all from Romania. In addition to English, they spoke a Romanian Yiddish that no one else could understand. When the family left Romania, they all traveled west. One of the brothers became seasick during the English Channel crossing and announced that he would go no further. This branch of the family became the English cousins. The rest of Steve's mother's family continued on to America.

I had always loved an English accent. It sounded so refined. Even when a small child was whining, it still sounded impressive, "Mummy, I *want* the candy!" Or it was laughable, as when a British waiter inquired whether I wanted "tomahto sauce" and presented me with a bottle of ketchup. I didn't know Morris and Thelma well, but from what little I did know, I liked them. I just felt my mother-in-law should not be offering more than she had to give. Her guest room was *our* room when we stayed in the U.S.

That first evening home was *erev Shabbos*. My mother-in-law had prepared brisket with kasha varnishka. Not only was the traditional Jewish meal special, but eating meat was a real treat. I had learned that there are few places in the world where you can expect the tender beef we've become accustomed to in the U.S. and the Philippines was not one of them.

My father-in-law asked Morris to say the *brucha* over the wine. I was amazed when the same nasal Ashkenazi Hebrew came out of Morris's mouth that I had heard all my life at *shul*. Morris's English may have been posh but his Hebrew sounded reminiscent of the Lower East Side of New York to my surprised ears. Morris's Hebrew pronunciation made the Ashkenazi Jewish experience seem more universal and the world that much smaller.

After dinner, we sat in the living room and discussed sleeping arrangements. Steve's sister Carol said that we could stay on the couch at her house, though she added that she had nothing in the refrigerator except ketchup and tuna fish. "What a gracious invitation," I thought. "How like Carol. Not only has she not bothered to stock her refrigerator, but we have no means of going marketing ourselves."

I told Steve I would not stay at Carol's. Our room at his mom's may have been given away, but at least we wouldn't starve to death here. We set up two small mattresses on the floor in Steve's old bedroom and pitched camp. Thelma came by the open bedroom door and noticed what we were doing and commented with dismay, "We've put you out of your room!" "That's okay," I replied. What else could I have said, even if it was not okay with me?

I came downstairs to help with the kitchen cleanup. Thelma came in, too. My mother-in-law and I tried to shoo her away, protesting that she was a guest, but she was having none of it. "And I expect you'll be telling everyone that I wouldn't even help with the washing up!" she teased us. My mother-in-law went into the dining room to put away the china and Thelma sidled up to me conspiratorially. "When my Aunt Esther first came to America," she said, "she stayed with her older brother, Nathan, and his wife in their small apartment in the Bronx. After the first night, Nathan's wife made a fuss about the indentations made in the kitchen linoleum by the weight of Aunt Esther's cot. The very next night, Aunt Esther was in a rooming house, paying board to strangers." She looked at me. "It's a terrible thing to feel unwelcome when you have no place else to go," she said. "We Jews have been wandering around this Earth unwelcome for two thousand years. We should know better how to treat each other. After Steve is finished with his studies, you come visit us in London. Now that the children are off on their own, we have plenty of room for you. You'll be most welcome."

Denise Bogard
The Song at the Sea

Marty Rubin sits alone in the last row of Temple Bayit Yisrael, where he struggles unsuccessfully to stifle a yawn. Not that anyone would notice. Just one more balding head and hawkish profile, he is as easily overlooked here as everywhere else.

Marty feels the tail of his spine as it digs against the chair. He has lost too much weight lately and his bones ache when pressed to a hard surface. He has not consciously sought to become thinner; he simply has lost his appetite for food, for drink, for life. When he closes his eyes, he hears his mother's admonishing voice: "Mortimer, you're too skinny and you slump like a *schlemiel*. Stand proud. You have your whole life before you."

His mother had her whole life before her, too, until it was cut short by a heart attack, following the same sad legacy of Marty's grandfather and great-grandmother. All of whom took their last ragged breath at age forty-nine.

The age Marty has just become.

"All rise," intones the rabbi. Marty doesn't like this rabbi, in fact, he doesn't much like any rabbi. He is particularly offended by the way they speak, in voices deep and sonorous, as though they have the direct number to God. A young woman also sits on the *bema*, legs primly crossed, dressed in a somber black suit, a muted *tallit* and shiny red heels. He's heard that the temple hired a female rabbi—in itself a bizarre concept—but this woman, who is yet to say a word, appears young enough to be his daughter.

"Turn to page 236 of the prayer book. Let us join together in reciting '*Veshameru*,' the prayer that sanctifies the Sabbath. And we remember that as the almighty God guards us, we guard the Sabbath." The rabbi's chin bears down against his neck, a well-rehearsed motion that lowers his voice by several octaves. As if on cue, the female rabbi mutely drops her chin as well.

Marty opens the prayer book, its binding fringed by generations of restless fingers. He can no longer read the backwards letters of Hebrew. After years of absence —how many years has it been anyway?—Marty has become a stranger to his own religion. What a farce it will be next week when he again attends services at Temple Bayit Yisrael, this time for the Bar Mitzvah of his son, Jason.

"Why a Bar Mitzvah?" Marty had asked. "Think of all the time you'll waste in Hebrew school. Three years of unnecessary tedium."

But Jason was adamant. It was important to him. More distressing, it was important to Jason's mother, blonde, green-eyed Sheri, raised Catholic, now a "Jew by choice." And what choice did Marty have? His own father the Temple Bayit Yisrael president for three terms—so long, in fact, they created a new set of by-laws to insure such tenure never occurred again. Marty had vowed that his son would have other options. "Go play ball, watch television, read comic books," Marty had implored. Jason had turned instead to Torah study.

Sitting here now, at the Bar Mitzvah of a stranger, Marty wants to feel a connection that goes deeper than his love of matzo balls and *kugel*. The music is nice enough; some tunes even stir something in him that might be the echoes of spirituality. But the praying. . . a bunch of meaningless words strung together. "*As the almighty God guards us, we guard the Sabbath.*" Ridiculous! For Marty, the world is what it is and what can't be seen doesn't exist. That's why he likes his accounting books; they're clean and straightforward with questions that have inarguable answers.

He retrieves the accompanying booklet prepared by the family of the Bar Mitzvah boy that explains the rituals and gives insight to the Torah portion assigned by birth date to all *B'nai Mitzvah*. Marty shakes his head in empathy. Apparently, this child has had to "conquer a passage that is not only long, but also extremely difficult—*Shirat ha-Yam*, the Song at the Sea, a compilation of three ancient *trope* melodies." Marty places the booklet face down on the empty seat beside him and for the first time considers Jason's designated Torah portion. He has a vague memory that the tutor is concerned whether Jason's Hebrew is fluid. Hopefully, Sheri is on top of the situation.

The rabbi is beginning to chant the "*Shema*." All around Marty congregants are shielding their eyes with their hands and gently swaying as they recite the centuries-old prayer that binds one Jew to another.

Marty closes his eyes. He sees again the doleful face of his boss, W. Reed Haine III, informing Marty yesterday that their biggest client has fired their firm. Marty sees in Haine's knitted brow the uncomfortable task of letting Marty go. Marty had turned away, so as not to observe the pity and regret on Haine's face, the ineffectual gesture of apology in his upturned palm. Marty had left the office, gone home, and slid into bed, shaking with the menacing image of unpaid Bar Mitzvah bills and Sheri's condemning scowl. He awoke today with an inexplicable urge to attend Temple. He has told Sheri he's going out for coffee and a walk, though she's so busy with the arrangements for Jason's celebratory luncheon, she has barely noticed him for months.

"You don't get it, do you? The centerpieces have to be PERFECT or everyone will talk for months about the dumb *shiksa* you married," she had accused, reminding him yet again of the supreme irony of her fervent conversion.

There is suddenly a palpable stirring in the room, the low buzzing of whispers as the Bar Mitzvah boy begins walking down the side aisle holding the Torah. The boy seems compressed under the weight of the Torah, "her" length reaching from above the child's *yarmulke*-covered head to below his ill-fitting suit jacket. He pauses every few steps to shift the heavy scrolls from arm to arm as congregants touch and kiss the silky covering.

As the Torah approaches, Marty can feel his neck begin to itch. His breathing becomes shallow and beads of sweat form behind his ears. The Torah with its thousands-year-old Five Books of Moses is three rows away. This most sacred of Jewish texts. Now two. The essence of his entire (discarded) history. Now one. Marty closes his eyes and lowers his head, overcome by exhaustion. He surrenders to the sensation of falling backwards as he slowly drifts away.

Then he hears it.

"Psst! Mortimer. In here."

Marty startles awake. He checks to see if someone he knows is sitting nearby.

"No, not out there. In here. Quick, Mortimer, closer. 'Atta boy. Okay, now put your fingertips on her, come on, you've seen how the others do it."

Marty's lungs have squeezed tight; the air has become too thick to breathe. He hears again, this time louder, "Kiss the Torah, Mortimer. Our lives depend upon it."

His body sways forward. Marty touches trembling fingertips to the Torah and presses them to his lips, mimicking the ritual of *real* Jews.

Abruptly, his hand goes numb. His arm is dragging against his side. His breathing is labored. And Marty knows with crushing sorrow that his time has come—Already? Too soon!—and that his forty-nine-year-old heart is collapsing. The family legacy has reached its cruel grip inside Marty's chest, squeezing out his life.

No. . . Marty silently wails and with the greatest effort heaves his deadened arm upward. He gasps, for there on his swollen palm is the fully developed form of a bearded, withered man not even two inches high.

"I need your help, Mortimer," this little man whispers in a voice husky with despair. "Pharaoh and his men are encroaching upon us. If we don't escape *now,* we will die or God forbid be once again enslaved."

Marty swings his head so fast his neck twists in sharp pain. He sees no one behind him.

"*Gevalt,* help me, please. They're coming." The little man's impassioned pleas jostle Marty's hand.

Once more Marty turns around, this time more gingerly, and to his dismay a band of men, three-hundredfold, are approaching with the menacing swiftness of a dark storm, carrying fiery darts, arrows and swords.

Marty looks forward and groans in alarm. Before him are the roaring black waves of the ferocious Red Sea. And instead of rows of stylishly dressed congregants, there now stand on either side of Marty hoards of frightened men and women clutching panicked children to their thin, tattered bosoms.

The clamor of the waves nearly drowns out the words of the thimble-sized man, who continues to stand atop Marty's palm. "I am Nachshon of the Tribe of Judah. And I desperately need you to save our people."

Marty throws back his head and laughs. "Boy have you got the wrong guy."

The little man jabs his forefinger against Marty's chest. "Ouch!" Marty reels back with fury.

"Now listen, Mortimer..."

"How do you know my real name? No one calls me Mortimer. Only my Mother could do that, and she's been gone for years."

"May she rest in peace," the crowd says in unison.

"Mortimer, please. The earth trembles with the advance of Pharaoh's men. Behind us are the Egyptians, on both sides the wild beasts of the desert, before us the sea. Follow me, Mortimer. Be a *mensch.* Show your faith in our God . . . and the people of Israel will follow in your steps."

"Into that sea? We'll drown, crazy fool. It's my son's Bar Mitzvah next week. I can't die today." Marty flings his hand, trying to topple Nachshon, but as hard as he shakes, he can't hurl the man off of his palm. Marty sighs and nods. He may as well—he with no job, mounting bills. . . and a hefty life insurance policy.

In the span of this thought, Nachshon has grown to the size of a Torah and now stands with one foot firmly planted on each of Marty's hands.

His facial features have become distinct and inexplicably familiar—bushy eyebrows, pronounced cheekbones, a clefted, square jaw.

Nachshon places his hands upon the crown of Marty's head, kisses his scalp and then both of his cheeks. "Bless you, Mortimer, for you are surely a vessel of the souls of Abraham, Isaac and Jacob." He jumps from Marty's palms and seems to float down to the earth, instantly lengthening to Marty's own size. Eye to eye, they stare intently at each other; for one glorious moment Marty can feel his entire soul become illumined and bare.

He hears then the deep, booming voice of a bearded man in a flowing robe, who holds in his hand a long black rod. Marty knows, without knowing how he knows, that this is Moses upon whose rod is engraved in Hebrew the names of the three Fathers, the four Mothers, and the twelve tribes of Jacob. As Marty watches, Moses lifts up the rod and stretches it out over the sea, saying, "I am the messenger sent by the Creator of the world. Uncover thy paths, O sea, for My children that they may go through the midst of thee on dry ground."

The sea, however, continues in its perverseness, roaring with ferocity.

And it is into this sea that Nachshon now walks until the water is up to his neck. Marty shuts his eyes, pictures his beloved wife and cherished son, feels with huge regret the emptiness of wasted years. Tears of grief trickle down his raw face as he follows Nachshon. Each step leads him further and further into the frigid water until his legs, his torso and soon his chin are covered. He senses behind him the frantic anticipation of the people of Israel.

Nachshon pivots and once again Marty is seized by a sense of familiarity. Then it hits: Nachshon bears the facial features of a grown-old Jason, his son as Marty will never see him. Silent sobs shake Marty's shoulders as he trudges ever deeper.

Suddenly, the sky seems to open and suspended before Marty is an angel dressed in flowing folds of lace and white. She croons a lilting song, the sound of velvet. Marty knows, though again he knows not how, that she is the bride of God, the *Shekhinah*. And then his mother stands before him crying out, "Mortimer! Mortimer!" Her raven-black hair is pulled loosely back, her hazel eyes bright, her face nearly unlined; she looks exactly as he remembers. For a moment, Marty acknowledges the absurdity of this dream, but he shakes off his cynicism as one shakes off drops of pelting rain. For decades he has longed for this *one more hour*. Marty enfolds himself inside his mother's arms, lowers his head to her shoulder and weeps with joy.

Moses once more raises up his rod, pleading with God, as a crackling sound splits the sky and a fiery right arm dips into—and parts—the Red Sea. Wondrously, Nachshon and Marty and all the Jewish peoples are upon dry land. Marty feels a thunderous wind gathering the waters back together, and the land that was dry changes into clay as the Egyptians step upon it. He sees among them a beautiful blonde with sparkling green eyes—Sheri? No! There is a huge mistake; she's one of *us!*—but before he can shout a warning, the walls of water are transformed into rocks, against which all the Egyptians are thrown. The screams of Pharaoh's advancing troops are swallowed into the brackish sea as they are dashed to death.

The tinkling trembling of a tambourine fills Marty's ears. It is the prophetess Miriam, the sister of Aaron, who stands upon dry land as everyone dances with joy. And to Marty's amazement, the words of *Shirat ha-Yam*, the Song at the Sea, fill his own head and he sings with the people of Israel. Marty feels his mother's caress upon his brow. She stands on tip-toe, places her hands on the crown of Marty's head, kisses both his cheeks and his scalp, and says, "It's not right, Mortimer, to eschew your people. It's not enough to simply be a gastronomic Jew." At his grin, she quips, "And it's not enough to eat Chinese food after a Christmas Eve movie." He laughs aloud even as he wipes away his tears. "*Do you believe?*" she whispers, and with trepidation he nods yes. "Then you, my beloved Mortimer, will dance at the wedding of your grandson, of my great-grandson. Our broken-hearted curse has ended." And with that his mother is gone, and Marty turns to find Nachshon.

He is stunned, Mortimer "Marty" Rubin, skinny, balding, unemployed middle-aged accountant. He stands, amazingly, dry, in the last row of Temple Bayit Yisrael, surrounded not by sea and fiery swords but by rows of fashionably dressed, well-fed strangers. Marty blinks his eyes several times in rapid succession. He shakes his head. What a bizarre dream he has had.

The congregation has grown quiet as the Bar Mitzvah boy approaches the opened Torah, leans forward, and begins his chanting of the Song at the Sea. Even with the boy's uneven squeaking voice, the melody is haunting. And eerily familiar.

With trembling hands Marty again opens the Bar Mitzvah booklet and stares transfixed at the full page of Hebrew letters. He begins to hum along, quietly at first, and then with confident exuberance. Out of Marty's mouth pours the *trope* of *Shirat ha-Yam*. In perfect pitch he translates the ancient words as effortlessly as he unravels numbers: *"Then sang Moses and the people of Israel this song to the Lord. The Lord is my strength and song, and he has become my salvation; he is of war; the Lord is his name: Pharaoh's chariots and his army has he thrown into the sea."*

Marty takes several cleansing breaths; his chest feels light and clear. The despair and confusion that have been his steady companions are replaced by an exquisite sense of calm. He pinches his arm until he feels the painful pressure that tells him he is, indeed, awake. Marty glances at his watch, and with no regard for the glares and whispers, he steps over the people in his row, walks with a skip in his step to the outside door. He must get home. He has only one week more to help Jason prepare for his Torah reading.

At the door, Marty stops to tie his shoe. He touches his ankle. The cuff of his pants is sopping wet.

Edward Farber
Papa's House

He added up the years on his fingers. He had been three years old when Papa had left Lachavitz for America; Uncle Yosel had told him the year had been 1912, before the war. Now he was thirteen. Ten years. He tried to remember what Papa looked like. Nothing. Sometimes the smell of saddle leather would stir a vague memory. Oh, he had built his own image of him from Uncle's descriptions and stories. Tall, strong, a thick black mustache. Of his mother he also remembered nothing since she had died at the time of his birth. Now he would be seeing his Papa here in America.

As he watched through the window of the automobile the buildings seem to fly by so quickly he was certain he would become dizzy. What grand and amazing things had happened to him in such a short time. Steamships, trains, and now an automobile. Soon they would be at Papa's house. A chill of excitement coursed through him just as it had when the ship had steamed into the great harbor and he had seen the giant statue which seemed to be welcoming him personally. What was it they had called him after he and Uncle Yosel and the rest of the family had left Ellis Island? Green Horn. Mendle Katzen, Green Horn! He smiled at the odd sounding name. Whatever it meant, he, Mendle Katzen, would soon be an American like his father.

The automobile, which also contained his uncle, aunt, two cousins and the driver, an American cousin of Uncle Yosel, slowed and pulled into a space at the curb. Unlike the streets they had driven along earlier near the train station--narrow, filled with people, carts, horses, children, with buildings crowding in on one another-- this was a quiet street. The houses were smaller, mostly two stories tall, with stone steps leading up to handsome doorways. Uncle Yosel laboriously climbed out of the car. "Cousin Itzy says that this street is Clara Avenue, and this is your father's house, Mendle. Say goodbye to Aunt Rivka and the girls. I will take you up there."

At the front door, Uncle Yosel dropped the carpet bag which contained Mendle's things, and rapped on the etched glass pane. The door opened. A stout woman stood there, an inquiring expression on her round face as she looked first at Uncle Yosel and then at Mendle. She must be my father's housekeeper, thought Mendle. Did they not say that Americans were wealthy? He listened as Uncle Yosel explained in Yiddish that he had come to drop off his nephew who was the son of the man who owned the house.

"I own this house," the woman said in four, tight, brittle words then turned a baleful eye on Mendle who cringed without knowing exactly why. "And my husband has no son that I know of."

"Does not Moshe Katzen live here?" Uncle Yosel asked. At the name, the woman blanched. Suddenly she grabbed Uncle Yosel by the arm and yanked him across the threshold into the house. The door slammed shut. Mendle could hear muffled voices, first hers then his uncle's, steadily rising in volume.

The door opened, and Uncle Yosel stepped out. Mendle could see that his uncle's face was red and wore the same angry look he remembered when Uncle had caught him smoking his favorite briar pipe. Uncle Yosel stooped down, kissed Mendle on both cheeks. "Goodbye, Mendle. You will stay here with your father--and the woman he neglected to inform me he had married. Six years ago." He put his hand on Mendle's shoulder, "I would wait here with you until he comes home from work, but, as you know, we must get back to the train station. I will write you from Chicago where we will be staying with Aunt Rivka's sister. Be a good boy. Now go in the house. The woman is waiting for you."

Mendle watched his uncle hurry down the steps and climb back into the big, black automobile. He waved as the vehicle pulled away from the curb and disappeared around the corner. He would miss his family, the only family he could remember. A tear welled up in his eye. Hastily he wiped it away with his sleeve. Was he not thirteen? A man? A man does not cry. Now he would go in and talk with the woman, his . . . his father's wife. Another tear trickled down his cheek.

"Well, come in, boy. Don't stand out there like a lummox."

Mendle jumped at the sound of her voice, turned and stepped past her into the house. When she shut the front door, he offered his hand. "I am Mendle Katzen and I am pleased to meet you."

She brushed past him ignoring his outstretched hand. "In my house we do not speak Yiddish. We speak only English."

"But I do not know English," Mendle said following her broad back into the warm kitchen which smelled wonderfully of baked bread.

"You will have to learn. Now you will go into the parlor and wait for your father to return."

"The bread. It smells so good."

"We eat at six. No more Yiddish. English only. Go."

Mendle turned and followed in the general direction of her pudgy, pointing finger. I will starve to death if I do not learn English quickly, he thought, as he slumped down in an overstuffed mohair chair next to the window. He glanced back down the hall and saw his father's wife cutting off a thick slice of bread from a freshly baked loaf. Aha, he thought, she is not as mean as she acts. Soon I will taste that delicious bread. But she never came back to the parlor.

"Mendle? Mendlele? Wake up it's me, your father."

Mendle opened his eyes. His neck was stiff and ached. "Papa?" Bending over him was a stranger who looked nothing like the image he had carried so long. No black mustache. Not so tall. A thin face with watery, red-rimmed eyes.

"My God, how you have grown. Come, give your Papa a kiss."

As his father pulled him close, Mendle could smell a sweet aroma like lilacs. Saddle leather smells better, he thought. He felt the bristles on his father's cheek rub against his face, and mingled with the lilac there was the sharp smell of schnapps.

"My son," Papa said, putting his arm around Mendle's thin shoulders, "We have a lot of catching up to do, like how you got that scar over your eye."

"And how come no one, not even Uncle Yosel, knew you had a new wife," Mendle added.

"In due time, due time. Now let's go in and sample your stepmother's cooking which, between you and me, is the best thing she does."

"Papa, what is English word for bread?" Mendle asked as they walked in for the first of many meals to come.

Mendle thought about that first day in America often in the months that followed. He had expected so much and found so little. Papa never explained why he had not told anyone back in the Old Country that he had remarried. Mendle figured that he did not expect to see them again. He certainly had not sent money to bring them over. He had not even asked again about Mendle's scar, received during the war when one side had shelled the other. Mendle couldn't remember which side had done the shelling.

The first big surprise was to discover that he had a stepsister, a big lump of a girl, a head taller than him and two years older. Her name was Sylvia. She had been a small child when his father had married her mother, Anya. Recently widowed and needing a man in the house and in the family business, Anya had sought out a likely prospect. She found him in Papa who was a frequent customer in the tavern which her late husband had owned. Papa, during his earlier years in America, had squeezed out a precarious living as a rag picker in a junk yard and was only too glad to trade his rat-infested, hole-in-the-wall quarters for the fine home of his former tavern keeper.

All this Papa had once told Mendle in maudlin confidence after imbibing more than usual of the tavern's stock, which he did frequently, adding-- more to himself than to his thirteen-year-old son-- that Anya's ample charms on a few cold winter nights had been enough to clinch the proposition. Soon after the wedding, Papa then complained, the widow began to mete out in diminishing portions the passion with which she had secured her former husband's successor. But Papa was satisfied with the bargain. He had a solid roof over his head, occasional bedroom privileges, a job in his favorite environment, food that would delight even a gourmet's palate, and no rats. The rest he could put up with.

Mendle, however, had no such compensating factors. His stepmother, from that very first day, had let him know that he was an unwanted visitor. She ignored his Yiddish questions. Even when he laboriously learned to make elementary conversation in English after going to a special immigrant's school, she often refused to speak to him. The few times she did was to scold him for something he did or did not do, or to badger him to quit school and get a job so he could pay for his keep. With her, Mendle decided, it was best to stay out of the way altogether.

With Sylvia, however, it was another story. Sylvia made it her life's work to torment him. If he tried to avoid her (which he attempted constantly) she cornered him, using her overpowering bulk to force him to her will. Once when Anya had gone to the market, she had pounced on him, pinned him down on his bed and pulled his pants down. Then, she had laughed at his embarrassment, telling him with a sneer that he had a lot of growing to do. Afterwards she leeringly called him names like "skinny pickle," and "puny little thing."

He comforted himself by taunting her in Yiddish which infuriated her because she did not understand. "What does that mean, you stupid greenhorn?" she would scream. When he remembered a particularly foul Yiddish curse, he would smile as he heaped it upon her with relish. She would then make up a complaint to Anya who would demand that he be punished without bothering to find out if it were true. (The time Sylvia had spied upon his private parts, she had scuttled up to Anya and told her that he had made a lewd comment.) These contrived complaints by Sylvia in her mother's willing ear cost him many scoldings and not a few hidings. Papa, fearful that his wife might decide to force him from that nice warm house if he did not do her bidding, (this much Mendle had surmised for himself) always sided with her and dealt the punishment vigorously.

"Mendle," Papa would say, "this will hurt me as much as it hurts you." Then he would remove his leather belt and and bring it down forcefully on Mendle's backside. Try as he may, Mendle could not see how the red welts on his rump could bring as much pain to Papa as they did to him. As painful as it was, however, Mendle never cried during his punishments because he knew his stepmother was listening on the other side of the door. Sometimes, after he was in bed the tears would flow, not tears of pain, but tears of sorrow as he thought about his father, his father's wife, his bully of a stepsister, and the unfairness of it all.

One day, Mendle observed Sylvia run screaming from her room. A tiny bug, it seems, had caused this outburst. Sylvia was afraid of bugs, even little ones. With this bit of knowledge, a plan began to percolate in his mind, a way to keep Sylvia at bay. He prowled the alleys behind the houses, over-turning rocks and debris. Whenever he came upon a sizable specimen he carefully placed it in the cardboard match box he carried for the purpose and added it to his growing collection. The big roaches were his favorites, and he would smile as he contemplated the confrontation between Sylvia and his new allies.

Sylvia, blissfully unaware of his plans, continued to harass him at every opportunity. When he protested, she taunted him. "So what are you going to do about it, tell my mother? She won't help you. Tell your father? He does what my mother tells him to do."

"I am warning you," he said summoning up all the menace he could muster. "If you don't leave me alone, you will be very sorry. Very, very sorry."

"Ha! What could a little twerp like you do?" Sylvia said and lumbered off to her room."

The next day when Sylvia opened her dresser to take out a clean blouse, a large roach scurried across the drawer. Sylvia screamed and screamed. Mendle smiled. The next day, when she bent to put on her shoe, another roach dropped out and disappeared under her bed. In hysterics she ran to her mother who immediately sent Mendle to the store for some roach poison. Mendle went willingly. With the roach powder sprinkled liberally throughout the house but especially in her room, Sylvia once more felt secure.

The next morning after her mother went to market Sylvia resumed her harassment of Mendle. This time, however, Mendle slowly opened his hand and smiled. A large roach stood there in his palm, feelers testing the air. Sylvia's eyes turned up into her head. She wobbled as if she were about to faint. Then, collecting herself, she screamed mightily and rushed from Mendle's room. Mendle laughed aloud. His days of torment were over. Maybe, soon, he would be treated as an equal member of the household.

On a gray, blustery November day, eight months after his momentous arrival in America, Mendle came home from work. Anya had been right in one thing. By working he could earn money. He earned almost as much as Anya allowed Papa. She had tried to talk him into working at the tavern, but he insisted on getting his own job which he had found in a shoe factory on Easton Avenue. As he walked up the steps to the landing, he noticed a bundle beside the door with a note attached. Curious, he bent and picked up the bundle. The note was addressed to him in Anya's spidery handwriting: "Mendle Katzen, you are no longer welcome in my home. Do not come back." It was written in Yiddish so that he would have no trouble understanding the message.

Mendle knew why. It was because he had refused to turn over his entire pay to his stepmother for room and board as she had insisted. Of the little money he earned, he gave half to the household, the rest he saved in a wooden cigar box under his bed. The cigar box! He ripped open the bundle and rummaged among his meager possessions. Not there. He began to bang on the door. He shouted for his stepmother. He banged and shouted until the chintz curtains over the window in the door lifted, and his stepmother's round, angry face peered out.

"Go away, you bad boy," she yelled through the closed door.

"My money in the box. Where is it?" he cried.

"It went to pay for all the time you lived here before you went to work."

"My father . . . he won't let you do this."

"He knows. He don't want you neither," she said with finality letting the curtain drop.

Mendle sat on the step shaking with anger. His first thought was to run to the tavern and confront Papa. No. Anya was right in one thing. Even if he were not a willing partner in this act, his father would do nothing. That much was clear. Tears streaked down his cheeks. Hastily, he wiped them away. He was a man, after all, was he not? A working man! He gathered up his clothes, tied them once again into a bundle, and stood up.

First, he would go back to the factory. Someone there would help him find a place to sleep. He would work and save his pay. All of it. Then he would buy a train ticket to Chicago where Uncle Yosel and the family lived.

Wait, he thought, could someone who was only thirteen years old travel alone to Chicago, wherever that was? Sure, he decided. It would be a snap. *A snap!* He smiled broadly. He had been thinking in English, not Yiddish. He really was an American now, wasn't he? And Americans can do anything. Mendle wiped the last wet streak of tears from his cheeks, picked up the little bundle of belongings and hopped down the steps. He looked back one last time at Papa's house--no, Papa's *wife's* house--then turned and walked away.

Jeff Friedman
Family

"It's the end of the world," my father proclaimed at the breakfast table, rising in his bear-checked pajamas. "Not again," my mother replied, emptying the scraps on the plates into the garbage and putting the dishes into the dishwasher.

He had that look in his eyes, and he had been up all night reading the Black Book and making notes in his journal in red ink. He showed me his notes, which were unreadable, except for the sentence, "Get out of town quick," underlined twice for emphasis. I was used to his predictions and prophecies, used to running down to the basement with our belongings because he smelled a tornado in the air or putting on a lead-lined jump suit and a helmet with a breathing tube and oxygen mask to prepare for a nuclear attack.

Once my father thought the chipmunks that burrowed under the patio were the souls of his ancestors. He carried on conversations with them at all hours and got advice on how to invest in the stock market. He actually did pretty well with his investments so my mother let him continue the conversations until they advised him to sell the house.

"Son, get the boat; it's our only way out of here." He said this with some urgency though we were landlocked and had been in a drought for two years. "He means the Cadillac," my mother interjected. "But we don't have a Cadillac; we have a Buick. "Get the car," she insisted and pull it up front so he can see it."

As always, I did as I was told. When I came back into the house, my father had put on his trousers and a sports coat, and my mother was dressed, but my sister was still strutting around in a night shirt and panties. My father put his hand on Rachel's ass, which caused my mother to hit him over the head with a pan. When he came to, he ranted on and on about spreading his seed to keep the human race alive.

"Ignore him," my mother said. "Dad's a perv," Rachel responded. I shepherded everybody out of the house because I thought the fresh air would do us all some good, but the air was thick and hot.

The sun caught fire, a blaze spreading across the sky. As we walked up the block, we could hear screams and shouts coming from our neighbors' houses. Ahead of us, the desert stretched toward the mountains. My fathered ordered us to march across the sand, to keep our faces forward, or a disaster would befall us. But my mother turned back to see flames raining down on her house—all her things lost—and bitterness plagued her the rest of the days of her life.

Appeared in *Quick Fiction*, Issue #17

Michael Getty
The Tower
Parashat Noach (Genesis 6:9 to 11:32)

I suppose we thought we were special. Looking back, that's the only way I can make sense of it all.

We could all understand each other when we were in Shinar, and everyone got along. But there were stories from before of big cities, as different from each other as night and day, cities that fought each other year after year.

We had to be special because that never happened to us. There weren't any settlements besides ours. The whole world was new.

After a few years, people began pushing out to the horizon. Soon they were arguing about how to divide the land and the water, even what to call the fruit on the trees.

We got scared, and the elders met for what seemed like weeks on end. Then one day, they had big news. They told us we would build a city, with paved streets and marketplaces and houses for everyone.

And in the middle of it all, we would build a tower with its top in the heavens, so high that people in even the farthest settlements would never forget where they belonged.

We wept with relief. We tore the straw from our donkeys' mouths to bring it to the brickyards. We dug up clay from the riverbed with our bare hands.

It sounds strange now, but I remember those days as some of the best ever. We sang songs and told jokes as we worked day and night, packing clay and carrying bricks into the heart of our new city. We ate like horses, and our bread had never tasted so good.

The elders appointed overseers for us. They were family, and they ate and worked alongside us.

One of them was a cousin from my mother's side. I remember the day I passed him on a freshly laid street. We had laughed together the day before, but on this day, he was hunched over, his eyes on the ground as he walked.

"Good morning, cousin," I called out to him. He raised his head, his face twisted up with worry, and grunted in reply.

The elders had grown impatient. The work was not going quickly enough, they said. Every day, there were new outposts beyond the horizon, permanent villages even, with strange names no one had ever heard of.

We'd work harder, we told them. We'd build the tower even higher.

Then one day I saw my neighbor's father-in-law. He was very old, but he worked with us the whole time, raking hay at the brickyard and pouring water for us. I was so thirsty that day, but when the old man went to hand my cup to me, he dropped it.

I got angry. I cursed him and called him names. I knew before the last word left my mouth that I'd gone too far. I could have told him I was sorry, but I didn't. I turned away and went to find more water.

I think that was the day people stopped smiling. We worked, we went to sleep, we woke up sore and exhausted. And still the word came from the elders. Faster. Bigger. Higher.

Soon the tower was so high that it took the bricklayers almost an hour to climb to the top.

I remember when the first of them died. He was just tired and lost his footing. That's what we heard from the people who saw it happen.

I was standing next to my cousin when the man's body hit the ground. We didn't know what the sound was at first, but within minutes, we did. My cousin asked if the man had been his son, his brother, his father-in-law. When it turned out to be none of those people, my cousin looked up at the tower again, then down at the ground. Then he told everyone to get back to work.

I hated the tower that day. I hated it more the larger it got. Even the elders and overseers hated it, even as they started beating people who wouldn't work, or couldn't work, or did something that set everyone back. Another one of us died, then another, then another.

One day, I dropped an armload of bricks and an overseer started hitting me. Didn't I know how precious those bricks were to the city? That's what he yelled as he beat me.

My cousin watched the whole time and said nothing, but when the overseer was done with me, he helped me get to my feet, and then he said this: It will all be worth it in the end. No one will forget our oneness, he told me.

But by this point, no one even talked about the other settlements any more. No one had left the city in months except to dig for clay.

People who couldn't work started disappearing or showing up dead on the streets. When the ovens ran out of wood, anything that could be burned was thrown in. Our grain, the beams of our houses, even the bodies of the dead. When the valley gave up its last handful of clay, people were made to march over the mountain to the next valley. Many never came back.

I ask myself every day if I could have done something to stop it all. But by the time we woke up to what the tower had become, none of us wanted to admit how empty it all was. How foolish we'd been all along.

Everyone knows what eventually happened.

I was on my way up the tower. An overseer was scolding a woman who had fallen down. She was so thin. We all were. Her hands and knees were bleeding, she was crying, and all the overseer could do was scream at her.

And then, in an instant, I couldn't understand any of his words. It was as if he'd swallowed his own tongue. All I could do was stare at him, and then he started screaming at me instead.

I can't understand what you're saying, I kept telling him.

He got angrier. He starting beating me. I pleaded with him to stop. Please, stop, I cried.

The poor woman's voice came from behind him, but she was talking gibberish too. The overseer stopped hitting me. He was breathing hard, a crazed look in his eyes as he just stared at us.

And then others came down the path. Dozens, then hundreds, all crying out, all speaking gibberish.

We went crazy. We ran through the city, grabbing anyone we could, pleading with them, "Do you understand me? Can you understand what I'm saying?"

No one could. People were crying, tearing their hair out. We scattered into the countryside in search of someone, anyone who could understand us. I walked for two days straight and found no one. By then, there were so few of us that I never saw anyone else from the city.

Somehow I found my way here.

I was so sick with hunger and grief that I don't remember how or when I got here. All I remember is waking up in the home of strangers.

I wept when they gave me food and water. I wept when they bathed me. I wept because it had been so long since anyone had been kind to me.

When I was strong enough, they took me outside and pointed off into the distance.

There, on the horizon, was the tower.

"Babel," they said.

Andrea Jackson
Second Thoughts

The sparkling new feeling dimmed as the waters receded leaving mountain tops littered with the carcasses of jellyfish and, below the tree line, dead branches dripping with soggy kelp. The excitement vanished entirely as He watched the comical Ark rock to the reconfigured shore and its human occupants stagger out, after the birds and beasts and insects and whatnot, dizzy with sunlight and shifting sands and the lack of instructions. The Holy One, blessed be He, shuddered as He anticipated the proliferation worldwide of human specimens bearing the character traits that this bunch had revealed during months of idleness and proximity: the jealousies and rivalries that erupted occasionally in violence and daily in irritability and pettiness; the obsessiveness and impulsivity, the arrogance and self-pity, and above all, the staggering depths of unreason. The Holy One, blessed be He, closed His great eyes and rubbed His great bald dome, trying to recall just what He had hoped to accomplish when He began that great cleansing operation.

Natasha Kaminsky
Jerusalem Stone

.A compact mirror. A box of cereal. A spool of "CAUTION!" tape. A Transformer action figure. A Bible. Purses can hold almost anything it seems. Sitting in front of the Ko-Op supermarket, Asher has caught glimpses of emerald colored thongs, lab jars of brown and yellow fluids, and movie ticket stubs. He has confiscated knives and knitting needles, nail files and scissors. On slow days he dreams about what he might find in his sister's purse, his girlfriend's purse, or his mother's purse. On busy days he keeps a mental count of how many averted gazes, forced smiles, and pink cheeks he encounters.

A woman in the city can't go a day without someone peering into their purse, and they wouldn't want to. On Sunday a woman with streaks of grey in her red hair and a Russian accent doubled back to him. "Mister, you didn't check my purse." Asher nodded to her and leaned forward as she extended an opened Ethiopian cloth satchel. He didn't find anything. He smiled at her and she stood a little straighter as she took a shopping cart and reentered the store.

Tal, half-sister, thinks this is all very adult. She is six and thinks of purses as part of a disguise. She wanders around the house with a pink plastic bag with daisies on the side and orders her father around. She orders Asher around too when he comes to visit. The last time he saw her was Friday night. She ordered him to sit down. Her mother had just given her a pocket notebook and she had to interview him.

"You just check the ladies' bags?" his sister squeaked at him.

"Yeah, Tal," he said.

"That's all?" She raised an eyebrow and sighed.

"That's all."

When University isn't canceled Asher attends evening classes. Being a security guard is temporary. While his professor lectures on poetry he stares out the window down at the city. The uniform white stone skyline glows through the dark and he wonders what it would take to make his girlfriend, Faren, move to Jerusalem. He has already agreed to move to North Carolina where they don't check inside ladies' purses outside the grocery store. Chapel Hill is clean and easy, he knows because he has spent five summers there. The trash gets picked up regularly and parents don't think twice about putting their children on school buses. The trees are different. Their thick oak trees shame the withering pines that litter

Asher's country. This is where his girlfriend wants to live. She says she fell in love with Jerusalem after spending her first and only summer there and Asher believes her. Chapel Hill is an easy city to live in but Jerusalem is an easy city to love. When she calls it's because she has heard something is wrong. When he calls she assumes something is wrong. He tries to call her when things go right, this is part of his plan to make her come to him.

"Hello? Are you ok? What happened?"

"Nothing has happened, you worry too much. This is a good call!"

When he calls there is always a delay. Clicks and clacks litter the quiet pauses in speech.

"Are you drunk?"

"A little, but we won!"

"Who won? What? Where are you?"

"Who won? Are you-- what? *Beitar* Jerusalem we got the uh, the state cup."

"Jesus Christ, you scared me. Don't call me when you've been drinking. Jesus..."

He sent her a *Beitar* Jerusalem sweatshirt for Hanukkah. She doesn't know that Maccabee Tel Aviv is more popular, she just recognizes the lettering on the front, *Yerushalyim*, Jerusalem, and it pleases her. The image of her in his team's colors, their emblem over the soccer ball, pleases him. She still won't come to visit him. He feels his own city is working against him. His own city wants him to go. When she concedes and starts looking for tickets a coffee shop explodes and she shies away from him. He sent her candy, *Pesek Zman* filled with chocolate and hazelnut, *Paskesz kilk* bite sized and crunchy, and *Elyit* aerated and bubbly. *You cannot find these in the States, you can't find these in North Carolina,* he wrote in a letter.

Asher's father thinks he should leave. He is a professor at the University and his young wife keeps him well dressed. He is an American but he looks like a Sabra, tall and narrow and long eyelashes that cast shadows on his cheeks. Asher looks like his father and that is all that connects them. His older sister says that they were for practice, a test run, and Tal is the real thing. Asher loves Tal, even if she is proof that he was just a failed experiment. She makes him laugh and she brags to anyone who will listen that her brother was very important when he was in the army. Asher's father tried to get him out of the service by sending him to visit his mother in Chapel Hill during the summers. Once he established residency there he was exempt from the draft, but he enlisted just like his friends did, just like his sister did.

"I don't know what to tell her. I'm not sure I can adjust."

"You've been there, you don't need me to explain it to you, son."

"I don't want you to explain it to me. I'm not asking you to explain it to me. I just thought we could go out for lunch, or coffee and talk. It doesn't have to be for a long time."

"This isn't a good week, my students are starting their presentations."

"You can't find an hour from your entire week? I just want an hour. I haven't seen you, just you, in a month, dad. When is a good week?"

"I don't know, call me next week, son."

Tal's mother, Asher's stepmother, was one of his father's students six years ago. He was sixteen and his sister had just turned fifteen. After his father got married he started sending Asher and his sister to see their mother in the States as often as their school schedule would allow. Asher still believes that he did this because he didn't want his children to be drafted and in danger. He can't get his father to have coffee with him but Tal jumps at the opportunity to spend the afternoon with him.

Last Friday they went to the zoo. He held her hand and pulled the hood of her jacket up every time it slipped down. While Asher walked Tal hopped from cobblestone to cobblestone. People smiled at them. He wondered if they think Tal is his daughter. He smiled back. Tal wanted to see the Flamingos so they went there first.

"They're pink!" she said. She tried to climb the guard rail and failed. Asher picked her up, setting her feet on the slick metal bar. "Are they all girls?"

"I don't think so, but maybe," he said.

"They must be," she said.

On their way to see the bears Tal spotted an ice cream cart and looked up at Asher. He treated them both and they sat on a bench together. Tal swung her legs back and forth and hummed happily as she licked the ice cream in the corners of her mouth. Asher sat up straight with his feet planted to the ground and methodically twirled his cone to keep the ice cream even as he ate it. Above them were the branches of a tree that was shedding pink flowers the size of thumb nails in the wind. These trees are all over that part of town. The sidewalk outside of the store where Asher checks bags is coated in a layer of muddy pink.

"Are you leaving?" Tal asked.

"I'm not leaving, Tal."

"Moving?"

"Maybe, but that's not the same as leaving, just so you know," he said.

"Why?"

He knew what she meant to ask is different from what she said. Asher nodded and took another lick of his ice cream before he lowered it to his side and turned to look at Tal.

"Because that's where Faren lives. Do you remember meeting her?"

Tal shook her head and the hood of her jacket fell. Asher pulled it back up for her, all the while she continued to lick at her ice cream. The frames of her oversized glasses had collected a few specks of mint chocolate chip. Tal doesn't need them but she begged for a pair of reading glasses at the pharmacy counter earlier that day and Asher bought them for her. She looked like the French women at their grandmother's nursing home, bundled up with wisps of blonde hair sticking out and glasses that reminded him of Woody Allen.

"She wants me to go live with her in the States. That way we can see each other more."

"But you won't get to see me more," said Tal. She sighed and shook her head again, a clear imitation of their grandmother who rants that no one ever comes to sit by her for Shabbat.

"I'll come back to visit a lot, and I bet you would come visit me too. Don't you want to see America?"

She shrugged her shoulders and turned her attention to her ice cream. The ice cream in America can't compare to *Nok Out*, *Naruto* and *Ro'lar*. Asher has been in Jerusalem and he has been in Tel Aviv. He has been in the Negev Desert on his base and on the coast of Ashdod with his cousins. In all these places there are ice cream carts, fully stocked. He tried ice cream at a parlor in Chapel Hill, candy cane flavor, and could not finish.

"There's something wrong with mine," he said.

"Really? Is it spoiled?" Faren leaned in and raised her eyebrows.

"It's hard."

"Well, yeah, Ash, it's cold, it's ice cream."

"It doesn't have to be hard."

They left the zoo, Tal on Asher's shoulders, and he walked back to their father's town house to drop her off in the neighborhood he grew up in. The buildings are different there. Instead of Jerusalem stone, limestone and dolomite, they use real red brick. These are buildings that will hold up against the next earthquake that people have been saying will come for the past fifty years. Pink petals coated the fences and sidewalks he passed. It was Friday afternoon and the city was winding down, there were no lawn mowers roaring, no cars or buses polluting. He walked by women washing windows and eager students already dressed for services.

This Friday Tal wants to go to the grocery store to pick out Sabbath dinner with her mother but she also wants to see him. Asher's stepmother says that he is welcome to join them. He finds himself back in his old neighborhood of red brick.

"I want to go to Asher's store," says Tal.

"But Asher's store is--"

"My store isn't as nice as the other stores, Tal," he finishes his stepmother's sentence for her. She purses her lips into a tight smile.

Tal gets her way. They squeeze into the taxi. Asher offers Tal his lap but she wants to wear her own seat belt. It's not a long drive but Asher never knows what to say to his stepmother. Tal babbles about her short day at school as she hugs her purse to her chest. Her mother tries to coax her into taking her oversized glasses off. Asher looks out the window and smiles as he listens to Tal insist that she must keep the glasses on as she wants to look grown up for the grocery store. Again, Tal gets her way.

"So what did you do last Friday for Shabbat?" asks his stepmother.

"Nothing really," he says.

Asher had visited his grandmother, her mother-in-law, in the nursing home last Friday after he dropped Tal off. After his grandfather died, Asher's father moved his grandmother to the home for the elderly on Emek Refaim. At first she spent all her time in bed reading but after a year she stopped reading and now only spends time in bed. He doesn't understand why his grandmother can't live with his father. His old bedroom is empty and Tal needs someone to watch her in the afternoons. He doesn't feel it is his place to tell his stepmother about these things. His grandmother speaks a strange dialect. It is a mixture of Hebrew, Lithuanian and English, something that might be labeled as Yiddish, but it's not quite Yiddish. Asher follows it well enough, but not as well as his father can. She was born in Lithuania and ended up marrying the American soldier that liberated her from the camp. After five years of thinking she had no family she was contacted by her brother in Israel who told her to come make *aliyah* and help build the land. This is Asher's family's story. The Levines own one of the oldest modern buildings on the West coast, the very one his grandparents and great-uncle built when Ashdod was still a wasted desert.

When he told his grandmother he was considering making America his home she shook her head. "Don't waste your time in America. This is where we belong," she said. "No one else wants us. There's no place else. America is just the next best thing. Here is where we take care of ourselves. No one wants us but we don't need them. We don't need anyone. I wish someone had taught me how to shoot, Asher. It's not a bad thing to be able to do, you know?" He thought about his country, the empty abandoned neighborhoods along the West and the dilapidated ones along the east. He thought about Haifa so close to Lebanon and he thought about the check point he spent a year guarding. The beige shack with the tin roof painted green where he checked for papers and checked for bombs. The thin air in the hot desert that made him forget everything good about his life. How he screamed at children trying to cross the Green Line in search of items their mothers sent them to find.

He held his grandmother's hand that day and felt a distance between them. Her voice wavered and he knew she was thinking about his great-grandparents. He doesn't feel anything when he sees Al-Jeezera cartoons depicting his troop as Nazis. He doesn't feel anything when he sees the faded blue numbers on his grandmother's leathery arm. He doesn't feel anything when people praise the three years he spent in uniform carrying his M-16. It was just what he had to do, like going to school or being bar mitzvahed.

Tal skips along the sidewalk, jumping over each crack she detects in the cement that leads to the Ko-Op. Asher makes small talk with his stepmother. He asks what she plans to make for dinner. He asks if his father's cholesterol is still high. His stepmother prepares for her purse to be searched as they approach the doors of the supermarket and Asher waves to his co-worker who is sitting at the front of a line of ladies rearing to get their shopping done before sunset. When they get to the front Tal tugs on the hem of Asher's shirt.

"I want you to check my purse," she says.

"Why can't Elad check?" he asks.

Tal gives an exasperated sigh. "Because."

Asher reaches for her pink plastic purse, and she pulls it back. "You're supposed to sit down in the chair first." Tal's mother starts to say something but Asher obliges his sister and takes Elad's seat for the moment. Tal shuffles forward, peering over her shoulders to be sure no one else is looking, and then she opens her purse. The inside is just as pink as the outside and the back of the daisies printed on the sides show through. Asher sees a wrapped mint, a pocket notebook and four large batteries. He furrows his brow and then looks up at Tal who is beaming. His throat feels tight and his chest hurts the way it does when he hears Faren say she can't visit.

Tal takes his hand and pulls him up from the seat, leading him into the grocery store. "I got my purse checked, I got my purse checked," she sings to her mother.

"I know, I saw," she says.

The sky is peach and grey, and everything is still. People are in synagogue now. No one passes him. Asher sits on the steps of his father's townhouse and looks down the street. It looks like a postcard. He tries to picture his grandmother as a girl, younger than him. She has no family left and she is dying and alone. He can hear his stepmother running the kitchen sink. He can hear Tal singing to their father.

"I got my purse checked. I got my purse checked."

Bob Karsh
Compensatory Advantage

When I introduced my beau to my family, they immediately sensed that he was not Jewish. It was not his appearance that gave him away. Jews come in all colors and shapes. My beloved was swarthy with brown eyes and hair, but his given name was Chris; not a name that Jews commonly employ.

My father's response, after Chris left, was so unexpected that it blew me away. I had always regarded my father as reasonable and unprejudiced in matters of religion. Now, I learned for the first time about his intense antagonism toward exogamy. It was a word he was unlikely to know, although it evoked his response. I had learned the word in Sociology 101.

I knew his opposition to Chris was really serious, when he resorted to the smattering of French that he had picked up during his wartime service. It was the language he employed only in his most vehement and distasteful arguments. "You are only twenty-five years old. You are smart and attractive. You can wait for an *homme Juif.* You don't have to marry *faute de mieux.* Why rush into exogamy? Do you know the word?" Damn it, he knew the word.

I decided, perhaps unwisely, to fight fire with fire, instead of with an extinguisher. I threw one of his Frenchisms back at him. "I am no *faux naif,* and I know what exogamy means." For good measure, I reminded him of one of his favorite aphorisms: "You are confusing perception with reality." And for a fillip, "Anyone unprejudiced would recognize Chris's *caractere superieur.*" By this time, we both had exhausted our limited French vocabulary and reduced mother to tears. "Stop already," she cried. "Stop with the French cursing."

I tried for weeks to break down the wall of religion. "True religion should be a bridge, not a wall," was my structural argument. "We are not practicing Jews. We don't keep kosher. We attend services only on the high holidays. We rally to our faith only when Jews are insulted, criticized or attacked. So there is no real difference. We are basically secular and so is Chris." The wall did not crumble.

As for Chris, he realized that he was being welcomed with more coolness than ardor. He chalked it up to entering into a different ethnic, a family habitually reserved, aloof and withdrawn. If he had heard me trading decibels with my father, he would have known how wrong he was.

My folks simply were incapable of greeting him with the same warmth they would have granted to a Jewish beau. We reluctantly gave up trying to win them over. Our solace was in a new mantra that we had devised. Sad, funny, whimsical and serious, it declared: "exogamy is excellent."

Passover fell before our June wedding. Chris was invited to his first *seder* and really seemed to enjoy himself. It was our usual family frolic, heavy on singing, food and wine, scant on prayer. He obviously was striving to participate. Afterwards, he confided, "You and your parents are Franklin Jews." "Franklin Jews? I don't know that label." The next day, he read to me about how our practices were described in Poor Richard's Almanac: It is easier to keep the holidays than the commandments. "Wise old Ben was talking about my family too," said Chris. We laughed and kissed. Exogamy is excellent.

What about the other side? They also knew, from the start, what they were getting. Rachel Greenberg broadcasts as loudly as Chris. In all fairness, I guess I was not easy to take either. I sat like a retarded log at the single Sunday secular service they tried on me. "Only the alliteration of all those esses cheered me up," I explained to Chris. "I recall you laughing and joking at our *seder.* You're really the stronger one, Chris. I wish I had some of your strength." I was accepted, not embraced, by his family. Like mine, they wanted marriage within the tribe. Chris and I consoled each other with "exogamy is excellent."

My parents gave us a lavish wedding to prove to all the friends and relatives that they, modern Jews, were true, unbiased liberals. No-one must suspect that the Greenbergs resented being diluted by *goyim*, or even secular humanists; Chris had said that was the Carter family faith. No, the Greenbergs would continue left of center as confirmed Democrats, no matter what the Carter faith or politics. To their credit, my parents, bless them, gave the Carters the same wedding that they would have given the Cohens.

Suspicious members of both families thought this was a shotgun wedding and started to count the months. Tough luck! They had to count to thirty-six. We were in no hurry. In the absence of parental support, we wanted to be sure that we had a solid marriage. After two years, we were convinced that we were the reincarnation of Romeo and Juliet, without the tragedy.

Our baby was a beautiful girl. I was delighted that her sex spared the Carters the ordeal of witnessing a ritual circumcision. We named her Sarah. What a coincidence! Unknown to us, each family had a great-grandmother who bore that same name. Both sides were delighted that we had remembered an ancient relative. Sometimes inadvertent pleasures are the easiest to confer.

The first sign that something was wrong was misinterpreted as a blessing by my father who was growing deaf. "This baby is a marvel. She can hear a pin drop from across the room." It was true. She would startle and cry out at the softest of sounds. On the other hand, if her hearing was four plus, I didn't think that her eyes followed my wiggling finger very well. "Just a new mother's over-concern," the pediatrician assured me. Indeed, she rolled over and sat up at the proper times. And then she forgot how to do it! At that point, the doctor agreed that "something is wrong". He sent us to a neurologist who looked into Sarah's eyes and found the something. He called it "cherry-red spots" on the retina. The diagnosis was Tay-Sachs disease.

Chris and I rushed to the internet to Google everything about Sarah's future that we feared to learn--that she would sadly confirm in the coming months. Yes, hyperacusis, her superb hearing, was an early symptom. She went on, as predicted, to swing between extremes of listlessness and irritability. Her arms and legs grew limp. She fed poorly. If she reached three years, we were told to expect blindness, spasticity, convulsions and blindness. What a prospect! And she would not live beyond five years. We were aghast. No longer were we Romeo and Juliet--without the tragedy.

Chris, the more scientific one of us, explained the inheritance, the genetics as he put it, to me. "This is a disease peculiar to eastern European Jews, Ashkenazim. Did I say it right?" He did, and I felt like one peculiar Ashkenaz. "When two asymptomatic 'normal' carriers of the defective Tay Sachs gene mate, they have a one in four chance of giving the baby two bad genes, one from mama and one from papa. With two defective genes, the baby is not a carrier; the baby gets Tay Sachs disease." The computer told us that it is possible to test for carriers, and even to test the embryo in the womb for the disease. But there is no need for such precautions when only one partner is Jewish.

My father seized with unseemly relish on the answer. "Of course, Chris is Jewish. I always thought he looked Jewish. And what about that Carter great-grandmother named Sarah, a Jewish name. And now this Jewish disease. That cinches it." Now my parents felt able to embrace Chris wholeheartedly. Nor did they forget to include poor, little Sarah in their embrace.

You expect a family to coalesce around a tragedy, if only from compassion. Still, my folks showered us with proximity. They brought clothes and babysat and played and fed her. They even took a weekly night call, no easy task with Sarah screaming at every sound, so Chris and I could escape to a hotel for some love and sleep. Chris's family was supportive too, although I felt that they could have helped more. Maybe they resented having a Jewish fore-bearer and a Jewish gene. Maybe it was just my imagination.

Despite all the help, such a child is still a terrific burden. As it turned out, Sarah was also a conjugal strain. We stopped having sex because Chris stopped having erections. "No problem," I said, "see the doctor and get some Viagra." "No, I'll wait. Time will cure it." Was he afraid of another Tay-Sachs? Or was he being altruistic about not bringing more carriers into the world, since two out of four offspring are apt to be carriers? We both knew that tests could avoid that.

"I'm sure it's a temporary response to stress," he winced. His explanation did not sit well with me. I was hungering for cohabitation. But, like a stubborn kid, he refused to see the doctor. My urgings only made matters worse.

Now I made another mistake. I was tired of rushing to the nursery to see if every startled cry was a crisis or a false alarm. I brought Sarah into our bedroom. That was too much for Chris. He had slept through much of the distant screaming, but now he awakened with each nearby cry. The next day he was pooped at work and out of sorts at home. No sex and not even a sympathetic husband to cuddle. Chris broke down first.

"Look, I have to move out until I get my head on straight," he sheepishly explained.

Some solid marriage! Some Chris, the stronger one! I guess adversity strikes each person differently. "If you must go, make it short and don't forget us." Chris moved in with his parents, much to their dismay. He called several times a day, and kept up his monetary support, as if he were still with us. What I really needed was emotional support.

I moved Sarah into our bed, on my left side, where Chris had always slept. The left side, you know, is nearer to the heart. Whether it was my warmth, my stroking, or my cooing, Sarah's nightly crying seemed to diminish. I was able to get some sleep. Even Chris might have tolerated her now, if he had been here.

Then one morning I awoke later than usual, because her cries did not rouse me. There she lay, on my left, poor little Sarah, blue, silent, motionless, dead. The autopsy revealed the cause of death was suffocation. I must have rolled over in my sleep and smothered her. That was my guilt-ridden reasoning.

"A hearing must be held to make sure that this is not a case of deliberate child-slaughter." Child-slaughter, I shuddered at the word when my lawyer uttered it. "The state has an obligation to protect its citizens." The state's interest in promoting Tay Sachs escaped me, but I did not voice it. I was too busy being disturbed by some awful doubts seething within me. Deep down inside, I could not be certain that I never wished for Sarah to die. Maybe I did long for her death. Wouldn't that be better than three or four more years of suffering? But whose suffering was I wishing to avoid, hers or mine?

At the hearing, Chris reappeared. He had sought out our lawyer and asked to testify on my behalf. His testimony was overpowering.

"I lived with this woman for more than three years, and I know her better than she knows herself. She treasured Sarah at all hours of the day and night. I was the one who fled because I couldn't take it. Rachel is incapable of deliberately killing a child, or of even wishing for her death."

Our lawyer said Chris was instrumental in terminating the hearing in record time. My parents, who were present, took Chris's performance as another evidence of his sterling Jewish character. His parents were relieved and delighted to have him move back in with me again.

In our reading about genetic diseases, we wondered, as had others, why these bad recessive genes persist. Shouldn't Darwinian 'natural selection' and 'survival of the fittest' have culled them over time? Chris found the answer on the internet, a phenomenon called 'compensatory advantage'. It means that the bad gene survives in a carrier, who has no disease, because this bad gene gives the carrier a survival advantage over the rest of the population who do not harbor it. The example cited in the article was sickle cell anemia.

Two bad genes and you have the disease. One bad sickle cell gene makes you a carrier whose advantage over the non-carriers is resistance to malaria, in Africa where the gene arose. Of course, the resistant carriers with their protective gene survived and multiplied while others succumbed.

For Tay Sachs carriers, the advantage is supposedly resistance to tuberculosis conferred by the gene. When Jews were forced into crowded ghettos where tuberculosis was rampant, the lucky survivors were the resistant ones with the Tay Sachs gene. Makes sense, we agreed.

Then Chris read about another 'compensatory advantage' in the New York Times. Some Utah researchers think it is the gift of superior intelligence that keeps the Tay Sachs gene going. The scientists are named Harpending and Cochran. Those names alone seem to free them from any taint of conflict of interest. They reason that generations of persecution and job prohibition forced Jews into occupations that depended on wits for survival. And the smart ones who survived did so by virtue of their Tay Sachs gene. These scientists even figured out how the gene nurtures intelligence. It makes a smart protein that stimulates the brain of Tay Sachs carriers.

How strange, I thought, that a double dose of smart genes should cause a disease that features dementia. "Too smart for their own good," joked Chris.

This Utah theory is so politically incorrect, or reprehensible, which is worse, that it is not yet widely accepted, except perhaps by the Greenbergs and their ilk. And when Chris explained it to his parents, we suspected that they were a bit prouder of their occult Jewish heritage.

Scars have an incomprehensible way of healing. Chris and I are back together. The in-laws find much in common, beyond genes. And I am pregnant with a fetus that has tested negative. That brings me to my own theory of 'compensatory advantage'. The Tay Sachs gene brings families closer together than families without it, and that perpetuates the gene. Both sets of in-laws are getting along famously with one another and with us. Chris and I are solid again. There is, however, one small change in our relationship. In bed, I keep him on my right side only.

Susan Koppelman
Her Mother's Chicken Soup

When Phyllis went out after the noon weather cast, she felt the dryness in the air. The Monsoon had ended. But it had been even wetter than last year, and the desert was more lush than usual. Under the bird feeder, three stray kernels of corn had fallen to the ground, taken root, and were now almost three feet high under the filtering shade of the beautiful old Blue Palo Verde. And the tree, too, had begun to stir in the way Phyllis was beginning to recognize as the Sonoran desert's version of what she had grown up calling autumn in St. Louis. Unseasonal tiny yellow blossoms were popping out all over the tree and hummingbirds were dive bombing them. The look of them, the Palo Verde, the hummingbirds reminded her of how the whole tree had been a glory of yellow when they had first driven into the drive of this hidden house high in the mountain foothills. The prickly pear was bursting into fruit at the end of each vertical lily pad. By *Sukkos* they would be ready to harvest. The house was For Rent and it suited them both perfectly. A split one story with a bedroom and bathroom at each end and all the common rooms in between. A big kitchen, one they could eat in, like the kitchens they had grown up in. It was perfect.

The moon had passed through the fullness of last week to just over half a pocked sand dollar in the sky. The High Holy Days were coming and it was time to think again, formally, about all those things that Phyllis thought about each year.

Phyllis could handle a dinner for six for Rosh Hashanah, but no more. Not like in the old old days, when her service for twelve had to be supplemented every year as one after another, Phyllis filled the chairs at her extended dining room table and then squeezed in extras for her husband's single colleagues and their children's friends, for out-of-town relatives, for the inevitable stranger stuck in town who called the local Hillel and was directed to their house. And not like the recent old days when there had been two of them to make dinner and host the guests. The *balabusta* in her had always been aroused by the holidays and now, widowed and alone again in a beautiful city chosen not because it was home but because she was so much less crippled by allergies and arthritis, at this time of year, the *balabusta* in her stirred as much as ever.

Even before she planned the guest list, Phyllis began to plan the meal. Of course there would be chopped chicken liver. And a round raisin challah, probably two. Although there was no Jewish bakery in town, the from-scratch bakery at Basha's produced a more than credible challah. Brisket, *tsimmis, kasha varnishkes*, carrot *kugel, tagelich*, honey cake, apples and honey to dip them in. It would be a sweet meal, everything with the special sweetness of the New Year to it, even the brisket with Heinz chili sauce added to the Lipton onion soup gravy because it was sweet. Chicken soup. Of course. As her mother would say, "*Vu den*?" "What else?" What did Phyllis want in the soup this year?

When she had been a little girl, her mother had always started with a fat kosher soup hen whose stomach was full of tiny unshelled eggs. Everything had been from scratch in those days. But things changed as her mother aged. After a while, her mother started with a base of College Inn chicken broth, because there was never enough broth and it took too many chickens to make enough. What were you supposed to do with all that cooked chicken? Nah, you supplemented with canned broth. But over the years, Belle had stopped doing any of it from scratch. It got to be too much work and not enough better to matter. So Belle would open a package of Croyden House chicken soup and matzo ball mix and make that and supplement that with College Inn. And she'd cut a few peeled carrots into coins and add them "for color and for sweetness," she would always say. And cut in some celery without giving any reason. And cut in sweet onions – at that time of the year Vidalias were usually still available – also without any reason being necessary. She sometimes added a little bit of ground ginger in the *knaidle* mix, but not always. Sometimes she would add a lot of ground ginger because it would be an old container of ginger, bought for a Passover *imberlach* several seasons past, but it was almost out of zing and had to be used up. It wouldn't be replaced until the following spring, when Pesach, *imberlach* time, came again. And towards the end she would shake in dried parsley, some kosher salt, and a few shakes of ground white pepper.

Of course, the soup Phyllis was making was her own version of her mother's chicken soup. Phyllis always thought of that as "the right way to make chicken soup" rather than "my mother's chicken soup" because all seven her mother's sisters, Ruthie, Henrietta, Laura, Leona, Faygela, Ida, and Celia, and her mother's first cousins, Ethel and Miriam, Vivian and Edith and Mollie, and even her fifth cousin Lillie, who was the daughter of her grandfather's nephew who was older than her own father, made chicken soup exactly the same way.

Phyllis had always made chicken soup her mother's way, the "right way," varying it only slightly, adding a lot of fresh cut parsley because Phyllis loved it when it went into the pot close enough to eating time that it was still slightly springy instead of totally limp when you ate it. And in her fancy young homemaker years when she'd even mixed her own curry, she had learned about parsnips and salsify and, liking the idea of them before she'd even tasted them, she had, of course, liked them, and so she used them in the soup when she was doing her big deal fancy schmancy holiday job of a chicken soup. She had used free range chickens and spring water. All her politics went into her cooking. And so did her ego. She always got a kick out of people looking at the white coins in their soup and not knowing what it was. And she got to tell them. She could do from simple, easy, and quick chicken soup to elaborate and gourmet – but whichever chicken soup she made, it was always an elaboration of her mother's soup.

Then she met Delores. And began to share a home with Delores, another displaced Middle Western Jewish widow. When she and Delores sat down to plan the first *Seder* they would make together, she discovered that Delores put potatoes in her chicken soup. Phyllis was stunned. Potatoes in chicken soup? It couldn't be. She just couldn't eat it that way.

It wasn't just that it was a different recipe; it was how it was different that Phyllis was appalled by. Potatoes in chicken soup? It was – just – wrong! The potatoes were too heavy, too starchy for chicken broth. And if you were going to use some sort of *lukshen* in it, *knaidlach* or *kreplach*, even just plain *lukshen*, thick or thin, even rice, however your family likes it, all these things she could compromise on, but to put in potatoes! It would ruin it, absolutely ruin it. Nobody in her family had ever put potatoes in chicken soup and she wasn't going to start now. She just couldn't. It would feel like – well, it just wouldn't be chicken soup by her. What would her mother have said about potatoes in chicken soup? Phyllis knew what her mother would have said – nothing. But the way she would have lifted her eyebrows would have said it all.

Delores was just as stubborn about her mother's chicken soup as Phyllis was about hers. By her it was the only right way to make chicken soup. They talked about alternating years, one year making Delores's mother's chicken soup with potatoes and the next year making Phyllis's mother's chicken soup one hundred percent absolutely without a hint of potato. But neither was willing to be the first to go through a *Pesach* without her mother's soup. Those fateful potatoes! So they talked about making both soups: each would eat her own and the rest of the people at the table could choose which they wanted, or a little of both.

They tried to find a way to mediate the unrelenting outrage and repugnance, each at the other's chicken soup recipe. They tried to distance themselves from the conflict, to laugh at it, that such a thing should cause such *tsuris* in an otherwise happy and peaceful home.

If they'd been honest they would have realized then and there that their relationship would never last, could never last. They agreed about everything – literature, politics, art, music, theater, where to vacation, financial planning, the importance of volunteering in their community, climate change, which rabbi was nice and which one was smart, what might make a late remarriage worth the problems it would inevitably bring. So could any other one thing be as important as all these other things? Well, yes. As it turned out, chicken soup with or without potatoes was the ultimate outward manifestation of whatever inward incompatibility remained undiscovered. They stayed together for another two years, another two seders, two Rosh Hashanahs, Yom Kippur break fasts, Sukkots, many, many Shabbats, but they grew increasingly unhappy sharing a home. All of these meals require chicken soup. They tried to quench the simmering resentment on Friday evenings by using different soups – mushroom and barley, vegetable beef, flanken, but with each mouthful of a *Shabbos* soup that wasn't chicken soup, wasn't her mother's chicken soup, the resentment would flare,

So they finally separated. *Vu den?* Each took her own soup pot and made a new home somewhere else, promising, of course, to stay in touch. And that's why she was alone again. And could hope to host no more than six.

After a few years, they no longer even exchanged Rosh Hashanah cards or even pre-Kol Nidre quick calls saying, "Listen, if there's something I should be sorry for, I'm sorry. If you wanna tell me about it, I'll listen; if not, I'm sorry anyway. Okay? You accept?" And the other would say, "Yeah. Me, too." And they'd hang up and go off to their separate pots of holiday chicken soup, alone, either with or without potatoes.

But then, this is real life, so the holidays continued to arrive in their proper order and the lives of the two women continued well beyond their three score and ten. Each was now preparing for her bat mitzvah. Delores was now settled in with someone new, someone whose mother's recipe for chicken soup was like her mother's recipe. Phyllis was alone but happier that way then with potatoes in her mother's chicken soup. And there was peace in each household.

Robert M. Levin
A Brief History of Howard

They turned into Webster University, into the parking lot of the Loretto-Hilton theatre. They sat for half a second, bracing themselves. Carolyn counted to three, they got out of the car, and then joined each other as quickly as possible, trotting in lock step to the doors. The coat-check was overflowing, they decided to bring the coats to their seats. It was an intimate theatre, every seat a good one. The rhythm instruments were already on stage, the drums, piano, and upright bass. Amplifiers, microphones, and speakers encircled the stage. Then the lights dimmed, the emcee came out, and there was mild applause. One by one, each musician walked to their instrument. They were ready.

Then from the sides there was a trumpet fanfare, notes upon notes, rapidly fired, popping like musical corn, a rolled out red carpet of harmony. And on this carpet walked the man playing these notes, one bullfrog stapled to each cheek, the bell of the horn, bent funny, pointing to the heavens. The crowd applauded so quietly, not wanting to miss one note. Dizzy Gillespie nodded to the crowd, and then nodded to the band. The drummer joined in, not beating a beat, but sizzling a beat like a piece of hip frying bacon. Then the bass player started to thrum, even strokes, the most beautiful of heartbeats, and finally the piano player dropping chords into the mix like he was seasoning a fine dish.

The crowd dropped into the jazz wave, actions meaningful and subtle, around the room, left to right, eyes closed, heads tilted back, feet quietly tapped. Used to be that jazz made you want to jitterbug, now it makes you want to dream. Carolyn and Howard reached for each other's hands, his thumb tapping her hand, her forefinger tapping the back of his knuckle. And gradually time changed, the daily tick tock slowly melted as it does in the deep of each night, where fifteen minutes of clock open into hours and days of a long dream. The air of the theatre, dried from hours of the running furnace, turned into the waters of a cool pond. The band was spinning ribbons and threads of tune, ribbons upon ribbons— Rumpelstiltskin rehabilitated, sweet and savory aromas of tunes, desserts of tunes, toys of tunes.

And then the bottom fell out, inside of Howard the bottom fell out. First his stomach, then his liver, his kidneys next, both intestines, his lungs, and then his heart fell ever so slightly, at least it felt like they were falling. Way inside, in the darkness where nobody goes, at the bottom of the anatomical sea, the alarms went off. No pain this time, beyond pain—the nervous system's telegraph was superseded by a clear, full awareness of imminent death. He held Carolyn's hand more tightly. The song ended, the applause was loud and long. Howard was as enthusiastic as his energy would allow. Another clear awareness—being completely at the mercy of this energy. Carolyn was standing and applauding.

Howard needed more awareness, he needed some sense of time— how much was there. He needed a sense of what to do, to leave now, to wait? And if he waits, what should he do after that? He closed his eyes, where else would the answer be? Dizzy was explaining the word Bebop.

"Okay ladies and gentlemen, all together, what sound does a dog make? Right, 'bow-wow.' (Thank you everybody for that wonderful bow-wow.) And a cat? That's right, meow. (Very good, y'all, very good.) But a dog doesn't really say bow-wow, and a cat doesn't really meow, that's what we say they say. We put words on the very pure sounds that they make. We do this all the time and don't even think about it. Like tick tock tick tock. Now back in the forties we would write some songs, and we would learn the songs before we would name the songs. Now you can see already, okay I can hear some of you giggling—which by the way is another example of this phenomena, the word 'giggle' sounds like a giggle. As I was about to say before some of you got too hip for your own good, that learning the song before naming the song caused a bit of trouble in rehearsal. You want to play the song, but you can't call the song. And so to rehearse we would say, 'Let's play that new one, you know, Oo Bop Sha Bam. Or Wee Dot, or Oo Ya Koo, or Bebop.' And, not to mention the one we're about to play, song that we finally named, 'Salt Peanuts.'"

He turned to the band and counted, "Ah Oh Ee" and then he stopped, and turned back to the audience. "And you can undo that process, too. You can take established words, like 'one, two, three, and four,' and change them back into their pure sound. Like so. He turned back to the band and snapping his fingers. "Right here. Ah Oh Ee Unh…"

Howard thought, the music played. If, he reasoned, I have only moments to live, minutes and seconds…salt peanuts salt peanuts…then dying while listening to Dizzy Gillespie is high on the list of Preferred Ways to Go…salt peanuts salt peanuts…If my moments are longer, days and weeks, if my soul or whatever, is trying to live, then I might have enough time to do something, in which case I can still stay for the rest of the concert…salt peanuts salt peanuts.

Laughing, Carolyn leaned to his ear and said, "the notes in the song really do sound like the words 'salt peanuts.' Her warm breath on his ear made Howard think of some other items on the list of Preferred Ways to Go.

"Okay, I'm getting it. I could love this music," Carolyn said, nodding, smiling. "Where I'm from is a very Country Music kind of place."

Normally the radio would be on, normally Howard would have responded by asking her more about where she came from. But both the radio and Howard were still.

"Are you okay?" she asked.

"Not sure," he said. "I had a moment of extreme clarity in there, I'm not completely sure what to make of it or what to do about it."

"I'm listening," she said.

"But it was more than just a thought. Something changed inside of me and…something's wrong," he said. "Something is very wrong."

She didn't say a word, she just reached over and held his hand. In silence, they drove the rest of the way and then parked in front of her apartment. Howard took a long, deep breath.

"I think that I'm going to die soon," he said. "That feeling in there, I've never had it, and I've never heard of it. But something tells me it's bad." He knew that it was extremely bad form to cry on a date, to get weepy and weak—no matter how modern people say they are, it could change everything, and in his swirling thoughts he decided to stay strong deciding he could handle dying better than another episode of 'Let's Just Be Friends.' "It feels like my internal organs are dropping and I've never heard of any symptom remotely sounding like this."

"Do you think that they're really dropping, because I don't think that they can do that."

"All I can say is what it feels like." They sat for a few moments, each watching their breath begin to ice the inside of the windshield. "Let's go upstairs," she said, tapping his hand.

They quickly got out of the car and ran up the walkway to the building's front door. Howard jumped up and down as she went through her purse, muttering "Key, key, k-key, k-key."

They went upstairs, into apartment 3. Jim was stretched out on the sofa eating some popcorn and reading a book. He was wearing a T-shirt and gym shorts, his skin had a mist of sweat and the side window was open ever so slightly. It was really hot in there.

"Either Randy's wife laid down the law or he's cheap the rest of the year just to crank the heat in the winter," Jim said. Randy was the landlord who owned this building, the one across the street, the Yoga center, and two on the next block. He and his wife lived in apartment 1, right underneath. "Whatever the reason," Jim continued, "I think I'll have to bake him a pie or something, do something nice. You guys want some popcorn?"

They took off their coats and sat around the bowl like it was a campfire.

"How was the concert?" Jim asked.

"Fine," said Howard. He looked at Carolyn, Carolyn looked at Howard.

"What's up?" asked Jim. "The guy's cheeks blow up or something?"

"No," Carolyn said, "nothing like that. The music was wonderful, the guy is fine."

"Then what's up?" Jim asked. "Wait, I know. Are you two engaged?"

"No nothing like that," Howard said.

"Howard had a bit of a revelation," Carolyn said.

"You're going to ask her to get engaged?"

"No no," Howard said. "It's actually not very good." He paused. "This is going to sound strange, it feels like my internal organs are dropping—not a lot, just a little bit, and I had the accompanying feeling that…"

Again a pause.

"That…" said Jim.

"That I'm going to die soon."

Now Jim and Carolyn looked at each other.

"I'll tell you what," Jim said, "when I was in Vietnam I had that same revelation every day. After a while I just looked at it like my five o'clock shadow. Even when I got shot," Jim continued, "it was my five o'clock shadow."

"You were shot?" Carolyn asked. Howard smiled to himself.

"Right here," Jim showed her a long, wide scar on his right calf.

"Did you get a Purple Heart?" she asked.

"My C.O. wanted me to put in for one, but it was just this jerk in the next bunk who wasn't paying attention when he was cleaning his gun." Then Jim looked at Howard. "You've got to spend the night here. If you feel bad you can't go home to that cold, drafty place of yours. You have to spend the night."

Howard and Carolyn reached for each other easily, without thought, as if they'd been together for years. They kissed softly.

"Then it's settled," Jim said. "I'll go make some more popcorn while you guys work out the details. But Carolyn," he said, "remember our boy's sick here, he probably needs all the warmth he can get." He winked and then walked into the kitchen. Howard and Carolyn walked into her bedroom, closed the door, turned out the light, and figured Jim would figure out the rest.

Normally, that is, if Howard were feeling normal, he would have undressed quickly. And he would have done it without the very audible sigh that just seeped out. Under the covers, as he touched her, he could feel from just that touch, the smoothness of her skin, how beautiful she was, as if his hands could electronically scan her image into his mind.

"We don't have to do anything tonight," she said. "We could just lay here. Don't feel as if there's some role or performance requirement. That's all nonsense."

"You say it's nonsense," Howard said weakly. "Shit, I'm feeling weak and tired," he said.

"No," she said. "It's nonsense. Men who feel like that, there's problems with that. I know."

He was so tired. He knew that he could probably ask her something personal right now, ask her what's behind the wall, and she'd tell him. Except that he was falling asleep. The last thought he had before he drifted off was that he had to teach guitar tomorrow, and he may have mumbled something about setting the alarm.

Howard pulled into the parking lot. There was a bright, cold sun that morning. The sleep did him well, although he was sore inside, underneath his bones, underneath his ribs, which didn't hurt as much as the thought of going one more time to the emergency room. He walked into the store, said hello to Ed and Chuck, picked out the guitar he would use that day, set up his studio, and walked into the front room to wait for his first student. He stood looking out the front window, at the cars on Olive, at the store across the street. Stupid. Howard thought, stupid. He was a guitar teacher for four years at Silver Strings, looking out at the same street scene for four years, looking across the street at the same Wang's Special Food store for four years, looking at the same small sign at the upper left hand corner of the building for four years, and until this day, never saw it. The sign had an arrow underneath, pointing, as it were, around to the back of the building. Above the arrow, as it has always been, was one word: Acupuncture.

Excerpt from the novel *A Brief History of Howard*

Stacey Levine
The Day of Silver Candlesticks
For Esther

I'm not a collector, but really a purloiner, and there's only a brief backstory to the silver-and-blue candlestick holders that now rest in my hands.

When my husband died, I sought companionship. I began to take walks in the little park beside the lake. I thought: Why is no one talking to me? Yet life can be surprising, so full of largesse. One afternoon a pleasant-looking man, younger than I, appeared on the lake path. In one hand he held an ice-cream cone and in the other a dog leash and a shopping bag. Beside the man stood an ancient, oblivious pug. As I passed, a scoop of chocolate dropped from the cone and onto the little dog's back; I offered to help, wiping the dog's back and tail with Kleenex. I realized this was not the best position from which to flirt, but I could not help myself. I winked. I couldn't understand why, either, at my age (I am a grandmother). The man smiled and said he was en route to a cousin's wedding. Did I want to come along?

I did. I wondered, though: Who eats a double ice-cream cone on the way to a wedding? It was not the only odd thing I observed that day. Still, the afternoon sky was lovely and open, with hordes of birds silhouetted against it. I was glad the man had invited me. Some of my grief scattered away then, white lace on the wind.

We talked and walked. I held the leash with the tottering pug. The wedding would be very casual, the man told me, so I would not need to change my clothing. A casual wedding? The man's name was Isaac, and his hair was wonderfully dark. I peeked into his shopping bag and saw almonds and snacks even sweeter than that.

He was a Moroccan Jew. He came from a family of bon vivants and bricklayers, he told me, and I thought this was a joke, so I laughed loudly, not realizing it might be true. When Isaac mentioned that his parents had recently divorced, I realized just how young he was. He told me it was hard to think of his parents apart, and that he had pain that would not leave because of the divorce—a torsion in his heart. The cousin's wedding today would be difficult as well, he said. But Isaac would weather these difficulties, I saw.

"My family is facing lots of changes, and that's hard. But the way life can change is a kind of miracle, too," he said.

I was impressed.

With the dog, we approached the house where the wedding would be held. Heavy rain broke out; we flew up the porch steps. Other guests streamed in, North African and white. Young mothers carried shoeboxes of homemade cookies, middle-aged men arrived in t-shirts; an entourage of musicians trailed behind a laughing singer.

The rooms of the house were unusually constructed—diamond-shaped, with hallways and staircases winding around them. We found the wedding party on the ground floor. In the press of the shifting crowd, Isaac held my hand. That action made my own hand feel shocked and dry. As I drew away, the two of us exchanged wary glances. He was so young, and I so old!

Isaac then saw some old friends across the room, waved, and ran to embrace them. Their group melted into the floor of celebrants.

I stood at the side of the big room and disliked myself for having run to this party so carelessly, eagerly, without my dead husband's company.

The *chuppa* leaned with its poles and cloth against a wall. Why leave the wedding canopy unassembled? That is ridiculous, I thought crossly. The conversation around me cued me in: the ceremony had been delayed because the rain had flooded the ground floor. Several family members swept water out of the kitchen.

I saw four men dragging a brand-new sump pump into the wedding room through the back door. Then bags of gravel. These items looked very heavy. Why start a big project like this now, right before a wedding? For a second time, I grew annoyed. The men unpacked the sump pump, beginning to install it just outside a closet door. I went over and told them they should install the pump inside the closet—but no, that idea made them upset. Yes, they owed up, ideally it should be placed inside the closet, but a hole for the device was already cut into the floor outside the closet.

The festivities continued. I helped clear the way, giving the sump-pump installers more space. One of the men extended a small shovel my way, and I agreed to dig alongside them. Why not? We needed to widen the pit. With the party's noise all around us, we discussed the pump's various attributes and how it should be positioned. The pipe fittings were puzzling. My feelings soared. I felt a part of something.

Hours passed. Savory music began. I forgot about Isaac. One of the men working beside me shouted to be heard.

"My hobby is taxidermy!"

"Great!" I shouted back.

The long evening rolled in. We caulked around the pipes, and later, the bride and groom walked toward us, smiling, admiring how tidily the pump fit into the floor, and the way its cover sealed the whole apparatus. They helped us connect and test its alarm. The small bride, beautiful in a satiny blue gown, laughed and slipped back into the crowd.

When the sump pump was fully installed, we cheered, and so did the rest of the wedding party. We had succeeded in mending the room. The *chuppa* went up; the wedding unfolded.

Alone, I wandered to the rear of the room and saw a table loaded with gifts. My own wedding, so long ago, had been vastly different from this one, and it was much less vivid to me than today's celebration. For this reason I became terribly sad. Long spells of time are difficult to comprehend and can render us frozen, like characters in old tales who drink unspeakably powerful potions. Yet the incomprehensible potion of time is also a gift, part of nature and God.

Across the room I saw Isaac dancing with his friends, his little dog dozing on the sidelines.

I dawdled near the gift table and saw the candlesticks made of uncannily bright silver and blue glass; they were wrapped in a plethora of ribbons. I touched the candlesticks' smooth metal. I am merely human. I suddenly thought: The bride doesn't need these. She has everything. I stole the candlesticks, dropped them in my black leather bag. What a coward I am.

I ran home and put them in a box, which I shoved beneath my bed. The candlesticks' silver burned white-hot through the box and the bed frame for days, making me nearly feverish with shame.

Days later, Isaac called and asked if I wanted to walk around the park, but I did not want to be reminded of the day of the silver candlesticks and how, on a day that gave so generously to me, I became a thief.

I sit here now with the candlesticks in my hands. They don't burn anymore. Their warmth is pretty. As with a developing tale, I will wait for the next turn of events to arrive, a change that may come simply because time passes and circumstances change. Or maybe I will gain insight and make the next move deliberately, pushing the tale forward with my own actions. Healing is part of time, a constant unfolding.

Charlotte Mielziner
The Secret

Perhaps one assumes my moment of rebirth was blasted by a dazzling surge of lightning with my creator, dramatically screaming to the heavens, "Life! Give my Creation life!" The reality was quite different. The good doctor, may he rest in peace, his equipment so primitive, gave but one tremendous blast to my system and then for weeks later, a tiny trickle of electricity equal to that of a normal human body ran through me, steadily feeding my physiology with the signals it needed to mend the myriad connections.

How much luck merged with skill in the doctor's success I can still barely fathom. That I am a compendium of over twenty various parts all found with blood type O+ still amazes me. The fact that none of my incisions became septic and that circulation was restored to each part must be credited to his obsessive cleanliness and attention to detail. God is not the only one to have performed a miracle.

I agree. The possibility of my existence is so improbable it is the stuff of gothic horror, is it not? True, but, this infinitesimal level of probability actually happened generations ago before even a true comprehension of the Herculean effort was understood.

Now we will finish the refinement my creator would have given me if he could. Your work in reconstructive plastic surgery is nearly as legendary as the good Doctor was in reanimation of inanimate tissues. By the way, I enjoyed your paper in *Lancet* on advancements in non-steroidal therapies for scar removal. It was cutting edge, if you'll pardon the pun.

You're quite welcome.

Please allow me to babble on as you work, it takes my mind off the procedure. I get so little chance for polite conversation. Perhaps this is why most surgeons would prefer their patients under sedation.

Thank you…you're too kind.

Consider my left hand, the fingers smooth and long, nails arched and thin; a sensitive hand meant for the arts, music or sculpture. I often imagine it was the hand of a classical pianist, well known for his innovative interpretations of Lizst. Yes, Lizst of the lilting waltzes and the demonic, pounding chords of Faustus. This hand could stretch across the keys of a fine Boesendorfer, feel the song within and give it voice.

Compare the left hand with my right. So different, with strong fingers, age spots, callused palms and a curious scar on the ring finger.

It has strength, but not gentility. This is the hand I use for...well, more menial tasks.

In the beginning, consciousness came slowly. What I remember is pain, all encompassing white hot pain. It racked my body and pounded me with its only reality. Imagine needing to scream and having no mouth. How long did I lay on the table unable to move, to voice my agony? It seemed as long as it takes a waterfall to etch away the threshold to a picturesque cascade. Be reassured, what your laser scalpel has inflicted on me is not even a prick from a rose.

My first recollection other than pain feels as recent as if it were yesterday. I heard music. At first, it was as if it were far away, echoing in a cave; drifting softly into my consciousness. I became aware of someone standing over me, assessing my vitals, quietly making notes and humming the loveliest song I've ever heard. It was melancholy, sweet and I clung to it like the lifesaver it was.

As if clarity rode in on the descending chords of music; I began to identify new sensations. I felt the brush of a cool, wet cloth on my face. The hands holding it were gentle, even loving. I fought through a fog of confusion for awareness.

I opened my eyes and slowly focused on my creator. To me, he was beautiful. He lifted my head to sip some cool water. Even though I was as massive in size and strength as you see me now, I was helpless in his arms. He tended to my needs in those next weeks with the care of a lover. He was my universe, my light, all things good came from him.

My brain tested its new connections, synapses firing and signaling movement. I began to stretch, flex and contract my limbs and the good doctor was there by my side. Coordination and balance had to be learned anew. Like a teenage boy who grows overnight, my brain needed to adjust to the capacity and range of movement of my limbs. The doctor celebrated my first halting steps like a proud parent.

That wretched little assistant Igor, perhaps the most famous hunchback since Quasimodo, limped through the laboratory incessantly. Remember, at that time research such as this was not only illegal, but considered evil, diabolical. Today, cutting edge research has the backing and protection of drug companies more powerful than governments. Malpractice suits pale in comparison to being burned at the stake by an angry mob. I, his greatest success had to be kept secret from the world and this scheming, greedy man was the only one who knew.

While I experienced love and nurturing from the good doctor, the hunchback was the opposite in every way. At first, I didn't understand taunting, but as my language comprehension grew, the meanings became clear. Tripping me as I tried to navigate the narrow stone steps to my chamber grew to threatening with a torch and beatings with chains. You may doubt it listening to me now, but speech came much later and I was unable to verbally protect myself or plea for help.

Like a child, I feared the night, fire, the unknown and the hunchback. My frustrations grew and anger deepened, but so did my curiosity. What world lay beyond the walls of the laboratory? I yearned for knowledge one hundred and forty years ago just like today. I am driven to learn, explore and live.

Yes, you're right, I don't appear to have aged since the day I was reborn. How reanimation kept me from the degenerative effects of time is another mystery the doctor will unfortunately never explain.

When that little troll threatened to reveal my creator's miracle to the townspeople, I silenced him. The secret had to be kept. It was actually easy. His twisted spine, a symbol of his life, was straightened in death. It felt as if my life force fed off his energy as he died by my hand. I felt power and it was exhilarating.

When I could, I explored the halls of the castle and found the first woman I ever saw. She was captivating in satin and lace. She moved with a sultry grace I had never imagined. To be near her I conquered my fear of the night. How was I to know she was my creator's fiancée?

Instinctively, I knew she mustn't see me. As she slept, I came to her room to touch her hair and breathe in its lavender scent. I knelt in adoration at her bedside and softly hummed the sweet song the doctor sang when I first became aware. It was the only gift I had to give. My heart flew when she smiled in her sleep. I wept with love and a tear fell on her cheek and awakened her. She saw me and a scream began to fill her fragile throat. I had to stop it before it got out and so my first love ended tragically.

I carried her lifeless body to the tower. I begged the same power that gave me life to bring her back, but my prayers went unheard. All that she was or ever would be was gone. I had taken a life in anger and now I had taken a life in love. Having been created from death, were all my relationships to end this way?

From the windows I glimpsed a world beyond the castle walls and it was to there that I had to escape. Torn between curiosity and terror, I found the door and freed the latch.

The night air washed across my cheek, cleansing me of my misdeeds and calling me to the world. I stumbled into the courtyard, dizzy with freedom and awed by the sheer openness. I thought the stars in the sky and the lights in the houses of the village below were the same. For a moment, I stood arms out, drinking in the vastness of simply being free.

Straining to listen to the sounds of the night, I heard music floating up the hillside from the village. Not the sad, sweet song of the doctor's, but bright, happy and inviting music. Reaching out, I went forward not to fame, but infamy.

Need I tell you how I fared in the village? That man fears what he does not know has been written about by philosophers for generations. It was as if the villagers looked into my eyes and saw a man without a soul. With the townspeople pursuing me, I panicked and ran to the only sanctuary I knew and that act brought wrath and vengeance upon the doctor.

We were tried by fear, found guilty by ignorance and executed by bigotry. Only I couldn't die again, I could only suffer. The emotional pain of losing my father, my creator, my God eclipsed the physical pain I had felt as my nerves, muscles and arteries rebelled at being awakened.

For all these years, I've lived a solitary existence. Secluded and rejected, I've searched the world and never encountered another being like me. I read, learn and observe unseen and unknown. I protect the secret. Never have I known acceptance by society. But now, through your surgical expertise, I can at least cosmetically appear to be the intelligent and sensitive creature I am. There is hope.

There is a lovely sidewalk café in town west of the park. It's a charming place well known for their homemade brioche. Oh, you know it. I dream of spending an afternoon there, drinking tea, reading poetry and watching passersby with no one taking more note of me than any other casual, however large patron.

Are you finished? Let me see. I've anticipated this for so long. Yes, this is much better. Excellent scar minimization, I must say. In a way, I'm nearly handsome. Your reputation is certainly deserved. You were well worth what you asked, but really shouldn't have pressed me for my story, because as you now know, I must keep the secret. Your fate was sealed when you made me relate my beginnings in exchange for your services.

You see, I am a miracle of science from a time when man first questioned his universe, explored his limits, but found no inner peace. For my creator to reanimate a concoction of cadavers was a feat of skill, a tremendous leap of faith so far past its time it has yet to be replicated. His secret must be kept. Don't struggle; your passing will be... indelicate if I must use both hands. It truly seems that all my relationships end this way.

My life is a metaphor for whatever theory the sages wish to posit. It could be man's struggle against ignorance, his inner need to create, the immorality of egocentrics, the futility of playing God, you name it and this humble tale will fit. I prefer to see it as an example of how shallow our veneer of civilization is. Oh, the tyranny of humanity.

I am a calculated culmination of my parts. I am of Man and by Man. I am quintessential nature versus nurture in action. I am the Monster. I am Frankenstein.

Lie still now, lie still.

Barry Nove
Isaac in a Bind, Again

"Isaac, how's my love letter coming along?" he asked me for the third time in Yiddish.

"Short and sweet, she seems like a lovely girl."

"If she could only speak Yiddish, we could have real conversation. Rather than these letters between my visits to Alton."

I laughed, "You could work harder on your English, Chaim."

"I workin' on it," he said proudly.

"Work on the accent... You still sound like you just got off the boat!"

"I have been here six months!" he protested.

I shook my head, wondering at Chaim's luck. He had come to Chicago, connected with his uncle's best friend in Indiana and was now engaged to her sister-in-law. I'd been here eleven years and my love life had led to disaster. I had fallen in love, finally gotten up the nerve to propose and she'd accepted, sort of. Her response had been less than flattering, "Oh, I guess that's alright. We can always get divorced if it doesn't work out."

Now, I'd been looking for a nice modern American born Jewish girl, but there was modern and there was modern. I'd walked off and muttered, "How about we divorce right now and skip everything in between?"

She had the gall to be affronted and tell me she'd never speak to me again, as if I had any interest in speaking to her after that.

So, here I was writing Chaim's love letters to the girl he was getting ready to marry in two weeks. I felt like an idiot as I finished writing, "Best Regards... Chaim." She wrote great letters back. She seemed the kind of level headed, witty, and based on the pictures she had sent rather cute, young lady I would have given my eye teeth to meet. My sister was having better luck than I was. She was getting married in seven months, in September to Izzy.

"Here's your letter," I said handing it to the smiling Chaim. He stuffed it into the envelope I had addressed for him and hurried out of parlor of the boarding house. My lantsman from Lanovitz, the lucky dog, he'd even had a Second Class ticket to America.

# # #

Chapter 1

Eleven years ago I came to America. Eleven years before that when I was eight, my father said goodbye and left Lanovitz behind forever to make a new life for us in America. Lanovitz was a very old shtetl, a village which many claimed was established back in the 15th Century. The town was basically two towns, one Jewish and one not. The closest city was Lvov in Galicia. Depending on the vagaries of history, the town was either Poland or Russia and because the train passed through Lanovitz, people could make a modest living.

Poppa felt we could do better in America and planned to work hard and make enough money to send for us. "It should be a year, two at most," he had promised. We cried, we didn't want him to go, but we didn't have the money for all of us to go. My Uncle Benzion, a few years younger than my Poppa, had written and said he had had to travel all the way to Missouri to find work. New York City was not so easy and our cousins there weren't in a position to help much. That was the last time Momma, my younger sister Surah and I saw him for years.

He stayed in New York for a time, but ultimately moved to Chicago where he got work rolling cigars with other immigrants who were from Lanovitz. He wrote that it was hard to save enough money for our three tickets, but he should have enough the next month. He promised that and we waited and waited for that next letter, when it didn't arrive for weeks on end we began to worry. Grandpa, Zayda Zvi and Grandma, Bubbe Bluma were both worried too. They lived down the street and lived for the letters Poppa sent us and Uncle Benzion sent them. It was two months before we got his next letter asking us if we had bought the tickets with the money he had sent.

Momma let out a cry at that, realizing that his letter had gone astray or as was more likely, the letter had been torn open along the way and the money stolen. "How can I tell your Bubbe and Zayda this?"

But it was worse than that. Business wasn't exactly great in Lanovitz for a mother raising two children. Momma had already begun making arrangements for me to travel to Warsaw and live there for several months to learn my bar mitzvah. She had hoped that she could save the money we had saved for the trip to America, but now it looked like I would be making the trip with my Zayda after all.

# # #

Chapter 2

I studied in Warsaw with the Hazans, the cantors, the city was famed for, and taught to chant the readings of my Torah and Haftorah portions. I had a good voice. That's what everyone had said in Lanovitz, and I was good with numbers and musical notes, I could do figures in my head and musical notation came as easily. The Hazans wrote to my Zayda and told me they praised the family's choice for sending me to them.

I received and wrote many postcards and letters, and learned that Poppa was heartsick over the money having been lost, but happy that I was studying in Warsaw. Momma also wrote that Poppa was again saving money for our tickets, but this time would purchase the tickets and not send the money. What she did not write was that it would take him years to save enough again.

Nothing was ever easy. But one thing I knew if you worked hard – and did a lot of praying, everything would work out for the best. Or so I hoped.

Yes, I was a bit naïve. Luckily, my voice didn't break until after my bar mitzvah in Lanovitz. Oh, did I mention that the war broke out about that same time? I am talking about the Great War as they call it here in America. Living through it, though, I assure you there was nothing "great" about it.

To say life was tough is an understatement. To say Momma was tougher, another. We fled Lanovitz as the battle lines shifted ever nearer. When the war receded, we came back to our home with our neighbors who had fled. We had to repair not just our roof, but our grandparent's, then the damage to our nearest neighbors' homes, all while foraging for food. The war was very hard on Bubbe Bluma. She fell ill… We buried her in the cemetery outside the shtetl.

Zayda visited her every day no matter the weather. Momma went into business. Not to say I plan to tell my children or grandchildren about that business, there's Prohibition after all. Explaining that we were bootleggers might be a bit embarrassing.

But we were in a bind and we had to make a living… and people do like to drink and are willing to pay whether it's legal or not, even in the Russian Empire, where drinking was considered almost a sport. Of course, those who wanted booze from the other side of town, the non-Jewish Lanovitz, often decided to skip the middlemen and came directly to us, which led to the day I had to hide in the oven.

Now, don't get me wrong, the oven wasn't lit at the time and it wasn't like we had much wood to burn lately. The men were drunk who broke into the house demanding the booze. They knocked Momma down and my sister threw herself over her and screamed so loud I could not fail to hear her say, "You hurt my Momma, you'll have to kill me first!" Had they found me, they would have beaten me to death to get the booze. We had known it to happen, which was one of the hazards of this particular line of business.

Now Momma could scream real loud, but Surah was no slouch, either. The men left, thank god, and never found the bottles I had hid out back… But let me tell you, don't hide in an oven, it's not easy to hold your breath with your knees up against your chest.

# # #

Chapter 3

So, we prayed for the war to end and what that got us was the Russian Revolution. The Communists killed the Czar, who thankfully had stayed far away from us… The Great War may have ended, but we had more to worry about. Momma wrote Poppa in America, but I had my doubts he would ever receive her letter. When we did start getting the mail again, Poppa's letters kept asking if we were all right and how his Mother and Father were. Well, it was clear from that that Momma's letter's weren't reaching him or hadn't yet.

News about the Revolution and fighting amid the factions made every day maddening. Yet one day the trains were running on schedule again and a batch of letters from Poppa arrived within days. I was twenty years old when Momma opened a letter with our tickets to America inside.

Eleven years we hadn't seen Poppa and now we were leaving Lanovitz. "Zayda, please, come with us!" I pleaded.

He shook his head, "I'll not leave your Bubbe… America is for the young. Just promise me this, Isaac. You'll tell your father and your uncle when you see them that I love them. They have my blessing always."

"Please, you've got to come with us. The fighting is only going to get worse."

"What are they going to do to me? I'm an old simple Jew. If I die, it's God's Will, and then I'll be with my Bluma… and as long as you live you'll never forget me."

My sister begged him too, but to no avail, "Just promise me, if you have daughters, name them after your grandmother as is tradition."

"We will," we promised, then Surah coughed and rubbed her eyes. When we came home, Momma was packing. Surah coughed again and again and Momma frowned.

Zayda hugged us all goodbye that next day at the train station, which was a bitterly cold winter day. We waved at him from the window as the train took us away forever from the town that had been our family's home for generations. I vowed to name my son after my grandfather, who had been more of a father to me than the father I would soon be reunited with.

My sister coughed some more. Now I was growing concerned. There was no doubt she was sick, "Get Surah some water."

I hurried from our seat as Momma put a blanket around her.

It took us days on the train to reach our destination, the port city of Danzig. Surah had been feverish for much of the trek. Our tickets were for the American Line's S.S. New Rochelle. We went to their offices, answered the questions they typed on the ship's manifest, then went through what they told us was a medical exam. They took one look at Surah's eyes, which were flushed pink, and told us we would have to leave without her. America wouldn't take her like this. The clerks said they'd exchange her ticket for the next sailing in a month, when the doctor said she should be fine to travel.

Momma listened, shook her head, then began screaming to High Heaven, "I'M NOT LEAVING WITHOUT MY DAUGHTER! OUR TICKETS ARE FOR TOMORROW, WE GO TOGETHER TOMORROW ON THAT SHIP!"

"Ma'am, we'll exchange your ticket for next month's ship!"

"WE HAVE NOT ENOUGH MONEY TO STAY IN DANZIG! MY DAUGHTER WILL NOT STAY HERE ANOTHER DAY! WE GO TO AMERICA TOMORROW! TOMORROW, YOU UNDERSTAND ME! I HAVEN'T SEEN MY HUSBAND – THEIR FATHER IN ELEVEN YEARS! WE'RE DONE WAITING! SHE CAN TRAVEL, SHE'S FINE!"

"Ma'am, you must understand. It's the law in America. They are afraid of a very contagious eye disease!"

"MY DAUGHTER DOES NOT HAVE THIS DISEASE! SHE HAS PINK EYE! KIDS GET PINK EYE AND ARE FINE! YOUR DOCTOR KNOWS SHE'S FINE! WE HAVE OUR TICKETS TO AMERICA! WE GO TOMORROW!"

Now, please understand, Momma had quite a temper and I may not remember all the words she yelled that day... But they made an impression on the shipping company men. They relented and told us we could go together the next day, but if Surah's eyes were still pink when we reached New York, Surah would be put back on the boat and shipped back to Danzig at the company's expense... They would not help us then. She'd have to buy another ticket once her eyes were clear.

Momma just glared at them, then turned and we left. The shipping company men did not speak to us when we joined the line to board the ship the next morning, but Momma glared at them for a time. Only once we boarded did she smile, then nearly fainted. "I'm fine, we are going to America."

Surah and I just looked at each other. Her eyes were pink as could be. Momma made me say Psalms once we settled in the hold with our over one thousand new neighbors on the voyage to New York.

# # #

Chapter 4

The trip took over a week. They told us we were lucky to get even an hour a day on deck after the First and Second Class Passengers went for their meals. I remember playing chess, I loved playing chess, with anyone who had a set... and I remember Surah staying in bed a lot as Momma brought her food and kept her as warm as she could.

Momma made me say a lot of Psalms for my sister's health and thanks that we would soon be seeing Poppa again.

Everyone tells me how happy they were once we were allowed on deck and the ship sailed across New York Harbor and saw the Statue of Liberty for the first time. I must admit, I did not see it. I only looked at Ellis Island and glanced at my sister's faintly pink eyes.

When we got off the ship there was a man passing out brown paper bags to all the Jewish families. He spoke to us in Yiddish briefly before moving on. He was from the Hebrew Immigrant Aid Society (HIAS) and had given us an apple, a piece of hard candy, a post card of New York City, a pencil, and a small book of Psalms. He said it was very important for everyone to stay quiet, particularly the children, and that we should take a few moments to write on the postcard to family that we had safely arrived.

Momma took the time we were standing in line to write to Grandpa Zvi and whispered one last time for Surah to keep her head down and try not to meet anyone's gaze.

Soon we were told to leave our baggage, then walked up a flight of stairs to the second floor. A soldier stood at the top with a piece of chalk in his hand. A woman with her hand on the railing, he marked with an "I" and separated from her children and husband, who cried out in dismay.

That made the man in front of me begin to whisper a prayer, the soldier glanced at him and when he reach the last step, he marked his coat with an "X" and separated him out of the line. The man was horrified, but didn't say a word.

Surah came up behind me, never looking up and the soldier ignored us. As we walked past, I dared to breathe. Then I heard Momma gasp, nurses and a doctor dressed in white coats were checking people's eyes with what looked like a shoe button hook.

They passed one person after another, then me, next they looked at Surah's eyes and stopped. The doctor gestured and a nurse came over and reached out to her. Momma shouted, "NO!"

Things got bad then. We all left the line and Surah was taken to the Ellis Island hospital. The man from HIAS was brought over to us and he explained in Yiddish that they were simply going to observe her. If in a few days her eyes were clear, we would be allowed to complete our processing and stay in America. If not, my sister would be sent back to Danzig.

I had never seen Momma so afraid in all her life. The man from HIAS spoke to us later that day and told us he had visited Surah in the hospital. She was well and in good spirits. He led all of us to the dining hall where kosher food was available. All of us delayed due to: the doctors certifying them healthy or those marked with an "X," who had been marked as crazy, or those who had other reasons to appeal the decision to send them back to Europe,

I had to laugh when I saw what our kosher meal was. Beet Borscht Soup and an odd crescent shaped yellow fruit that I bit into. It had a leathery peel that I quickly learned wasn't exactly edible. "Not like that, you peel it like this," one of the fellows who was appealing the decision to send him back to Russia said. "It's called a banana."

I've never told anyone this. But I hate bananas to this day. Lunch and dinner were borscht and bananas for three whole days until the hospital released Surah once her eyes cleared.

Momma was crying as we left Ellis Island and found Poppa waiting. Surah and I were crying too and dropped our baggage at the sight of him. The only thing I remember saying when he hugged me was, "What happened to your hair?"

"You look like Zayda!" Surah said.

Poppa laughed, then looked at Momma and said, "Welcome to America."

# # #

Chapter 5

Five weeks later I returned to the boarding house after a hard day's work. I was feeling miserable again, having realized that by now Chaim was on his honeymoon. I had no sooner sat down in the kitchen, when I heard someone enter the boarding house. I turned in surprise to Chaim with his bags. "What are you doing back here? You should be married by now!"

"Isaac? Oh, there was a bit of a misunderstanding… Sadie didn't understand that, well…"

"What?"

"I saw no reason that we shouldn't get to know each other a little better before the wedding – and she slapped me and called off the wedding."

I stared at him. He was an idiot. I'd read him her letters. She was a proper young lady. What had he been thinking? Then again, I could guess what he had been thinking… He just really hadn't gotten to know her, not through the visits where she spoke to him in broken Yiddish or through her love letters.

I shook my head and watched Chaim go back up to the room he had shared with his friend. Sadie had slapped him and called off the wedding – good for her!

Then the urge to write to her came over me. I couldn't, could I? But I felt I knew her through the letters and what could it hurt. I took out my pen and stationery, then wrote that I had heard, refraining from mentioning I'd heard it from Chaim, that she had not gotten married. What should I say? Ah, I wrote and asked her if she would write me a long letter back, if she felt writing me back was something she would like to do, then I signed it, "Best Regards, Isaac."

Before I could chicken out, I mailed it to her, feeling very foolish indeed.

A week later she wrote me back, first neatly and narrowly typed on a roll of adding machine paper. I laughed, I had asked her to write me a long letter, but apparently the roll was a bit limiting. She had stapled strips of notebook paper to it and finished writing the letter by hand. It was the funniest thing I'd ever read and she wrote she looked forward to my next letter!

Ahem, we resumed our correspondence and I took the train to Alton as soon as I could. Sadie accompanied me to my sister's wedding; a month later Sadie married me. My baby brother Joe was eleven, he, Momma, and Poppa were the happiest I think I had ever seen them. A month after getting married, Sadie and I opened a store in a small town, Robinson, Southern Illinois. I chose the town with care, well, some care. Hey, the candy shop across the square was doing good business, even opened a factory to make toffee bars. Okay, I tasted a few and thought them pretty good. Those working for the Heaths needed uniforms, dresses, shoes... And so did the Marathon Oil Refinery folks in the neighborhood. A smart couple like Sadie and I could do worse, and living upstairs above the store wasn't so bad in the summer – not if you poured water on the mattress to stay cool, anyway.

Oh, last I heard of Chaim, he had moved to Mexico City to become rich. Knowing him, he probably would too. He was a lucky guy like I said before, but for all the binds I've been in, I think I may be the luckier one.

Howard Schwartz
The Celestial Orchestra

Once it happened that Reb Nachman woke up in the middle of the night, and instead of the deep silence that usually pervaded, he heard something like faint music. At first the sound seemed no more than an approaching wind, but soon he realized it actually was a kind of music. What could it be? He had no idea. But he continued to hear it, ever so faintly, sometimes present, sometimes about to disappear. And as it did not grow any louder, he had to strain to listen. One thing was certain, though: Reb Nachman felt drawn to this music, as if it were a message coming to him from a great distance, which he was trying to receive.

Then Reb Nachman got up and went into his study and sat down by the window. And yes, from there the music seemed slightly louder, as if, he were a little closer to its source, but it remained very faint. It did not seem to come from any instrument with which he was familiar, for it did not sound like a violin or a flute; not like a bass fiddle and not like a drum. Nor did it have the sound of voice or voices. If only he were able to hear it better, he thought, he might be able to identify its source.

Then Reb Nachman left the house and walked out into the field beyond the gate, under a sky crowded with stars. There he had no memory, except for questions that concerned the origin of the mysterious music. And while his eyes were fixed on the heavens, the ground remained unknown beneath his feet. And for that time he did not impose patterns on distant stars or imagine the life they might sustain. Nor did he count the gift of the stars as riches. Instead he listened for a long, long time.

At first Reb Nachman thought that what he heard was coming from a single instrument. But soon he was able to separate the instruments that wove their music together so well. Yet this new knowledge did not satisfy his longing and curiosity; in fact, it only served to whet it. Where was this distant music coming from? Surely it was not drifting there from any orchestra in Bratslav, or from anywhere else in this world. Of that Reb Nachman was certain. No, this was some kind of celestial music, music of the spheres. It was then Reb Nachman realized how much he wanted to follow that music and discover its source. And this longing grew so great that he became afraid his heart would break. Then, while he was staring upward, he saw a very large star fall from its place in the heavens and blaze across the sky like a comet. He followed that star as it fell, and shared its last journey. And somehow it seemed to Reb Nachman that he was falling with that star and was caught up in that same motion, as if he had been swept away by an invisible current, and he closed his eyes and let himself be carried.

Now it happened that when Reb Nachman opened his eyes again he found himself seated inside a chariot of fire that blazed its way across the heavens. And he did not have time to wonder how this had happened, or what it meant, but merely to marvel in awe as the wonders of the heavens passed before his eyes. Before him he saw two kinds of luminaries: those that ascended above were luminaries of light, and those that descended below were luminaries of fire. And it was then, when his eyes had become adjusted to the sudden illuminations crossing his path, that Reb Nachman became aware of a presence beside him and began to perceive a dim body of light.

That is when the angel who drove the chariot first spoke to him, and said: "Reb Nachman, I am the angel Raziel. You should know that your calling and your prayers have not gone unheard in heaven. This chariot has been sent to bring you to the place you long for, the source you are seeking." And with each word the angel Raziel spoke, the light surrounding his ethereal body grew brighter, until he appeared to Reb Nachman as a fully revealed human being. This was the first time Reb Nachman had ever been face-to-face with an angel. And yet, strange to say, he did not feel the fear he would have expected, but rather felt as if he had been reunited with a long-lost companion.

Just then the chariot approached some kind of parting of the heavens, which resembled a line drawn across the cosmos. As they drew closer, he saw it was actually an opening through which an ethereal light emerged. Raziel recognized the question taking form in Reb Nachman's mind, and he said: "We are approaching the place where the Upper Waters and the Lower Waters meet. This is where the Upper Worlds are separated from the Lower Worlds, and what belongs to the spheres above is divided from what belongs to the spheres below."

No sooner did the angel finish speaking than the chariot approached close enough to that place for Reb Nachman to catch a glimpse of what lay on the other side. And what he saw was a magnificent structure suspended in space. And from that one glimpse he knew that whatever it was, no human structure could begin to compare with it. But then, before he had time to question the angel, the chariot passed through that very aperture, to the complete astonishment of Reb Nachman, for it was no higher than a hand's breadth. It was at that moment that Reb Nachman grew afraid for the first time, for he realized he was flying through space at a great height and did not dare to look down. Then he said to the angel, "How is it possible that we have passed through that place which is no more than three finger-breadths?"

Raziel said, "In your world of men, Reb Nachman, it is possible to contain a garden in the world. But in this kingdom it is possible to contain the world in a garden. How can this be? Because here, whoever opens his heart to the Holy One, blessed be He, as much as the thickness of a needle, can pass through any portal."

Even as Raziel spoke these words Reb Nachman had already been captured by the radiant vision that loomed ahead. And again, without his having to ask, Raziel replied, "The place you are about to be taken to, Reb Nachman, is the very one you have been seeking. Yet since even this chariot is not permitted to approach much closer to that sacred place, you must soon depart from it and remain suspended in space, like the Sanctuary you see before you."

And without any other explanation, Reb Nachman realized that the wonderful structure he saw must be the Celestial Temple, after which the Temple in Jerusalem had been modeled, and with which it was identical in every aspect, except for the fire surrounding the heavenly Sanctuary. For the marble pillars of this heavenly miracle were illumined by red fire, the stones by green fire, the threshold by white fire, and the gates by blue fire. And angels entered and departed in a steady stream, intoning an unforgettable hymn to a melody Reb Nachman heard that day for the first time, but which he recognized as if it had been familiar to him all the days of his life.

That is when Reb Nachman realized he was no longer within the chariot but suspended in space without support for his hands or feet. And it was then, with his eyes fixed on that shimmering vision, that Reb Nachman was first able to distinguish the Divine Presence Of the *Shekhinah* hovering above the walls and pillars of the Temple, illuminating them and wrapping them in a glowing light, which shone across all of heaven. It was this light he had seen from the other side of the aperture, before the chariot of fire had crossed into the Kingdom of Heaven. And so awestruck was Reb Nachman to witness the splendor of the *Shekhinah*, he suddenly experienced an overwhelming impulse to hide his face. He began to sway in that place and almost lost his balance.

Had it not been for the angel Raziel speaking to him at that instant he might have fallen from that great height. The angel said, "Take care,

Reb Nachman, and know that the Temple remains suspended by decree of the Holy One, blessed be He. And you must remember above all to keep your eyes fixed on its glory, if you are not to become lost in this place. For should you look away from the Temple for as long as a single instant, you would risk the danger of falling from this height. Even a mere distraction would take you to places unintended, from which you might never return. So too should you know that no living man may enter into that holy dwelling place and still descend to the world of men. For no man could survive the pure fire burning there, through which only angels and purified souls can pass."

And it was then, when he had regained his balance, that Reb Nachman finally discovered the source of the celestial music that had lured him from his house in a world so far removed, and yet so close. For as he followed that music to its source in the Celestial Temple, his eyes came to rest on concentric circles of angels in the Temple courtyard. Then he realized that the music he had been hearing was being played by an orchestra of angels. And when he looked still closer he saw that each of the angels played a golden vessel cast in the shape of a letter of the Hebrew alphabet. And each one had a voice of its own, and one angel in the center of the circle played an instrument in the shape of the letter Bet.

And as he listened to the music, Reb Nachman realized it was the long note of the letter Bet that served as its foundation and sustained all of the other instruments. He marveled at how long the angel was able to hold this note, drawing his breath back and forth like the Holy One Himself, who in this way brought the heavens and the earth into being. And at that moment Reb Nachman was willing to believe that the world only existed so that those secret harmonies could be heard. And he turned to the angel Raziel, who had never left his side, and once more the angel knew what he wished to know, and said, "The score of this symphony is the scroll of the Torah, which commences with the letter Bet, endless and eternal, and continues with each instrument playing in turn as it appears on the page, holding its note until the next letter has been sounded, and then breathing in and out a full breath."

And when Reb Nachman listened to that music he arrived at a new understanding of the Torah and realized that among its many mysteries there was one level on which it existed only as pure music. He was also aware that of all the instruments in that orchestra it was only the letter Bet that spoke to him and pronounced his name. Then the angel Raziel turned to him and said, "The souls of all men draw their strength from one of the instruments in this orchestra, and thus from one of the letters of the alphabet. And that letter serves as the vessel through which the soul of a man may reveal itself. Your soul, Reb Nachman, is one of the thirty-six souls that draw their strength from the vessel of the letter Bet, which serves as their Foundation Stone and holds back the waters of the Abyss."

Then it happened that when the angel Raziel said the word "Abyss," Reb Nachman forgot all of his warnings for one instant and glanced down at the world so far below. And the next thing he knew, he felt like a falling star. That is when he realized he was still standing in the field beyond the gate. And the celestial music, though faint once more still echoed in his ears.

Joe Schwartz
King of Hearts

"Are you ready?"

"Yes. I am."

★★★

Paul woke up but was not startled by the stranger sitting next to his bed. The man's pale white face seemed even more so against his black robe and long red beard. Paul presumed the man's head once matched the lush facial hair that was now almost entirely bald save a crown that ran from ear-to-ear.

The man looked familiar, yet he was certain he had never met him. He wasn't the kind easily forgot. His large hands complemented his massive shoulders that were as large as a defensive lineman in uniform. The hands, that were big enough to strangle a horse if he had wanted, were folded neatly in his lap. The undeniable strength of the man did not worry Paul, but comforted him. Instinct told him this man, this stranger, would not hurt him.

Paul sat up. He felt exceptionally well. Not a single ache or pain. The chronic hurt in his lower back was gone. A first in sixteen years of constant suffering. He twisted to his left, then his right. The remarkable agility made him laugh, happy to feel so good, surprised to have his youthful body again.

He smiled at the man and the man returned the exact same grin. Paul stood up. Practically a leap with his renewed vigor that made him feel as if he could fly. The loose muscles that had begun to atrophy were strong cords again.

Paul went to the bathroom to confirm himself to himself. The mirror's reflection, though one he had not seen thirty years, was one he instantly recognized. The young, healthy, invulnerable body he had had when he was twenty-five glowed back at him.

He had forgotten his youth. Married and a father by thirty, his life had become automatic. Paul was an unconscious character in the story of his life occasionally spiked by sex, work, movies on television, and most especially by pain. The healthy man in the mirror with thick black hair, unblemished skin, and a flat stomach, although familiar, was impossible to believe ever existed. One thing though had not changed. His eyes were not sparkly with the optimism youth foolishly granted. They were still the hard stones crafted through disappointment being alive long enough made of all good men.

The man still sat in his bedroom. He waited for Paul with no more urgency than one might a slow bus. Eventually it would come.

Linda was a middle-aged woman now, but Paul still saw the nineteen-year-old girl he married. Her crow's feet and laugh lines were invisible to him. The gray hair and loose skin, if she were another woman it might be repulsive, but because she was his beloved Linda, the only woman he could ever love, they were the things he found erotic.

"We got married young," Paul said to the man.

The man nodded thoughtfully in agreement with Paul.

"Back in the day, we were wild as hell," Paul said. He was beginning to remember a thousand random things at once. However, an annoying question kept interrupting his pleasant thoughts. "You seem so familiar, but I'll be damned if I can remember your name."

The man smiled. His teeth were perfectly straight, large, and white. His smile made Paul momentarily forget his question or that he had asked anything at all.

"My name," the man said, "is irrelevant. But if it is helpful, you can call me Jack."

Paul mulled it over for a second.

"Jack," Paul said as if getting used to the name crossing his palette. "Okay, Jack it is. I like that name."

"I had a feeling you might," Jack said and stood with the opposite force a tree falls. He was well over seven feet tall. The long robe that disguised his body gave the illusion that he floated rather than walked.

Paul believed he was a person like him, not a ghost. First of all he didn't believe in ghosts, gremlins, aliens, or angels. Second, why would a ghost be bothered by such trivialities as clothes, flesh, or choose to be bald? No, Paul decided whoever he was, he was a man like him.

Paul had begun to lose his hair in his forties and had hated it. Linda said it made him look sexy. Her lie gave him comfort, but didn't change a damn thing. Still, it could always be worse. His friends complained mostly about sex. Top of their lists was an inability to perform, followed closely by frigidity their spouses developed after menopause or so they claimed. Although he had a bad back and Linda had undergone two knee surgeries, they still found happiness in each other's body at least twice a week. Paul never dared to mention this to his suffering friends. It was something they wouldn't have believed anyway. Instead he found it better to simply agree with them, to join them in their misery even if it was a lie.

Paul held his wife's hand. He petted her soft skin and the fine, pale downy hair of her arm. She mildly stirred, but did not wake. A small grin appeared for a moment as he stroked her arm then melted away. It was that secret smile that she saved only for him. To remember each one was impossible, but he cherished them all.

Bent low to her face, Paul kissed her forehead. This skin to him was sacred and reserved. He had to share so much of her body with doctors, girlfriends, and family that this spot was his alone and Linda was always careful to keep it exclusively for him.

★★★

In an instant, Paul was no longer in his home, but on the sidelines at his son Brian's soccer game. He was amazed to watch his young son run with his teammates. A game like so many others he missed until his boy was no longer a boy, but a man now with toddler and another on the way.

Paul held few regrets. He worked hard to provide a good life for his family. His father had gotten him the job at the brewery when he had graduated high school. As his friends went off to distant colleges or joined the military never to be heard from again, Paul learned to load trucks with beer.

Paul's father was also the dock foreman. A stern man who showed no mercy or favor toward him at work, he treated his son especially worse than the other men as to never be accused of favoritism. Ten years later when his father retired, Paul took his place.

Now as he watched Brian sweat and grunt to control the ball, his knees stained green from grass and red with blood, he wondered how he could have been so stupid.

"Don't be so hard on yourself," Jack said.

Paul had forgotten about his companion. The giant stood behind him with his hands on his shoulders. In Jack's enormous presence, he felt sheltered. Safe to speak exactly what was on his mind without regard to the discomfort that truth brought.

"I should've been here. Brian got his only goal that year at this game. He tried to tell me about it, but I ignored him. They lost, and all I could think about was the money going down the drain for shoes, and lessons, and soccer camps. It never occurred to me he was good despite the score."

"You did the best you knew how."

"I was an asshole," Paul said, "just like my father."

The soccer field blurred as a sea of people filled Paul's vision. A light breeze, cool and filled with the smell of fresh cut grass, rushed his senses. The wonderful smell that reminded him of a thousand summer days instantly made him feel better.

A crowd of thousands watched as their little Johnny or Jane ascended a stage to receive their hard won diplomas. Brian had graduated cum laude. He would parlay his biology degree into a terrific job with the same college he graduated. Unlike Paul, his son would sit in an air-conditioned lab all day. His salary to start was shamefully close to Paul's after thirty years riding forklifts, walking picket lines, and hoping to God the union wouldn't fuck him for his pension.

"His life is gonna be good," Paul said.

"There are no guarantees, only choices," Jack said.

"That's horseshit. I worked my ass off to make sure that kid got a head start."

"True," Jack said, "but the future is blank pages in an infinite book. Brian will write his own story as did you, as did your father and grandfather, back to the beginning of time and everything before that."

"You sound like a goddamn tree-hugger."

"I have nothing to gain by lying."

"The old angels can't lie bit, eh?"

"I'm not an angel."

"Then what the hell are you then?" Paul asked sarcastically. "A genie?"

Jack laughed at Paul's attempted insult. His laughter was a boom that exploded through his lungs to his mouth and into the atmosphere.

Paul took a step away. He wasn't scared. Furthermore, he wasn't tired, hungry, or thirsty. He simply was not anything.

"I am your friend," Jack said.

"Then why don't I know you?" Paul asked.

"Because you choose to forget. Or rather it was the life you preferred to live."

"You're confusing the hell out of me."

"Funny," Jack said as he took hold of Paul's hand. "You always say that."

Paul was surprised he didn't automatically try and jerk his hand back. Such displays he considered queer and himself likewise by association. However, he was not uncomfortable. If the enormous man were to pick him up and cradle him to his chest, Paul would not have resisted.

★★★

They walked together for minutes or days. Paul could no longer grasp time. With Jack, that concern was futile. Time was nothing more than an ignorant hoax played on humanity. An invention conceived by mankind to define living that failed miserably to measure life.

Although not tired, they sat beneath a great tree. Paul remembered the perfect tree in sense of déjà vu. It was like recovering from long-term amnesia. This place was so familiar, yet so foreign that it made him yearn to remember more and more.

All around them were people. Unaware of each other, Paul felt like a spy invading their presumed privacy.

Beautiful, naked women surrounded a young man with brown skin and a spotty black beard. The women were unashamed as they either waited for him or were yielding to his will. Sometimes he took one at a time, sometimes three or four. No matter the vigorous energy the young man expended, he no sooner finished with one than he began anew with another. With every triumph the women applauded, giggling and clapping as his every whim was satisfied.

Across from him, oblivious to the other, stood a thin, dark skinned warrior. Long bow in hand he slew beasts great and small. As one fell, he re-loaded his bow and took aim at another. The game stood no chance against his expert prowess to kill.

Another sat on a throne amidst a great feast. Adorned with a gold crown and a luxurious purple silk robe, he ate as acrobats and belly dancers moved to entertain him in a marble courtyard.

The visions were too numerous to count. They clustered the landscape unconscious to the others existence.

Then Paul saw his father straddled upon a tavern stool as he enjoyed the company of other blue-collars. The men cheered for the never-ending sports that came to them through a nineteen-inch black-and-white television. With every score the men cheered, clinked their glasses together, joyfully cursed, and drank non-stop.

"Is this heaven?" Paul asked.

"No," Jack said as he plucked the petals from a daisy. "This is paradise."

The answer made Paul even more curious. It made sense. Although not a religious man himself, he knew men who were. Their unrelenting faiths in their particular theological supremacy were something he envied. Freedom from doubt was a splendid delusion.

"You seem sad, Paul."

"Disappointed. That's all."

"Every man's highest ideal is separate and different."

"But what if…" Paul hesitated a moment. He had hidden something all his life, but never dared to confess his secret to anyone. Paul had wanted to be like everyone else, but could not. It made him feel abnormal, and had determined through casual observation, it most certainly was.

"I don't believe in God," Paul said in a whisper.

"That's okay," Jack said standing up. "He believes in you."

Paul had been ready for any number of responses except that one. It was such a plain, beautiful answer. Why had it never occurred to him before now? Maybe all these men too had struggled with the same thing. Maybe.

"Let's move along," Jack said subtle in his command over Paul.

Without thought of resistance, Paul stood and took Jack's hand.

★★★

They walked together through the tunnel's archway. Past the threshold all light evaporated and the darkness swallowed them whole.

The dark slowly gave way to a green hue that reminded Paul of mucus. Jack moved steadily forward gently pulling Paul by their mutual tether.

Paul saw openings, offshoots from the main path that held hallowed eyed, haunted men. Without bars these men could leave their prisons, but seemed to have no interest in escape.

The incarcerated were obsessed, stuck on some kind of perpetual pause, slaves to their personal twisted logic. While one sat in a corner strumming his electric guitar and singing softly to himself, another played chess against an invisible opponent, losing and cursing in German as he flayed his bare back with a cat-o'-nine tails.

Before Paul could ask, Jack explained.

"Free will, my friend, is a double edged sword that every man is given. Some will choose to seek enlightenment while others can never get past the false glory that is vanity."

"How could any man choose this?"

"A question that is as old as the universe itself, but new and different to each man it is asked of."

"So, the answer is there is no answer."

"The answer," Jack said, "is as convoluted as each individual's perception to the question. If you truly aren't convinced in the existence to the divine, that all this, in spite of what you're experiencing now, then nothing will convince you otherwise."

"Then whatever comes next---"

"Is your choice," Jack said finishing Paul's sentence.

★★★

The door was locked. Paul stared at it thoughtfully, but Jack said there was nothing that could be done. A key, if one existed at all, was to be patient. When it was time it was time.

There was no negotiation, no middle ground, nothing to do but wait. In the meantime, Jack recommended that Paul try to enjoy this moment. Once he crossed through that doorway he wouldn't remember any of this anyway.

★★★

Linda sat next to Paul. She held his hand thinking over what the doctor had said.

It was her choice, but her husband's condition would never improve. He could technically live with the aid of life support almost indefinitely, but he would never be alive again.

For all intents and purposes he should have died when he collapsed at work. His well-meaning co-workers had kept him living by performing CPR until the paramedics arrived. The continuation of Paul's life had passed hand-to-hand in vain, desperate attempts that eventually proved pointless.

"Darling," Linda said in hope that Paul could somehow hear her, "you were always so strong. I can't imagine my life without you, but you're already gone. I'm gonna miss you so much. My entire life is in you. I don't have a memory without you and I will never forget you, ever. If you were me, I know you could do this without blinking, but you were always so decisive. It was something I always admired about you and one of a thousand things I've already begun to miss.

I love you and to see you like this is worse than death itself. Forgive me darling, but I can't stand to see you suffer anymore. Maybe I'm being selfish or maybe this is what you would have wanted. I can't believe we never talked about this. We were such fools to think we could live forever. Hopefully, I will see you again. Goodbye, darling."

Linda stood and bent over her husband. Tears streaming down her face, she kissed his forehead, then turned and left the room.

She needed to find Paul's doctor. There were forms to sign, and afterwards, she would have Brian take her to make arrangements for Paul's funeral.

★★★

The door lock clicked. Paul didn't need to check or for Jack to tell him that it wasn't locked any longer.

Jack stood. His long arm draped and resting across Paul's shoulders.

"Are you ready?" Jack asked.

"Yes," Paul said, "I am."

Rachel Schwartz
Leaving Anatevka

Shelly and Gabe hadn't had a real conversation in 10 years. The telephone, their ally in maintaining a safe distance, transmitted the occasional stilted exchange about where their daughter Becky would spend her birthday or the holidays this year. Every six months or so they'd nod politely at each other as they sat in a teacher's conference, or catch each others' eyes across a crowded auditorium during a choir concert and wave tentatively. Gabe thought of these encounters as a chance to size each other up — who had managed to keep off the weight, whose hair was holding off the grey, who was aging best. But there had been little occasion for more than that, and even less interest.

Still, Shelly knew exactly how Gabe would react to Becky's news if he was there to hear it. How much he would enjoy saying "I told you so".

"Like mother like daughter," he'd pronounce, sure he'd finally exposed the conspiracy he'd long suspected.

But really, wasn't it just the opposite? Becky had won a lead in the school play. But when Shelly was that age, she was one of three religious Jews in a public school. There were no weekend choir trips for her, no Saturday swim team meets, no proms or mixers unless they fell on wintery Saturday nights when the sun set early and Shabbat was over by 7:00, no Friday night talent shows, and no matter how well she read her role in English classes or sang the show tunes in chorus, absolutely no part in the school play. This time things would be different.

"I warned you, if she turns her back on tradition and marries a goy…." Gabe would add, as if that's what Shelly had been planning all along.

Shelly would reply in the exasperated tone one used with the other parent - the one who doesn't get it. "It's just a musical, Gabe."

"But the rehearsals, the shows, she'll have to drive on Shabbat. She'll miss services." Shelly imagined him trying to figure out how he could explain to his new wife, his new children, his parents. But of course he'd blame Shelly — hardly a new strategy. She didn't mind. Things had gone so far that it was too late for him to do anything about it anyway — at least not without seriously damaging his relationship with Becky.

Shelly would pause for a few breaths, as if tacitly conceding Gabe's point — which, in fact, she was, just not the way he wanted her to concede.

Yes, she had encouraged Becky to audition for the part, and yes, she had known full well how it would upset Gabe, but no, there was nothing wrong with what she'd done. "Becky can stay with me whenever rehearsals fall on Shabbat – if it's a problem," she'd add mildly, the very calmness of her tone a rebuke to him. Of course, there really was no right way to speak with Gabe. And suggesting that he give up any of his already limited visitation with his daughter was bound to raise trouble.

He would counter indignantly that this was more than a problem – his daughter (always his, not theirs) playing the part of a Jewish girl who disobeyed her father and ran off with a goy. Kissing a goy onstage, in front of the entire school. And rehearsing it all on the Sabbath? A problem? It was much more than a problem.

Shelly would listen as he worked himself into a self-righteous knot, a regular "keeping up with the Cohens" fury. Anyone listening would imagine he must be an orthodox Jew, a real pillar of the community, rather than a convenience conservative, as Shelly called it. How he hated that term. Perhaps because it fit so well. For what was his religion but a matter of convenience? Two dishwashers in his kitchen, one for meat dishes and one for milk, yet he'd eat the meat lasagna at Bertoni's without a qualm, ordering a coffee with cream afterwards. He paid to send the children of his second marriage to a Jewish day school, yet if there was a football game across town, would drive straight there from Saturday services.

Shelly would keep quiet but wouldn't hang up, and soon, as she had known it would, his anger would begin to abate.

"The youngest lead in the cast, you say?"

"And the only Jew," she'd add.

"Hmmm…" she imagined him rubbing his chin as he reconsidered. Probably thinking how he could impress his friends and family with the news.

"I know Fiddler is your favorite." Shelly would add. The comment would unsettle Gabe – that she still remembered, was still privy to his personal tics after all these years. Despite the divorce, despite her rejection of his return to the religious fold, despite his having created what he believed to be an entirely new life for himself in which, he liked to believe, Shelly played no part.

But she was right. He still sang snatches from Fiddler, *Sunrise, Sunset,* *Sabbath Prayer,* and his favorite: *Tradition* around the house, his children joining in the chorus, swept up in his enthusiasm.

When they were married he would suddenly break into the song, waving his arms in the air, snapping his fingers, and then turn his face toward the sky to shout, "Tradition", throwing in a little shuffle and stomp – Topol in a T-shirt she teased. She had found it endearing.

Gabe and Shelly met and married in Jerusalem where both were studying biology on a 2 year program. They each considered themselves rebels, having left behind in America not only their families, but the Jewish tradition they'd shrugged off like a scratchy sweater in midsummer – keeping a kosher home, keeping the Sabbath holy, keeping the Passover. Why, they'd asked each other, was it always about "keeping" anyway? Their parents had kept, clung to the outdated rituals as if all that stood between them and some awful fate, some oblivion that awaited Jews who strayed from the prescribed path, was having two sponges in the sink, one pink for meat dishes, one blue for milk.

It wasn't that Gabe and Shelly rejected Judaism completely, they explained to all who would listen – except, of course, their parents. It was that at 22 years old, they were confident in their identities without props like prayer shawls, Havdalah candles, phylacteries. The very fact of living in Israel – of being where it had all begun, surrounded by their own people, not having to think about being different or not fitting in, this was enough. They looked not to the mumblings of fusty rabbis from long ago, but to the tanned faces and self-reliance of the new Israelis. They were building upon the past, not trapped in it.

They were what most people called a "handsome couple" – which is to say that they looked better together than they did apart. Both had the dark eyes, curly, black hair, and olive toned skin that fooled people into thinking they were native born Israelis. Even their Hebrew sounded Israeli. Gabe was a lean 6 feet tall, though he insisted on adding an inch when asked. At 5'5", Shelly fit comfortably into the crook of his arm when they wandered down Ben Yehuda Street making up stories about the people they passed, laughing so hard that they had to lean on each other for support, ignoring the looks cast in their direction by the subjects of their mirth. It was as if they had not so much married as joined forces.

One week before they were to return to the States, Shelly decided to surprise Gabe. Most Friday evenings they partied with friends or drove down to Tel Aviv for the night life – Jerusalem was dead on the Sabbath, stores closed, no busses, no restaurants, only the synagogues on every corner packed with the devout. But instead of finding her on the phone arranging to borrow a car or to rendezvous with classmates, Gabe opened the door of their tiny apartment to the scent of herb roasted chicken, baking potatoes, and sweet yeasty bread. Shelly was in the kitchen bent over the oven, wearing, of all things, an apron. He didn't even know they owned one.

"What's the occasion?" he asked, sniffing the air appreciatively. He couldn't remember the last time Shelly had cooked a festive dinner, much less a traditional Sabbath meal.

Seeing his surprised pleasure, Shelly was gripped by the same question. She had told herself it was in honor of their last Friday evening in the holy city. The meal itself was easy enough to make. Burn a few stray feathers off the chicken with a candle (usually around the tail, where the thigh met the back, and on the front edge of the wings), pull out the slippery giblets, rub olive oil, garlic and sage into the skin, throw some sliced white potatoes into a pan, two challahs into the oven. It was a meal she'd learned to cook at her mother's side, and had eaten it so many Friday nights that the smell of roasted chicken alone was enough to evoke the Sabbath. Gabe, too, was raised on such meals and, it appeared, still loved them with the unquestioning certainty of childhood habit. It was only food, she told herself, and yet, as she lit candles that evening (just for the atmosphere, she thought, no blessing involved) she was overwhelmed by a feeling of suffocation as if in striking the match she illuminated a demon better left buried.

"Any occasion you like," she said, concentrating on not burning herself as she maneuvered trays in the oven.

The loaves of challah came out steaming and fragrant, perfectly browned, double-braided, and studded with sultanas, just the way Gabe liked them. He reached out to pry off a raisin.

"Ouch! That's hot." He thrust his two fingers into his mouth, the tang of slightly burned fruit, the sting evoking memories of the half-hearted scoldings his mother dispensed weekly when she caught him picking at her Friday night baking. Shelly, however, said nothing.

In the dining room she placed the loaves on a plate, tucking them under a velvet cover with intricate embroidery spelling out the words "Shabbat Shalom" in gold thread. The table was set with wedding gifts they had never used. The cloth was thick and white with a delicate pattern of interwoven roses. The challah knife was fresh out of its bubble wrap, a nacre handle matching the design on the challah plate. He recognized crystal salt shakers as a wedding gift from his Aunt Leah and Uncle Art.

Shelly had even filled the matching crystal vase with a tumble of brightly hued poppies, and the whole room was lit by the glow of candles.

"Boy," he said, "I could really get used to this."

"Well don't," she said, only a little more sharply than she'd intended.

At the table Gabe clipped on the yarmulke Shelly had crocheted for their wedding. She had worked his name into a wreath of flowers against a white background and though she could see that he had put it on inside-out, she ignored it. He raised the Kiddush cup. A gift from his parents, it had been accompanied by a blessing. "You should always have a good Jewish home, God willing," Gabe's father had intoned. The new couple had shared a secret smile, thinking of weekend barbecues and the taste of breaded shrimp. But now, over the silver filigree of the goblet as bright and untarnished as a Rosh Hodesh moon, habit, as Shelly preferred to think of it, took them through the very rituals they had rejected. They chanted the Sabbath blessings from memory. Gabe's eyes were closed as he swayed slightly, his voice, like his father's, deep and sweet, while Shelly's rose, a light soprano that twined a delicate chain of notes around his.

Gabe drank deeply from the goblet and passed the wine to Shelly. Gripped by a strange resistance, she tipped it to her lips and handed it back.

"But you didn't drink any," he said.

"I tasted it," she'd replied.

"You did not! I watched you."

"Ok, so I didn't. So what?"

"If you don't drink the wine it's a wasted blessing," he said. Shelly knew this. Knew it like she knew why there were two loaves on the table that night instead of one. Like she knew what kind of wine she must use, and when to sing Kiddush and grace. She knew it all, but it had been so long since she had chosen to lay the knowledge aside. She looked up at Gabe. Was it only the reflection of the candles that burned in his eyes?

"Drink." Gabe thrust the goblet at her, sending a wavelet of wine slopping over its rim onto the tablecloth. The sight of still more waste infuriated him. She had gone to all this trouble to recreate a Shabbat straight from their childhood – even better because it was their own – and just as he was beginning to settle into it, to remember the comfort of ritual, she had to mess it up.

Why had she done it? If she was honest with herself, Shelly had to admit that part of her had expected something like this – had feared it almost since they'd met. She had known that despite Gabe's insistence that driving on Shabbat was liberating, despite how he enjoyed making flight reservations for Saturdays so they could avoid plane aisles crowded with black-clad orthodox Jews, their children always underfoot, crying or kicking at the seat backs, and despite his announcement that cheeseburgers were "a revelation," – as if two of his best friends, meat and cheese, had been meeting behind his back for years – it was all really just a fling with the forbidden to him. And now, like a discarded toy long set aside once resurrected could become a favorite again, he had rediscovered the Sabbath. If this was a test, one of them had failed.

Shelly ignored the goblet he held out and reached for the pitcher of ice water. Gabe pushed it away.

They glared at each other, his fury meeting her defiance.

"We will have a traditional Jewish home," Gabe announced, "For our children's sake."

"Children? Who said anything about children?" she snapped back. Behind her, the candle flames trembled, sending a cascade of shadows across the table.

But just weeks ago they had been sitting at a table in a downtown café. Hot, dry *hamsin* winds sent dust whipping around their ankles as they drank Turkish coffee with cardamom in clear glasses, shared a piece of baklava swimming in a puddle of honey. They watched a heavily bearded man in a dusty fedora pushing a stroller past their table, close enough so they caught the unwashed, sour smell of him. A few feet behind him, a woman in gray, her hair hidden under a scarf, her eyes vague and tired, dragged two resistant toddlers in matching *yarmulkas* and runny noses up the hill after her. Her belly, over-ripe to the point of bursting, seemed to pull her after the man.

"We'll have four – two girls, two boys" Gabe announced, stabbing the pastry with his fork. Shelly watched as a fly landed in the honey sauce and struggled to free itself.

"How about three," she said, thinking that maybe two would be enough.

Now the goblet stood between them on the table. Around it, the wine stain spread, slowly bleeding into the cloth. It's too late, she thought. It will never come out.

"Callbacks are in!" Becky gave a screaming war whoop and leapt up from where she'd been hovering over the computer monitor all morning.

"Well?" asked Shelly, trying to sound calm.

At 15, Becky was already as tall as Shelly, and looked just enough like her, the same swift flash of a grin, curly, dark hair that was always falling into her eyes, and that skeptical expression with one eyebrow raised and lips pursed that made Gabe feel that even though they'd been divorced 10 years, Shelly was still around every corner.

"I got the part!" She enveloped her mother in a stranglehold of a hug

"That's just great," Shelly laughed, absorbing a wet kiss while steadying her coffee cup protectively.

In Shelly's day, callback results were scribbled on a piece of paper torn from a notebook, posted with a scrap of tape or a scrounged tack on the corkboard outside the gym door. Students would arrive early at school and form a jostling mob around the board, parting to let each hopeful through, cheering those who got their part and commiserating with those who ended up in the chorus or with no part at all. Shelly tried to avoid the gym at those times, but was inexorably drawn back in the afternoon after the news had spread, to look at the two lists, the roles on one side and the names of the newly cast students – now complete with smiley faces, congratulations, and jokes scribbled in the corners. Already the lucky ones – among them some of Shelly's best friends - would be carrying themselves differently, as part of their own little clique, planning their first pre-rehearsal meetings, their cast parties, cracking their "in" jokes, and she would be out.

"When do you start rehearsals?" Shelly asked.

Becky was texting the good news to everyone she knew – though not, Shelly was sure, to her father. That would require a more diplomatic approach

"First read through Friday night," Becky said, pausing a moment as if she had picked up on Shelly's thoughts. "I'll talk to Dad tomorrow," she said, frowning.

On opening night Gabe and Shelly walk into the school at the same time. They have not planned it this way, but they sit together because they have no good excuse not to. Not knowing how to behave, they treat each other as if they were somehow fragile. Gabe opens the theater door for Shelly. Shelly offers to hold his coat and program as he pushes down the flip bottom wooden theater seats where they will sit.

Should I have worn something nicer than jeans? Gabe wonders as he notices other fathers in suits and jackets. Of course Shelly is well dressed – neither of them will look directly at each other -- but he can tell by the precise seam of her slacks and the soft polish of her brown pumps. He leaves the armrest between them to her, and claims the other for himself. What will Becky think if she looks out at the audience and sees them together?

The show is sold out, and as people squeeze past them to take a seat, the entire row, bolted together and to the floor, shudders slightly like an unanchored pew. Shelly waves at a couple sitting across the room and smiles at several more. It's not his fault he's too busy to get involved at Becky's school, he thinks. He has the other children to look after, his wife, his business. Still, it bothers him that he goes unrecognized. Worse still, that he has to depend on Shelly for introductions to Becky's friends who stop to congratulate Shelly.

"This is Becky's father, Mr. Hirschfeld," she says, introducing him as one might introduce a stranger. He is gripped by the old anger that Shelly took back her maiden name after the divorce, as if even his name wasn't good enough for her. But he can be charming when he wishes, knows how to work a room, dispensing smiles, jokes, invitations to drop by, pronouncing each name aloud and shaking hands so that they will remember him and tell Becky. "Your father's really nice," he imagines them saying – perhaps with a touch of surprise – he knows divorced fathers are always cast as the bad guys.

They sit down together and the seats squeak beneath them. Shelly looks around embarrassed at the others in the row.

"So, this boy," Gabe speaks abruptly, surprised at the sound of his own voice, "the one she kisses."

"John Ryan, the one who plays Vyetka," says Shelly.

"Vyetka". Gabe is staring at the back of the person in the seat in front of him, his only concession to their conversation, a slight cocking of his head in Shelly's direction. "What do you know about him?" It galls him to have to ask.

"Nice guy." She says, "A Junior. Plays football."

"Becky said he was a nice guy?" Gabe's eyes turn sharply toward Shelly.

The house lights go down, and the familiar tunes of the fiddler bring an attentive hush to the room. Shelly is saved from the question she knows would follow her reply.

How simple it is to evoke a *shtetl* on stage. A wooden crate, the
suggestion of a broken down fence, a gate hanging by a single hinge, a
few bales of hay, a milk wagon. Anatevka. It could be anywhere in Poland
or Russia, Latvia, Lithuania, my grandparents or yours. And there, from
behind the rough plywood forms – silhouettes of hovels, homes, the cast
appears, dressed in drab browns and grays, heads covered, all with their
burdens: baskets, bundles, an axe, a bucket, a baby. And over it all, the
plaintive scratching of the fiddler and the singsong voice of a teenage
Tevya:
> A fiddler on the roof...
> Sounds crazy, no?

A man sitting behind them is whispering to his companion – something
about dinner after the show. Gabe and Shelly turn simultaneously and
train twin glares at him, sending a shudder through the row of seats.
Turning back to the stage, they share an unguarded glance. Suddenly they
are aware they are the only Jews in the audience. They feel protective of
this village conjured out of cardboard, string, and bits and pieces of their
own histories, their roots. They feel protective of their daughter.

> You may ask,
> why do we stay up there
> if it's so dangerous?
> Well, we stay because
> Anatevka is our home.

Becky, dressed in a heavy overcoat, a shawl and a babushka is onstage
now, singing with the others. Gabe thinks he can hear her voice above
them all, high and clear. Does she understand? Soon, maybe ten or fifteen
minutes into the show, the acne-afflicted Cossacks will sweep through
this little outpost of Jews, leaving behind them the dead and the dying.
Homes will be looted, the *shul*, the holy books set on fire. Does she realize
that after intermission, these people – her people - when nothing is left
but the rags they wear, their burdened lives, her ancestors, they, not some
burlap-wrapped, fresh-faced teenager with a smudge of brown makeup
on his cheek, will be forced to leave this scrap of land? Will be homeless,
stateless, wandering and afraid with nothing to anchor them but their
God?
And the people in the audience, the tall blond women with their

gold earrings and manicured nails, the crew-cut gentiles whose own grandparents might have mounted black horses in the service of the Tsar, and the Andersons, Smiths and Chartwells, how many generations since the Mayflower? Who is Tevya, what is Anatevka to them?

> ... how do we keep our balance?
> That I can tell you in one word!
> Tradition!

Out of the corner of her eye Shelly sees Gabe's lips moving to the words of the song, feels a slight motion in her seat as his foot taps assent to Tevya's cry, "Tradition." On stage the entire cast is singing. Shelly reaches out in the dark to touch Gabe's hand.

Pat Lorraine Simons
Snippet

For a change, Fran arrived early for her regular haircut with Shirley,
a grandmotherly lady who had been cutting Fran's hair every month
for years. Fran liked going to her. It wasn't so much the haircuts as it
was spending a little downtime with someone like Shirley. Fran had a
stressful job as a lawyer, and it was nice just to kick back and laugh about
bad movies, the changeable St. Louis weather and the antics of Shirley's
grandkids. Shirley was an easygoing sort of lady—relaxing to be with for
an hour.

"Well," Shirley offered, "I'm glad we got some sun this morning." She
nodded at the window. "I had to wear my dark glasses in the car coming
here, it was so bright."

"Half a day of sun this week—not bad for the middle of December in
St. Louis," laughed Fran. She sat down on the black vinyl chair at Shirley's
station, and Shirley stood behind her, as always. They were a pair of faces
talking through the mirror.

"I sure hope it stays nice through Christmas," Shirley said. "Just a
couple of weeks away and I hate shopping in bad weather."

Fran nodded.

Shirley took out the black plastic smock, shook it out and laid it over
Fran, tying it at the back of her neck. "I'm glad you washed your hair
before coming over today," she said. "Saves me some time."

She deftly took some of Fran's straight brown hair between the index
and third fingers of one hand and snipped with the other. Fran relaxed,
closing her eyes.

"Well," Fran said, "I really shouldn't complain about the weather here,
since I got to see the sun in L.A. all of last week."

"What were you doing in L.A.?"

"I went there to see my uncle," said Fran, eyes still closed. "He wanted
to talk about his childhood in Germany, so I tape-recorded what he had
to say."

"Boy! I'll bet that uncle had some stories!" said Shirley.

She parted Fran's hair and tilted her head slightly, regarding the way
the hair was falling. Then she started trimming again.

"He sure did," said Fran, her eyes closed. "He told me he was in
Munich in the mid-1920's. And Hitler and his friends sometimes sat and
drank at the rathskeller that he went to."

"Really?" asked Shirley. "Did he ever hear him speak?"

"Who, Hitler?"

Shirley nodded. "Uh-huh."

"Yeah, he said the guy was quite an orator. But everyone thought that he and his friends were a bunch of degenerates. No one paid much attention to them at the time."

Shirley said, "You know, I have a girlfriend who was a teenager in Germany during World War II. In fact, she was in the Hitler Youth. Do you want more cut off the top?"

Fran's eyes popped open. She regarded herself in the mirror. "I guess . . . if you think so."

Shirley was again busily cutting Fran's hair, and Fran thought maybe she should drop the subject. But she didn't. It was the lawyer in her.

"So . . . did your friend know about the Jews?"

Shirley was looking down now, concentrating on an unruly cowlick. "Well, I don't know . . . maybe. Some German relatives of hers hid some Jews, I think." She looked up suddenly. "But really, you know, they were kind of arrogant."

"The Germans?"

"No, the Jews."

"Huh? What did they have to be arrogant about?"

"You said it!" Shirley laughed.

She stopped then and eyed Fran in the mirror, her scissors aloft. "Yeah," she clucked, "You give 'em an inch, you know, and they'll take a mile."

She smiled affably and pattered on. "I mean, some of them are all right, but most of them are like that. You know what I mean?"

It had been a long time since Fran had heard an anti-Semitic remark, although it had happened several times before. There was the teacher at Cleveland High School, who was shocked to hear that Fran was Jewish, because she didn't have horns. (Fran could hardly believe that one!) And there was the judge Fran had clerked for, who practically fell over when she asked for the day off on Yom Kippur and then spent an uncomfortable few minutes trying to make things right by saying that from her looks and her last name, he'd never have guessed. And then there was the fellow tourist who said he was moving to St. Louis soon, but not to the central corridor because all the Jews lived there.

Whenever this sort of thing happened, Fran was abashed. It always seemed to come out of nowhere. And she didn't know why, but she never knew what to say afterwards. Not that she hadn't thought about it. She had, every time. After the fact. She thought of all sorts of quips, castigations, and words of wisdom. But now, once again, she felt at a loss for words. *You'd think*, she told herself, *that I'd know what to say by now.*

Fran pondered. Shirley's comment was what it seemed to be, wasn't it? So why shouldn't I answer back? Tell her I'm Jewish, that I find such remarks offensive. Or <u>not</u> tell her I'm Jewish, since the woman obviously doesn't know, and simply say that I hate stereotypes and generalizations?

Instead, Fran said nothing.

Now Shirley stopped fooling with Fran's hair and looked at her in the mirror. The Fran in the mirror looked back, watching Shirley standing there behind her, scissors aloft, one eyebrow raised inquisitively.

Fran remained quiet, so Shirley went on.

"This one customer I have, well, *she's* one, you know. Always starts out acting nice, you know, but then she gets demanding. Wants me to do this and that, do more and more. You know. There's no pleasing her. And then of course she whines about the bill and all that. But," she laughed sarcastically, "she always comes back. Well, you know what I mean. That's how they are."

She looked down, noticed some uncut hair around Fran's ears.

"You want it shorter around your ears?"

Fran nodded.

"Well, that's just how they are, you know." She sighed.

Fran still said nothing.

Shirley bent over and retrieved a blow dryer from her drawer, while Fran sat staring at her own 40-ish face in the mirror.

I guess I don't look Jewish to her, whatever that is, she thought. And it's true that I'm not religious or anything, but so what? I should say <u>something</u>. If I don't, she'll think I agree with her.

Maybe I should teach her a lesson. I should say, 'Guess what, you idiot, I'm Jewish. How do you like them apples?'

She considered. No, that would be getting in the mud with her, Maybe I should tread lightly, not embarrass her too much. After all, maybe I egged her on. What if I just say, 'Do you think I'm like that? <u>I'm</u> Jewish.'

But what if she really knows I'm Jewish and is just trying to see how far she can go? That seems cynical, but what if?

Fran quickly dismissed this idea. Not Shirley. She likes me, and besides, why would she want to risk losing a good customer?

She obviously doesn't know, Fran decided. It isn't malice—it's ignorance. So wouldn't it be good to let her know that some Jews aren't really like that other customer of hers? I'm not that way.

But shouldn't Shirley know better anyhow? She had to be at least sixty years old. She's a bigot, plain and simple. She's not going to change that, is she? No matter what I say or don't say.

Anyway, telling this woman that I'm a Jew—no matter how I say it—isn't going to do anything but embarrass both of us.

Fran's ruminations were interrupted by Shirley, who was now standing up straight and staring at her through the mirror, holding the blow dryer aloft. It was aimed nowhere, just blowing air out into the room. Shirley smiled. She was waiting. She was waiting for Fran to say something.

Finally, Fran stammered, "Maybe you don't know that many Jews. I know a lot of Jewish people who aren't like that."

Now Shirley aimed the blow dryer at Fran's hair and quit looking her in the eye. "Well, I know quite a few," she said matter-of-factly.

Well, Fran thought, I know more than you do!

It was a silly retort. And it came to her in that sing–song of the little kid whining, "My daddy's bigger than your daddy."

"Jews are just people," Fran blurted. "Good and bad, just like everyone else."

In the mirror, she watched Shirley wielding the blow dryer. Her eyes wouldn't meet Fran's.

"Well. I guess," Shirley said, shrugging.

She turned off the blow dryer.

"There now. You're all done."

She smiled and handed Fran a small hand mirror and swiveled the chair around so she could see the back of her head.

"Nice," Fran said, handing the mirror back.

Shirley untied the smock, and Fran got up and paid her. She made sure to give her an extra tip for Christmas.

Shirley pocketed the extra money and grinned.

"Merry Christmas!" she said.

Fran smiled back. "Thanks!"

"Well," Fran muttered under her breath as she left the shop, "*that* was something!"

She got in her car, stuck the keys in the ignition and sat there letting the engine warm up. She was mad at herself. She'd handled the discussion badly. *What's the matter with me?* she asked herself. *Am I ashamed of being Jewish?*

Bullshit, she thought. I was just caught by surprise. Next time, I'll be ready.

Pamela Singer
Letter to Frieda in Antwerp

Sunday

Dear Frieda,

Thank you for asking about our trip to see your daughter Mieke while she's working in Majorca as a scuba instructor. It was a kind of we-are-not-in-control, "Alice in Wonderland" experience for the most part. (Did you ever read that book in your English classes? It's hard to follow even if English is your first language, so probably not.) For one thing, Mieke insisted on renting a house for us instead of letting me reserve a hotel, telling me I'd be "happier" (really? Cooking and cleaning on my vacation makes me happier than... what?) ; and then also rented a car even though we told her not to. As it turned out, the house was way out in the middle of nothing, with the nearest neighbor a half mile away, so we did · need a car. But she rented a Suzuki SUV model that was banned in the U.S. for safety reasons, and I wasn't comfortable having my children ride in it especially on unfamiliar terrain, so we ended up trading her for her tiny car. This seemed to make her really happy; she even said that she had rented the Suzuki for us because "I think I look really sexy in it." Okay. We went to the car rental place with her to pick it up and unfortunately nothing else was available for us, apparently. So we paid for a car for her to look sexy in for a week.

Before we went anywhere else from the airport in Palma, we stopped at some tiny shop where we were all starving while Mieke and her German boss (George?) had drinks, smoked and compared tattoos. My litte fairy-tale princess cousin with the long blonde braids? How did she become a smoking, drinking, tattooed European who ignored hungry children? We did buy the kids ice cream there, and agreed to a drink ourselves, but that was probably a bad choice on empty stomachs since we were totally out of sync (do you know that expression?) once we finally got to the house. When I was taking suitcases into the rooms (a light, airy one with twin beds for the kids; a darker one that I assumed would be ours), I winced at the large black crucifix next to the bed in the dark room. I reached to take it off the wall and move it, but it fell (leapt out of my hand?) behind the night table. When I told Seth about it, he informed me that the home's owners had the right to decorate any way they wanted. Well, of course, but did he want to sleep next to a large crucifix? I noticed that he never did dig it out from behind the night table, but somehow things shifted with him in Spain, where I guess we weren't supposed to be Jewish or something. Oddly, my born-Jewish husband seemed to align with my Catholic cousin more than with me, who'd converted and had Solomon Schechter children. Oh well. After we went to the car rental place and then took Mieke to dinner, we still weren't in tune with each other, and I was really hot, so I went upstairs to read in another bedroom with more windows to open, and fell asleep there.

About the house: Mieke had described it as amazing, and that someone would be coming in to clean and wash the linens. She repeatedly said, beginning with our trip from the airport, that she would love to have a party there. Interestingly, it turned out that not only did our "deposit" not count against the house rental, and was an additional amount so we had to pay again; but also the rental period didn't last until the end of our trip to Majorca, so we had to find someplace to stay for the last two nights of our visit. Though the last day, when I packed everyone up while Seth slept late, no one came in to clean (no one ever had! I scrubbed the whole disgusting kitchen so we could use it, washed the towels etc. constantly while we were there); and certainly it seemed that no other guest was imminently appearing. So, since we weren't allowed contact with the actual owners, with Mieke insisting on being the middle person/ only communicator who took our money including the extra "deposit," I assume she'd planned a party there for the last night. On us, financially. Also she hadn't said that, unlike a hotel, there was no telephone or TV. Television we didn't miss, but with Seth's father being seriously ill, we would have liked to have a phone available. Though I guess you don't think of these things if you're merely looking at a house as a party venue that your "rich" American cousins are paying for.

Everything was so disorienting: we wanted to experience Majorcan (which I knew was different from Spanish) culture, but mostly encountered British vacationers (nice, though they smoke a lot), and Germans strutting nude on the beach and using vulgarity at restaurants, especially if the bilingual menus didn't also include German (funny how they pretend not to be able to read English or Spanish, but they know the "m-f" word to fling at the servers). The one "cultural" thing we went to on Saturday night in Palma, at Mieke's insistence, featured a lot of American and English musical impersonators. The few Spanish dancing troupes wore scary Inquisition-type robes for at least part of their routines; what is that

about? Why would they want to remind people of that terrible part of
their history, murdering anyone who disagreed with their church, and
sending their Jews far and anon five hundred years ago? Or does their
local memory even include the hapless Jews at all? You see no feeling, only
the powerful technical synchronization in the dances, almost an overt
display of cultural triumph as the red and black robes swirl to throbbing
drums. I felt chilled, while Seth complained about the photography
vendor hawking her wares. Sometimes I feel like I don't even know

Monday

Dear Frieda,

   Thanks for asking about our trip to see Mieke in Majorca. When I
think of all the things I want to tell you about, Carmen at "The Three
Dolphins" café comes to mind the most. Have you ever heard of soul
fragments, or parallel lives— someone else is part of the essential material
you were made of, but they live separately from you, maybe in another
country? Sometimes you might even have dreams of this person's life as
if it's your own. If this is true, Carmen is my soul fragment, or living my
parallel life, or whatever. She is half-Spanish, half-English, with a red-haired
husband from Yorkshire; you know how I feel about redheads, and about
the U.K. Their café is outside their home, which you have to walk through
to go to the restroom; and you know my doll collection in our family
room? She has the same dolls displayed! And we just communicated so
well, even in sentence fragments. Seth has a way of believing anyone but
me about something, and it was a little eerie seeing him take in Carmen's
advice when he wouldn't have even listened to what I said, using the
same exact words. Oh well! She also told us about the area where we're
staying, that vacationing neo-Nazis take over parts of Majorca, calling it
"Little Germany," and having their meetings even though it's illegal to be
a Nazi in Spain. (Question: Why is it not illegal to call yourself a Nazi in
the U.S., though it's forbidden throughout Europe? Should I be proud of
this, or just confused?)

Tuesday

Dear Frieda,

I appreciate your checking on our visit with Mieke in Majorca. What I really enjoyed about that episode is that I'd secretly wanted to stay in a house in a place like Provence or Tuscany, and now I've done a similar thing, only on a Spanish island. So it was certainly an adventure, especially with the house having so many rooms and not really being in a town or village, which is what I had pictured when she mentioned renting a place for us. We all enjoyed not being part of a busy hotel and being able to escape the loud tourists in town. How many times can you hear people singing, "We're going up to LONDON! We're going to have PIZZA!" in a night without wanting to leave the island? You've been there to visit too so you probably know what I mean.

It was thoughtful of Mieke to make arrangements for us, and it's always good to get out of our American routine. I've been thinking a lot about who I really am since we got back.

Love always,
Your cousin Shulamith

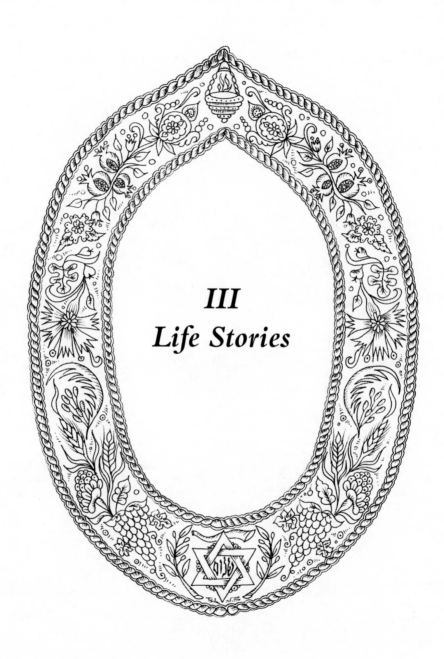

III
Life Stories

Beth Arky
Hello Muddah, Hello Faddah, Sure Did Love It, at Camp Sabra

As I watch friends and neighbors ship their kids off to sleepaway camps in Maine and the Berkshires, nostalgia kicks in for the summer of 1970, when The Partridge Family was must-see TV, Michael was still the fifth Jackson and I was a girl setting off on my maiden voyage to Camp Sabra.

As I hugged my mom goodbye in the JCCA parking lot in suburban St. Louis to board the bus for the Lake of the Ozarks, I knew that water sports, arts and crafts, and my first taste of freedom awaited me. What I didn't know was that I was embarking on a years-long journey that would end in strong friendships and sweet memories, along with a deeply personal Jewish identity and my green awakening.

Once we arrived at Sabra, we discovered that we'd be roughing it, relatively speaking, as we toured the bare-bones cabins, shower rooms and mess hall. We learned to build lean-tos and campfires for overnights in the thickly wooded – and tick-infested – hillsides; we skinny dipped, rode horses and stargazed with our nature specialist, who earned his "camp cred" by virtue of having lost a sizable chunk of one heel to a Missouri viper. There were no computers for emails home; instead, quaint as it now seems, we rushed to mail call, where we waited anxiously for missives from our parents.

All the while, Judaism was woven into daily camp life, with nature serving as the backdrop. For every time we barked out "Sound Off!" as we marched up the steep gravel road from the swim dock or wept inconsolably to "You've Got a Friend" around the final campfire, we sang rowdy versions of the Hebrew mealtime prayers, traded loud "Bubbe Bubbe Bubbe Zayde's!" during "David Melech Yisrael" and danced the hora under the night sky.

On Friday nights, we dressed in white and walked to the Chapel in the Woods, where we sat on rough log "pews" and helped lead services in Hebrew and English, performed "creative expression" – fellow camper Terri Grossman, now Sabra's director, recalls doing an interpretive dance to the Amidah – and swayed arm-in-arm as we sang "hinay ma tov."

These joyful communal experiences stood in stark contrast to my religious life, such as it was, back home. Although my family didn't keep kosher, there was no bacon, shrimp or Chanukah bush at our house, and

I did feel Jewish. But during services at Shaare Zedek, the Conservative synagogue my family attended, I was bored beyond belief. I didn't know any Hebrew – my father grew up in an Orthodox family and didn't press the issue, though there was no question that my older brothers, Carl and Michael, would have bar mitzvah ceremonies. There was a lot of davening, very little English and no transliteration, let alone children's services. Still, I loved many of the melodies, so I hummed along and faked the words. But in some important way, I felt left out.

At Sabra, I was an outsider no more. My lack of Hebrew didn't matter. In fact, according to "How Goodly Are Thy Tents": Summer Camps as Jewish Socializing Experiences (Brandeis University Press), I was part of a much larger movement to get Jewish youth involved in their religious and cultural traditions, long before Taglit- Birthright began sending lucky kids like my nephew Jake to Israel.

Attending camp was also a family tradition. My mother, Bea, and her two younger siblings – and later Michael – went to Camp Hawthorn, the precursor to Sabra, while Carl and I attended Sabra. Founded in 1938, Hawthorn offered Depression-era children the chance to flee the hot city and live in nature alongside other Jewish kids. But my mom's "baby sister," Fran (Podhorzer) Goldberg, says that for immigrants like my grandmother and grandfather, who hailed from Warsaw and Vienna, respectively, camp wasn't just about instilling a Jewish identity. As my Auntie Fran told me, "They really wanted us to experience America – to be American."

When I was 15, I graduated to Masada, Sabra's oldest and, by definition, coolest unit. We were living off the grid, so to speak, in isolated canvas tents nestled high above the boys' and girls' villages. But the peak experience was our wilderness camping trip to Colorado, where we slept in meadows filled with mountain flowers, bathed in frigid streams and hiked amid the awe-inspiring Rockies. We learned to respect and preserve the land. And we sang "Rocky Mountain High" without a trace of irony. The trip was an epiphany – a truly religious experience.

I live in Brooklyn now, so I don't know whether my 7 year-old son, Matthew, will go to camp in Missouri. But regardless of whether he makes it to the Lake of the Ozarks, I will strive to instill in him the lessons of Sabra, both in terms of an appreciation of our religious heritage and the planet we call home.

first published in the Boston-based *Jewish Advocate*, July 2010

Abby Bader
Bubby

Bubby was the keeper of our family history, our traditions ... and our recipes. Anyone who has ever been to a Seder knows just how important food is to the Jewish tradition. Passover was the time of year when our entire family gathered together -- dozens of people: cousins, aunts, great-grand-nieces and nephews -- and Bubby fed them all. Year after year, she managed to produce enough food to feed us all, and all of it delicious. It seemed like some sort of Bubby magic, to get it all done.

When I was a bit younger, I thought of Bubby's cooking as the height of all things Jewish: recipes that were surely passed down from her mother by her grandmother and her grandmother's mother. So in eating the Passover matzoh ball soup, I felt connected to a family that stretched back long before I was born.

It wasn't until I started having my own seders that I learned a little more about Bubby's style of cooking. She was always generous with her recipes, so I had all of the old favorites: Bubby's sweet Russian chicken, instructions for matzoh ball soup, and, of course, Bubby's brisket. And here I found something different from what I expected. The Russian chicken? Its tangy flavor comes from a bottle of Russian dressing. The matzoh ball instructions? straight from the Manischewitz package. And the brisket? Let's just say it involved 7-Up.

When I was preparing for my first Seder, I had to laugh at that. I had imagined that Bubby's recipes themselves were what connected our family to a deep history. I don't think our Polish ancestors cooked with onion soup mix; Bubby's food legacy was uniquely her own. And in this, I think you can find a much deeper family tradition: feeding your family, lovingly, in whatever way you possibly can. Bubby's passover recipes are the product of needing to cook a lot of food to feed a lot of people, and, surely, of wanting to feed them food that tasted delicious. So while the recipes that I've inherited aren't exactly mystical relics of our Jewish past, they are certainly a connection to a very deep tradition of loving and caring, one that I'm honored to inherit.

I live in Colorado, which feels pretty far from New Jersey, where most of this history happened. I live on my own, and I'm forming my own new traditions. But when Pesach comes around, or when somebody I love needs some special caring, Bubby's are the recipes I turn to. Like her, I want to be a woman who is steadfast, loving, and fiercely loyal.

That's our real family tradition.

I never got to know Bubby in the ways that others did. Since her passing, I've heard so many people comment on her strength, her discretion, and her fierce loyalty. As a beloved granddaughter, I never had the occasion to meet her like that. She was too busy loving us grandkids in other ways.

Debra Solomon Baker
Plenty of Wednesdays

The quibbling during dinnertime is the worst. There's something about the dinner table that's supposed to be holy. You know, we sit down together, savoring the home-cooked meal, swapping stories about our daily triumphs, cheering each other on. We are not supposed to be erupting over who got stuck with six baby carrots, rather than five. We are not supposed to be complaining about a freckle-sized brown spot on our slice of pear. The elder, impatient for chocolate chip ice cream, is not supposed to be commenting on the sluggish pace of his younger sister's macaroni eating, or tallying the word count on her roundabout stories. We are supposed to be giggling like the Bradys.

Tonight's fracas, however, is delightfully oxymoronic.

It stems back to last night, when Max and I arrived at our synagogue at 7:30, armed with crocheted blankets (stitched by my student's grandmother), a deck of cards, some picture books, a few toiletries, and a change of clothes for the morning. We were there to camp out on air mattresses with the homeless women and children who depended on open doors in 59 churches and one synagogue. It was the 3rd Wednesday of the month, Congregation Shaare Emeth's turn to host a program called "Room at the Inn," and I had read that volunteers were needed for the overnight shift. I signed up. And Max insisted that he wanted to join me.

Six hours later, I lay restlessly awake on my air mattress and wondered about the others asleep in that same room. I had wrapped up shivering Ashley with one of the donated blankets, and she had boasted that when she was just eleven, she had learned how to crochet in foster care. What had happened in her life? And then there was the woman with the boldly-colored head scarf, the woman whose name I never learned, the woman whose five-year-old daughter announced to me that she and her mama were going to the zoo tomorrow and then, guess what, skating the next day. She may have been without a toothbrush and in a filthy pink t-shirt, but life sure sounded perfect in that little one's imaginary world. And I thought about this nomadic trudging from church to church to church, night after night, and the carting back in the mornings to the day shelter, and how gratefully one of the women accepted my offer of a bar of soap and a tiny vial of vanilla body lotion, and how I just wished that I had more to give to her than some stinkin' toiletries.

And then I thought about Max, asleep beside me. I remembered his final question to me before he fell asleep on this bed, in this room, with these strangers. "Mommy," he had whispered, not wanting to be overheard, "does Jimani get to go to a good school, you know, like mine, or does she have to go to one of those, you know, those other kinds of schools?" Exhausted, I had answered abruptly, a quick, I'm not sure, and, it's really time to go to sleep. But I realized now the meaning behind Max's question, Max who understands the bitter cycle of poverty. He wanted to know if Jimani had a chance, or not. I just don't know, Max. I don't know if your new-found friend, the little girl to whom you read "Fancy Nancy", the little girl to whom you so patiently tried to teach the card game, War, the little girl who made you laugh with her cartwheels, that you chased around the room, pretending she was too fast for you, I don't know if she will get out from under this mess. I wish I could tell you a fairy tale, but I am too tired for that and, you, my son, are just too smart.

So, tonight, at the dinner table, Max is sharing tales of the evening and suggesting that his little sister is too young to volunteer, that she would be too tired, that she might get frightened in the dark room. This is big guy work, he seems to be saying. And, seven-year-old Sarah, of course, is asserting her strength, attempting to slash his argument, bit by bit, whining that she wants to go next time, that she wants to help the homeless.

Yes.

This is one beautiful little brawl.

And, in the end, I assure both of my dear children, that there are, and will continue to be, plenty of Wednesdays.

Debra Solomon Baker
To Piwniczna

Last night, two children, Max and Sarah, vacationing at their grandparents' home in Boca Raton, Florida, traveled far, far away from there. They landed in Piwniczna, a town that, today, is captured by just a single sentence in Wikipedia: "Piwniczna-Zdrój [piv'niţşna 'zdrui̯] (until 1999 Piwniczna) is a town in Nowy Sacz County, Lesser Poland Voivodeship, Poland, near the border with Slovakia, with 5,744 inhabitants (2004)." There is nothing there (of course) about Max and Sarah's great-grandmother, Hene Federgrun, or about her parents and her grandparents, or about her ten younger siblings, all of whom, long ago, shared one house in this one-sentence town. There is nothing about their family's butcher store or about Max and Sarah's would-be aunts and uncles, then mere children, lugging water from the well to wash their small bodies.

The word shtetl does not appear in the wikipedian glimpse into their great-grandmother's town, a town that had just 14 Jewish families. It is a word that makes Max and Sarah giggle, such a silly word to pronounce, *shtetl, shtetl, shtetl,* over and over and over again.

It is my 72-year-old mother who has been guiding my children, page by page, on this journey to Poland. She has been reading aloud to them from the book that my father plucked away on typewriter paper, 25 years ago. It is a book dedicated to me, to my sister, Amy, and to my brother, Andrew, "so you can pass these remembrances on." It is quite dusty.

Tonight, I listen to my mom's hoarse voice describe my grandmother's decision to leave behind her bustling family, to "convert" from Hene to Anna, to head to America with a bunch of withouts — without a trade, a language, a fortune, a home– but with determination to carve out a decent life for herself and then, of course, to send for her family. Tonight, my children learn of Anna's father's imprisonment, and the word pogrom. They do not think this one is quite as funny to say.

They are mesmerized by Mom's reading, asking question upon question. But, perhaps it is time to travel back home now, to suggest that my mom close the book, for another year or two, that the kids go swimming or watch Spongebob. They are my babies, after all. And though they are 10 and 8, not babies at all, maybe that is still too young, for if my mother keeps flipping pages, there will be descriptions of Anna's parents and of her ten siblings. This one to the gas chamber. This one, to a firing squad. And this one? We never knew how. They will see photographs with captions that say, "Brother-Name Unknown." Name. Unknown.

They will see toothless babies, my grandmother's nieces and nephews and cousins, babies who would be my parents' age now, nameless babies, who died simply because they were Jewish in Piwniczna. They will learn that there were hundreds of relatives, all gone. They will learn the details of why Anna's plan did not work.

I still remember being 20 years old, living in Florence for the semester, and standing in a hallway, listening to other college students make travel plans to visit this relative in Germany or that one in Holland. I sobbed. I suddenly felt lost and alone, and deeply homesick. Though my father had always told us the importance of the Holocaust, I never really understood. He talked about relatives and gas chambers. He talked about people who stood by and did nothing. But, it was vague and far away and surreal. But there, standing in that hallway in Florence, I suddenly and unexpectedly grieved for Grandma's siblings, Henry and Rebecca and Samuel and Rachael, and I even grieved for those without names, for all the relatives that I could have called, that I could have visited. If only...

And, today, although I am a teacher, or, perhaps, because I am a teacher, I fear that, in Max and Sarah's school, the Holocaust will be reduced to yet another lesson in yet another unit in yet another class, that it will be just another piece in the massive curriculum glob. I worry that, in an effort to cover so much, students are emerging from our classrooms with a dangerous level of simplicity about all kinds of topics, in this case, a Jews-died-sucks-for-them version of events. But I also know that far too many parents have relinquished their own duty to teach their children, relying solely on the educational system, and that this, in many ways, is negligent.

I am not sure what Max and Sarah should learn right now. Is pulling out this book a good idea, or is it not? I don't know. I am just one mother trying to raise two kids in this world. I will answer their questions and I will try to be truthful and sensitive. I will try to rely on my instincts. But, of course, there is nothing simple about any of this.

In the end, I suppose I do believe that, even as young kids, they should know who they are. They should know about their great-grandmother's forgotten town and about the human beings who inhabited it. They should know that this, and she, and they, are all far more important than a one-sentence summary on Wikipedia might suggest.

I will ask my mom to keep reading to them. At least, I think I will...

Originally published by *Teaching Tolerance*, a project of the Southern Poverty Law Center.

Diann Joy Bank
My Bubbela
(My Precious One)

It was 103 degrees. The hottest day of the year in St. Louis. It was 2:03 p.m. and I was exhausted. At last, my miracle had arrived as the nurse placed my son carefully in my arms on July 1, 1966. The day I will never forget. I became a mommy.

He had hazel eyes, just like mine. He had brown thick hair, just like mine. He had a turned up nose, just like mine. What can I say; he had a sweet smile, just like mine. The doctor told me my son only had gas, but I was his mommy. I knew better.

From that moment on, I called him my 'Bubbela,' my precious one. In a blink of an eye, my Bubbela began to grow, and grow, and grow. "Bubbela, wash your face; Bubbela, put your toys away; Bubbela, flush the toilet!" Bubbela, eat all your chicken soup, so you can grow up big and strong."

Then it happened, like it does to all moms. Where did the time go? My sweet Bubbela was five years old. That dreaded day was here. The first day of kindergarten; the first day he would leave the safety of my arms. He was going where he had never gone before, leaving me behind. "Was I ready? Was my Bubbela ready?"

My Bubbela was going to school on that yellow monster school bus all by himself. I told my son, "Bubbela, listen to your teacher. Bubbela, be sure to share at school. Bubbela, wear your coat when you go outside. Bubbela, eat your delicious peanut butter and applesauce sandwich."

As he finished his Cheerios, he looked up at me with his brown thick hair, just like mine. His turned up nose just like mine. His hazel eyes just like mine. He had a sweet smile, just like mine. He said, "Mommy, I'm ready."

I took hold of his little hand, and stepped outside of my kitchen door. We walked, hand in hand, up our blacktop driveway and one block to the corner. Turned right and walked half a block to the bus stop. I saw that monster bus turning the corner toward us. I watched those accordion doors open up. He climbed up the three giant black rubber steps. I'll always remember his little red tennis shoes, the ones with the alligator on them, his brown shorts, and his red shirt with the little green alligator, as he was swallowed up behind the doors. He sat by the window, and waved to me with his little hand. I yelled, "Bubbela, I'll be waiting for you when you come home!" I watched as the monster bus took my little boy away.

I walked back home around the corner into my kitchen door, and did what any other loving, worried mommy would do. I cried, "Who will take care of my Bubbela!" I had to pull myself together. I looked at the hands of the sunflower kitchen clock moving so slowly from minute to minute. What was I to do? "Keep busy," I thought to myself. First, I washed the kitchen floor, then the bathroom floors. I vacuumed all the carpets, cleaned out the closets. I glanced, once again, at the sunflower kitchen clock. Oy, the clock hands moved so slowly. I knew what to do. I'd make my Bubbela his favorite treat. Have you guessed my five year old's favorite cookie? Not just any chocolate chip cookie, only Nestle Toll House cookies. They must be timed perfectly so they are hot from the oven when he comes home. Ding! The bell rang. The tips of the chocolate chips were half melted over just right. Quickly, I poured the cold white milk in his Nestle Bunny cup. Put two hot chocolate chip cookies on the plate. The clock hands moved faster now. It was time to meet my Bubbela at his bus stop. It was 12:05 p.m. I ran to the bus stop Here it comes. The giant monster bus pulled up right in front of me at the bus stop. I waited anxiously. It's accordion mouth opened up. Down those big steps came my little Bubbela. I kneeled down on the sidewalk looking at him eye to eye.

I gave him a giant squeeze. "Welcome home, Bubbela!" He looked up at me with his brown thick hair, just like mine. His turned up nose just like mine. His hazel eyes just like mine. He had a smile, just like mine. At last, my Bubbela was back home.

Hand in hand we walked quickly back around the corner to the kitchen door. As we stepped into the kitchen, he lifted up his head with his nose wiggling. "I made you a surprise. Your favorite snack is waiting for you, Bubbela." The sweet aroma tugged his nose straight to his chair at the kitchen table. He reached for the warm chocolate chip cookie. I put my hand on top of his hand. "Bubbela, before you take your first bite, tell mommy the first thing you learned at school today?"

My Bubbela gazed up at me, as our hazel eyes met, and in his small child voice he said, "The foist thing I loined at school was that MY NAME IS NOT BUBBELA! ITS NATHAN! " But to me, his mommy, he'll always be my Bubbela, my precious one!

I dedicate this story to my firstborn son. You guessed it. His name is Nathan!

Henry Berger
How I Came to My Jewish Identity and Did It Matter
Delivered at Shaare Zedek Synagogue on
the Occasion of the 60th Anniversary of
Henry Berger's Bar Mitzvah, July 24th, 2010.

I was received as a son of the commandment on July 29, 1950 in Beth Sholom synagogue, at that time the only Jewish congregation in the place where I was born, Frederick Maryland, a relatively small town which is situated midway between Baltimore and the nation's capital. Frederick had become famous because it was the subject of a poem composed by a mid-19th century American poet laureate, John Greenleaf Whittier. The poem "Barbara Frietchie," is about a ninety year old woman who in 1862 allegedly hung the American flag from her upstairs window in defiance of an invading Confederate Army commanded by General Stonewall Jackson. In Whittier's words, Dame Frietchie exclaimed as she waved the stars-spangled banner: "Shoot if you must, this old gray head, but spare your country's flag." To which Stonewall Jackson allegedly replied, again in Whittier's words, "whoever dares to harm the head of yon gray head, dies like a dog, march on! he said."

The incident almost certainly never happened and we kids in Frederick replaced Whittier's Dame Frietchie's exclamatory remarks in the poem with the following words: "Shoot if you must this lovely young maid, but please spare the boys upstairs!" she said." Whittier's poem nonetheless figures in what I am going to say in a few minutes about the creation of my Jewish identity.

By 1862 there had been Jews living in Frederick for over a hundred years, small in number, but they were there. Among them were several of my relatives whose descendents were important in sculpting my own Jewish identity.

My bar mitzvah itself was a bittersweet moment. My mother had died two years earlier, just a few months before my brother's bar mitzvah. The nation had just entered the Korean conflict the month before, on June 25th 1950, and the military situation for South Korea, the United States, and the United Nations did not look good. The Cold War was dominating and poisoning American culture, politics, and foreign relations. Secret chemical and biological warfare research was being conducted at the United States military installation at Fort Detrick on the edge of Frederick and, from time to time, individuals working there would suddenly disappear. Only much later was it revealed that they had either been reassigned, purged as security suspects, or had died doing dangerous experiments.

Most immediately and frustratingly, from my early teenage perspective, the New York Yankees, the team my brother idolized and thus I detested, were in first place in the American League while the Brooklyn Dodgers, my favorite team, and the Philadelphia Phillies were in a virtual dead heat for first place in the National League. The Phillies would win the pennant in the 10th inning of the last game of the season but then lose four straight games to the Yankees in the World Series. My brother was jubilant! I was anguished if not devastated.

That, however, was two months later. On my Bar Mitzvah Day, unlike just a short time ago, I chanted the whole of the Torah Parsha. The small but handsome Schule was crowded. It was, however, very hot, there were no fans, not to mention air conditioning, in the sanctuary. I was sweating profusely in my starched white shirt and jacket. I was nervous, right? Beth Sholom Congregation did not have high quality gabbaim like Rudy Oppenheim and Steve Keyser. Somewhere in the second or third aliyah, I skipped a whole line. The Rabbi got excited, I stopped, an unmistakable undercurrent of Yiddish-English babble could be heard from the ranks of the congregation. I may have taken a deep breath. I raised the Yad, the Torah pointer, into the air and went back to the beginning of the Parsha, the Torah portion, and did the whole thing all over again - much to the confusion and consternation of the congregants but much to the satisfaction of the Rabbi. The bar mitzvah and the service ended happily for all concerned.

★★★★★★★★★★★★★

In the rabbi's charge to the bar or bat mitzvah, it is customary for him or her to remark that the occasion marks a culmination but also a new beginning of one's Jewish journey. This observation is wholly true, but today I want to give a specific, personal content to the notion because, in retrospect and from the vantage point sixty years later, I realize that whereas I did begin a new chapter in my Jewish journey upon my bar mitzvah, the arrival at my Jewish identity had already happened before I ever mounted the bimah and executed the rituals of the bar mitzvah.

My decision to address this topic is, I should acknowledge, inspired by Rabbi Fasman's Kol Nidre sermon this past September about Jewish identity. The Rabbi may be flattered that anyone would remember what his sermon on Yom Kippur was about, let alone what he said last Shabbat. As a classroom teacher for over forty years, I want to reassure him, albeit at long distance, that I know the feeling.

That said, four individuals and two events before my Bar Mitzvah shaped my Jewish identity. I am telling you this now so that, among other things, you will know when I am coming to the end of these remarks. The four individuals influenced the construction of my Jewish identity in different ways, each providing me with a piece or, better stated, a "key" to a part of my Judaism. You may be surprised when I tell you that neither my mother nor my father were key holders. The reason was that for much of my pre-bar mitzvah childhood, my mother was grievously ill, my father consumed by her illness while at the same time carrying on the bookstore business they had established, and he was trying to pay for the immense medical bills in the age before health care reform by buying and selling stamps and old and rare books at night and on Sundays.

And so it came to pass that others provided the keys. The first was my great Aunt Jeannette. In her earlier life, she had been an accomplished violinist and in the 1930s became one of the first, if not the first, woman president of a synagogue in the United States. She paid great attention to me at a time when neither of my parents were able to do so. By the time I was seven, eight, and nine she had become increasingly pietistic but also authoritarian and could be quite stern in her manner. To defy her word was to risk severity. If I was fearful of doing so, I was also hugely impressed by her authority and her own disciplined life style. She instilled in me an understanding of Jewish ritual, an appreciation of custom and prayer, a respect for her observance of kashrut and above all else, I now realize, provided me with a personal connection to Judaism.

But then a terrible thing happened. I was coming to understand that Aunt Jeannette's Judaism was rigid, intolerant of views other than her own, an intolerance driven largely by fears of the other, and that she was controlling of other people's feelings and behavior even as she worked overtime to restrain and deny her own emotions. Something in my gut began to tell me that I could never be the Jew she wanted me to be which meant, in her view, expressed many times, becoming the rabbi of Beth Sholom Congregation. On most Saturday nights I would join my Aunt Jeannette in her upstairs parlor to daven ma'ariv, the evening service, and observe havdalah, the ceremony bringing to a close the Shabbat, the Sabbath. As we prayed, we faced east. I began to find it ironic that as we davened, what we were facing was a cluster of church steeples, the same church steeples Whittier had written into poetry in "Barbara Freitchie" with the beginning words: "Up from the meadows rich with corn, clear in the cool September morn, The clustered church spires of Frederick stand, green-walled by the hills of Maryland." The most prominent of these steeples, bathed in light at dusk and in the dark, is the tall tower of St. John's Catholic Church atop which rests a large cross illuminated by a powerful lantern light. When, on one Saturday night, I had the audacity to point out what I thought was a humorous irony – praying facing the cross - to my Aunt Jeannette, I received a vicious tongue lashing that cut to the core of my vulnerable early teen-age soul. This I never forgot and I also came to realize that there had to be more than this, a more positive affirmation of Jewish identity.

The second key to that identity was provided by my maternal grandmother, Leah Rae Weinberg, who married my Aunt Jeannette's brother, Leo, my grandfather. Shortly before her marriage to Leo, my grandmother became a Jew by choice. Of German Protestant origins, her adoption of Judaism in 1908 was regarded by her family as far less offensive than the conversion of one of her sisters to Roman Catholicism. Such were the realities of religious politics in Frederick Maryland at the time.

My Grandfather Weinberg, who died when I was four years old, and his wife, my grandmother, gave the building which houses the Beth Shalom Synagogue, to the Jewish community of Frederick. In his own time, the first three decades of the Twentieth Century, Leo Weinberg was a brilliant, well known lawyer in the state of Maryland and a famed orator. When he died in 1942, my grandmother continued to live in their house, which was right next to the synagogue. Suddenly widowed, she was left penniless and rented out five rooms in her house to make ends meet.

She was a committed Jew, a lovely woman and caring person to whom I was increasingly attached in the wake of my mother's fatal illness. More than any other individual I knew at the time, she taught me about the possibilities of humanity, about humility, and about perseverance in the face of considerable adversity which she herself had endured, including the loss of a husband and a first born, my mother, in a half dozen years. Above all else, she was to me the embodiment of righteousness – Zedakah. She read widely and appreciated good music and theatre as did my mother and father, interests I also absorbed. She studied and quoted from Torah but also from psalms and the prophets, the latter whom she revered. It was because of her that I began to appreciate Isaiah, Amos, Micah, and Hosea even when I am sure I did not understand much of what was written in their names.

There was, however, a flaw in my grandmother's personality: Like virtually all the people living in Frederick, Jew and non-Jew alike, she had grown up observing the racial code of her era. She seldom strayed from the color line. While respectful of African-Americans, she conveyed a paternalistic attitude which was also class rooted. She insisted on separate and equal justice but had no ready answers to the obvious inequalities of racial and economic segregation which dominated race relations. She also ill-disguised her suspicions and fears of the Roman Catholic Church and clergy at the very moment when I was being befriended by the local priest, Father Jordan, who counseled me to observe, practice, defend, and never stray from my Jewish identity, the same Father Jordan, who when I asked on a very hot day how the flock of congregants could be lured to mass, replied with the snap of a finger: "It's all right Henry, we just tell them it's a dress rehearsal for hell!"

The third key to my Jewish identity, if he were alive, would be sitting in this sanctuary today. Rabbi Bernard Lipnick was a very young man when, in 1945 and 1946, he served as the Acting Rabbi at Beth Sholom Congregation. At the time he was simultaneously a student at Johns Hopkins University and at Baltimore Hebrew College. Bernie, as we kids called him, was one of many students, some of them studying for the rabbinate, who served time in Frederick. He instantly connected with the youngsters at Beth Sholom, myself included. Extroverted, dynamic, even-handed, handsome, Rabbi Lipnick possessed a wonderful singing voice, a thoroughly captivating bimah presence, and a gifted teaching ability. None of that changed throughout the remainder of his life as I am sure most of you know.

Most of all, Bernie was real and reached even my brother who hated Hebrew School and, at the time, really did not want anything to do with religious instruction. Bernie exploited my brother's love of sports, especially baseball, and also created space for my brother who had a severe stuttering affliction. Bernie provided an important male Jewish model for me and appealed to my love of history. He helped to cement my commitment to education and inspired me to be confident in my Jewishness but not arrogant about it, on the one hand, and on the other hand, by his own example, to resist victimology which, in the wake of the recent holocaust and the emerging awareness of the shocking and horrific nature of it, was an all too easy trap into which to plunge. His attention to equal educational opportunities and advancement for girls as well as boys was also impressive.

But then a terrible thing happened. Bernie left and went on to bigger and better things. We did not have any contact for nearly twenty five years until Mary, my son David, and I came to St. Louis on New Year's Day, January 1, 1970.

A towering figure, Bernie's death in April of this year was a loss for his family, the Jewish and non-Jewish communities of St. Louis and, for me, a personal loss. He is missed by all.

The last person who keyed my Jewish identity was also someone who stood at the pulpit of Beth Sholom synagogue each year, for many years, on the High Holidays. His name was Maurice Shudofsky.

Shudofsky had a magnetic, yet calm personality, an exquisite and learned sermon delivery, and a deep reservoir of knowledge of Hebrew, English, French, and American literature and culture. He was also a courageous individual.

Born in Russia in 1916, Shudofsky left that country sometime in 1921 during the Russian Civil War and the invasion of Russia by Poland, France, Great Britain, Japan, and the United States, an assault which was accompanied by a wave of anti-Semitism. Shudofsky received his elementary and high school education in Baltimore and his undergraduate and Ph.D. degrees from Johns Hopkins University. After a short stint as the editor of the Baltimore based American Jewish Congress Bulletin, he received an appointment in 1940 in the English Department at the University of Wisconsin in Madison where he taught English and American literature and reintroduced the study of Hebrew at that institution after a lapse of twenty years.

Shudofsky was still a member of the faculty at Wisconsin when I knew him before my Bar Mitzvah. He went on to Wayne State University and Long Island University in Brooklyn during the remaining years when he came to Frederick to officiate at the High Holiday services. He died prematurely at age 47 in 1963.

Shudofsky was an academic and on many matters he pushed beyond accepted wisdom and spoke out on issues of the day, including racism and the Cold War. A committed Zionist, Shudofsky organized a now long forgotten series of panel discussions on that subject in Madison in 1945 and 1946. His Zionism was not uncritical, however, and he reached out to academic and political figures in the Arab communities of Palestine, Egypt, Lebanon, and Iraq. I was not aware of these latter activities at the time

and only discovered them when - earlier this year - with the assistance
of officials at the University of Wisconsin and Wayne State University, I
researched Shudofsky's complete biography.

Shudofsky made the occasion of the High Holidays extremely worth
while. His addresses were awe inspiring, intellectually exciting, and bridged
the worlds of the religious and secular with references to non-sectarian
literature, the Bible, and Rabbinic sources. He helped me, I now realize,
to become a Jew in the United States.

These four people were critical to my emerging Jewish identity, but
there were two events in which I myself was an important actor that also
mattered. Those of you who are high adventure film goers may recall
the character Jason Bourne that Matt Damon portrays in The Bourne
Supremacy and The Bourne Ultimatum. An amnesiac super assassin,
Bourne does not know who he is until he sees what he has done. Though
not a murderer and not afflicted with amnesia, I also had two such
moments of self recognition.

The first occurred when I was in elementary school on a certain day
in October, specifically October 12th The teacher began the class that
morning by asking us, the children, what significant event had occurred
in 1492. My long, skinny arm shot up, and the teacher called on me:
"That was the year," I proudly announced, "that Jews and those other
people" whose Muslim identity I either did not know or could not then
remember, "were expelled from Spain." That was most definitely not the
answer for which the teacher was looking. There was a moment, probably
not longer, of deadly silence in the room and then derisive laughter and
taunts. I was completely embarrassed and humiliated. Only later did I
realize that, as the only Jew in the classroom – a fact likely unknown to
most, if not to all, the other kids – I had inadvertently, to use a current-
day phrase, "come out." I understood then, if I did not know it before,
that I was a minority in a majority Christian all-white school which was
operating under the laws of racial segregation at the time and for as long
as I was enrolled in the public school system.

Episode Two: Sometime later, again before my Bar Mitzvah, in a
certain year and on a certain summer day my brother, together with an
older African-American teenager whom my brother had befriended at
the local YMCA because of a common interest in baseball, and I were
in Frederick's largest and most prominent park, hitting and catching
fly balls. At that time it was forbidden for any but whites to enter the
park. My brother, two years older than I, knew this to be the case as did

his friend. I have no idea whether at that time – I was about nine years old – I fully understood the totality of the color line. I was now going to find out about it. For on that particular summer day, seemingly out of nowhere, there suddenly appeared four or five white teenagers, armed with bats and other objects, walking towards us, shouting racial epithets and anti-Semitic slurs and demanding to know why WE, my brother and I, had allowed HIM, a "Colored" whom they described using the racist term, nigger, into the park. It was clear that most of the furor was directed against my brother and my self. I was frozen with fear.

What happened next was, however, extraordinary. It was extraordinary, because it was rare, if ever, at that time for an African American daringly to defy whites, especially when outnumbered. But my brother's friend, older than either of us, grabbed our baseball bat and told us to leave the park. We hesitated and then my brother, with no hesitation and without stammering, said to me:

"Go run and call Pop," his name for our father. "Do it now and do it fast." I was always simultaneously afraid of my brother, who had a ferocious temper, and at the same time I also considered him a heroic figure and almost always obeyed his commands.

I ran as quickly as I could up the hill, across the street and into our house, and called our father at his book shop. My father did not even wait for me to end my sentence so speedily did he react. I then raced to the front door, nearly colliding with my brother who had slowly walked up the hill, then turned, and watched as his friend swung the bat from hand to hand and stared down the advancing gang of boys marching towards him. They slowed their pace, then they resumed walking. Before, however, a confrontation could take place, a car carrying my father, the chief of police and another officer arrived on the scene. The chief ordered the whites to leave the park and severely scolded my brother's African American friend and told him not only to leave but also never, ever, to come into the park again. What the chief told my father I do not know but, in retrospect, I can easily imagine he read him the riot act about preserving the color line. I do not recall ever seeing the African American youth again, but what was seared into my pre-adolescent conscience or perhaps sub-conscience was the reality that I was simultaneously a member of a majority as well as of a minority, certainly in the eyes of others, white and black. To be sure I doubt that at the time I intellectually so clearly formalized the idea in these terms, but the event did influence me afterwards in the way I came to see the world and my place in it. I understood, in a moment of truth, that I as a Jew was not the only one who had an identity to uphold and, when necessary, to defend and that I was in most fundamental respects a privileged person in a society, dominated in my youth and after, by the racial divide which was and is a primary fault line of American society. I came to understand that in the context of American white society, I was expected by other whites to behave as a white and to uphold the prevailing racial code. I came to realize the injustice of this situation and that it demanded my attention as a Jew and as an American. This then was also a piece of how, by the time of my Bar Mitzvah, I was constructing my Jewish identity and has remained part of that identity ever since: That what I was and am is defined by what I did and do even more than by what I believe, that the values I came to embrace were worth a great deal but only in the practice of them. In this I recognized the wisdom of the Russian writer Anton Chekhov's words: "Man will only become better when you make him see what he is like."

By now, the answer to the question, "did any of it matter?" should be obvious. The two pieces of eloquent advice from Hillel, the Elder, in answering the question are the most relevant. The first: "If I am not for myself, who will be for me, and if I am for myself only, what am I? And if not now, when?" The second: "Separate not one's self from one's community." In the United States this means the several communities in which I reside – Jewish, non-Jewish; local and national. I would be the first to acknowledge that I may not have always followed these injunctions as well as I might have, but I'd like to think I've tried. I mean, if not, then what has been the point of it all?

Saramina Berman
B'Sharet

"Kiss me so it means the end of life as I know it," pleads the hero of the movie, *P.S. I Love You*. Alone in the darkened theater, I start to cry. My own true love and I realized that life as we knew it ended with our first look into each other's eyes. Kiss me as though it's for the last time," I used to tease, borrowing a line from Ingrid Bergman in *Casablanca*. Forty-five years later, my true love died.

When he landed on Omaha Beach on D-Day, I was a freshman at Northwestern University in Evanston, Illinois. While I was donating my blood to the Red Cross on the home front, he was serving in the 17th Battalion Signal Corps, U.S. First Army, on the war front. We had never met, never heard the other's name spoken, and yet we shared a mere two degrees of separation. It was 1944.

Allied armies marched confidently across France, headed for Berlin. Then, at the confluence of borders of Belgium, Germany, and Luxembourg, all hell broke loose. The Germans launched a last-ditch offensive of unanticipated numbers and ferocity. Allied victory went from "guaranteed" to "touch-and-go." Those seven weeks of fighting – December 16, 1944 to February 7, 1945 – came to be known as The Battle of the Bulge.

My love, a first lieutenant, was billeted outside of Spa, Belgium. Orders were to "hole up until further notice." During the day, the lieutenant kept busy monitoring the coding equipment for which he was responsible. At night, he relieved boredom by accepting dinner invitations extended by local Belgium women whose men were dead, imprisoned, or fighting in the war.

At these dinners, the lieutenant ate well but held his liquor poorly, for along with his army-issued equipment, he carried a heavy load of painful memories of an alcoholic father who abandoned wife and children when the lieutenant was three years old. So that one night, returning to his barracks after a delicious home-cooked meal and too much liquor, upon discovering a young buddy scribbling away at a letter, the lieutenant felt compelled to slap his buddy on the back, and cry out, "You dope! You should have come with us tonight! The food was great, and it was fun! Besides, we may all be blown to smithereens before tomorrow dawns!"

"No thanks, lieutenant," the buddy replied. "I'm writing to my gal back home, and, as you can see, she's the most beautiful gal in the whole world."

The lieutenant took one look at the nearby photo of his buddy's girlfriend, and blurted out, "She is not! I'll bet there're at least three females back in the U.S.A. I've never even met yet who are prettier than she is!"

The lieutenant was not an unkind man. Surely it was the liquor in him that spoke those unkind words. Nevertheless, everyone within earshot understood that a gauntlet had been flung down. The young buddy stopped scribbling, pulled himself up, and snarled, "For how much?"

In the end, the lieutenant won almost $10,000 and a wife on his bet. But I get ahead of myself in telling my story.

The soldiers set up a mock court-martial proceeding, with the commanding officer agreeing to be judge. A date was set many weeks ahead for deciding who was prettier: the buddy's gal, or the lieutenant's three unmet females. Rules were few and simple: the lieutenant was to write to a college sorority in the U.S., asking for photos of three of the most beautiful amongst its members. He would have to swear to the CO that he did not know any of his contestants. The soldiers' pockets were full of back pay, and it didn't hurt that the whole thing was tinged with sexual innuendo. Betting became a welcome and popular diversion.

Having once dated a Sigma Delta Tau sorority member at Northwestern University, the lieutenant immediately wrote to that sorority, asking for pictures. A few days later, for insurance, he wrote to an old friend who was 4F, meaning unfit for military service, who lived in Chicago, and asked him to please call the nearby SDT's at Northwestern, and make sure they understood that the lieutenant was dead serious about needing the photographs.

Lo and behold, the following announcement boomed over camp loudspeakers: "Due to increased German fighting on the battlefield, delivery of all mail is halted." Confident now that the lieutenant would lose his bet purely by default, the odds lengthened and the betting intensified.

What the lieutenant had no way of knowing was that his 4F friend in Chicago, newly married, had a sister-in-law, me, who was an Alpha Epsilon Phi sorority member at Northwestern University. Naturally, then, I, and not the SDT's, got the insurance call from my brother-in-law explaining and promoting the lieutenant's bizarre request. I complied at once, sending photographs of three gorgeous AEPhi sorority sisters, a snapshot of myself, and a note explaining how I came to be writing to a total stranger. But alas, after all that effort, I failed to put sufficient postage on the package I sent off to the lieutenant!

Mail delivery to the 17th Signal Battalion was resumed before the designated day of judgment, in time for the lieutenant to have received a huge package from the SDT's at Northwestern containing a professionally-shot photograph of every member of the sorority. His real problem was picking only three photos from the whole batch to use as his contenders. The lieutenant easily won his bet, and sent the winnings home for safekeeping.

The German siege was broken, and First Army crossed the Rhine and the Elbe rivers. Somewhere in Germany, my postage-short package showed up in the lieutenant's mailbag. In his return letter of thanks for my efforts, he enclosed two snapshots of himself, and wrote, "You look like a very decent sort. Your pic indicated it, and your letter had a certain 'I love life' aroma! This is good. I shall have to see for myself upon my return. …"

We exchanged letters once more before the Nazis surrendered on May 8, 1945. In his letter, dated May 1, 1945, he briefly but profoundly described his devastating experience of having entered Dachau and other neighboring concentration camps. A month after I received that letter, the lieutenant showed up in Chicago.

The lieutenant was on leave before being redeployed for the upcoming invasion of Japan, which was preempted, of course, by the dropping of two atomic bombs. He had wired ahead to my brother-in-law, saying he was coming to Chicago for three days, and asking him to "take care of my social life." Everybody knew what that meant.

It was mid-June, and the lieutenant was betting, correctly, that I had finished my finals, and was back home in Chicago. Never mind that his own home base was now in New York City; the lieutenant was coming to Chicago "to see" for himself.

As we sat together on the sofa in my parents' living room, I could feel the lieutenant eating me up with his eyes. It was a repast that began with our first look into each other's eyes, when life as we knew it ended.

We spent the three days at the beach, sunning and talking, and the three evenings dining, dancing, and talking some more. When the lieutenant got to his new Army base in South Carolina, he telephoned and said, "I think I've fallen in love with you." Frightened by the swiftness of the whole thing, I answered, "I like you very much, too." We agreed to write to each other every day. Once, he sent me three letters written in the same day. After another leave spent entirely in Chicago, and our exchange of more than 200 letters, my share of which I still keep safely and handily stored, our fate together was sealed. Rabbi Solomon Goldman officiated at our wedding, in Chicago, on May 19, 1946.

I may be a little biased, but this is my favorite how-did-you-meet story. Someday, somebody is going to make the movie.

Ben Fixman
My Mother

There is a Yiddish expression: "*Siz nishto a schlecter mameh.*" The English translation is: "There is no bad mother."

Deep inside the hearts of the five Fixman children, we all felt nothing but love and respect for our mother, Rose, despite the scoldings and beatings we received when we got out of line. Our mother was always our Queen, our Rock of Gibraltar, a fearless woman with a spine of steel who did her best to raise her children against a backdrop of suffocating and grinding poverty.

Our mother controlled our lives – and that was a good thing because, without her, we would all have ended up in orphanages or have perished.

She would often tell us, "We may all starve, but we will starve together as a family." Her words and deeds sustained us and kept us alive. Without a word of complaint, she toiled as a cleaning lady, sometimes working for as little as 13 cents an hour to bring in some income.

She was so desperate and driven to find money that she even tried making bootleg wine in our bathtub. But it was a failed enterprise. She also tried making comforters stuffed with feathers but that didn't work out either. She had a grocery store at one time, a confectionery at another, but she was always undercapitalized. After all, how could you open a store with just $30 of capital? (I think the man who gave her the money was her lover. My mother was single at the time, but married twice after that. As my success in the business world grew, I supported all of her marriages.)

My mother, a strict Orthodox Jew, always saw to it that we lit the candles on Friday night and had a pre-Sabbath supper. Most of the time it was chicken because chicken was cheap, it tasted good, and chicken soup was supposed to be the panacea for anything that ailed you – from the sniffles to a raging fever.

My mother was a born improviser. When I needed new shoes – and there was no money to buy them – she took me to a surplus store and bought me some used tennis sneakers. When the soles got to the point that they were full of holes, I stuffed newspaper into the holes. That's how you survived in the ghetto.

Over and over again, my mother would tell me as a child, "*mein zindele, deigeh nisht,*" which meant, "don't worry, don't have a care." And then she would add in her broken English: "It will be all right. Someday you will grow up and be a businessman." She drilled those words into my head repeatedly. It was a refrain that never stopped. Later on in life, I realized that my mother had street smarts, and she somehow passed them on to me, her youngest son. Without them, I never could have made my mark in life.

I also respected my mother because she was a physically strong woman who could defend herself when trouble came along. One day she went to collect the back rent from a woman in our building. As she was demanding the money, the woman suddenly lunged at her with an ice pick. My mother wrested away the ice pick, and after that incident the rent money was always on time – and the landlord was happy.

One day, when I was 13 years old, my mother sat the family down and told us some truly wonderful news: We were moving out of the ghetto. I couldn't believe it, and neither could Celia, Nina, Martha and Hymie. I think we all cried, but they were joyous tears.

At that time, our family had just gotten off of relief. We were all working steadily and bringing in a little more money. That money made our exodus from the ghetto possible.

So in 1938, the Fixman family relocated five miles west to 1384 Clara Avenue, a West End neighborhood that was predominantly Jewish, a neighborhood that was much nicer than where we had come from.

What a difference five miles can make. We were now living in a neighborhood where I was still hustling newspapers but it was a place where you could walk the streets at midnight and still feel safe. Rarely was anyone attacked, but if a woman were accosted her attacker would wind up in a sewer – compliments of several Italian men who policed the neighborhood and saw to it that people acted properly and abided by the law. It was a kind of vigilante justice.

I was now enrolled in a new school, Emerson Grade School. Naturally, as the new kid on the block, I had to prove myself with my fists. But these were not gang battles; they were exhibitions between kids to see who was the best "duker." That's where my ghetto experience as a fighter kicked in. I won every one I fought. Not a single loss in the bunch. Pretty soon the challenges all faded away.

My reputation as a fighter soared when I beat the living shit out of a kid named Eddie Cola, a neighborhood tough guy with a big reputation as a duker. Eddie tried to pick my pocket one day and I made short work of him. When kids heard that I had cleaned Eddie's clock, they never gave me any more trouble. None at all.

At Emerson School, I always wanted to dress nicely to impress my classmates, especially the girls, who were just starting to bloom. But there was always the problem of money. Money went to pay the rent. New clothes? Out of the question.

Once again, my mother came to the rescue. She got a neighbor to lend her $10. She then took me to Safron's Department Store in Wellston and bought me a navy blue suit. I was so proud that I didn't take it off for eight months. I wore it every single day to school. At night, I would press the suit, putting a wet cloth over it and steaming it so I could keep the trouser creases as sharp as the edge of a knife. But the kids at school, kids who came to class every day in different outfits, were not dummies. They soon figured out that the navy suit was my only outfit, and I took a lot of ribbing from them. But I didn't care because I owned that navy suit.

After Emerson, I was a freshman at Soldan High School on Union Boulevard. Attending Soldan was a bittersweet proposition. I really enjoyed the classes and my teachers, but there was a downside, too. I hated to go to school every day wearing the same old clothes, while my classmates wore many different outfits. But the worst was sitting in the school cafeteria and watching everyone having lunch. I skipped lunch most of the time because lunches cost money and I didn't have any. It made me feel like an outsider with a big chip on my shoulder.

After just eight months at Soldan, I was forced to drop out to help support my mother and the rest of the Fixman family. At this time my brother, Hymie, was in Koch Hospital suffering from tuberculosis. He was in the hospital for three years.

That time at Soldan was the extent of my formal education – just eight months of high school. As I walked down the steps of Soldan for the very last time, tears streamed down my face.

(Excerpt from *The Ben Fixman Story: from the Ghetto to the Gold* by Ben Fixman, Artful Tale LLC, c2009.)

Harris Frank

Whatever Happened to the Sunday Family Dinner?

During the Depression years and certainly continuing until the beginning of America's participation in World War II, a fixed tradition in our family was the Sunday dinner.

Memory tells me that this event was a staple in a great many American families a century ago and certainly continued until the mid 1900's. I'm sure it continues today, particularly in the more rural areas. Of course, it varied in size, scope and grandeur according to the family's means, religious beliefs and size.

For whatever reason, our family (my mother, especially) viewed attendance at this weekly ritual as mandatory. No exceptions. Golf must be completed before noon. Ball games with the kids could wait. Sunday lunch was as must, as was dressing properly for the occasion.

It was our usual practice to have from two to four invited guests. Most often long-time friends of my parents; but every once in awhile there would be uncles, aunt or cousins. I liked the latter group especially because they were full of tales about my father's "way back when" family. I loved those old memories, but my mother, whose family originated in England, never could cotton to the ways and delights of the old German Jews.

We never were served family style. Each course - soup, salad, entre and dessert - was served separately. No one's plate was cleared until the last person was finished. It always seemed to me that the biggest eater was the slowest eater and the biggest talker; so our meal was always protracted in spite of the fact that a whole bunch of friends were already outside playing ball on what was an unusually glorious summer day.

The menu didn't seem to vary too much, I seem to recall. But why should it...the "anchor" standing prime rib was always cooked to perfection. Mashed potatoes with think gravy. Creamed spinach. Just about nothing on the main menu would be considered healthy by today's more rigid standards (and alas, rarely followed).

Once in a while a turkey was the featured attraction, and a couple of times a year it was fried chicken. But the poor cow provided the usual repast. We all loved it and to the best of my recollection, no one ever worried much about the unhappy bovine!

Oh, yes, the meal was always topped off with all cream, ice cream - with topping - a bit more health food excellence from the good old days.

From time to time we had some very rotund people at our Sunday board. In those days, either because of the depression, or the dearth of fast food restaurants or simply the fact that many people didn't gorge themselves too often, really fat people were much more of an oddity than today when it seems that fully half of the folks you see are overweight... oftentimes grossly so.

I do remember that these folks – I'll name no names, but God bless them all in their final resting places – always were the ones who (1) talked about their diets, either now on, going on, or should be on; (2) ALWAYS ate the most; and (3) ALWAYS were the last to finish because of #1 & #2. The main course, in particular, was sheer agony for me. I desperately wanted to have at the dessert and then to get out on the ball field. Our guests very obviously wanted to have at the dessert, too, but they were never in any hurry to get there.

There was some divergence of opinion as to whether our Sunday repast was *lunch* or *dinner*. My father called it *lunch*. It was *dinner* to mother. It was NEVER *supper!* No matter the name, it was always bountiful (even in the days of our deepest depression). The cast of characters was often amusing, and generally it was followed by a brief walk and a long nap for the elders with an afternoon of ball playing, touch football or ice skating for the kids...depending on the season and the elements.

I am guessing that for a great many families the Sunday Lunch (Dinner) is only a long-gone memory...if even that. I imagine that the tradition still endures for many who live in rural areas where farming is the principle enterprise, Sunday church is still an established custom and families have an enduring closeness due to the tight-knit communities in which they reside.

70 or 80 years ago those Sunday meals might have been bad for the waistline and hard on the cholesterol count...they were for sure hard on the patience of young boys aching for the playground...and cleaning up afterwards, without the aid of an automatic dishwasher, had to be a beast; but they were a part of a quieter, more relaxed time...a bit of solid American tradition which sadly is no more.

Shelly R. Fredman
Writing Towards Home

Smack dab in the middle of my life, I moved my family from St. Louis to New York City. We'd been mulling it over for years, and then, on a fated bike ride the summer before the move, we rode down to the bottom edge of the city. My sixteen-year-old daughter spied the spread of green around Rockefeller Park, the ferry boats plying the Hudson, men soaring toward net on the basketball courts and in America's version of a fairytale, the speck of Miss Liberty out there in the water.

We would live here, Anielle decreed. And so my husband and I found a two-bedroom on the twentieth floor of 22 River Terrace. We'd lived so long landlocked that all of our forces gathered around the idea of life at the rim of the Hudson, where you would actually be reminded, daily, that Manhattan is an island.

I signed my daughter up at a private school which would embrace her in its cushy arms, and then dashed the walls of our three-room apartment in familiar yellows and lavenders, thinking to hoodwink my husband into believing he wouldn't miss our two-story house on a tree-lined cul de sac back home.

As the school year loomed, and my husband returned to St. Louis on his new weekly commute, the other price—loneliness--set in. Borough of Manhattan Community College, four blocks and a world away from my door, was the closest college, and I'd heard they had forty sections of English Composition to fill.

The next day, I had a job. BMCC is a college of minorities, immigrants and immigrant's children—tired students of all ages who come to evening classes after a full day of work. In St. Louis, I'd been teaching at the University of Missouri Honors College, in a lovely old house set on a hill; twelve young people gathered around a seminar table. Now, I'd be teaching in a trailer, because some of the classrooms were blown up on Sept. 11.

Anielle was at my side as I headed out to teach my first class at 5:30 Monday night. She had recently gazed in upon my maladjustment and announced, "You can go back to St. Louis if you want, but I'm staying here." Now she was talking me into letting her walk by herself to Taco Bell and by herself home to the apartment. Meanwhile, I'd be at class, unable to know she got home safely. So she set up the silent mode on my cell and said she would text message me. All of this was happening in the two minutes before I was to teach my first class in NYC. Thirty students of God knows what mood and inclination waiting for me. So we're poised at the West Side Highway, watching the cars zoom by and Anielle is swinging her pink purse, which she purchased the day before in Chinatown, pink like cotton candy, pink like a Broadway spotlight shining through the gray Manhattan streets, screaming pink, begging someone to come by and swipe it.

Are you scared, Mom? she asks. "Yes," I say, not wanting to go into the 4,000 reasons why, the main one being the fact I've now got to teach a new class and worry about whether she got home. And I'm dependent on technology to make it all happen. We cross the highway, she waves goodbye and I walk into a classroom of 25 people before me, looking wary, confident, apprehensive, relieved, bored, depending on the face.

I introduce myself, and immediately forget to have them say their names—I'm running at breakneck pace, going through the syllabus, trying to inform and keep it lively. There is one Jamaican girl in the left corner, Samera, I learn later, and she is nodding and smiling as I speak and I want to go over and hug her.

I tell them we're going to do a bit of writing, to see where they are, how their sentences look. No grade; no pressure. Just for fun. I ask them to write about a place that is meaningful to them. And I sit, amazed, yet again, as twenty-five hands take up their pens and begin to write. On command. Having a teenager, it's always a wonder when someone actually listens to you.

They write away, and afterward, I ask them to introduce themselves and to say a bit about what they had written. Lorenzo Segarro, to my right in the front row, in a hot pink button down shirt, jumps in. He has written about his grandmother's apartment, where he and his father grew up, where he can still eat the same good food (his words) and hear the Yankee game playing. Hazel, behind him, in her tri-colored hairdo, wrote about where "her dreams became tangible," at the House of Blues in Myrtle Beach. Traysie described the day when her aunt Rey died, how the orange trees outside were filled with oranges while Rey went away somewhere where Traysie couldn't follow. We had Ayanna on the Tranquility Government Secondary School in Trinidad; Kareem, 6'3", in tattoos and muscleman t-shirt, on his first snowfall, after moving to 162nd St. from Belize. Quan Fang Chen, whose name I can write, not pronounce, sat in the back row. She was afraid to hand her paper over to me, and Ivan, about 55, from Moskow, was telling her it would be alright.

At some point, I glanced down at my cell and read Anielle's text, "You can stop worrying now. I'm home."

Reading Ivan and Kareem's papers late that night, I'd felt I'd stumbled into a treasure box. All those hearts. All those places. All those secrets. A writing class is one of the most sacred places still left on earth. Hearts and souls on the page, misspelled, mispunctuated, grammatically incorrect. I had my work cut out for me, and yet… I felt a new kinship with the Lady sitting out there in the water. Odd, me being an alien species here, and I'd be the one to lay out the welcome mat--their introduction to America, to college, to writing, to analyzing, coherence and notes on the side of the page. The Lady holds her lamp. I've got my pen.

Yonason Goldson
Shylock in Jerusalem

There are no accidents in Shakespeare.

Hardly a week passed without Professor Levin impressing upon us yet again this paramount lesson, and no one passed Professor Levin's class without learning it well. So learn it I did, but with no inkling of how its echo would reverberate beyond Shakespeare's era by thousands of years, and beyond Shakespeare's England by thousands of miles.

Levin was cheery, almost spritely (in spite of his erudition), a short, energetic, New York Jew who amicably prodded us to challenge him on every point, then mercilessly undercut our arguments whenever we contested him. So effortlessly did he draw from the Complete Annotated Works of William Shakespeare in defense of his assertions that no one dared attack him without the most thorough consideration, not even the cockiest among us.

That would have been me – a headstrong senior at the University of California, Davis. Having recently returned from half a year circumnavigating the globe, I had acquired just enough sophistication to cringe at the cultural shortcomings of my fellow undergraduates, if not quite enough to recognize my own; by my reckoning I had out-paced them all, and I fancied myself nearly an English professor in my own right, momentarily denied the recognition I deserved by the patriarchal myopia of those higher up in the ivory tower. Graduate school would rectify that soon enough.

In the meantime, I was still short one faculty recommendation and, with this deficiency in mind, my advisor had suggested that I take Levin's course in Shakespeare, advising me to introduce myself to the instructor at the start of the term and declare my intention of impressing him with my scholarship. In retrospect, the absurdity of such counsel seems staggering, although at the time it struck me as eminently reasonable.

"You're an English major, I suppose?" Professor Levin asked at our first meeting. I nodded. Non-majors took *Shakespeare for Non-Majors.* "And what are your plans after graduation?"

"Graduate school," I replied. Then, matter-of-factly, I added: "I'm still short one recommendation, so I'm planning to do quite well in your class this term."

He laughed condescendingly, but was impressively gracious considering the audacity of my remark. I went on to outline my idea for a paper on *Romeo and Juliet*. He replied that I should write on the *Merchant of Venice* instead, then hurried me out of his office.

Half a lifetime later, I can still visualize Levin's introduction to the *Merchant of Venice* as if I were sitting in his classroom. Clearly, he would have preferred to ignore the editor's remarks that prefaced our edition, and if he could have assured himself we would all skip over it I'm certain he would have done just that. His overarching fear, however, must have been that some of us might indeed read it, and that it might influence our approach both to the play and to Shakespeare in general. So he couldn't leave it alone; the risk was too great.

The editor described the play as a romance, Portia as a young innocent longing for love, Shylock as evil incarnate. To his credit, Levin tried valiantly to be judicious. "Perhaps the editor intended to present the foundations upon which one can build an appreciation of the play," he suggested at first. But as he continued, he had more difficulty finding room for magnanimity, eventually reconciling himself to observe that the editor "seems to be overlooking a rather critical third dimension to all the major characters." But he couldn't stop there. Love's labors lost, together with the patience of a scholar wishing to impart scholarship to his students. "There's nothing else to say," he finally concluded in exasperation. "The man's a fool."

There are no accidents in Shakespeare. Every word is in place. Every repetition purposeful. Every omission calculated. Every nuance measured. And every theme directed at the very heart of Elizabethan society in a way that pricked the sensibilities of the times without drawing the ire of the monarchy or the church. And as Professor Levin taught us, as he opened our eyes to the meter, the rhythm, the seemingly infinite complexities of character and plot, something dormant in my brain stirred to life, woke with a start, and burst forth into the dawn of enlightenment with all-consuming passion. Here was wisdom that had not been mastered, that could not be mastered, in which yet undiscovered pearls of insight lay deep beneath the surface waiting to be recovered by any dedicated diver and revealed to the world.

Trapped within the cushy walls of my suburban, secular-Jewish upbringing, condemned to a life of comfortable mediocrity by what I called *the upper-middle-class curse*, I projected my own frustrations onto Portia, empathizing with her subjugation to her father's will and finding couched within her words both the intent to manipulate her father's scheme and the resolve that no man would ever again hold her under his thumb. With euphoric abandon I peeled away layer upon layer of meaning and insight as I composed my midterm essay.

And so, when Professor Levin bustled into the classroom with his stack of graded papers, I could hardly have failed to notice, from my conspicuous vantage point at the center of the front row, my own paper lying atop the pile. The professor lifted it up, carried it about as he made a few comments about the papers in general, then set it down and picked up the one beneath it, from which he began pointing out examples of a well-written critique.

I wasn't listening. If he had intended to read from this paper, why had he not placed it, rather than mine, on the top of the bundle? Would he read from mine next? No, he went deeper into the pile, citing further examples of what makes a paper work. Then he picked up mine again, and I tried desperately to read the silhouetted grade showing through the back of the last page as he paced up and down at the front of the class. "Now from the best paper in the class..." he began, and I swallowed air as my heart swelled up into my throat. I labored to pay attention, but directed even more effort toward keeping an even expression and not grinning like an idiot; presumably I failed, since the guy next to me kept shooting glances my way, even though there was no way he should have been able to tell that the paper was mine.

Today, I empathize with my own students, to whom I rarely return exams until the end of class. It was an hours-long fifty minutes that afternoon, and when the professor finally did hand back the papers, I quickly flipped to the back page from where, at the bottom of a long paragraph of Levin's blue ink, an A+ jumped off the paper and into my arms.

I sauntered casually out of class, then cantered down the stairs to find a bench in the hallway where I could pour over my professor's remarks, all of them glowing. After a few minutes I felt a presence standing over me. It was Professor Levin, and I leapt to my feet.

"A really first-rate paper," he said. "Are you an English major?"

I nodded. Evidently, our first meeting had not left much of an impression. "And what are your plans after graduation?"

"Graduate school," I replied. "As a matter of fact, I'm still short one recommendation, and I'm hoping to be able to ask you for one."

He smiled, with no hint of condescension this time. "I'll be happy to write you a recommendation," he said. "Just let me know when you need it."

Professor Levin had accomplished what few of my other professors had, and what none had accomplished to the same degree: not only had he challenged me think, but he had made me think with an intensity and a fervor that drove me to produce the major opus of my college career. Which, I now understand, was exactly what he had intended. What I'm sure Professor Levin did not intend was to set the chords of Jewish disharmony resonating in my heart and mind through the tragedy of Shylock the Jew and his daughter Jessica.

But this latter effect would have to incubate for several years and, in the meantime, Professor Levin drove me on in the study of Shakespeare with even greater enthusiasm. I finished the term with a dissection of *Henry IV, Part I*, followed by a second term with the same professor and a chance to sink my teeth into *Hamlet*.

Sink, yes, but it was I rather than my teeth that sank amidst the swirling tides of the bard's most famous play. Projecting as I had done with Portia, I superimposed my own sophomoric hopes and fears upon the Prince of Denmark, crediting him not with simple indecisiveness, but with a trepidation born from a crystalline vision of myriad futures, every one of them converging inevitably upon a common destination of death and disaster. I gleaned the play for evidence, developed arguments, established proofs, anticipated counterproofs, neglected the other plays Levin had assigned and even my other courses as I grappled with the task of interpreting the unsteady psyche of the young prince in whom I saw myself.

The result was a six-thousand-word thesis, more than twice the length of anything I had ever written. Too long, in fact, as I found myself thoroughly lost in the turns and twists of Shakespeare's subtleties. When I reached the end I knew I hadn't made my case, but I was drained of the desire to go back and work it through again from the start. My professor rewarded me with an A; I suppose my treatise was impressive work from an undergrad, but he was unconvinced by my arguments and let me know it with his trademark smile, albeit with hardly any condescension.

Graduate school, however, remained a fancy as distant as Shylock's Venice. An unusually slow reader and typically undisciplined student, I had barely passed my lower division survey courses and had absorbed far too narrow a cross-section of English and American literature to prepare me for the Graduate Record Exams. As they stood, my GRE scores would have qualified me very nicely for engineering or law school, but I didn't need an advisor to tell me that no respectable English Lit. department would be impressed or interested.

A cultivated talent for picking apart great literature is not a greatly sought commodity in the general marketplace, and my penchant for creative writing was neither saleable nor especially refined. And so, with the looming specter of matriculation and frighteningly few alternatives, I buried my hopes of becoming either scribe or scholar, slung a pack over my back, and set off to hitchhike across America.

After all, it had worked for Kerouac.

From November to April I traveled east, from L.A. to Boulder to New Orleans to Key West to Charleston to Washington, D.C., before I burned out and headed home. I had satiated my appetite for travel, I thought, and the vague notion of a master's degree in social work was now buzzing about my head. But as way does indeed lead on to way, the following autumn found me not back in the ivory tower but on a street corner in Vienna, so travel-weary after half-a-year of European wandering that, although headed nowhere in particular, I found myself quite incapable of making up my mind whether to turn left or right. After five minutes agonizing over one or the other road not taken, I finally made a decision: I needed to stop – or, at least, to slow down.

My focus drifted across the Mediterranean to Israel, the land of my people, and – more importantly – the land of *kibbutzim*. A month or two of highly structured mindlessness on a collective farm picking oranges or harvesting bananas sounded like just the prescription for recharging my emotional batteries. So I caught a flight across the Mediterranean, confident that after a brief respite I would be off again, this time to Kenya and Botswana and, after that, to India and perhaps an ashram in Nepal.

I arrived in Israel together with the winter, when the earth slumbers and, with it, the field hands. I also arrived together with many thousands of twenty-somethings who had exactly the same idea I had. They were camped out at the government placement offices like teenyboppers waiting to buy tickets to a Rolling Stones concert. Even more discouraging were the signs declaring, NO VOLUNTEER OPENINGS – COME BACK NEXT YEAR.

Next year? I wanted to go to Africa or Asia next year, but I couldn't afford to just hang out, nor would a month or two of indolence restore me to sanity. I needed a routine, something to keep me busy until my psyche recovered and I could return to the road.

A long-forgotten, foreign-sounding word surfaced amidst my foundering thoughts: *yeshiva*, a term I had picked up in my earlier travels, an institution dedicated to the study of ancient talmudic laws and the traditions of the Jews. Scholarships were freely given, I had been told, and also room and board, particularly to college-age Jewish men and women who had grown up dispossessed of their ancestral heritage. I didn't contemplate for long: I needed something to do, and this would do as well as anything.

Better still, I didn't even have to find them; they found me. As I arrived at the Western Wall, before I even made it down the stone stairway into the vast courtyard, I had been identified, classified, and virtually tagged like an endangered fauna, given a place to stay, and set up to visit yeshiva the next day.

Like a toddler thrown into the deep end of the pool to sink or swim, so was I tossed unforewarned into the sea of Talmud. There, sitting around a table overlooking an array of oversized volumes filled with indecipherable writing, Rabbi Moshe Carlebach read and translated for us, then cheerfully endured our relentless questions.

"The Talmud wants to know," he chanted, rocking back and forth in his chair in time with has singsong intonation, "why the Torah prescribes that the bondwoman 'goes out for free, with no money.' Someone explain to me what's bothering the Talmud."

We looked around at each other for a moment. What was bothering me was how the antiquated legalistic minutiae of indentured servitude could have the slightest relevance to my life.

"If she goes out for free," suggested the fellow seated beside the rabbi, "then obviously there's no money."

"Excellent!" cried the rabbi, rewarding the boy with hearty slap on the back that made his eyes bug out.

"But maybe it's just for emphasis," someone else suggested.

"But what's being emphasized?" asked the rabbi.

"That she goes out for free."

"But it says that already."

"So it repeats it to make sure."

"To make sure of what?"

"That we're paying attention."

"No," laughed Rabbi Carlebach. "No, no, no, no, no! The Torah assumes that we're paying attention. Like I keep telling you, if there's any repetition, anything appearing extra or unnecessary, any seeming omission, it's there for a reason, and it's there to teach us something. That's what learning Talmud is all about."

My mind clicked up several gears, and I leaned forward with sudden interest. "Are you saying," I asked cautiously, "that *there are no accidents in the Torah?*"

"Exactly!" he roared, as he tried to give me a slap; fortunately, I was out of reach.

"And if the Torah could have expressed itself in one way but chose another," I pressed on, "is that also relevant?"

The rabbi could scarcely conceal his joy, as if this were a concept that normally had to be drilled in for weeks or months before his students finally grasped it. "Yes, yes!" he exploded. "Nothing in Torah is by chance. Everything is relevant. *There are no accidents.*"

That was all I needed to hear. For as much as William Shakespeare had been deified by the literary community, per force the bard remained an icon of mere flesh and blood. The Torah, however, claimed to be a direct transmission from the Almighty. As such, it provided not merely inspired insights into the nature of man and his world, but a revelation of divine guidance, a veritable tree of life, whose fruit not only nourishes but sustains the soul.

At least that's what it said on the flyleaf. Oddly, despite this direct line of communication from above, there was still much to debate, as evidenced by the furious volleys of argument exchanged by the scholars on all sides of us in the yeshiva's enormous study hall. The tricky part was learning when to argue, and when not.

"A man wished to betroth a woman," intoned Rabbi Carlebach, "but in place of the requisite amount of currency, he gave her a cow. Is the betrothal binding?"

Predictably, a novice student asks, "Why did he give her a cow?"

Patiently, the unflappable rabbi answers, "We don't know why, and it doesn't matter. That's the case. Now we want to understand the ruling."

"But if he'd just given her money we wouldn't need to know."

The observation, although valid, is irrelevant in the context of talmudic discourse. The only *why* of interest to the Talmud relates to proving either similarity or dissimilarity between one case and another. In this I found it deliciously Shakespearean, seeking not to debate the workings of the world, but to accurately reproduce them and render them comprehensible.

"A man was discussing marriage plans with a woman," chanted Rabbi Carlebach, "in the course of which he gave her the requisite amount of money for betrothal without articulating the purpose for which the money was given. What's the ruling? Rabbi Yehudah says that even where the intent is clear, he needs to specify his objective or else the betrothal is not binding."

"I don't think that's right," said a boy across the table.

The rabbi clapped his hands in delight. "Ah, you are *so* lucky!" he cried. "*You* can argue with Rabbi Yehudah. I wish *I* could argue with Rabbi Yehudah. You're just like a six-year-old kid arguing with Einstein. A professor of physics would never *dream* of arguing with Einstein, because he knows who Einstein is, so he knows he can't argue. But a six-year-old who never heard of Einstein, he goes right ahead and argues."

The boy looked back blankly, but again I heard echoes inside my own head, this time not the resonating memory of Professor Levin, but of a different instructor, Mr. Byrd, the only other English professor who had convinced me that he was smarter than I was. Byrd had little in common with Levin; he was the seminal college prof, with his conservative suits, neatly trimmed beard, and round, wire-rimmed glasses. His sense of humor was witheringly dry, he almost never cracked a smile, and always he insisted on *Mr.* Byrd, never *Dr.* Byrd and certainly not *Professor* Byrd. I was too intimidated to ask why.

Paradoxically, Mr. Byrd wrote trashy mystery novels, Mickey Spillane style thrillers that made for lively speculation about the incongruous secret life our bookish little professor might be leading off campus.

What I remembered at that moment, however, leaning over a massive tome and attempting to follow the arcane ruling of Rabbi Yehudah, were Mr. Byrd's comments on the first day of his class in Swift and Pope. He confessed that there were certain authors (including Bellow, I think, and Nabokov) for whose works he had never managed to acquire an appreciation.

"These are flaws," said Mr. Byrd, "because authors without merit do not gain respect in the eyes of the literary community. It is our job, therefore, to teach ourselves to appreciate them."

Mr. Byrd might as well have been speaking Aramaic. As a college junior, the idea that my opinion of quality should subordinate itself to the opinions of others seemed about as sensible as marrying a woman with a cow. Nor was that the only time I failed to learn this lesson. I missed it again in Professor Levin's class, as did Portia, when it was spoken by her waiting maid, Nerissa:

Your father was ever virtuous; and holy men at their death have
good inspirations: therefore the lottery, that he hath devised in
these three chests of gold, silver, and lead, whereof who chooses
his meaning chooses you, will, no doubt, never be chosen by
any rightly but one who shall rightly love (I, ii, 30 - 36).

But Portia refuses to recognize her father's wisdom, even after all
her unwanted suitors have departed in exasperation as a result of the
conditions of her acquisition.

In the context of Rabbi Carlebach's sermon about Einstein, Mr. Byrd's
remarks came back to me as clear as the Jerusalem sky. The integrity of
any discipline, whether legal or academic, depends upon the establishment
of an historical hierarchy of expertise within that system. Mr. Byrd would
present the same lesson later when we studied *A Tale of a Tub* and pondered
Swift's satiric proposal that the Ancients must of necessity be viewed as
inferior to the Moderns. But not until I heard Rabbi Carlebach's own
satiric proposal concerning the egocentricity of a six-year-old child did
the lesson finally strike home.

Having received Mr. Byrd's admonition that great literature establishes
itself neither by appointment nor referendum but by weathering the
criticism of scholars over generations, I could now appreciate that the
rulings and syllogisms of talmudic scholars had been canonized not by
virtue of simple dogma, but because their authors had earned the respect
of their contemporaries and of succeeding generations. And having
witnessed Professor Levin's contempt for the Shakespearean scholar who
failed to look beneath the superficial interplay of character and plot, so
too could I accept that the Torah presented a depth of design far more
complex than simple narrative – all the more so according to the claim
that it had been penned by the Almighty, whom one could reasonably
expect to be at least as competent a writer as William Shakespeare.

My assertion that the study of Shakespeare had brought me to Talmud
raised more than a few skeptical eyebrows among my fellow scholars.
But it was my suggestion that Shakespeare might offer some positive
contribution to the world of Jewish thought that placed me within
distance of virtual excommunication. For although few of my fellow
students of Talmud had given serious consideration to Shakespeare, nearly
all of them assumed him to have been an anti-Semite, knowing that he
had written an unflattering characterization of a Jew.

A person should always fear heaven, privately and publicly, acknowledge the

truth, and speak truth in his heart. These words begin the morning liturgy
of the observant Jew and, with them in mind, I felt it only right to defend
Shakespeare, not for his own sake (since surely he wouldn't care what a
handful of talmudists thought of him four centuries after his death) but for
the sake of truth. It was not, however, merely an abstract devotion to truth
that motivated me, but my conviction that within Shakespeare's depiction
of Shylock's Venice resided a universal relevance to contemporary Jews
and contemporary Judaism.

Since Jews were banned from living in England in Shakespeare's time,
it's unlikely that the bard ever met a Jew, or that he formed any strong
opinions about Jews one way or the other. But his reservations about the
sincerity of the Christian world are self-evident, nowhere more clearly
than in the very work that has drawn upon him accusations of anti-
Semitism.

> Mark you this Bassanio,
> The devil can cite Scripture for his purpose.
> An evil soul producing holy witness
> Is like a villain with a smiling cheek,
> A goodly apple rotten at the heart:
> O, what a goodly falsehood hath! (I, iii, 98 – 103)

So does Antonio indict Shylock for his manipulation of the Holy
Word to justify his usury – the very same charge that has often been
leveled against talmudic reasoning and the syllogistic hair-splitting
through which Torah law is sometimes explicated. Ironically, this is the
very method Antonio gloatingly applauds when it saves him from the
consequences of Shylock's scheme.

> Therefore prepare thee to cut off the flesh.
> Shed thou no blood, nor cut thou less nor more
> But just a pound of flesh: if thou cut'st more
> Or less than a just pound...
> Thou diest and all thy goods are confiscate (IV, i, 324 – 332).

And then, not satisfied at saving Antonio's life and depriving Shylock
of his note, Portia awards half Shylock's fortune to Antonio, at whose
request she commits the rest to Jessica, (who has already deceived her
father and disavowed her heritage), then further imposes the condition of

conversion to Christianity. All this while impersonating a judge.

Conversion, however, does not a Christian make, at least not in Shakespeare's Europe. For even as Shylock is coerced into becoming a proselyte, his daughter, Jessica, embraces Christianity as an escape from the restrictions of her heritage and her father's name. Sadly, Christianity does not return her embrace, for even after her conversion Gratiano comments upon her approach: "But who comes here? Lorenzo and his infidel?" (III, ii, 221).

By the final scene, Jessica herself regrets her apostasy from the faith of her ancestors. Having abandoned her own people, she has come to realize that she will never be an equal within Christian society, counting herself among the tragic figures of Thisbe and Medea when she responds to Lorenzo's romantic banter, concluding:

> In such a night
> Did young Lorenzo swear he loved her well,
> Stealing her soul with many vows of faith
> And ne'er a true one (V, i, 16 -19).

Jessica has learned, too late, the lesson her father articulated in his famous soliloquy as he rails against the fate that has placed him in a society that allows Antonio to torment him:

> He hath   disgraced me, and hindered me half a million;
> laughed at my losses, mocked at my gains, scorned my nation,
> thwarted my bargains, cooled my friends, heated my enemies;
> and what's his reason? I am a Jew (III, i, 56 - 61).

Such was the fate of most Jews in medieval Europe; prohibited by the state from supporting themselves by means of "honorable" professions, they often had pitiful few options aside from money-lending, for which they were reviled by nobility and peasantry alike. And while some sought escape through conversion like Jessica, most bore their burden like Shylock, bitterly, but at least with the recognition that their ancient heritage provided them with the inner strength and resolution to persevere and survive against overwhelming odds.

Some of this I had articulated as a student in Professor Levin's class. Yet the full force of the Jewish condition never penetrated deeper than the intellectual musings of a dilettante. Indeed, so ignorant had I been of my own culture that I wondered why Sir Lawrence Olivier, in his portrayal of Shylock, had given the doorpost a violent slap whenever he passed into or out from his house. I had never heard of a *mezuzah*, the parchment scroll inscribed with two paragraphs from Deuteronomy, which hangs encased upon every doorpost in the home of every observant Jew. Nor had I ever witnessed a Jew press his fingers lovingly against the *mezuzah* case when passing through a doorway and touch those fingers to his lips as a sign of respect and adoration. The brilliant subtlety of Olivier's Shylock, perverting reverence into impotent fury, passed me by as surely as if I had been an uninitiated gentile.

I never did make it to Botswana or Nepal although, like Jessica, I would once have readily opted out of my culture and forsaken my heritage in pursuit of some imagined better life. Of course, I could claim neither the religious nor the social oppression that make us sympathize with Jessica and her plight, but in this I was no different from so many other thousands of middle-class, college-educated Jewish American princes and princesses who afford scant notice to the ancient teachings of our people.

The Jews have long been called "People of the Book," and there may be no better explanation of our unnatural survival than the unbroken chain of scholarly tradition from generation to generation. But the chain in my family had broken three generations back, leaving my grandfather, my father, and finally myself to grow up in America with no knowledge of "The Book," with no appreciation for its wisdom and its legacy. Doubtless, I would never have strayed from the road of cultural ambivalence had not the long departed ghosts of Jerusalem come back to life to teach me the lessons of my people, lessons I had once studied but failed to learn.

Of course, I was only one of many American Jews for whom yeshiva was only one of many stops along the road to nowhere. Of those who dabbled in the ancient teachings, some capitulated before the mind-bending intricacies of talmudic reasoning, while others never looked beyond to appreciate the brilliant contemporary relevance of talmudic wisdom. So I've wondered, looking back across a quarter century, what made me heed this echo from the past when so many others continued on unchanged?

Twas the bard, of course. After Shakespeare had fanned the embers of erudition in the hidden caverns of my mind, it seems almost inevitable that the holy sparks of the Talmud would ignite them into a blaze. And who knows? If not for Professor Levin's felicitous instruction in Shakespearean analysis, if not for Mr. Byrd's uncompromising elucidation of Swiftian respect for the ancients, I might well have remained in the company of those poor souls destined to fade away into the same cultural oblivion as the bitter Shylock and his misguided Jessica.

James Stone Goodman
Jackie

I met Jackie in front of Schnucks one summer night, as I was tying my dog up to a pole.

Nice doggie, she said. She had a grocery cart with a couple of bags in it. I don't think she had any dogs with her the first time we met.

I love doggies, she said. I have two of them. Big dogs.

I also love doggies, I told her.

Where did you get this one?

Pet store. She was so ugly that no one wanted her. She is the sweetest dog.

She's not ugly, Jackie said, she's beautiful. I'm Jackie. I'm around here all the time, I'll see you again. Maybe next time I'll have my babies with me. Can I have your phone number?

Sure.

We would run into each other now and again over the years. In the next phase, we both had new dogs.

Where did you get this one? Jackie asked.

I found her on the street. She was a kind of rescue dog. She was a terrible dog for two years, then I gave up and one morning I said to her, all right, you win, the house is yours, I give up. I took you in and I am going to stick with you. You can do whatever the hell you want in my house and I'm not going to take you to doggie school anymore, I'm not going to tug on your collar, I'm not going to spank you or rub your nose in your doody. I'm not going to put a leash on you and walk you up and down the street, stopping and starting like storm troopers. I'm not going to yell at you when you chew up my carpet downstairs. I surrender.

Then what?

She became the greatest dog I've ever had. Within a couple of weeks, she stopped doing every stupid thing that had been driving me crazy. She just loved me, followed me around the house, and begged me to take her whenever I went out. I take her everywhere.

I love that story.

Do you still have those big dogs?

Little dogs now, Mickey and Minnie. They are Mexican hairless something or others, I got them from a friend in New Mexico. They're so sweet. Don't you love them? She kissed them.

Every now and again Jackie would call me. I would meet her at

Schnucks and we would have our dogs and sit down on a bench near Barnes and Noble and talk.

Sometimes we would talk on the phone. Jackie talked fast and talked a lot. She would tell you ten years of her life in a couple of paragraphs.

Here is one of the first conversations we had on the phone:

It happened on Wednesday, May 26, some time in the late 1980s.

Wednesday, May 26

We met in the early eighties, when she had just returned from New Mexico, studying shamanism, sitting Zen, tracking the wild weebee bird in the wildernesses of Mexico. Now she is taking care of aging parents ("he's just like a baby! I clean up after him everywhere!") with no money, no place of her own to live, a big dog and a grown daughter who (finally) is on her own feet. "I don't do anything anymore, I have no money, no friends, I can't pray anymore, I never meditate, I don't know why I called..."

The window is open in my third floor office, and just then the wind blows a paper off of my desk onto my lap. The paper is page two of a class I taught a couple of years ago. I pulled the file a few days ago to teach it again. I often recycle my computer paper, and this piece of paper has one address on the uppermost margin of the paper from a long-ago defunct mailing list, in addition to the text of the class which I had several years ago printed on this piece of old mailing list paper.

The name is Jackie, the woman on the phone, with her address, circa 1983. I tell her this. I also tell her what is written on the paper: instructions on prayer and meditation techniques from the great Rabbi Nachman of Bratzlav. Rabbi Nachman calls these techniques "conversations with God." If you cannot think of anything to say, instructed Rabbi Nachman, begin with a more structured meditation, like a mantra. I tell Jackie the mantra that Rabbi Nachman liked to use. At the bottom of the page is a quote from Rabbi Nachman, "when you bring your problems to God, they cease to exist." And then he quotes the Psalm, "Place your burdens on God, and God will carry (it for) you." (Ps. 55:23).

Jackie is crying as I tell her this, she thanks me and makes me promise that I will send her a copy of the page, with her name on it and the teachings of Rabbi Nachman, in the mail. I do.

I talked to Jackie periodically, sometimes visited with her, and then Jackie got sick.

After she got sick, she asked me to come visit her in the hospital.

I don't do those medicines, she told me. I am going to meditate and read this, read that, but I am not going to take those medicines.

She had surgery.

A lot of people thought Jackie was goofy, but she wasn't goofy. She was loving and open and giving and completely beautiful. You could not make a better friend than Jackie.

She ended up in some humiliating places, and she would not allow anyone to diminish her beauty. While almost completely incapacitated in one of the most humiliating places of all, she sent me on a mission. I was wearing a scarf that she liked. She liked the colors. Jackie was a collector of snatches of beauty, unfinished, the kinds of things she found in the street, in garbage bins, she carried them home and decorated her apartment with them.

Where did you get that scarf?
Some head shop on Delmar.
I like the colors. Can you get me some?
How many?
I want five or six of them. How much do they cost?
Why so many?
Presents.

So I went to the head shop with my cellular phone and described the different colors that the scarves came in. She picked out four of them over the phone.

The last time I visited her in her apartment, she gave me a piece of pottery that someone had thrown away. It was disfigured but had a beautiful blue luminous patina. That's why she brought it home. She had found a small setting to lay the disfigured piece of pottery into and it sat in a privileged place in her living room, where the sun would liberate its hidden beauty, not in form, but the delicate patina of luminescent blue.

She loved African violets and she had figured out how to grow them. She told me the secret of the African violet. She only grew plants with round leaves.

She also told me this: The one thing I can do is die well. Maybe I didn't live so well, but you watch, stay with me, I am going to die well, Jackie said.

And she did.

She died as well as anybody I have ever seen. I have been with many people around death, but no one did it with as much awareness, as much dignity, even joy, as did Jackie. She asked for those she wanted to be there to accompany her, and those she did not want there, she let them know it. That was the hard part for her, I don't want my space corrupted, she said to me, know what I mean?

After her death, we held a memorial service for her at her kid's house. A lot of people came. We talked about all the wonderful qualities that made Jackie extraordinary.

I spoke at Jackie's memorial and I told all the stories that I knew about her. There was not a person in the room who was not crying.

If there was anyone left who thought Jackie was goofy, at her memorial she was described as the heroic, sensitive, clever, beautiful, soft heart of the world that she was, who had the rare gift of bringing out the same in those who survive her.

This is the story of a *lamed vov-nik*, one of the thirty six, without whom the world would cease to exist. That is the nature of the *lamed vov-nik*, that they are agents for the expression of something that would remain hidden without their presence. They are agents for the revealing of that which is hidden. I remember this every time I stare into the luminous blue patina of the disfigured piece of pottery that is displayed in my living room. Jackie's presence continues to sustain the world, years after she left it.

Felicia Graber
The Old Woman

"The Old Woman," as I call the woodcarving that hangs in my dining room, is ugly. Nobody wants her. Nobody likes her but me. My husband dislikes her. I offered her to my children, but they refused to take her. "She is hideous and depressing," they both said, their feelings echoed by their respective spouses. But I like her, so I hung her in my dining room, opposite my chair, where I can see her almost daily.

Why do I like her? What attracts me to her, even though, I admit, she reminds me of an old witch?

She used to hang in my parents' living room in the 1950's in Frankfurt, Germany when I was growing up, and makes that area come alive for me. She reflected my father's tastes for exotic art, Russian and Asian antiques, and anything that was different, or out of the ordinary.

That living room served many functions simultaneously – music room where I practiced piano, bedroom where I slept on the sofa bed, den where our first television set took center stage, and sitting room where we entertained friends. But, for me, that area reverberates mostly with memories of our annual Passover Seder.

I remember as if it were happening today. The table is set with mother's best linen, china, and crystal. Our guests, all Holocaust survivors from Poland, are seated on each side of an elongated table. Mother is hurrying back and forth bringing in tureens and platters from the kitchen. And Father – Father sits at the head of the table leading all assembled in the ritual reciting of the *Hagadah*, the story of the liberation of the Hebrew slaves from Egyptian bondage. He recites whole passages in Hebrew without even glancing at the text; he still remembers it all by heart. He sings the traditional tunes to his heart's and his guests' delight and intersperses it all with stories from the "old days," from the days before 1939, from the days before the war, from a world that has disappeared –the world of Polish Jewry.

Even after all these years, I can still almost hear Father talking about **his** beloved father, a *chassid* (a member of a branch of Orthodox Judaism), who wore a *shtreimel* (a fur hat) and a silk *bekishe* (a long silk coat) on the Sabbath, and immersed himself in the *mikvah* (ritual bath) every morning. Father also delighted relating stories of how *Chassidim* tried to outdo each other in telling tall tales about what marvelous deeds their *Rebbe* (term for rabbi used in that community) was capable of performing. One favorite was the following.

"Several *Chassidim* were comparing their *Rebbes'* miracles. Each tale surpassing the other, one of them who was listening quietly, finally said, 'All your tales are nothing compared to the miracle performed by my *Rebbe*. He was walking one day and was confronted by a gigantic lion. The lion opened its huge jaws and was about to have my *Rebbe* for lunch. My *Rebbe* stuck his hand into the lion's mouth, reached for his tail, pulled the tail through the lion's mouth and turned him around so that he faced away from him.' The group was speechless, 'How is that possible?' One man asked. 'Well, you see, it happened,' was the proud reply."

Father also often expanded his narration recalling **his** parents' youth and Jewish life in a *shtetl* (a small town) before World War I.

"My grandparents had five children three girls and two boys. My grandfather worked in a brewery and my grandmother sold cloth at the market by the size of her forearm – that is how they used to measure in those days. At the age of ten, my father, Leib Israel, went to work as a toll collector. When farmers drove their horse-drawn wagons to the city to sell their produce, they were supposed to stop at tollbooths and pay a toll, which the government used for road repairs. As a ten-year-old boy, my father staffed one of those booths. His job was to collect the money. Often, however, the farmers tried to avoid paying, attempted to force their wagons through, and whipped him to scare him away."

Father also recalled the hassles Jewish boys endured growing up in a small Polish town, the fights by which he had to defend himself and the teachers' disparaging treatments. Instructors never addressed the Jewish students by name but referred to them as *Zydkowie* (Jew boy). His Jewish education took place in the in the *heder* (Jewish religious school), where he learned Hebrew prayers as well as the *Hagadah* he can still recite by heart. Above all, however, Father remembers the dire poverty of many Jews who had to borrow a few zlotys to buy bread for their family.

However, Father always included one of his many jokes, which illustrate the immense lore of Yiddish humor but also often poke fun at the Poles among whom Jews lived in uneasy relationships. The following was of Father's favorites, "A Jew and a Pole were riding on a train. The Pole asked the Jew, 'Tell me, how come you Jews are so smart?' The Jew answered: 'That is because we eat a lot of herring' 'Really?' came the reply. 'Would it also work for me?' 'Sure.' said the Jew, 'I happen to have some with me and can sell it to you for thirty zlotys.' 'Great,' answered the Pole. He took thirty zlotys, got his herring, and ate it. Some time went by, and suddenly the Pole said, 'Say, how come you charged me thirty zlotys for a piece of herring when I can get it on the market place for ten?' 'You see,' answered the Jew, 'It is already working.'"

Almost all Jews in town led a strictly Orthodox Jewish life style. Several days prior to Rosh Hashanah (the Jewish New Year), when Jews recite special prayers at dawn, the synagogue's sexton would go around town in the Jewish neighborhood, ringing a bell and shouting, 'Jews, wake up, it is time to go to *shul* (synagogue) to say *selichos* (the penitential prayers).'

Yes, the old woman heard many stories during those post-war-years, humorous ones, as well as tragic ones of spouses and children murdered. She witnessed both celebrations and sad good-byes as friends moved on to the United States, to Argentina, or to Brazil when their visas arrived.

And, for the last twenty years, she witnessed the rebirth of Jewish traditions in our home here in St. Louis. She saw many Passover Seders, led by my husband, and attended by our children and grandchildren, and the lighting of Chanukah candles. She heard joyous songs on Chanukah and Purim, numerous hymns and prayers during festive Holyday observances, as well as dozens of happy birthday songs, during group birthdays celebrations whenever the whole family was in town.

I hope that someday one of my children or grandchildren will adopt her so that she can continue to witness the unbroken chain of Jewish survival despite Hitler's attempt to annihilate us.

Rita Horwitz
Childhood Memories of the World War II Years

I was born in 1933 during the Great Depression. We were poor. As children, we were not aware of this because everyone was poor. Though there was not much money, my father brought home a newspaper every day and sent his three girls to Hebrew School (*Cheder*).

Entertainment, that I remember, was a trip to the library once a week, movies on Sunday or an outing to Forest Park to the zoo and art museum where we would run to see the mummy's toe. Always Jefferson Memorial and the Pavilion so my father could visit with his friends and take pictures. We traveled by streetcar. Some people had a car. A machine as my father called it. When we were a little older, my mother packed a picnic lunch and we were off to a cruise on *The Admiral,* an excursion boat that cruised the Mississippi River. My sisters and I stayed on the dance floor most of the time. It was comfortable and the only floor that was air-conditioned, that I remember.

Everyone walked from the streetcar on the cobblestone streets to the boat. The most delicious aroma from Switzer's Licorice Factory filled the air and my memory forever.

Airplanes were a marvel to my friends and me. We would run outside and watch this wonder of the world. We had no telephones, TV or air-conditioning. The radio brought us together as we sat around listening. My father always listened to the news with Gabriel Heater.

I was eight years old in1941. December 7th, I was unaware of the news. December 8th, I was in the kitchen dancing with my four-year-old sister. My mother was holding our one year old sister. My father came in with tears in his eyes and told my mother we were at war. My sister Phyllis and I were dancing and singing, "What is war, what is war."

Our secure little world was about to change.

Everyone participated on the "homefront." At school we bought Savings Bonds and Saving Stamps. I could buy two ten cent stamps each week. I was so excited knowing that when I had enough stamps, they could be exchanged for a bond. Not too vivid now, but I don't think I got my bond till the war was over.

I doubt if I had tasted a Hershey Bar, but I knew there was none to buy. At my young age, I remember saying, "Hershey Bars are for our boys who are fighting for us." After I was a little older, I helped collect scrap metal and paper.

At school we learned all the songs for each of the "armed forces" and patriotic songs. I can still remember the words. We had a little newspaper at school, *My Weekly Reader*. I don't remember if much was written about the war. We learned to crochet in grade school and crocheted squares to be crocheted together for an afghan, of course, for our boys.

"Loose Lips Sink Ships." My friends and I were aware of this and whispered if we thought something was important. Not much to do during an Air-Raid Practice (Blackout, I watched the stars for a while and then went to bed.

My friend Pauline and I were always planning trips. We walked most of the time or once in a while took a streetcar. During these years, all of us would tell our parents we were going for a walk or something and they would say "OK, be back in time for supper."

Pauline heard that Carmen Miranda was sick at Barnes Hospital and we decided to visit her. I don't remember why but we didn't get there. One day, I think we were about 11 years old. We walked to DePaul Hospital and told the nuns we were 16 years old and wanted to work as Nurses Aides. I knew they were trying to keep from laughing but they told us they didn't need help at this time but to come back again.

I know my parents were concerned about ration stamps. The only time I remember it affecting me was when I needed a pair of gym shoes. They took it from my little sister Barbara's allotment.

Everyone participated in some way in the war. The rationing was difficult for the families but they got through it. Many people had victory gardens and grew their own vegetables.

Anti-Semitism was rampant. My mother told me For Rent signs said. "No dogs and No Jews." I can't remember anti-Semitism at my grade school. We were a melting pot. We played together, sang together, belonged to a conservation club and tried to take each other's holidays off. But in some neighborhoods, usually by the Hebrew Schools, older anti-Semitic boys would torment us, call us names and throw rocks.

Some Friday's after school, I would take chicken, soup, compote and more to my grandpa when he wanted to stay home. My friend Natalie would help me. Grandpa's house was close, but at times the anti-Semitic boys were around to torment us. Natalie and I decided to take a short cut by a house and then walk down the steps. Natalie dropped the compote. The rest of the day is sketchy. One boy fell down the steps. I think he slipped on the compote. His nose was bleeding. I bent down to get my pot and both boys were crying loudly. Grandpa's food was OK except no compote.

No one ever said anything to Natalie or me. Actually, we did nothing. Probably the boys thought it best not to say they were pushed or beat up by two little Jewish girls.

Everyone loved the war movies. They were romantic and we saw how other families were coping with the war. Before the movie, a newsreel was shown about the war. Usually we saw two movies, the news and a cartoon and then stayed and saw it all again. The movie musicals served as a relief from worry for a short time.

The entire nation participated in the war effort. We as children played, sang patriotic songs, laughed, crocheted, danced, joined the Brownies and did a lot of walking.

Sometimes at night, this little girl would think about little girls my age in the war. I would ask my mother, "How far away is Hitler?" Alone with my thoughts, this little girl was scared.

Sharon Katz-Weintraub
An Eternal Flame

An alabaster-like candle flickers rhythmically, like the ebb and flow of life, and silently brings back cherished memories. The flame casts a reflection on the surrounding glass and upon a pool of melted wax. The glass encircles the wax in a warm embrace, reminding me of his loving hugs. For this is no ordinary candle, nor is today just any day. I traditionally light this *Yahrzeit* candle in memory of my father, on the 12th anniversary of his death. As I watch the candle's flame, I am reminded of his strength of character, perseverance against all odds and unconditional love of family. I can feel the lasting bond of love between father and daughter. So I take a seat among the shadows of this eternal flame and bask in the glow of his memory.

Around the Corner

This scene, like a movie frame, is etched forever in my memory. My mom predictably appears from around the corner adjacent to her front door. She stands, 4 feet, 8 inches tall, with tinted reddish brown, thinning hair, a few wrinkles framing her dark brown eyes and rosy round cheeks. She is wearing a red, short-sleeved, knit top snugly pulled over black, polyester slacks. White ribbed socks and slightly worn, brown Dr. Scholl's oxfords complete her outfit. She stares down the hallway, expressionless, waiting for me to approach.

Before my 90 year old mom died last year, I visited her at least twice a week, sometimes just stopping by to chat, change a light bulb or to check if a form letter she had received was "kosher." Weeks before *erev* Rosh Hashana or the Passover seder, we'd engage in lengthy discussions about who would make which dish, including *gefilte* fish, kugel, turkey, brisket, fruit compote and matzah ball soup. She always made the same things and so did I. It was tradition.

Today my mom's condo was sold, and so I decided to walk down her hallway for the very last time. Even though I knew she wouldn't be turning the corner, standing and waiting for me, I could still see her there. I followed her into the living room and imagined us sitting down at the far corner of the dining room table. I touched the soft, beige, lace tablecloth lying atop its matching plastic cover.

"You want some *kmish* bread? I still have a few pieces," she asked.

"Sure," I replied. "Nothing to drink."

We picked up our conversation from the last time we'd spoken, she asking me about my job and her grandsons, who affectionately called her Nana. Finally, I stood up and slowly walked toward the door. I stopped and gave her a tight hug goodbye. "Talk to you later," I said.

After a few moments, I gathered up my cherished memories and gently tucked them back into the corners of my mind. I stepped haltingly over the threshold and refocused my attention. Then I walked from room to room, packing up the few remaining items - a rug, a broom, a lamp and some cleaning supplies. I envisioned everything as it had been, trying not to acknowledge the current staged décor of modern furnishings and flowered wall paintings. Instead, a history of family photos embraced each wall, testimony to a life well lived, a life full of loved ones past and present.

Returning to the living room, I walked toward the front door and slowly turned the knob. Pausing, I reached my hand up for the first and last time and kissed the mezuzah which had blessed this Jewish home.

"Goodbye. I love you," I whispered. Then I turned the corner and walked back down the hallway as a warm, fine mist filled my eyes.

Cissy Lacks
From **Miriam's Way**
(a story about nature and about humankind)

Miriam's Way is based upon the experiences of Miriam Kenisberg from 1941 through 1946 as told by Cissy Lacks.

In September of 1941, German armies marched through eastern Poland into Russia, and a Polish Jew, Miriam Kornitsky, only thirteen years old, was sent by her parents into the dark forests of White Russia to hide from the invaders. This book is not about the events of World War II; Miriam did not know the history that forced her parents to send their child into the forest and isolate her from them and her brothers. This book is about a young girl's will to survive, and her ability to live with loneliness and the constant threat of death. Miriam's father taught her that the forest could protect her. Few people who escaped to the forests survived until the end of the War. Young Miriam Kornitsky (the character based upon Miriam Kenisberg) was one of them.

*(***Excerpt is Chapter 4***: Miriam cannot face another harsh winter in the forest by herself. Overcoming her fear of being caught, she wanders into a village.)*

After a winter in the forest, Miriam was like the wolves that stayed alive but were reduced to near skeletons.

Their eyes and bones seemed to be the only parts of them that didn't shrink. They no longer traveled in packs because the competition for food made them dangerous even to each other. When Miriam saw a lone wolf, his skin hanging loose across his side ribs and his eyes bulging from their sockets, she thought about herself. She didn't know what she looked like, but she recognized herself in the desperation of the wolf.

The second winter she refused to confront the wolves, deciding instead to make her way into one of the villages. Her clothes were no more than rags; in preparation for the journey, she searched to find some in better condition. Until now, Miriam took little from dead bodies in the forest. Now, she must take more.

Miriam wrapped herself in an orange scarf of soft wool and a long brown coat, which she tore at the bottom so it wouldn't drag. The scarf came from the body of a young girl, not much older than Miriam, who had frozen to death huddled against a big tree, as if she thought the tree would give her warmth. Miriam wondered why the girl didn't know that trees take warmth for themselves. Only snow gives warmth back.

The coat came from the body of a woman lying close to the girl. Miriam thought they might have been mother and daughter, but then she wondered why only the woman's body was covered. She thought a mother would have shared the coat. Miriam thought of her mother giving her the coat when she sent Miriam into the forest, the coat left on the cart after Lisper died.

Miriam's fingers searched for a place on this newly found coat to put her parent's wedding ring, the ring she tore from her mother's coat lining before she and Sonia abandoned the cart and most of their possessions. It was hard to find a hiding place on a coat with no hem and with holes where pockets should be. "Papa, she didn't know to move her fingers in the cold. She pushed them deep into her coat pockets until she wore away the lining. Where shall I keep the ring, papa?" For the time being, she wrapped it in a piece of hem she tore from the coat and put the small package in her pant's pocket.

Miriam wore the coat and scarf in the hope that villagers would think she was no more than a runaway. The coat hid what was underneath, a thick yellow cotton blouse and boy's short red knee pants. Her feet were bound with thin tree bark softened with a lining of brown oak leaves, moist and pliable in the forest even in the winter. Miriam took clothes off the dead in the forest but she didn't remove shoes. She slipped clothes off bodies but taking shoes meant holding onto someone's foot while she pulled off the shoe. She couldn't wear shoes she took from a dead person.

The snow was heavy this winter. As Miriam walked, it came up over her shoes and pressed coldly against her calves. Walking through snow, instead of on top of it, was not a good idea, but she didn't have the patience to build snowshoes. She plodded through a small field, hoping to find a village close by where she could stay until spring.

When she finally saw a larger clearing, it turned out to be fields and more fields of snow. Grayish white clouds hung in oblong patterns from the blue and gray toned sky over this white floor. The open fields would be her path, even though she knew similar fields were the death walk for Lisper and Sonia. She could not return to the forest where only the starving wolves were waiting for her.

Miriam didn't understand the weather and its connection to the war, anymore than she understood the war itself. If the weather was pleasant, the forest was good to her and food was everywhere. If it rained too much, fruits rotted, and if it was too cold, plants died.

She wished for pleasant, dry weather while everyone else in Poland was grateful for heavy rain in the spring and harsh cold in the winter. If the usual rains had come in the spring when the Germans invaded Poland, the forests would have flooded and the marshes would have been impossible to pass with troops. The mild weather, which made it tolerable for her the first months in the forest, condemned Poland to a pathetic defeat by the German army.

Miriam didn't know she had little to fear in crossing these snow packed fields. Harsh weather stopped German reconnaissance, and the threat of more snow, suspended in the hanging clouds, was almost a guarantee that German soldiers wouldn't make a surprise appearance.

When she walked through the fields, the snow reached her knees and soaked through her ragged coat, hanging on like it would to a tree branch. Snow seeped through her braided, bark shoes and stuck between the leaves that coated her feet from the bark. Instead of soft protection, these leaves were becoming a menace. Taking away the leaves meant dealing with cuts and bruises from bark rubbing against her feet, but the wet and snow covered leaves were too heavy and now, she could barely drag herself forward.

Slipping out of one shoe and bending over to unwrap the leave binding, she lost her balance and fell face first into the snow. She didn't have the power to get up and when she moved, she sank further into the snow. She thrashed her hands and feet, splattering snow everywhere. She started to yell, "Papa, Papa!" but snow filled the inside of her mouth and when she tried to spit it out, more packed itself in. Her teeth and gums were like one ice mass that would crack with the slightest touch.

Just as the cold exploded in her head, she heard echoes of "Don't panic, Miriam. Don't panic." Her father was talking to her and she heard him. Her body relaxed. First, her legs bent slowly at the knees and shifted her body forward. Then her waist, chest and shoulders pulled upwards and finally, her neck and head lifted slowly. A twist of her neck sent snow off her head but she had to pull the snow out of her mouth, wiping her fingers against her gums to get rid of the cold moisture sticking to her tongue and mouth lining.

She unwrapped the orange scarf, removed the coat and jumped up and down, slapping her hands against her body. She reached around as far as she could to hit her back and shoulders, but her arms weren't long enough to do much good. Her father had always rubbed her back for her and she wanted him now.

"Papa, I'm doing as you said," she whispered, waiting for a warm hand across her back. When it didn't come, she rubbed her coat with the scarf, shook out the scarf, put both back on and continued across the field. She walked for hours and was so much into the habit of expecting no view that she was past two farmhouses before she realized she was entering a village.

She walked toward buildings, more than she saw together anywhere in a small town. If she hadn't been so determined to leave the forest, she would have feared the numbers. Now she looked forward to mixing, perhaps unnoticed, in the center of this village.

The overcast sky was a weather forecast. Already, snow started to fall lightly but anyone who watched the clouds knew another storm was close by. Townspeople were lined up in front of the stores. Miriam didn't know it but most villagers had used up their winter supplies, and this new bout with the weather was unexpected. People were anxious to buy whatever food they could with the little money they had.

Shoppers were talking to each other about how happy they were that winter kept the Germans away. Those closest to shop windows were examining the products inside. Miriam stopped to look with them.

At the butcher shop, she saw chopped beef shaped into large molds, chickens and smoked pork swinging from the window top, stew-meat soaked in onions and garlic piled high on top of each other, and herring marinated or creamed in barrels along the window.

She didn't move from the window, and the conversations, repeated with each new group that passed by, were meaningless to her. Two women complained to each other.

"We won't have any meat at all soon."

"Look, there's hardly any in the window and it's only late morning. The butcher says they take more meat than they let him sell. If his prices are high, he doesn't want the blame. Each week, he says he doesn't know if he'll be in business the next."

"He's been coming to the farms, hoping to butcher directly for the farmers, but they found out about it and are asking for supplies from the farmers as well."

"I buy what I can and hope it will last."

Miriam didn't know Nazi soldiers took food from the merchants. Nor did she know that local collaborators told on people who tried to hide any of their merchandise.

Miriam turned to look at the women, trying to discover how such misery could come from so much food. The women looked full, maybe even fat, although she couldn't tell because their bodies were covered in thick, black fur coats. Their matching fur hats covered everything but their round faces, and their boots came up well under their coats.

The boots tempted Miriam to look away from the trays of meat. Her feet were cut everywhere and only the cold was keeping them from bleeding. It was hard to decide what she wanted more, their boots or the food. At least the food was possible. She wanted to go in and grab a piece, at least of the herring, and swallow it before they caught her. But the idea of taking anything from the store scared her. She heard they cut off people's fingers for stealing. In the forest, she tried not to steal but sometimes her survival depended upon it. If she were to make a new life outside the forest, no one would have taught her what to do. Perhaps she would have to steal. But if she had no fingers, she couldn't take a thing.

She wandered up and down the street, stopping at each window displaying food. The bakery window showed loaves of dark pumpernickel, rye crusted with corn meal, and puffed white egg bread all in twists like the challah she had at home on Friday nights. Although the window was piled high, she saw that inside the shelves were empty. This bakery had no pastry, no rolled dough filled with prunes and raisins, the smell of which could change freezing winter air into a warm, Shabbat, Friday night, kitchen.

The grocery store wasn't made for window-shopping. Windows were small, and the line of people waiting to get in was so big that it covered the view. Woman after woman held empty sacks crocheted of twine and meant to expand to many times their unfilled size.

Miriam stood across the way from the line, watching people leave the store. Sacks were still limp as people left. She imagined herself packing such a bag so full that the twine would make ridges against the food, food to last more than one winter in the forest.

As she imagined herself with such a package, she made her way into the line toward the small market, her hand limp at her side but her fingers clutching at imaginary thick rope handles of a bag.

She continued forward as the line moved, always holding her hand down, as if raising it would somehow allow the bag to disappear. A woman behind her brought her son and daughter into town but they were getting bored with the long wait. They poked and pulled at each other but they were bored with that too now. Then they saw Miriam. At first, the girl made faces at her. But making faces wasn't enough for the boy. He started pulling at her scarf and stepping on her feet. When Miriam didn't respond, the boy, no more than ten, shouted, "Mother, it's a girl animal in front of us." Then, he grabbed Miriam's orange scarf and pulled it off.

Miriam yanked up her hand, clutching both arms tightly to her chest to protect the bag she was sure he was going to take from her. The mother must have thought Miriam was going to hit her son because she stepped in between the two. But when she looked down, all she saw was a frightened girl grabbing on to a torn brown coat. Miriam's eyes were darting everywhere at once. Her hair was sticking out in all directions, almost as if it was frozen that way. Her bark shoes, now dried out, had warped on her feet.

The woman's hand rested on Miriam's shoulder, maybe as an apology for her son or maybe as a warning for Miriam not to do anything to retaliate. While the woman's hand was on Miriam's shoulder, Miriam leaned in her direction.

"Mama, Mama, she's a crazy one," the boy shouted. Then he danced around Miriam, hopping and jumping to his own chants. The woman ignored her son and Miriam. He stopped teasing when he realized Miriam would not respond and began to fight again with his sister.

The line moved forward and Miriam followed as if being pulled slowly and methodically by a long rope. At the door, she stopped and the woman, as if she expected it, moved around her. Miriam stayed at the front door, close enough to smell the onions and garlic hanging from the ceiling on long ropes. Even the flour had a special odor and its powder, invisible before, now filled the store with a white cloud so thick she was sure she could bite into it if only she could get into the store.

She was in the same spot when the woman and her two children left the store. The boy was carrying a bag, the weight of which he easily managed with one hand, while he slapped at Miriam's orange scarf with the other. "Look, the crazy one is still here."

Then the girl noticed Miriam or at least she watched her brother go after the scarf as a boy would pull at a dog's tail for no reason other than it was there. For perhaps no more reason than her brother, she said to her mother. "Let's take her with us," as if she wanted a stray dog to have a home.

The mother bent over Miriam – examining her hair, her eyes, her coat and even her bark shoes. Miriam stood still, head down, but her hands clutched ever harder at the bag against her chest. The woman straightened up.

"You can come with us," she said.

She reached for Miriam's hand and her daughter reached for the other one. Miriam's eyes darted down, watching for the bag to fall to the ground. Nothing happened. She was pulled along the road and she didn't fight, not even when the boy slapped at her.

Llama lo arba?

In the US, I am a garage sale junkie, always looking for the hidden gem in a pile of junk.

I am a photographer, too, always looking for the picture that tells a thousand stories.

Often times, the two searches go together.

When I'm in Israel, though, the game changes. Israel doesn't have garage sales.

But one city in Israel has something I can't find in the US. Haifa – the Haifa at the bottom of the Carmel, the part of the port city without a view – has the *Shuk Pish Pe Shim*. Literal translation: the street market of the bugs.

Some might say another translation is flea market, not such a negative connotation, but it's nothing like a flea market. It is stall after stall of bent aluminum pots and pans, broken bicycle parts, metal scraps from objects unknown, piles of *schmattas,* and a good layer of Middle East dust covering most everything.

Surprisingly, one thing it doesn't have is beggars. And I'm glad of that because I don't like to pay subjects for taking their pictures, and I take a lot of pictures at the *Shuk Pish Pe Shim*.

Another thing it doesn't seem to have is happy people. They appear as worn out as the items they're selling.

One person, though, and the picture I took of her, changed my view.

She was a round-shaped woman who greeted visitors with an infectious albeit two tooth smile. And she was a woman of texture. In the hot summer and sun of Israel, she wore a herringbone tweed coat over a flower patterned long skirt, plaid flannel house slippers and a layer of three *tichels* or *mitpachot* (scarves) covering her head.

I had to take pictures of her.

She let me click away on my camera, picture after picture.

I decided to break my rule. "*Bevachasha, hena shekel achad beschvel lach.*" (Please, here's a shekel for you.) At the time, it was about 50 cents. (I'm embarrassed to admit it could have been a quarter.)

I don't know if I expected *toda reba*, (thank you), but without a second's hesitation, she laughed and asked, "*Llama lo arba?*" (Why not four?)

And I laughed too. "*Lama lo?*" (Why not?) and I handed over three more shekels.

Now, I'm sorry I didn't give her 25 so she would have seen that I learned my lesson.

Morton Levy
The Saturday Debating Society

As a pre-teen I was usually home alone with my grandparents on Saturdays. After breakfast I would park myself on the floor in front of our 10 inch black and white Zenith TV while Grandma Bessie and Grandpa Louis sat on the couch and began their weekly ritual.

Bethsheba (later Americanized to Bessie) had been born and raised on a *shtetl* outside of Kiev in that part of Greater Russia known as the Pale of Settlement. She was educated in the ways to make a "good Jewish home," but had no formal education. Illiterate in 1882 when she came to America, she remained so throughout her life. An aunt, Mima Esther, who had come into some money, brought Bessie and her siblings to America, but only after they had toured many of the capitals of Europe. After arriving in Dublin they boarded a ship traveling in a stateroom to New York.

Louis was also raised in the Pale of Settlement, but was from Lodz, Poland. He had received both a religious and secular education, but due to the restrictions placed upon Jews by the Tsar, his formal education was limited. He was trained to be a tailor like his father. At the time of the family emigration Eliezer, or Lazer as he was known then, was a teenager who had fallen in love for the first time. He left the girl behind with a promise to see her again. Throughout his life he avidly studied the works of the great philosophers, had been active in labor causes and had been a Socialist Party supporter, voting for Eugene Debs for President even when the latter was in prison. Like most immigrants he came to New York steerage.

In 1891 Bessie and Louis were joined in an arranged marriage

On Saturdays Grandpa would sit down with Grandma on the couch and open up his most recent copy of *The Daily Forward*. This Yiddish language newspaper that is still published in New York was a major part of the lives of the Eastern European Jews who came to America between 1880 and 1920. He would read the paper to her and eventually they would come to the section called the Bintel Briefs (Bundle of Letters).

The Bintel Briefs were letters to the editor seeking advice on how to deal with the problems the new Americans were having in adjusting to their life in a land totally different from the one they had left behind. Following the letters were the editor's recommendations. Ann Landers admits that the Bintel Briefs were the inspiration for her column.

Louis' readings of the letters and recommendations were followed by heated debates about the correctness of the editor's comments, which Bessie usually won. The following scenario is an example of one of these Saturday debates.

"Dear distinguished editor," Louis began to read, "I have been in this country for six years. When I left Minsk I had a wife and two children. I said I would make enough money in no time and send for them, but times have not been good. In the rooming house where I live we eat together every night. A young woman, whose name I won't mention out of respect, lives there and helps the owner prepare meals. She is very attractive and a wonderful cook. She could have any man around, but has taken up with me. We want to get married and start a family, but I do not know what to do about what I left behind in the old country. Should I bother with a divorce or just assume that none of that is binding in this new world?"   Signed; Unsure

Bessie interjected, "What a *momser*! What did the Editor say?"

Grandpa went on, "Dear Unsure: You have no one to blame but yourself for this dilemma. If you had been honest with your wife in Europe, when you went looking for someone in America, your current romance could flourish, and you could marry again. Now however, you have doubly betrayed your wife, and also been unfair to your boarding-house love. Explain your situation to both women and ask your wife to obtain a divorce, even if you must send her a cash settlement. If the woman you now love cares for you enough, she will wait until you are free to pursue a life with her."

Grandma once again spoke her mind, "He could rot in hell before I'd divorce him."

"No matter," Grandpa added, "I think he should forget about the old country and marry the girl in New York soon. The old capitalistic European ideas should be ignored."

"Don't you think he did something terrible?"

"Terrible no, stupid yes, and now he can only make it worse by following the

Editor's advice."

Then, as was often the case, the discussion got personal.

"You and your socialist ideas. What good have they done except keep us from becoming rich. You should have gone back when the communists took over," Bessie began.

"I might have if they hadn't murdered Trotsky, the Stalinist bastards."

"Back to that *nafga* you left behind."

"I stayed didn't I, and married you. I followed exactly what I just said the man in the *Forward* should do."

Then Bessie launched her weekly coupe d'gras, "Vot do you know."

"What do you mean 'Vot do I know.'"

"You know vhat I mean. Vot do you know?" she repeated.

"You say that all the time. It means nothing to me." he fought back.

"It means, vot could you know better than me. You came to this country steerage. I came foist class."

Grandpa shrugged his shoulders, lowered his gaze and complained of a headache as he climbed up to the sanctuary of his bedroom. I turned up the sound on the TV having learned that while you can win some arguments with logic others can result in a favorable outcome by the absence of it.

Bobbi Linkemer
Unconditional Love

In 1987 a new Stephen Sondheim play opened on Broadway, and I wanted to see it. This was not an idle whim; it was an obsession. It was also highly unlikely that it would ever happen. I couldn't really afford to go or to stay in a hotel. I had used all my vacation time. My company wouldn't pay for me to join a professional association let alone to send me to New York. Talk about dreaming the impossible dream. Yet, in October of that year, I watched the curtain rise on *Into the Woods* from what was surely the best seat in the house. What followed was magical.

Into the Woods is a morality play about fairy tale characters who all inhabit the same story. Their lives intersect as they seek the one thing they think will make them happy—a handsome prince, boundless treasure, adventure, freedom, lost beauty, and a baby. And when they get what they yearn for, they live happily ever after. And that's the end of Act I.

How could a 50-year-old woman be obsessed with seeing a bunch of make-believe characters, including a frustrated witch, two womanizing princes, and a cowardly baker, sing and dance their hearts out for hours? And what does this have to do with my father? Well, that's the real story.

Stephen Sondheim didn't know my father, but he captured his essence when it came to make-believe. My father was a gentle man with a beautiful, deep voice and a vivid imagination. He thought it quite natural to have characters show up in each other's stories, where some of my friends insisted they didn't belong. The original versions paled in comparison to his.

Into the Woods opened the same year my father died. The play was, in my mind, a kind of memorial. They say people we love hang around a while after they die just to be sure we are OK. He surely did, at least until I saw that play. In a theater full of people, I watched it alone, except for the very real presence of my father, who stayed just long enough to watch it with me. My father never considered himself a successful man, and that always puzzled me.

Perhaps he felt he should have made more money, but I can't imagine what he could have provided that we didn't already have. He always had a generosity of spirit and of self that I have found in no other human being. His whole life gave testimony to the philosophy that the more love you give away, the more you have to give. And give it he did—consistently, constantly, endlessly.

Most of all, he gave it to my mother, for fifty years, in small ways and, occasionally, with extravagant gestures. No woman, I think, has ever been more loved by a man than she. He gave it to my sister and me and then to our daughters, three more additions to what we always called "Frank's harem." But, he gave it, as well, to everyone he met on his journey through life—to his parents and brothers and sisters; to those he worked with on the Long Island Railroad; to friends and to total strangers; and to every child he ever met who wanted to sit on his lap and hear his wonderful, slightly rearranged fairy tales.

I could list the things he did, his accomplishments, the specific acts of kindness I remember or others told me about. But, in truth, I would prefer to gather and share my own special memories of this man, who held my hand as we walked through the park and swept me into a magic world of imagination with his wondrous stories and fanciful pipe dreams.

The things I remember may seem inconsequential—not the stuff of which a man's life can be defined. But, they are significant to me and help, somehow, to explain what made my father so special.

He could fix anything with his wonderful hands, no matter how mangled or hopeless the damage might seem. He could take himself and any child who wanted to accompany him into a world of fairies and princesses and wonder. He was a marvelous dancer, effortless and smooth, somehow trapping the music in his every movement and transmitting it to his partner. He was a helper, always rushing to do something for my mother or for us. He woke me in the morning with a hot cup of coffee; he was always first to do the unpleasant chores he wanted to spare us; but he is best remembered, I think, for removing the saucers from beneath our cups so he could beat all of us to cleaning off the dinner table.

He was a collector—of everything—especially memories. His dresser drawers and closets bulged with wonderful things he had saved for his children and grandchildren, and his mind was equally full of recalled treasures from the past. He loved history and baseball and things made of wood, but most of all, he loved the railroad. All his life, no matter how far from trains he may have strayed, Frank Levay was a railroad man.

I grew up on the railroad, riding back and forth between New York and Chicago. I slept in upper and lower births, in tiny compartments, and in spacious bedrooms. I ate meals in dining cars with white tablecloths and heavy silver coffee pots. I was watched over by tall, dignified porters who had promised to keep and eye on me during the trip. This was my father's world, and so it was mine.

I was an only child for the first eight-and-a-half years of my life and spent much of that time with him. My memories are like slides flashing on a screen: flying through the air on a swing until all I could see were thick green leaves dotted with patches of blue ... watching beautiful ladies, whom my father called debutants, sweeping though fancy hotel lobbies ... eating chicken chow mien in New York's China Town ... walking on top of a wall made of rocks and holding tight to his hand ... and riding with the engineer in the cab of a brand new diesel engine.

We built a life together during my early years, and we rediscovered each other when I was a grown woman who reached out to my father and found that he was reaching out to me. He went blind, very suddenly, in his seventies, and never really adjusted to the loss of his sight. He was seventy-nine when he died, leaving an unfillable void for the six of us who loved him.

All my life, he gave me one priceless gift—unconditional love. No strings, no living up to expectations, just being me was all I had to do to receive it. Few parents have the wisdom and strength to give that to their children. My father had both.

Liz Lippa
My Jewish Identity

How did I become aware that I was Jewish? As a very young child, I remember my mother and I saying the *Sh'ma* together every night before I went to sleep. I didn't know what it meant, but I knew it was a Jewish Prayer. On certain Jewish Holidays, our house came alive with a special meal that the entire household ate together, and we said some Jewish prayers, and chanted some songs in Hebrew.

I knew I was not living in the country where I was born and we spoke a language at home that was different from what other people around us were speaking. We were living in Montevideo, Uruguay as refugees from the Holocaust. My Viennese family could no longer live in our homeland if we were to survive. As I grew older, maybe four or five years old, I began to understand that, at one time, I had grandparents and relatives who lived in other countries. Some were trapped in Vienna and sent to concentration camps where they were killed. All this was happening to us because we were Jewish. Hitler wanted to kill us all because we were Jewish. How does a five year old understand this?

In the streets of Montevideo, we were sometimes called "Russos" in a tone that I knew was not complimentary. I did not know what the word meant, but I knew it was not a good thing to be. My parents had no friends in the community, even though they owned the neighborhood grocery store. When my brother and I started going to school, we never made friends with any of the other kids. We lived in our own small family world, and somehow I knew that had something to do with being Jewish.

We never went to a synagogue, and I believed there were none to go to in Montevideo. If there were other Jews there, I never came into contact with them. I knew a Polish Jew had helped my father learn how to open a business there, but we never visited with him or his family. I was not unhappy about all of this. It was just the only life I knew at the time.

When I was almost nine years old, and World War II was over, my mother's brothers were able to bring us to the United States to Richmond, Virginia. I was enrolled in Hebrew school and Sunday school. It felt good to finally be surrounded by other people who were, like us, Jewish. I also loved going to Temple services and learning the songs and prayers and looking at the Hebrew letters. My parents rarely went with me. They were busy, working in the family delicatessen restaurant. Friday nights and

Saturdays were their busiest times.

On the major Jewish holidays we still had the big family dinners with Hebrew prayers. In the United States, the only friends my family had were other "newcomers" who had somehow survived the Holocaust and found their way to Richmond. The Jews native to Richmond loved to come to our Deli, but they had no intention of making friends with the "immigrants." The Jewish kids in my temple rarely invited me to their parties, since their parents did not know my parents. We were just "the folks from the New York Delicatessen." Few people in Richmond even knew our names. As a teenager, I joined the B'nai Brith Girls and the Jewish sororities "pledged" me as a member. I worked hard to earn a place in this community, but I always felt like I was on the periphery of it. When I was in the Jewish homes in Richmond, I was introduced as the girl from the New York Deli.

In school, we were on our own to figure out how catch up to our American classmates. There was no special assistance in learning English or adapting to our new environment. My brother fought with the boys, and I tried to be likeable and accepted. Our parents could not help us with our schoolwork, so our grades were just passable. Mostly, we tried to stay quiet about being Jewish. We said The Lord's Prayer every morning with our class and we sang the Christmas carols in December. Chanukah was never mentioned in the school, although we did light the menorah at home. On Christmas morning, we got a few presents so that we would not feel left out of the holiday. My mother thought that it was the American thing to do.

As the years passed, I learned more about what happened to the Jews in Europe during the war. I was told that my grandparents and other family members were killed in Auschwitz. The problems of my pre-teen and teen-age years were nothing compared to what "real problems" were. I was told over and over how lucky we were to be alive. My job was not to make any trouble for my mother....she had enough tragedy in her life.

I never discussed my background with any of my friends. I assumed that they all knew my history, but it was never spoken about. I knew I was different and I would never really belong to the community, but I learned to fit in and even became a leader in some of the youth groups. When I went to my 50th high school reunion, I discovered that the kids I grew up with knew nothing about my family's Holocaust history. This came as a shock to me.

At age eighteen, I married a Jewish boy from Chicago. We met at a Jewish Community Center picnic for the Jewish Servicemen stationed at Fort Lee, Virginia. After a very small wedding, we moved in with his parents, who lived in a predominantly Jewish neighborhood in Chicago. There were kosher butchers and synagogues, and Jewish bookstores. I loved it, but soon found out that my husband's family was not really practicing Judaism at all. On our first Passover together, my mother-in-law made a ham! Hams were on sale for Easter, you see. All my in-law's friends were Jewish. And they would have been devastated if their son had married a non-Jewish girl. It was a strange mix for me.

I had six children in the next ten years, and brought them all up to be Jewish, although we never went to Temple services. When they became school age, I begged to join a Temple so the older children could go to Sunday School. My husband reluctantly agreed to do so, but he never attended services with us. Even so, most of my children had either a Bar or Bat Mitzvah, and they considered themselves Jews. They may have been aware of my European background, but the Holocaust was not discussed in our house. My husband and I also did not talk about my family's Holocaust history. It just did not seem to be relevant to him.

When we moved the family to Springfield, Illinois, I heard my 12 year old son say that he was not going to tell anyone at school that he was Jewish, and that propelled me to the synagogue. Before any of my children gave up their Judaism, they had to learn what they were giving up. A mother walking into temple and Sunday School with six children was very visible. People in the congregation welcomed us. I joined the Sisterhood, taught Sunday School, and became a leader in the Jewish community.

At some point, I was appointed to be the liaison between the Jewish Community Relations Council and the Public Schools. I facilitated in-service training about Judaism for public school teachers and even gave a few talks about my Holocaust connection and family experience. My identity changed dramatically, and I fully owned my Judaism publicly for the first time in my life. It felt liberating and it honored my family history.

I have lived in different communities since my time in Springfield, and none of them had a strong Jewish presence until I moved to the St. Louis area in 2003. I had never experienced such a large and active Jewish community, and I was fascinated and also intimidated by it. I found a group of Holocaust survivors who were children during the Holocaust and somehow managed to escape or be hidden in order to survive. I had been looking all my life for such a group. Even though we were from different countries and had a variety of experiences, we were more like each other than we were like anyone else. I had found the last piece of my Jewish identity at last.

I cannot imagine being anything but Jewish, even though I am not very religious. My history and my culture are very dear to me, and I am proud of Jewish values and of the phenomenal things that Jews have contributed to this world. I feel wonderful when I find out someone great is a Jew, and I feel terrible when a Jewish person perpetrates an evil act. In some way, I am in all of them and they are all a part of me. I guess you could call that quite a strong Jewish identity. I certainly do.

Gerry Mandel
Under the Red Goose Sign

I stand on the littered sidewalk, staring through the grimy plate glass window into a dark and empty store. This was once my father's shoe store, a business he ran for more than forty years and was as essential to him as food and air. The store, and the entire street, once resonated with shoppers and colorful window decorations and a transcendent energy, all accompanied by a soundtrack of voices and traffic. Now the store, on this street of deteriorating storefronts and struggling businesses, holds only ghosts and memories. Outside the entrance, over the name Proper Shoe Store, hangs a huge Red Goose Shoes sign. Suspended in immutable splendor, it is a happy reminder of the line of children's shoes he once carried.

My father evolved from a four-year-old immigrant from Russia into a respected and well-liked businessman who made friends with aldermen and mayors, prize fighters and comedians, rabbis and priests, maitre-d's and cops. Even now, twenty years after his death, I still am fascinated by the photographs he so proudly displayed: Dad with Jimmy Durante, Rocky Marciano, Joe Garagiola, Shecky Green, Henny Youngman, Rosemary Clooney and even Buster Workman, a notorious racketeer from across the river in East St. Louis.

Yes, Dad knew them all. But he did not know me. And I, sadly, did not know him. Over the years we went to ball games and boxing matches together, family dinners at restaurants and large dances at hotel ballrooms for organizations he and Mom supported. And we had lunch together, usually at his suggestion. But our conversations never seemed to go beneath the surface. The job is fine, business is good, the Cardinals are playing great, Aunt Minnie isn't doing so well. Even when I knew his heart was weakening and a fearful look in his eye had replaced the confident smile I had always associated with him - even then, we couldn't get past the mundane. I must have been fifty years old before I could say 'I love you" to my dad. It took him even longer to return the sentiment.

Don't get me wrong. I loved him. He loved me. But it was unspoken. My entire life was, if anything, too easy. I never wanted for a car, a new suit, a college education, and - of course - shoes. He frequently would bring home shoes for me, even after I was grown and out of the house, shoes I didn't need or like. They were his way, I think, of saying "I love you." Shoes were his language.

Dad had a knack of associating people with the size of their feet. He forgot people's names occasionally, but never their size.

"You see that guy over there?" he'd say to me. "Size nine Charlie."

"Who is that, Dad?"

"I don't remember his name but he wears a 9-C."

Dad had everyone pegged by their shoe size. The waitress at the diner down the street with the petite 5-B. The cop in the neighborhood with the gigantic 14-EEE. Dad specialized in hard-to-fit feet, and drew customers from the entire St. Louis area. His name was Milt, his nicknames were Smiley and Uncle Miltie and Curly, even though he was bald.

He'd proudly introduce me as his son. I was the piano player. My brother was the baseball player. I gravitated more to mom, who also played piano. We knew each other better. But here's the strange part: In my dreams today I dream about Dad frequently. Not Mom. In my dreams, Dad is with me, healthy and happy, as he was when I was growing up. Even as I talk with him, I know he is dead. But we are together and that's all that counts. Sometimes the dream seems to go on for hours, and I fear his departure, but he stays. And I treasure each second, impossible though I know it is. I wake up still locked in the magic of the dream, feeling fulfilled and sad and privileged.

I often wonder why we have such difficulty getting in touch with our fathers. How and where the distance began. He was born on the other side of the world. He entered a strange land, made his way to St. Louis, learned the language, the hustle, the do's and don'ts of making it in America. He ran his own business for four decades, survived The Depression, recovered from a devastating fire that put him out of business for almost a year, at a time when Mom was pregnant with my brother and Pearl Harbor was just months away. Even then, he never stopped, never looked back. I don't think I could have achieved what he did. At one of our lunches, instead of telling him I got a raise or was thinking about buying a new Monte Carlo, I wish - God, how I wish - I had told him what an incredibly beautiful job he had done with his life and mine.

So many people migrated to America during the early part of the last century, became men and women of respect and accomplishment. Many of them died without ever talking about how they did it, why they did it, how they felt about it. This is a personal loss of lore and legend we must now seek out in other people's books and experiences, to see what, if anything, applies to our own lives.

I touch the cold glass. In the darkness I can see Dad pull a shoe box from a shelf, flip open the lid, pull out a size five beige pump and present it to a seated woman who has one shoe off. He looks up at the window, sees me, and smiles. Then he slips the shoe onto the woman's foot.

Maryellen McSweeney
Mrs. Rubenstein

I grew up in San Francisco in a neighborhood once called Carville that was two blocks from the Pacific Ocean. It was literally the end of the line – for the streetcar and for anything the city found too large to keep and too good to discard. The city's castoffs included old streetcars that were sold to residents for $10 each (or $20 with seats intact). Some people de-wheeled the streetcars and converted them to one or two room homes. There were also 14' x 18' Earthquake Shacks left over from the temporary housing the city had put up for people made homeless by the 1906 earthquake and fire. Even in 1948, some of the neighborhood housing consisted of repurposed streetcars and a few single room Earthquake Shacks. The abundance of tiny, cheap, street-level homes attracted many low income older people, especially widows who lived alone.

A long-time resident, who was part of this group, acted as an informal economic matchmaker. She linked neighbors with specific needs (such as for food, transportation, or health care) with other neighbors likely to be able to meet their needs, sharing a little background information about each with the other. This was how my family met Mrs. Rubenstein. She was a heavy-set older Jewish woman from Russia who lived in one of the tiny houses. Her hugely swollen feet and legs and her shortness of breath made it difficult for her to get around. But the problem that brought us together was that her deteriorating teeth were making it very hard for her to eat, and my dad was a dentist. After several home visits and a trip with my mother downtown to my dad's office, Mrs. Rubenstein's dental problems were resolved. In the course of conversation we learned that she was the daughter of a scribe and was proud of her ability to read and write Hebrew as well as Yiddish.

We did not see her for several weeks, then suddenly on a Sunday afternoon in spring, she was at our door with an enormous box of prepared food. She was nearly gasping from the exertion of having carried the heavy box up the street and then up a steep flight of stairs to our door. She explained that she had brought us dinner, but that it was no ordinary dinner – it was a special Passover dinner. She described the various dishes she had made with pride but would not join us for the meal.

We enjoyed the meal greatly. What struck me was my dad's response. I don't recall ever seeing him so touched by a gift. As a literal-minded child, I thought it was because he realized how hard it must have been for her to walk eight blocks for the round-trip to the grocery-deli, cook, and then carry the heavy box of food to us. In later years I thought there must have been more to his response. My dad must have realized that Mrs. Rubinstein, living alone with no family nearby, probably had not cooked a special Passover dinner in years. What bittersweet memories cooking that meal must have elicited! Doing so for us – not family and not Jewish – was an exceptional gift of trust – that we would understand and appreciate what she gave us. This was our first *seder* – no Maxwell House *haggadah* or formal service included – but Mrs. Rubenstein gave us an object lesson in welcoming the stranger. The memory of this *seder* meal enriches each *seder* I've attended or conducted since.

Miriam Friedman Morris
In the Aftermath of the Holocaust, St. Louis was Home

We were a unit. It was my father, my mother, and I. We left Israel on the SS Jerusalem and arrived in the United States with thirty borrowed dollars and immense hope for the future. Besides the typical baggage of immigrants, we brought along something unique, a trunk carefully packed with extraordinary artwork created after my father's liberation from the concentration camps.

My father David Friedman(n) was born in 1893 in Mährisch Ostrau, Austria-Hungary, now Ostrava in the Czech Republic. At age seventeen, he moved to Berlin and studied etching and lithography with Herman Struck and painting with Lovis Corinth. He achieved acclaim as a painter known for his portraits drawn from life. In 1924, his quick sketching ability led to an additional career as a freelance artist for Berlin newspapers and magazines. He became one of the leading press artists of his day and sketched hundreds of celebrated personalities from the Arts, Music, Theater, Sports, Politics, and Industry, such as: Albert Einstein, Arnold Schoenberg, Yehudi Menuhin, Leo Slezak, Ramsay MacDonald, Hugo Eckener, and Emanuel Lasker. This talent played a central role throughout his career and saved his life during the Holocaust. After Hitler came to power in 1933, his prewar career abruptly ended. In 1938, he fled with his young family to Prague, only to be deported in 1941 to the Lodz Ghetto, and in 1944 to Auschwitz-Birkenau. His wife Mathilde and daughter Mirjam Helene were murdered by the Nazis. The Gestapo looted his oeuvre of 2000 artworks in 1941. After his liberation he began to paint a new collection.

My mother Hildegard Taussig was born in 1921 in Berlin. The Taussig family lived in Gleiwitz, Oberschlesien, then a part of Germany. In 1935 they fled from the Nazis to Prague. Czechoslovakia was occupied in 1939 by the Nazi regime. Older Sister Else immigrated to Eretz Israel on an illegal ship. Hilde was deported to Thyeresienstadt in 1941 with her father, Karl. He survived the Holocaust, but she never saw her mother Irma and twin sister Ingeborg again. Hilde survived Theresienstadt, Auschwitz-Birkenau, and Christianstadt. After the camp was dissolved in early February 1945, Hilde escaped from the death march and lived in hiding until her liberation. In January 1946, she met David Friedmann and helped him hang his first exhibition of Holocaust art. They married in Prague in 1948, but only a year later fled the Stalinist Communists for Israel where I was born. Israel was in poor economical circumstances. My father was determined to succeed with his art and set his ambitions on America.

He applied for the job of pictorial painter at General Outdoor Advertising Company, Inc. It didn't matter that he spoke little English or had never painted billboards; he surpassed the firm's expectations in a trial period of only three days. GOA moved our family from New York City to Chicago, Illinois, the company headquarters, and then in February 1956 to St. Louis, Missouri, where he had accepted the head position for this branch. A great triumph for anyone under ordinary circumstances, but my father accomplished this in just fifteen months.

David Friedman writes To Mr._____:

> …When we arrived in New York in November 1954, I had to forget about art paintings and I had to forget what was hidden in the inner part of my heart, the pictures from the concentration camps. I had to work first to make a living and to be one of the top painters in the company. I had to work hard because my age was 61 years. However, General Outdoor Advertising didn't care about my age, they were looking how fast I could produce the gigantic paintings…[1]

This opportunity gave him reason to believe that there was still a place where his ability as a painter could be honored. He painted 150 billboards in Chicago and St. Louis, among them the iconic Budweiser Clydesdales. This new profession brought recognition and satisfaction with life in America and the Friedmann family made St. Louis their final home.

By the age of five, I already sensed we were different. Most of my parents' friends spoke with accents and I was aware that they also had tattooed numbers on their arms. There was an aura of sadness in the air as the survivors tried to create happy homes in a foreign land for their children. They found the strength to rebuild their lives and raise children in an environment of love and learning. However, despite the efforts, there was always that current, that unexplained something and the hushed tones when we children came around.

---

[1] To Mr. ___ Draft of a letter by David Friedman, 1964. The addressee is unknown.

I never had a babysitter. Everywhere my parents went along came Miri, as I was called. It wasn't so much that my parents doted on me, it was just our way of life. Together we would go to the swimming pool, the movies, symphony concerts, and visit friends. They delighted in taking me to Disney movies, especially enjoying "Fantasia" because of the classical music. We joined a synagogue where I attended Sunday school and became members of the Jewish Community Centers Association.

Almost every Sunday afternoon was spent at beautiful St. Louis Forest Park the site of the 1904 World's Fair. My father would take along his camera and sketchpad to draw the scenery. Soon a crowd would gather around to watch him sketch. We took advantage of Forest Park, the exceptional zoo, the art museum, and outdoor amphitheater known as The Muny. (My father contributed his expertise in painting scenery for several productions.) Going to the zoo was an adventure and always my favorite Sunday. I loved the animal shows and the miniature train that wove its way through the zoo. The three of us enjoyed many picnics, long walks, and pleasant times together.

I attended Hamilton Elementary School just a block from our apartment on Westminster Place. I had many friends, some of them also children of survivors. In first grade I joined the Brownie Girl Scouts. My father was shocked and outraged when he saw me in the brown uniform reminding him of the Hitler Youth in Nazi Germany. Eventually he calmed down and always came along with my mother to the programs. I learned to ice skate, play the piano and violin. I excelled in school and loved to read and draw. Encouraged in all activities and possible talents, my parents were my most ardent fans. My father hung my crayon drawings next to his paintings and from the time I was a small child kept a portfolio of my art. Having a love of music and art were seeds that were planted early in my life.

My father was 27 years older than my mother. This didn't seem possible to me because he walked with a jaunty bounce and was full of vigor. My mother said she didn't want a younger man, she fell in love with David Friedmann. When they met, he immediately wished to draw her portrait. Over the course of their life together, David portrayed her in numerous paintings and drawings. Hilde was his best model and she loved to pose for him. Not a holiday would pass without my father bringing her flowers. Sometimes he painted these very same flowers, dedicating the artwork to his darling Hilde. In his eyes she stood on the highest pedestal.

David Friedman writes To Mr._____ :

>...In the face of the SS man she was able to save the life of
her father in Theresienstadt and Auschwitz without fear. She was
a real heroine. I was highly impressed as she told me the story
and immediately I decided to do everything possible for her and
make her happy. My age for her was never a hindrance...

A great passion of his was the violin. He played etudes, compositions
published by violin virtuoso Carl Flesch, under whom he had studied
in Berlin. When I became adept at the piano we performed duets
together. My father had an abundance of interests. He was a Freemason,
a chess enthusiast, and an avid stamp collector. He spent long hours at
his typewriter keeping up with correspondence and working on his
autobiography, *Trieb zur Kunst* (Driving Force to Art). There was an
ongoing intense correspondence with his father-in-law Karl Taussig and
friends from all over the world. He also delighted in writing poetry to
honor friends and family. I can never remember him not being active in
some pursuit.

One of his great pleasures was taking multitudes of photos of us.
When my father set up the tripod and timer, we knew he meant business.
I was dressed in my best and would pose with my mother. At the right
moment he joined us, we smiled, and the camera would flash. I remember
sitting with my mother in a rented boat on the lake in Forest Park. My
father was standing at the edge with his camera and I felt apprehensive
that he would fall in. "Smile" he said, and so we did. He created photo
albums with poignant and lively descriptions on the page:

>This picture seems especially enchanting under a magnifying
glass. I am going to have a cutout enlarged. All this gives us a
great deal of pleasure. To enjoy this when you are eighty is too
late. Just now, the time has come for us to really enjoy life and
total harmony.

Photos and sketches were also made of our homes. I am grateful to
my father for creating this legacy of happy memories.

It was usually just the three of us celebrating holidays and special events.
My parents made hearty toasts with wineglasses raised. Sometimes, I felt
there was a forced gaiety; they wanted to create happiness. We embraced

the American holiday of Thanksgiving. My mother would prepare a wonderful turkey dinner with all the trimmings and frequently invited guests who were also without extended families. About Thanksgiving, November 1958, my father writes:

> This time we have had our own Thanksgiving, small but fine, mmm it tasted good and it was a joy. And we have a good reason to be grateful to the Almighty to be in this land that has been so good to us.

Thanksgiving indeed had special meaning. My parents were caught in the brutal web of the Nazi regime; their path was a horrific and tumultuous journey until they reached St. Louis. Thus, it was an exciting day in 1960 when the Friedmann family became United States citizens and symbolically dropped the double "n" spelling of their surname.

By this time we were living in the University City Loop. We didn't own a car and walked or took the bus. On Friday nights we attended services at Congregation Shaare Emeth especially to hear Rabbi Nodel's inspiring sermons. Sometimes Saturdays or Sundays, my father accompanied me to activities toting a sketchbook or a camera or both. In addition to his artist's materials, he brought his folding stool to sit for long hours. I recall an excursion to Lewis Park on a beautiful, cold afternoon. The ice had frozen over the pond and while I skated, my father sketched. He not only enjoyed observing people and their activities, but nature and the world surrounding them. Another time we went to the Science and Natural History Museum at Oak Knoll Park. My father sketched the forest landscape and we listened to the birds singing. In 2003, my warm memories of that day brought me back to the park that now housed the Artists' Guild. Coincidentally, my father had been a member of the Guild from 1956. My visit resulted in a special exhibition of his Holocaust art in 2005. The two drawings my father sketched of Oak Knoll Park were donated to the Artists' Guild in his memory and that perfect day in 1963.

I was long aware that my home was different from other homes in that it resembled a museum. My father always had a studio where he would disappear for hours at a time. The apartments where we lived and later our house on Lynn Avenue were characteristic of my father, vibrant and colorful. Artwork was hanging from every available space on the walls. We were surrounded by landscapes, still life, portraits, religious, and abstract art executed in diverse media.

The paneled walls of the downstairs of our house, the *Rathskeller Gallery* as it was called, also had a beautiful selection of art. However, these paintings hung alongside those of a different nature, a dark history that seemed from another planet. The tormented faces show the misery and terrible hunger that forced people to search in trash cans for crumbs of food that frequently brought on disease. Friends commented, especially about my father's depiction of the evil Nazis. SS men smirked and nonchalantly smoked cigarettes while watching helpless Jewish prisoners brutalized before they were killed. Often they dug their own graves before being shot. We would sit and gaze in wonderment and revulsion at the images trying to comprehend the incomprehensible.

In 1962 my father retired from his commercial art career at GOA. At the age of 68, he still had the temperament and drive for self-expression and new challenges. He looked forward to the freedom to paint at liberty, similarly to the rich, artistic experience he had known in Berlin and Prague. This was another beginning and he set forth with great zeal into numerous projects. Now there was time for his autobiography, *Trieb zur Kunst*. He wrote about his life up to 1915 with the intention of completing his story, hoping to interest a publisher in his work. However, this was the 1960's, a period when there was little interest in the life and art of a Holocaust survivor.

Nevertheless, he was a "free" artist and painted what he liked: still life and genre themes, landscapes, and abstract art. He developed the unique series, *Enjoyment in Libraries with the Candid Pencil of David Friedman*. The life studies capture the essence of the public's enjoyment of the library. The drawings transmit the ambience of the library, the quiet concentration of the people, and the hushed tones of the spoken word. I often accompanied my father and enjoyed watching him quickly and deftly capture the likeness of his subjects. Young and old were portrayed. Discreetly he sketched with his pad under the table or from behind a bookcase. Realistic portraits and some wonderful caricatures were produced. It was always amazing to me as the image on the page magically appeared. During the exhibitions that followed viewers were amused to see themselves as the subject of a drawing.[2]

Traveling by bus from one library to another, 100 portraits were sketched. Even in wintry weather, his enthusiasm for his work was

---

[2]   Drawings from the series, *Enjoyment in Libraries with the Candid Pencil of David Friedman*, were donated to the Finkelstein Memorial Library, Spring Valley, NY, and St. Louis Public Library.

unbounded. For a change of pace, he roamed the streets, alleys, and parks capturing the diverse landscapes of St. Louis resulting in the series called *The Urban Scene.* Because of my father's special bond to his beloved town, I donated a charcoal drawing of City Hall to the citizens of University City. During the heartwarming ceremony attended by dear friends of our family, Mayor Joseph L. Adams proclaimed April 30, 2007 as *David Friedman Day.* The drawing hangs among other historic documents in the second floor office of the City Manager.

The trips to the library and the numerous projects offered respite from the anguish of his memories. My father had sought refuge in his work, but still he could not forget. He was never truly "free". The responsibility of bearing witness weighed heavily on his conscience even before his liberation. It took several months to make his way back to Prague, arriving sick with a nervous breakdown in June 1945. Instead of finding loved ones, there were only memories of what was lost. Like other survivors he had to adjust to a new way of life, one without family. He struggled to rebuild his life.

> ...The strongest will of mankind, the will to live gave me the power again to start from scratch and to practice like a schoolboy with pencils only, because at this time there was no chance to get any materials like oil paints and brushes. When I was able to get the material, I started to paint. During the next four years I once again arranged large exhibitions with new paintings, among them motifs of the life in the concentration camps...[3]

Although his exhibitions in St. Louis were well received, they did not compare to his success and loyal following in Europe. Occasionally, he was commissioned to paint portraits. Newspaper reporters interviewed my father and published nice stories about his life and work. However, the truth was that here in America, David Friedman was an unknown artist.

Setting his disappointment aside, he listened to his inner voice. He decided to continue with a subject closest to his heart and always in his thoughts. Disturbed by the fact that people were forgetting the Holocaust, he strongly desired to make an indelible statement to all humankind. He wanted to impress upon their consciousness the ruthless persecution, torment, and atrocities practiced by the Nazis, so that it would never happen again. His tortured recollections would be transferred to paper

---

[3] *The Story of David Friedman,* by D. Friedmann.

and show the dehumanization and suffering of the Jew under Nazi rule. There would be no imagery or symbolism; his art would show the reality that only one that had been there could produce.

David Friedman writes To Mr._____:

...After I was retired in 1962, sometimes I had the idea to try again, but was afraid to start, had no courage also in consideration of my wife Hilde, I had to lock my feelings in a kind of *jail* and close the door. So sometimes I went out, painted pictures from nature and worked on my book, later I went to the libraries to make sketches, also in the streets, parks and alleys. In March 1963, I had a small exhibition in the Central Library, but it was not satisfying. I thought about the time between 1946 and 1948 when I was a successful artist.

Then in December 1963 I had enough. I told myself that all the paintings on the wall mean nothing, they no longer satisfy me, anyone can paint like that. I have to do something that nobody can do in the same way. I opened the door of the *jail* and in the night quietly left our bedroom, closed the door of my studio, placed a piece of paper on the easel, took charcoal and made my first sketch. Now I was free again and from that time nobody was able to stop me. In a short period of only four and one-half months, twenty-eight new drawings were finished. The Jewish Centers here are interested in these kinds of painting and drawings. They want to show their members and children what happened in the Nazi time. Now I am satisfied because what I am doing is not only for myself. I wish everyone had to take a good look at the artwork. They have to look at what persecution under the Nazi regime was, and it can happen again, for in America to be a Nazi, to be a Communist is not prohibited.

Against an evil world I will work further and try to put my feelings down on canvas or paper against anti-Semitism, against race hatred of all people. My wife Hilde has the same opinion...

He named the series, *Because They Were Jews!* My father relived his tribulations to capture the scenes he could not erase from his memory.

David Friedman was in Auschwitz again. He believed this would be his most important accomplishment and worked passionately and relentlessly, ignoring his health much to the anxious concern of my mother. Although she understood the significance of his work, it was difficult to see this tragedy constantly before her eyes. It was enough that she had to live with her own vivid memories. My mother wanted to enjoy the present.

My father spent long hours working in his studio where I often observed him. He used a mirror to portray himself. With one hand he held the mirror and drew with the other. Because he was a victim, he painted himself on many canvasses as the prisoner with the glasses. "I was there. This happened to me," he would say with emotion. The new drawings were produced with firm charcoal strokes as if the pent up feelings of his lengthy wait had exploded over the paper. He was baring his soul for the world to see. David Friedman did not forget one horrific detail of what the Nazis did to human beings. His paintings, drawings, and etchings show the evolution of the Holocaust from deportation to the ghettos and concentration camps until liberation. Hunger, forced labor, torture, murder, and the death march are the subjects. He supplemented his artistic testimony with descriptions of the scenes portrayed in his works to create a singularly detailed pictorial and written record.

Artwork depicting experiences that were impossible to understand were the images that I grew up with. When I left for school in the morning, my father was already busy with his work for the day. When I came home, he was still at his easel. One could see the concentration on his face as he was bringing his past to life on the canvas. After dinner and the news, it was back to the studio to access the work he had completed and plan for tomorrow. Often he worked past my bedtime and into the night as if possessed. I was from the generation that would learn from his art and experience. The words that were never said aloud were drawn on the faces of victims in scenes of such overwhelming tragedy, that certainly a child would not comprehend it. But his suffering was my suffering; I could feel the pain. Later as an adult I would share my father's frustration and difficulties in exhibiting these works.

In 1964, successful exhibitions of *"Because They Were Jews!"* were held at both branches of the Jewish Community Centers Association (JCCA) in St. Louis County. The paintings and drawings produced in Prague were included in the exhibition. In a letter dated May 21, 1964, William Kahn, the Executive Director writes:

Dear Mr. Friedman:

As I expressed to you at the Yalem Building a number of weeks ago, the JCCA shall be forever indebted to you for your very significant and moving art exhibit relating your experiences in the concentration camp. You have conveyed the complete horror of the Hitler era and certainly no one who has been exposed to your show will ever forget this bestial period of man's history.

Again, I want to express our deepest appreciation for your allowing us to present your art to our membership.
P.S. Please convey my best wishes to your gracious wife.

In a continued effort to publicize his art, my father contacted Zurich's *Israel Weekly Newspaper*, May 21, 1964:

...In any case, the exhibition seen by thousands, were full of enthusiasm and amazement at the art that it represents. It was such a success that the exhibition was extended for fourteen more days in a second location. People were asking me what compelled me after nineteen years to begin again. Right after 1945, I painted my first series in Prague, which were shown at diverse establishments and lastly at the Prague War Museum [Památník Osvobození]. In 1947, there was a major exhibition in memory of the 300,000 deaths by Hitler in Czechoslovakia, which was mentioned in an article in the "Ceske Slovo". It [the government] was still under Beneš,[4] who viewed the show and stopped in front of my paintings...[5]

The excitement and publicity gradually declined except for several devoted friends and supporters such as Rabbi Julius J. Nodel[6] and Rabbi Jeffrey Stiffman[7] from our temple, Congregation Shaare Emeth. The Holocaust was not a topic of great interest to the general public. Many

---

[4] **Beneš, Edvard** (1884-1948) Served as Czechoslovakia's first foreign minister (1918–35) and its president (1935–38). Reestablished a government in 1945 and resigned in 1948 in the face of Communism.

[5] Author's translation.

[6] **Nodel, Rabbi, Dr. Julius J.** (1910-1992) Senior Rabbi Congregation Shaare Emeth, 1959-71, Rabbi of Temple Emanu-el in Honolulu, 1971-81, and Rabbi Emeritus from 1981 until his death in St. Louis.

[7] **Stiffman, Rabbi Jeffrey** (1939) Assistant Rabbi, Congregation Shaare Emeth, 1965-68. Co-rabbi 1970-71. Senior Rabbi, 1971-2004. Rabbi Emeritus, 2005.

people, among them Jews, felt this subject did not affect them and this greatly upset my father. He expresses his thoughts about a forthcoming exhibition to Karl Taussig, December 12, 1966:

> ...Naturally, for the American Jews it will be a great shock, because they are reminded of what happened under the Hitler regime. Not everybody is so well read that they know about the nine Crusades that began with the blessings of Pope Urban II during his reign 1095-1099. The German Hordes started to rob the Jews first in the Rhineland, then murdered them and this they did everywhere on their way, all the way to Jerusalem. There they robbed and murdered not only 70,000 Jews, but thousands of Muslims all in the name of Jesus Christ. And all this because afterwards there would be a Paradise, the Kingdom of Heaven. But such stupidity will never come true. There will always be more stupid people rather than less. So it will take another few thousand years.

However, it is quite good that at the very least, the Americans can see what our suffering was about, because many have no concept. They should know that something like this could happen again. Take a look at the new Nazi Party in the damned Nazi Germany, it should be destroyed and burned!!![8] If not for me, no one would remind them not to forget! Who reads all the books that were written about this anyway, certainly not the Americans. However, paintings the way I created them show more than the printed word, they show the reality!!!

This Friday, December 16, they will have the opportunity to view the exhibition of fifteen paintings and twenty-eight drawings each 22 by 28 inches, and afterwards, to think about it, that this could have happened to them. Rabbi Nodel will give a speech. He personally came early this morning with his assistant rabbi [Jeffrey Stiffman] to pick up the artwork, a total of eighty-two pieces.

The concentration camp artworks are not for sale of course. Therefore, those artworks that are intended for sale will hang in a second hall and the rabbi will take care that some of them will be sold. I told him that this year only one painting was sold in the size of 25 by 75 centimeters and this was to a Catholic, namely a Yemenite beggar whom I painted while

---

8   D. Friedman refers to the NPD (Nationaldemokratische Partei Deutschlands). In 1966, the NPD won parliament seats representing some federal states of Germany. It was rather a shock. To avoid misunderstanding: they did not represent those states, they were represented in the parliaments with ca. 10 or 12% of those states.

still living in Hadar Yosef.

I imagine that I will sell at least two or three artworks. This would be a nice success after all. In Israel, there are plenty of people with substantial money but not for art. So, here it is exactly the same.

And now we are curious about what else will happen. This month we have a great deal of taxes to pay, especially for the house, and for this reason even a small sale would be appreciated.[9]

During an exhibition held at Congregation Shaare Emeth, several artworks were stolen off the wall. One was different from the others, an impressionistic work of a pianist performing on a grand piano in a concert hall. A sea of faces represented the audience. The closer you moved towards the canvas, the more the audience looked like fluid abstract strokes of the brush. The thief had good taste. The painting was a favorite of mine.

Inspired by Israel's victory in the Six-Day War in 1967, my father produced etchings depicting scenes of the country and from the Lodz Ghetto and concentration camps. At the age of 72, he still had a steady hand to create such detailed and painstaking work. However, he didn't own a printing press as he explained to Karl Taussig, April 4, 1967:

> ...I wanted to let you know that after a forty-year break I have dedicated myself to the art of etching. I have completed my first etching, that of a Yemenite Jew, one I had painted in Israel. At first I tried to produce a proof by hand on Japanese Rice paper, then I searched for a copper printing press and found one at Washington University. I asked the instructor if I would be allowed to use it. He was very surprised. However, after I introduced myself, he was right in the picture as to who I was. He had read about me in the St. Louis Post Dispatch and therefore, he had nothing against it. He made me very familiar with the brand new machine and I saw how easy it was to use in comparison to my old, similar looking one in Berlin, only considerably larger. The students were impressed how quickly I was able to prepare for and then produce a successful print from the plate...[10]

My father continued to create art. He also enjoyed making his own frames and working around the house and garden. No longer having the energy to go out as often as before and practically living in seclusion, he

---

[9] Author's translation.

[10] Author's translation.

found solace in painting a series of intricate abstract art. When he was scheduled for surgery for another pacemaker, seven in all, the sketching materials were packed along to the hospital. Despite being encumbered by tubes connected to medical devices, he sketched his physicians as well as himself and wrote a poem to honor the doctor who had saved him this time.

Several years later at the age of 84, he summoned the strength to produce a large self-portrait. As was her custom, my mother watched him paint while classical music played. The finished portrait shows a man of advanced years wearing his precious glasses, head held high and proud. This was his last work; his final defiance of that world he could not forget. The portrait now hangs on the wall next to my desk in New York where I often look to my father for inspiration. His strong painted image looks down on me as I work and for some reason this has a calming effect.

The portrait was painted in 1978, the same year that Gerald Green's mini-series *Holocaust* was telecast on primetime television. This fictionalized drama was a commercial hit and generated interest about the Holocaust. A local television news station discovered that there was a survivor living in St. Louis, who like in the movie had been an artist in the camps. The co-anchor made an appointment and arrived with a film crew, but the sudden attention was much too late for my father. He was emotional and could hardly speak when interviewed. Instead it was Hilde who told their story and showed the art.

Soon after the newscast, Elsie Shemin-Roth arrived at the door. Moved by the interview, she came to buy a painting so that her children would never forget their heritage. My father was surprised at the unexpected interest. Else chose a scene of three Lodz Ghetto inmates with the yellow Star of David sewn on their coats. She took the painting home the same day. Else teamed up with renowned Christian scholar and friend Dr. Harry James Cargas[11] to publicize and find a permanent home for the Holocaust works.

Elsie reminded me about a torrential rainstorm that suddenly hit St. Louis. Together with Dr. Cargas, they rushed to the *Rathskeller* to bring the works upstairs and save them from the impending flood. In 2002, Else generously donated her painting to the St. Louis Holocaust Museum and Learning Center. She wanted everyone to have the opportunity to "remember" through the art of David Friedman. In 2003, the painting

---

[11] **Cargas, Dr. Harry James** (1932-1998) Holocaust scholar and Professor emeritus of literature and languages at Webster University, St. Louis, Missouri.

became part of the permanent exhibition.[12] In 2005, the HMLC hosted a major exhibition of his works.

My mother called me in New York. My father's health was failing and I immediately flew to St. Louis. Despite his weakened condition he managed to voice his concern about what would happen to his concentration camp works. I reassured him that this was a lasting and important contribution to the world; I would take care of his legacy. I will always remember what he said. Silently I made a promise that I would not let David Friedman and his art to be forgotten. My father died February 27, 1980 at the age of 86.

We were all deeply saddened by this great loss. My mother continued to speak about her experiences, the Holocaust art, and her life with David Friedman. Hilde was dedicated to "remembrance" never forgetting the elderly and sick she helped in Theresienstadt and Auschwitz-Birkenau. She was invited to address various organizations, schools, and temple youth groups. My mother would tell the audience about the inhumanity of the Nazis and warned them to guard their democracy against the extremist groups that were a serious threat to our freedom. Wherever Hilde spoke, she made an impression. After an engagement for the Bridgeton Kiwanis Club, she received this letter dated February 26, 1981:

Dear Mrs. Friedman,

Thank you very much for coming to our luncheon today and sharing a painful part of your life. It was a privilege to listen to your story. If you should publish any part of your story, I would be most honored to purchase a copy for each of my three sons (ages 8, 6, 3). As a matter of fact I was tempted to talk you out of a copy of your speech.

God bless you and the best of luck in selecting the proper home for your husband's paintings.

Sincerely,
Bill Bates

P.S. I am the young man who assisted Charlie in carrying the paintings to his car.

---

[12] Friedman family photos are also included in the permanent exhibition, *Renewing Lives in St. Louis.*

The following is a letter dated October 18, 1983, from Rabbi Julius J. Nodel. He played the cello and was also a painter. The mutual talents of Rabbi Nodel and my father drew them together and occasionally they would perform a duet. Rabbi Nodel had moved to Honolulu and my mother informed him of David's death and our continued efforts to show and publicize the artwork.

Dear Hildegard,

...Yes, we were very sad to learn of David's death, and I know how much life without him has changed your life; but I am sure the many fond memories that survive him will always be a source of comfort to you and to Miriam. And, I guess, after all the many difficult experiences you went through, and that he went through, you are fortunate to have shared a life together for the number of years that you had; and also that David lived long enough to welcome his grandchildren into the world. I know that I shall never regret the times that he and I spent together both at the temple and in the graciousness of your home and studio. David had a remarkable talent; and it is a great tragedy for the art world that the personal tragedies in his life interrupted the growing brilliance of his artistic career. I am happy that you and Miriam were able to arrange an exhibition of some of his works at the *American Gathering of Jewish Holocaust Survivors* in Washington D.C. I am sure that his paintings were not only admired as great art, but also were deeply moving for those who attended the exhibit. Else and I still cherish two paintings we have that were done by David. One is the Western Wall in Jerusalem, and the other is a landscape of Holon in Israel.

Has any book been put out with a collection of only David's pictures about the Holocaust? That might be a worthwhile project, providing some interested party or parties could be persuaded to underwrite it. It would add greatly to the history of the Holocaust and provide a deeper insight into what happened at that time.

Express my regards and remembrance to Miriam when you next

write to her. I still recall what a lovely young lady she was even when she was one of my Religious School students.

With all good wishes from the both of us, and with Shalom and Aloha,

Faithfully and fondly,
Julius J. Nodel

Hildegard Taussig Friedman died January 25, 1989. She survived three and one-half years in the ghetto and concentration camps, loss of family, fiancé, friends, her home, and everything she owned. Throughout her horrific ordeal she maintained her dignity, spirit, and courage. What made her pull through and keep going was her zest for life, love of family, and the desire to help fellow Jews. These were the important values for her, not material things. She was warm, loving and despite everything that she had been through, had a good sense of humor. These traits helped Hilde survive the hell of her incarceration and were apparent to all those that knew her. She supported David emotionally so that he could focus on his work. My father could not be without his darling Hilde. She devoted the remainder of her life promoting his art and speaking about the Holocaust. My mother wrote:

> ...Our memories and pain will always be in our hearts; we cannot forget six million Jewish people. In time we could learn something about history. I only hope and pray that such injustice will never be repeated and that America is strong and alert and willing to fight to the end. This I pray and wish for the whole human race...[13]

From the time I was a small child, my father let it be known that my mother was special. He wanted to be sure that I gave her all the respect and love that she deserved. He needn't have worried, because a mother and daughter could not have been closer. Her death at the age of 67 was a painful loss for me; it was too soon.

David and Hildegard Taussig Friedman emerged from the destruction of the Holocaust with the passion to live and found a welcome home in St. Louis. Watching them, I learned persistence, tenacity, and not to

---

[13] Excerpt from Hildegard Friedman's speeches dated February 26, 1981 and February 20, 1983.

give up. This has inspired challenging pursuits focusing on the legacy of David Friedman. History has a curious way of confirming itself. After 30 years and monumental odds, astonishing proof of my father's lost years and art have surfaced: paintings, drawings, etchings, lithographs, and 400 published portrait drawings signed in a variety of signatures, among them: D. Friedmann, Dav. Friedmann, DaFrie, DF, Fried or just Friedmann. Most amazing was the surviving evidence of his art from the Lodz Ghetto.

David Friedman made important contributions both in the realms of 20th century art and in the creation of materials that play a powerful humanitarian role in educating Americans about the reality of the Holocaust. He has been recognized internationally as materials continue to surface. A number of his works can be seen in the permanent display of the Holocaust History Museum, Yad Vashem, in the archives of the State Museum Auschwitz-Birkenau, Poland and the United States Holocaust Memorial Museum in Washington D.C. The United Nations Headquarters in New York, the Terezín Memorial, in the Czech Republic, and the Berliner Philharmonie, in Germany have hosted significant exhibitions of his works.

My father lost his works three times: before, during, and after World War II. As a successful artist he sold his work, but would also give it away. Certainly his art can be found in St. Louis, but his works could be anywhere in the world. I would be grateful for photos and leads to artwork by my father. My aim is to create a catalogue, a confirmation of his brilliant career the Nazis could not destroy. Thus, I appeal to the reader to join my search for the lost and stolen art of David Friedman(n) and preserve the legacy of this remarkable artist.

Notes:

- Excerpts were edited by author

Steven Moskowitz
Funeral Blues

Even though I have served as a rabbi for over eighteen years, some of the most important and lasting lessons were learned in my earliest years prior to earning the title of rabbi. Many times our first experiences teach us far more than we can then admit. I still remember my grandfather teaching me how to ride a bike, his loving hand guiding me and his shouts of joy encouraging me.

There in my mind is a tableau of first memories. And so I continue to be drawn to the memory of officiating at my first funeral.

In 1987-88 I served as a student rabbi in Clarksdale, Mississippi, the birthplace of the Blues. Since the 1870's Jews had found a niche in this community and there thrived in many businesses. Once a month I flew from Cincinnati where I was attending rabbinical school to Memphis and then rented a car, driving through the cotton fields of Northern Mississippi to Clarksdale. There I served Congregation Beth Israel, a synagogue built in the 1930's.

By the 1970's its membership was declining. The synagogue could no longer afford a full time rabbi and so it became a training ground for young student rabbis, until ultimately closing its doors in 2003. It was there, in Clarksdale, at the age of 23, in the first days of June 1988 that I officiated at my first funeral.

Harry Lipson Jr. died after a long battle with cancer. I carved out a few hours to visit with him and his wife Dottie during the course of my weekend trips. At the funeral I recited the words from the perfect, unused pages of my new Rabbi's Manual. "Death has taken our beloved Harry. Our friends grieve in their darkened world…" Some of the words felt empty, and some even cruel. "For when we die we carry nothing away; our glory does not accompany us." Others felt comforting. On some words I stumbled. On others I discovered strength.

I have never before revealed this but the next day I returned to the cemetery and sat by myself at Harry's grave. The warm, humid Mississippi air was heavy with moisture. I asked Harry to forgive me for being the first funeral at which I officiated. I begged him to ignore my mistakes. I apologized over and over again for all of my weaknesses and flaws. I was overwhelmed by feelings of inadequacy and incompetence in facing death.

And then I remembered that death is not a failure. I recalled that I became a rabbi rather than a physician because I wanted to have a manual that worked for moments just as these. I did not want to say, "There was nothing more we could do…" but instead, "I am sorry. I promise I will walk this path with you. We will face this death together. This is what our tradition says we must now do."

The pages of my Rabbi's Manual are now torn and wrinkled from snow and rain. The pages bear scribbling and notes as well as reminders that I no longer require. There are a few pages wrinkled from my own tears, from funerals still too painful to recount. Many have stood expectantly, looking up at me as I read from this small, holy book. There were days when I did not know how I might summon the strength to greet these expectations. Nearly every time I am drawn to remember Harry.

I recall that there is no perfect path through the valley of the shadow of death. I remember Dottie's observation that the very words from our tradition that I found harsh and cruel she found soothing and comforting. She explained to me that it was the comfort of a familiar voice reciting what generations of Jews have spoken for thousands of years. I worried too much about the meaning of each word. She listened instead to the voice. I learned then that there is our tradition's manual and its guidance. There is the strength we draw from our community, from each other.

I still find it remarkable that people ask me to stand by their side at countless occasions such as these. I am thankful that there have been far more *simchas* than tragedies in these eighteen years. In these years I have studied Torah with over 200 b'nai mitzvah students and watched as their parents welcomed them into the age of Jewish responsibility. I relish the smiles of parents and their tears of joy. I find it to be an unparalleled privilege that my congregants want me standing there at the absolute best of times and the worst. I am grateful that they see fit to call me rabbi.

I cannot promise that I will always say every word perfectly. I can promise that I will continue to call it a privilege and blessing to serve as a rabbi.

And as I learned as well in the birthplace of the Blues, from the master B.B. King: "You better not look down if you want to keep on flyin'. Put the hammer down. Keep it full speed ahead."

Jordan Oakes
The Jews of Rolla

Growing up Jewish in the small town of Rolla, Missouri reminds me of the old stand-up routine by comedian Steven Landesberg. Reminiscing about being one of the Promised People in the deep, deep South, he used a hillbilly drawl while imitating the way people would point at him and say, "See that guy? That's our Jew." I wasn't the only Jew in Rolla. There was my family. And there were a few other Jewish families, as well; together we comprised a religious minority in a town that was heavy on the Catholics and Fundamentalists. Rolla was also a college town – but instead of the academic environment clashing with the more rural aspects of our locality, they created a kind of synergy. UMR was full of smart, calculator-toting students who seemed to have the dual objectives of graduating cum laude and drinking themselves to death. Fraternities were everywhere –in buildings built to be fraternities, in houses near the campus that had been sloppily converted; in apartment complexes that, with the nailing-in of a few Greek letters, became party central.

If the town didn't have UMR as an anchor, clearly it would have been adrift on a sea of geographical irrelevance. My father, who taught philosophy of religion until the early '90s, was never fulfilled working at a school that offered only a whiff of the humanities, while positively reeking of chemical engineering. Inevitably, most of the other Jewish families worked at the university, too, and we all – by virtue of sharing a culture and a religion -- knew one another. Of course there were also the transient Jews – students who were in town only long enough to get a degree; faculty members who came and went after being denied tenure; and the occasional Jewish drifter, if there is such a thing. Whenever there was a new Jewish person in town, the news circulated – at least among the Jews. At least we would have that one thing in common. And being Jewish in Rolla meant having the unlikely cache of celebrity. We were essentially a loophole in the Bible Belt, particularly on exotic-to-Rolla holidays like Chanukah and Rosh Hashanah. We were famous.

Though I was admonished in no uncertain terms by my Christian friends that someday I would burn in hell if I didn't accept Jesus, it was ultimately a mixed message, because I was also told regularly that the Jews were the apple of God's eye. In fact, I was faced with this cliché so often that at times I wasn't certain whether the world had been created by a higher power or planted by Johnny Appleseed. (Perhaps Appleseed himself was a

rural Jew, and had a core connection to the original sin.) Being Jewish in
Rolla also meant being in limbo, because ours was an insular identity that
could never be reinforced by the local culture. Though I never felt like an
outsider, or even worse a pariah, my Jewish identity deprived me of having
things. For instance, a Christmas tree – which I've always felt is a staple
of childhood as much as Christmas. I was jealous of my gentile friends,
who enjoyed annual rites like slowly transforming pine trees into ornate,
silvery boscage. Even fake Christmas trees seemed to grow wild during
wintertime in Rolla. That said, Jewish people were reportedly entitled to
have something called a Chanukah bush -- but I don't think I've ever seen
one, and therefore have come to believe the concept is either a joke or an
attempt to level religion's botanical playing field. Frankly, looking for any
hint of Chanukah in the backwoods was like trying to find a pine needle
in a haystack. My family wasn't observant. In fact, my father – don't forget
he was a philosopher of religion – at times seemed spiritually restless,
flitting from church to church like a religious secret shopper. He was
testing the waters of Christianity (undoubtedly to see if they'd part). And
Rolla had quite a menu of churches – one for every appetite. For a while
we even attended the Unitarian Fellowship, wherein the sharp edges of
religious difference became one dull convention.

Rolla also had a lot of Baptists, who to me represented the panicking,
fear-mongering extreme of fundamentalism. Remember when people
used to burn rock and roll records? It doesn't happen much these days,
mainly because CDs have taken over and they're not very flammable.
Actually, I doubt record burning ever occurred in Rolla – but I was
subjected to rock criticism one day when I was buying the hit single "Live
and Let Die" at Woolworths. The checker berated me for purchasing the
"devil's music" (the devil must have a hell of a record collection). I could
tell it was painful for this woman to play her own small ding-ding of a
song as she rang up my purchase.

In Rolla, very little occurred that was newsworthy. We had no
celebrities in town. There was very little crime. Therefore, things like
bar mitzvahs got into the newspaper. In Rolla, my own ceremony was a
huge story in the Rolla Daily News -- in the Leisure section, which was
appropriate considering I wore a leisure suit, as did my grandfather and
several other men who donned what was less a fashion statement than a
fashion question. Though my bar mitzvah reception was held at our house,
the event itself – all 45 minutes of it -- took place outside the city limits.
We had to drive to Fort Leonard Wood, which was about an hour each

way. I'm sure that at times my parents wished we grew up somewhere like New York or their native Philadelphia, any place we could fit in and be part of a common culture – namely, our own. Ah, but in Rolla we had more value. By being scarce, I suppose we were special. Were it not for my family and the five or six other Jewish families, the good people of Rolla may have never seen a Jew.

Miriam Spiegel Raskin
Bedtime Stories

I.

Sometimes technology brings unexpected benefits. Here I was, stashing a new air mattress with its incredible built-in electric pump back into the closet after the departure of a visitor, when suddenly, out of nowhere, I got this flash of recollection of a folding bed I used to sleep in. It was so primitive that I forgot totally about it. Never thought about it at all, never even told my children about it though they would certainly have been interested, at least in the strangeness.

"What?" they would have asked. "You slept in the dining room?"

I have always tried to be open with them. I don't deliberately withhold information, even when I should in order to protect my dignity, my immortal reputation. I risk telling them the truth because I want them to know me, neuroses and all. And love me anyway; that is the subtext. I have told them the whole story of this poor little undersized refugee girl I was when we found a haven in America and I, wholly unprepared, was thrown into a strange school in a strange city, among strange children speaking a strange language, and told to swim. Or the equivalent.

This they know: the story of A-Ging, how embarrassed I was, reading aloud in a semicircle of first graders in that Chicago elementary school and, running across the word "aging," saying "a ging" to peals of laughter from my classmates. And that pronouncing the name of Arkansas was equally intimidating (well, why isn't it pronounced arKansas? tell me that!). And this: how I went to the neighborhood bakery on a regular basis with a nickel in my hand to ask, rolling my r's in the way the German language had required and my tongue had not yet unlearned, for a "rrrye brrred frrrrrrom yesterrrrrrday." And that it wasn't just for reasons of thrift; we were looking for texture in our bread and had only found the likes of Wonder Bread.

But the folding bed I did not tell them about because I forgot. There wasn't much to remember: a single mattress pad on a flat spring in a metal frame that flipped up lengthwise and was then covered by a curtain so that its presence could melt into the elegance of that dining room. That was my space. All of it. Behind that curtain. There was no closet -- it was, after all, our dining room -- so one may wonder where my possessions went. Indeed, I do wonder.

Of course I wanted a room of my own. But I knew we were living in desperate times and I could not have everything I wanted. "Close your eyes," my father would say, and I would comply. "Everything that you see now belongs to you." Nothing. That is what he meant for me to understand. Nothing belonged to me. Don't misunderstand. He was not cruel, not my darling daddy. He said it with a half-smile, a smile halved by his own sadness, and said it only because it was the truth. I had nothing and should expect nothing; the latter proved to be a hard habit to break.

I slept in that folding bed and feared that it might snap shut with me inside, smashing me to smithereens. Though there was little actual risk involved, I stayed half awake nights to be on the alert for disaster. But then, I was always preparing for disaster. The only disaster that occurred in connection with that bed, and there is no reason for this, no logical connection at all, except that it was the way it happened, was the arrival one day of a telegram from the International Red Cross that was placed on the closed bed and so we all stood around it as we read that my uncle in Shanghai, where he had found temporary refuge after escaping with minor shotgun wounds to the stomach from a concentration camp in Germany, was starving to death and in urgent need of our financial aid. The telegram helped me keep perspective. Having no space to call your own was not the worst thing that could happen to someone.

II.

The bed in which I made my first personal-disaster coping plans was the one I occupied in my parents' bedroom in an apartment in a converted cigar factory in Bünde in Westphalia. My father's textile business was in the same building. I slept in an oversized crib although that seems impossible for even me to believe. I was eight years old when we were lucky enough to be able to escape from under the Nazis' thumbs and make our way to America. Furniture needs had not been a major preoccupation in the times leading up to our departure so I brook no criticism of my parents for their incredible laggardness in getting me out of their bedroom. But my children would certainly have screamed on hearing this account. "Oh no! You can't mean that. You were eight years old and in a crib? in your parents' bedroom?"

Well, yes, but that was not the bad part. The bad part was that I was scared half to death when they left me alone in that bed while they went out at night. The windows were barred (remnants of the security policies of the one-time cigar factory the building had been in a prior era), and I had persistent images of being sealed up in the room forever and ever. I could see that no one could get through the windows and worried that the solitary door might somehow get irrevocably shut and I would starve to death. Unless, and this is how I became the heroine of my own disaster tale, I devised a solution to save myself from starvation. There was a narrow space under the door, through which my parents could roll those tiny pastel-colored candies I loved, the ironically named *Liebesperlen* (love beads). Transported (or should that be sub-ported?) in copious amounts, these tiny sweets, exactly like the white candy sprinkles found on nonpareil chocolates, would keep me alive.

Luckily, the efficacy of my plan was never put to the test. The door remained operable, and my parents always returned home, a fact I would discover by repeatedly switching on and off the light switch (it was within my reach if I stretched my arm way out over the foot of the bed) until I could see their familiar shapes under the covers of the bed next to me. In fairness to her, I must report that my mother says now she never would have left me alone, at that age and in those times, for more than a few minutes. Ah, but she does not remember this the way I do. I was alone for ages. I can still touch the fear of being alone and enclosed by all those bars on the narrow windows.

III.

During my twelfth summer I traveled to the Wisconsin Dells with two cousins and their parents. We drove up the hilly roads from Chicago, the ancient Ford chugging its way with sputtering difficulty across the miles. I wasn't sure the old thing was going to make it. In those days hills were hard, even for newer cars; engines spurted, motors died, tempers flared. I wasn't sure I was going to make it either. I started feeling queasy, unsure, questioning the wisdom of my decision to make the trip. I had forgotten that these people thought differently than I.

We arrived, checked out the cabin, carried in the luggage, and had my worst fears confirmed when my aunt and uncle announced the sleeping arrangements. I was to sleep in the same bed with my two cousins, one male, both older than I. They did not know whom they were dealing with. I should sleep in the same bed with a boy? I was indignant. What was wrong with that? they asked me. I don't know what I answered because God knows I did not know exactly what was wrong with that arrangement. Naive as modest girls once were, I only knew that girls weren't supposed to sleep with boys, and I wasn't about to be tricked into wickedness.

Not without a smirk or two at my expense, they reconsidered and sent the boy, complaining at the unfairness of it all, off to sleep on a couch on the sleeping porch. It was a small victory in the battle to keep myself pure in an impure world. I could not wait to get home to tell my parents.

IV.

Not long ago, my husband and I toured through a few western states, traveling past vast unpopulated areas that no urban dweller can imagine and through the magnificent natural parks that add to the bubbling mix of America's natural beauty and grandeur. Our days were glorious with absolutely perfect weather and views of sky and mountain as breathtakingly beautiful as can be found on earth. So much natural glory should satisfy all the soul's longing for transcendence, but mine evidently was not satisfied. I could not sleep.

Despite my appreciation of the setting, it was not rest but tedious, detailed mental activity that I found when I lay my head down on the pillow. It is nothing new. I should be accustomed to this. Quite regularly, going to bed sets my mind flitting from one unnecessary task to another, chores so ridiculous that I laugh as I watch the screen of my quasi-dreams. I don't have to do all these things, I tell myself. I don't have to solve all these problems. They are not difficult, taxing chores, just time- and en-ergy- consuming. I wear myself out doing nothing. After a while, I stop, wake myself and try one or another oft-tried remedy – breath control, visualizations, recital of some numeric series or the Hebrew alphabet – but soon I am off again, retracing my creative steps looking for a lost glove or key ring or searching for the owner of a puppy that has wandered my way.

In my "sleep," I wonder why I occupy myself in this fruitless way. Who is this "I" that sets my mind to spinning when it should be at rest? In my waking state, I am calm enough, but this nocturnal "I" is a model of mental disturbance. Shhhhhh, I say to myself. Don't even go there. If I even think such thoughts, I will start palpitating, break out in a cold sweat and never get back to sleep – never ever get back to sleep. It is my greatest fear. From early childhood, the inaccessibility of sleep has been the monster in the closet, the ogre that will destroy me if I let him.

One night we ended up in Laramie, Wyoming, landing without reservations at a decidedly un-sumptuous Super 8 Motel. The room was small but adequate to our needs. All we wanted was a night's rest before pushing on, and it even had a television set to lull us to sleep – some of us, at least. My husband, disappointed by the lack of closed captioning that would make it possible for him to enjoy television, turned onto his side and slept. I don't exaggerate. I have watched this phenomenon over the years and without understanding a bit. The man is able to close his eyes and sleep. Even when he could hear, there has never been a way to penetrate his consciousness once he closes his eyes and leaves the waking world behind. It is a skill I have long envied.

I, less lucky, watched a *Law and Order* episode I had seen before, turned off the set, and faced the darkness. Wind was whistling outside the windows. "Wild Wyoming winds whistling," I started a nocturnal exercise. Perhaps it was the genesis of a poem waiting to be born. Wild, Wyoming Winds, too mellifluous a phrase to be easily discarded. I know nothing about Wyoming other than the emptiness of places we have crossed, the undistinguished nature of the few dozen people who dined with us at the quasi-Victorian Cattlemen's Ranch. What could I say about Wyoming: or even its winds flapping everything loose outside our door? Pondering the possibilities, I closed my eyes and listened to the sound of trucks rushing by on the interstate a few hundred yards away.

"Wild Wyoming winds," the thought reappeared unbidden, "whistling while I sleep." I was wide awake now, stirred by the sound of the extended line. Perhaps if I sat up, took a place at the table, I might be more creative, but, not wanting to disturb my sleeping mate, I stayed prone, unsleeping, uncreative, regulating my breathing while wild Wyoming winds rode over my mental processes. Hours later, still unsleeping, I curled my body next to his, seeking the comfort his presence gives me even when he is asleep. I lay quietly, untouching, feeling the lack of contact along my back, and simultaneously recognizing my neediness, my ubiquitous neediness, thinking that perhaps my mother was right when she described me, when little, as *Liebesbedürftig:* requiring a lot of love. More love, perhaps than she could give. And I flashed back to the sensation of being alone in my childhood bed, in the dark bedroom of that converted factory where I dreamt of love beads to sustain me. Of course, clear as the sky above. Why did it take so long to figure that out?

When morning came at last, the winds outside had quieted. The world was beautiful again.

"How did you sleep?" he asked me.

"OK," I answered, "And you?"

"Lousy," he said. "I can't wait to get back to our own bed and get a good night's rest."

What a lucky man he is. He knows by instinct the truths I struggle toward, like this one: there is no bed like your own, if you are seeking comfort, although it may take time to find the one that really deserves the appellation. It certainly took me time – centuries, I believe – to make the long journey from sleepless, anxiety-filled nights in that tiny barred bed of my childhood to the undisturbed sleep I now enjoy in our luxurious, oversized marital bed.

So much has changed, and so little. I have a light switch located conveniently right over the headboard. I can switch it on if ever I should feel an instant's doubt about my safety. But I don't need to. I have never, in my lifetime, felt more safe.

Questions without Answers

I thought I was done thinking about it all but then I came across an article on the internet about Minsk that made me remember my maternal grandparents again. And wonder.

It took a good chunk of the twentieth century to teach my grandparents how small the world is. Their own ancestors had wandered from Iberia towards Germany after the Inquisition and had stopped wandering when they found a safe base in Hamburg. They never considered wandering again. Certainly not as far as Minsk, which in the early 1930's when the Josephis considered themselves firmly settled in Hamburg, was a large, predominantly Jewish city in Belarus, a continent away. Nor did they learn from their heavily censored newspapers that Stalin's Russification strategies had shrunk the Jewish population of Minsk to just 30% of the population by 1939. Shocking as it is to us, in retrospect, that Stalin was methodically killing Jewish intellectuals whose views did not coincide with his, the murders did not bring Minsk to their attention.

Truth be told, my grandparents might well have felt no sympathy for those distant Russian Jews. From the sample they confronted in their own city, they knew eastern Jews to be unsympathetic characters: dirty, uneducated, vulgar, garlic eaters, Yiddish speakers who could not speak the German language properly and were generally un-Germanic in their habits and customs. That was perhaps the worst thing, that in their dark and gloomy clothing reminiscent of seventeenth century *shtetl* life, they could never be fully assimilated into the sophisticated modern country in which they lived. As it was, their appearance made it likely that real Germans might misapprehend them as representative Jews, typical of their co-religionists. And that was bad for everybody.

Barely in the middle class, the Josephi family never had much money, which deficit did not stop them from having cultural and social aspirations. My grandmother especially admired the lifestyle of the upper classes, both Gentile and Jewish, and tried within her means to emulate it. If one did not have the money to buy books, one could, after all, still read reviews and be knowledgeable. If one could not afford theater tickets, one read the plays themselves. One tried to fit in, and not make trouble.

During the same years that Stalin was decimating his Jewish community, that notorious fourth decade of the last century, the Germans were also -- was it in the air?-- implementing their own anti-Jewish bias by means of restrictive laws so my grandparents had more than enough antisemitism in their own neighborhood to have to worry about what was happening to the far-off Jews in Minsk. But things got worse in Germany. There were arrests of Jewish men on the streets, followed by violence against Jewish shops and institutions, and then, far worse things.

My grandfather, reading the handwriting on the wall, packed his old leather suitcase with his toiletries and other necessities and stationed it at the door to be ready when the dreaded knock at the door sounded for him. He was realistic. He knew they would come for him. He may have feared the worst, but I think not. He did not have so cruel an imagination, so black a worldview nor so evil an intellect as to be able to imagine the fate that awaited not only him but both of them. He may have thought of a labor camp outside the city, slave labor in a war plant or perhaps a concentration camp in Poland; Poland was just across the border from Danzig. But Minsk, Minsk? That could not have entered his mind. Being pushed alive into a mass grave, he and his beloved wife together with hundreds of other poor souls, before being shot to death, or, worse, not to death? Certainly he could not have imagined that! He waited for the knock on the door but it did not come. They feared and hoped. They tried to make the best of the situation. In the long run, God would protect them, they believed.

We, by then safely ensconced in America, could not know even the little he knew about their situation. We could only worry and be fearful. As the years went by, we learned from official sources the dates of deportation and death for both of them and later we learned from ordinary people who had been with them, some of the gory details of the tragic endings of their life stories. So we knew of their deportation from Hamburg and their transport to Minsk. We knew from one person that my grandmother had peeled potatoes in the sorry kitchen that served the captive Jews and from another, the facts about the execution at the gravesite. It was enough to know. I didn't need to know more. Eventually I stopped thinking about the cattle cars into which they were crowded for that horrendous caravan to the fields of death.

But then, almost accidentally, I garnered more facts. I was myself in Hamburg when I learned that the knock on the door to arrest my grandfather was a pure figment of my imagination. There was no such private invitation offered. It turns out that by the end, the apartment building in which they lived was turned, along with its neighbor, into a ghetto for all the neighborhood Jews, all of them cramped together in limited space. I don't know the absolute numbers so can't imagine the population density achieved there but it was not good for anyone, that I know. When the day came for their deportation, there was only one summons barked at all of them, and they all obeyed. As would we all. I don't kid myself about that.

From the web article on Minsk that I stumbled upon, I learned about the then resident Jewish community, and the institution of a Jewish ghetto in July of 1941 after the city surrendered to the Germans. The Nazis filled it with local Jews and then started killing thousands of them before the importation of fresh German Jewish fodder for their death machine. So they were ready in November when my grandparents arrived in one of the first transports.

It was reading this that made me realize that my grandparents may have spent time in this ghetto before their execution. I have no way of knowing how speedily their execution followed their arrival though of course I am hoping it was fast, speedy and efficient. But if it was not speedy, if my grandmother, the culturally and socially ambitious aspirant who was so beloved by her daughters to the very ends of their lives, if she had to actually mingle and live and peel potatoes and worse within the degraded population of the ghetto, was she able to make the best of that situation? Was she able in that environment to overcome her prejudices against the Yiddish speakers? Did she stop caring about what people looked like or sounded like? Did she give up her defenses when they proved themselves to be utterly useless? Did she stop thinking altogether? Did she perhaps lose her mind, little by little or all at once? As I would have? As I surely would have?

These are the questions I have now.

I do not even want them answered.

Warren Rosenblum
Philosemitism: A Berlin Story

Back when I was a poor graduate student, researching my dissertation in Berlin, I tried to make some money on the side playing guitar and singing in the subway. I figured Yiddish music was the way to go. Never mind that I don't really speak Yiddish, and that my repertoire was limited to about 8 songs I'd learned off a poorly recorded cassette tape given to me by an overly earnest Dutch engineering student in Ann Arbor who played the squeezebox. And never mind that I'm a pretty awful guitarist with just a passingly ok voice. I figured Germans loved this stuff, and with my big curly "Jew-fro" and vaguely Jewish features I'd be sure to seem authentic, and the coins would pile up.

I advertised in the classifieds for a fiddler or an accordionist to accompany me. A Brazilian violinist called me -- I wasn't sure if it was a man or a woman -- who spoke such awful German that we were barely able to make an appointment, but we arranged to meet at a cafe in Prenzlauer Berg. The prospective fiddler was short and slim, with a shock of brown curly hair, a smooth attractive face, and beautiful blue eyes. He/She said his/her name, but I barely understood it, and not knowing Brazilian names I didn't recognize it as male or female. I began carefully listening for German gender endings (as a violinist, one must be either a "Geiger" or a "Geigerin") and posed various baiting questions, but it quickly became clear that whatever German-lessons he/she was getting, gender-endings in general were not a big theme. Maybe Portuguese just has one gender? I dunno.

Well, anyway, Joao turned out to be a guy - happily married in fact to a lovely Portuguese-speaking German woman -- and he was a pretty good fiddler too, though he didn't know anything about Yiddish music and was going to have to learn the songs from the same miserable tape that I used.

We practiced the songs a bit and played some other stuff too, 12-bar Chicago blues and some American folk songs, then headed off to play in the tunnel at a transfer point between two subway lines. I quickly started to feel absurd. People walked by so rapidly that we could have been playing ANYTHING. We could have played the same line over and over, and I'm not sure they would have noticed. Most people avoided looking at us and stared straight ahead. A few people smiled knowingly or sympathetically and then tossed a trickle of small coins. The best response

we got was from a group of burly black guys from Baltimore who were
visiting to play football. They gave us more than anyone and then danced
raucously to "Die Grine Kusine" as they continued through the passage-
way. I suddenly thought of the Nazis' bizarre theory of a "Jewish-African
symbiosis," which, in their view, was at the origins of jazz and was a major
cause of cultural degeneration in the United States. (Benny Goodman
was the American musician they most loved to hate.) Well, I thought, long
live the "Jewish-African symbiosis!"

After a couple more disappointing efforts to make money in the
subways, I decided to advertise our services in the classifieds. I'd christened
us (so to speak) "*Die Grine Ganoven*" (the green thieves), and I was careful
to put my last name in the ad -- ROSENBLUM -- just to underscore
that this was *Ekht*.

To my surprise someone called right away. To my even greater surprise,
he said he was organizing a birthday party for a 90 year-old Jewish woman
who had been living in Israel. He didn't ask me for a demo tape or even
for references but just wanted to know if I was Jewish. "Well, *Ja!*," I said,
slightly annoyed. And then he asked about our fee.

I hadn't given any thought to a fee, and I was suddenly washed in
guilt at the thought of charging money for some poor old refugee's
birthday party. This woman probably grew up with these songs! She was
probably a native Yiddish speaker! Certainly she'd see right through us:
A graduate student in German history from suburban Chicago with his
hermaphrodite Brazilian fiddle player pretending to be *klezmorim*. *Oy,
Vey!* (And I really am a terrible guitar player.)

Certainly Joao, however, was entitled to some money. I told the
gentleman on the phone that 100 Deutsch Marks would be fine. We
finished making plans, and I hung up. Five minutes later the phone rang
again. "Herr Rosenblum?" It was the same man. "This is about the fee."

"Ok," I said, feeling guilty again and certain that he was now going
to ask for a demo tape.

"I have to insist that you take more. We'll pay you 200 Deutsch
Marks." We argued, but he wasn't budging. "Ok," I said finally, "let's see
how it goes, and then you pay me what you think it was worth."

Two weeks later, Joao and I showed up at the party site. It was a
little convention center in Wansee, and the party was in a meeting room
overlooking the lake. As we entered, they were finishing dinner. A cheerful
looking fat man ran up to me, shook our hands, and told us we should
sit and have dessert. They were going to give some toasts, and then we

would perform.

He pressed a wad of bills into my hand and led us to our seats.

The cake was fantastic, but as I ate, I snuck a peek at the bills. There were four 100-mark notes.

A young woman stood to give a toast. This 90 year-old woman, it turned out, was a Berliner. In fact, she had been one of the few women to qualify as a judge in the Weimar Republic, a career which was denied to her only because of Hitler's rise to power. It occurred to me suddenly that having been an assimilated German Jew, she probably didn't speak a word of Yiddish and could care less about Yiddish music. (In fact, she confessed later, she did not have much of any Jewish identity. She would never have gone to Israel if not for the Nazis.)

When the speeches finished, we got up to play, and, sure enough, it was clear that the guest of honor and most of her friends were indifferent to the songs, no matter how much angst, loss, and yearning I tried to pour into the ballads. I decided to make an unauthorized trip to another genre, and Joao and I played "September Song" by Kurt Weil, which got a wonderful response, especially from the birthday lady. What to play next? The only thing we knew that was remotely similar was George Gershwin's "Summer Time" from *Porgy and Bess*. After that it had to be the blues. So we played a Blind Lemon Jefferson song and something by Muddy Waters, and I told Joao to let it rip, and he gave the folks a bit of his Jimmy Hendrix on the fiddle routine, and I think it all went over ok, though I remember the fat man giving us funny looks. Long live the Jewish-African symbiosis.

And then that was it. We got ready to leave, and the organizer came running over to me, enthusiastic and cheerful again. "Herr Rosenblum," he told me, "Frau Proskauer loved the songs. Come, she'd like to speak with you."

I sat with the lady, and we talked about German legal history and the Weimar Republic, and then she asked if I realized that "September Song" was by Kurt Weil. Of course I did. In fact I'd recently been reading an interview with Weil's widow, Lotte Lenya

She told me she had been at the opening performance in Berlin of Brecht and Weil's *Mahagony*.

"Wow," I said. I was a huge fan of Brecht and Weil. I told her that Lotte Lenya had written something funny in the interview. "She said that if all the people who claim to have been at the opening of the *Three Penny Opera* had really been there, they would have had to perform the play in a football stadium."

"That's what I meant," said Frau Proskauer. "That's where I was: the opening of *The Three Penny Opera*, not *Mahagony*."

She paused for a moment and then said sharply, "That's crap what Lenya wrote." ("*Das ist ja Quatsch was die Lenya geschrieben hat.*")

I decided I had earned my 400 DM. We finished packing our instruments and said "goodbye." I think I even grabbed another piece of cake on the way out.

Leah Rubin
Millicent's Journey

Our rabbis teach us that birth is a beginning, death a destination, and life is a journey. Millicent's journey took her on unpaved roads full of hazards and even, or especially, dead ends. The sudden death of her brother. The murder of her father. Her mother's losing battle with breast cancer. Millicent Routman experienced all of these before most young women her age were married.

Her beloved brother Samuel died at age 13, when Millicent was only eight. When she was 14, her adored father Mike was murdered in his tobacco store during a robbery that netted the thief and murderer two dollars. This left Millicent and her mother, Ida on their own in 1931 St. Louis.

Millicent left school after the eighth grade, and was soon working as a secretary to support herself and her mother. Ida was diagnosed with breast cancer when Millicent was eighteen, and Millicent spent the next six years riding the streetcars to Jewish Hospital on her lunch hours and after work to spend time with her mother, until she too was gone in 1941.

A cousin took her in, and Millicent lived for a time in a home filled with humor and conversation, in sharp contrast to the bleak and despairing atmosphere that had overtaken her family life from the day of Sammy's death. It wasn't always like that. Many photos remain of Ida and Mike, and the pre-loss images are marked by their smiles and overt signs of happiness that typify a young family. After Sammy died suddenly of meningitis, all such indicators disappeared, leaving a stony-faced family in their stead. After Mike's murder, the photography all but stopped, and there are few pictures of Ida after that at all.

Almost by default, Millicent's work became the focus of her life. Her bosses and co-workers admired her for her competence and resilience. She worked for Jewish men in the garment district, and quickly became indispensible to her bosses. She learned quickly and took responsibility eagerly. Her employers were men she spoke of with respect and fondness all of her adult life. Her journey went on.

The United States entered World War II, and while the young men all seemed to be enlisting and going into uniform, the women of Millicent's circle of friends continued to work close to home. The dress business may have been impacted by the focus on the war effort, but Millicent's job was secure. And everyone at work called her Millie.

One night in the spring of 1942, Millie and her girlhood friend Bella took a bus to a U.S.O. dance. It sounded like fun, wrapped in a cloak of patriotism. Wasn't it an act of generosity to go dance and drink punch with soldiers serving their country?

The two met a couple of buddies from New York, G.I.s temporarily sent to Jefferson Barracks from their home in the Bronx. Abe Rubin and Joe Kaplan must have thought they were being watched over by a Jewish cupid, because Abe fell for Millie like a ton of bricks, and it was mutual. Incredibly, Joe and Bella were similarly enthralled, and both couples would be married—Abe and Millie, before Abe went overseas, and Bella and Joe, after the war. Both marriages endured.

When Abe left Jefferson Barracks for Oakland Army/Air Base in California, he and Millie wrote letters to each other every day. In the summer of 1942, she took a train to visit Abe, with the approval of her loving cousins, and with a letter of caution and warning written to Abe by her watchful employer. I still have the letter he wrote to Abe, which may be summarized as follows: "You had better be worthy, young man. I'm sending you the cream of the crop, and if you are not entirely deserving of this fine young woman, I will hunt you down and make you very, very sorry."

Millie came back to St. Louis, knowing she and Abe would marry before he shipped out. Abe completed the Air Corps Technical School course in airplane mechanics in August of 1942, and was sent to Walla Walla Army Air Base in Washington State. Millie took the train out to meet him there in mid-October, and they married on the seventeenth.

They cobbled together a traditional Jewish ceremony, even though none of their family members were able to share it with them. Both of Abe's brothers were also in the army, but not stationed near enough Abe to be present. And travel at that time wasn't feasible for his parents or sister. So they had their tiny wedding, with just Abe's army buddies and their wives, and made a life on the base. They were pretty darn happy to be Staff Sergeant and Mrs. Abraham Rubin.

Abe shipped out to northern France on December 28, 1943. Millie was eight months pregnant. Once again, she got on a train, but this time she wasn't bound for St. Louis. She went to the Bronx, where Abe's parents and sister welcomed her with open arms and full hearts. Their three sons were all overseas, and the fact that the youngest had a wife and a baby on the way, brought them great joy.

In January of 1944, with Abe still in France, Millie gave birth to a baby girl. They named her Ida.

Abe came safely home in October of 1945, and the little family set up housekeeping in the Bronx near the rest of the Rubins. Before long Millie was pregnant again, and Michael was born in October of 1946. Now she had honored her mother and her father.

Abe and his brother Eddie had a little candy store in the neighborhood, and worked it until Eddie's health made that impossible. They sold the store, and Abe went to work for the Veterans Administration, while Eddie nursed his ulcers. Meanwhile, Millie gave birth to a baby girl, Leah, in June of 1949. This baby was supposed to have been a boy named Samuel, so they gave her the Hebrew name Shmuel. That's me. Call me Ishmuel.

While rents were high and apartments small in New York, friends and relations in St. Louis encouraged my parents to bring their brood to my mother's home town. Opportunities, a suburban lifestyle and reduced cost of living beckoned. Having worked for the VA in New York, my father thought that he could grow with their new offices expanding in St. Louis. So in July of 1950, our family of five pulled up stakes and moved to St. Louis.

My parents bought a house in University City and sent their kids to the public schools.

Dad often said he could tell who among their friends had known his wife since girlhood, as they continued to call her Millicent throughout her life. Only people who met her as an adult called her Millie.

My father did get that VA job, but within a few years found himself training people who were being promoted over him, and my parents always believed that there was anti-Semitism to blame. And because they were not people who ever claimed bias as an excuse for anything else, the accusation was credible. There had to be a change.

My father went to work selling insurance, and spent the rest of his working years going door-to-door in the city neighborhoods where his was the only access to insurance available for most residents. He was well-liked among his co-workers, and frequently turned down promotions because he liked being on the street and working with his customers. A couple of times he was persuaded to take a supervisory role, but he always returned to the role of agent. He blamed his first heart attack, suffered in his 40s, on the stress of knowing he was going to have to fire one of his men. After that, he resolved to remain a footsoldier, rather than an officer.

My mother continued to work as a stenographer as they raised their family. They had a nice circle of friends, but were not ones to join clubs or get involved in organizations of any kind. They were never affiliated with any temple or synagogue, but Mom kept us kids home from school not only on the High Holy Days, but also for the first two and the last two days of Passover. She did not light Shabbat candles, but lit her many Yahrzeit candles with emotion and intensity.

My mother didn't keep kosher, but she kept separate 'pesadich' dishes, and kashered her kitchen, driving out the chometz for the holiday. On these holidays we were forbidden to watch tv, play games, listen to the radio, play records or use the sewing machine. We could read and we could write. My mother always said that her religion was the Golden Rule, and she lived by that. But we wondered how that accounted for her ban on the use of appliances.

Mom had a heart attack in her early 40s, after she playfully took a snow shovel out of my hands to give me a few pointers. Dad had just brought Mom home at the end of the work day, and it was starting to get dark. After only a few shovelfuls tossed to the side, she stopped, sensing what had happened. Dad rushed her to the hospital, where she spent two full weeks recovering. While we all learned about cholesterol and adopted a low-fat, heart-healthy diet in the aftermath, Mom returned to smoking her Kents almost immediately.

Millie was a watchful mother. No, more than watchful, she was vigilant. After all, her brother was healthy one day, and died the next of meningitis. Her father went to work one morning, and bled to death on the floor of his small store. She never saw him again. Her mother's illness gave her time to prepare, but it turned out that knowing and anticipating that loss didn't change the outcome. It only took away the surprise. But that didn't outweigh the fear and expectation of death and disaster. Who had a greater right to loss and abandonment issues than my mother?

She worried excessively about her husband and about her kids. Every late arrival was fraught with tension. She was ready to call the hospitals if one of us was not home when expected. She always expected the worst, and chain-smoked her way from the front windows to the back, watching for the straggler to come safely into view.

Life went on; we kids grew up and got married in sequence. Ida and Mike both married other U.City alums. My parents became close with their in-laws, their *machetunim*, all of whom lived in St. Louis. My in-laws were in California.

Then, in 1976, after a reasonable period of normalcy following her sad beginnings, Millicent, Millie, Mom's journey took a sharp turn onto a dark and unmarked road.

Six weeks after I gave birth to my first child, my daughter Rachel, Mom became reacquainted with breast cancer; this time it was hers. She had a modified radical mastectomy just days after her 60th birthday.

Her outlook was grim. If ever there was such a thing as a self-fulfilling prophecy, this was it. Mom had always assumed she would get breast cancer, and follow her mother's path. This was 1976; she was given no chemotherapy or radiation. They removed her breast, pronounced it 'done', and she was supposed to get over it. She did, and she didn't.

She became forgetful; she became withdrawn. We blamed depression. She had a right to be depressed, given her fears and expectations. We sought help for her, but the offerings were like Band-Aids, and my mother needed a tourniquet. Her problems grew.

She referred to Rachel as Rebecca. Not a good sign, when you can't remember your first granddaughter's name. When we tried to cheer her up, she'd say, "I'm sixty years old, what do you expect?" More than once I tried answering that with, "You're sixty, not ninety—sixty's not that old!" Of course I was forgetting that her mother died at 49, her father at 41, and her brother at 14. She never expected to see sixty. To her, sixty might as well have been 100.

Over the next five years her memory declined even more. Her actions and behaviors became more and more peculiar. She exhibited the classic *leave-a-pot-on-the-stove* danger, and once went across the hall to a neighbor's apartment in great fear because her oven timer was buzzing and she didn't know what it was.

With my father's permission I went to see Mom's doctor. I said, "You know her blood pressure and her heart rate, but here's what you don't know." He told me that I was describing early senility, but that my mother was too young for that. I didn't point out that maybe that's what the 'early' meant. I wanted this guy on our side. My greatest fear was that her breast cancer had metastasized to her brain.

The doctor admitted her to the hospital for tests. She was disoriented to the point of near-panic. Every day she cried, and pleaded with my father to take her home. I was thirty-two years old and had never seen my mother cry before; it was shocking. It hurt him deeply to see her in such a state, but he held firm, and consistently sweet-talked her into handling it "just for one more day."

After a week of scanning, probing, testing and scoping, they had found nothing.

Enter Dr. George Grossberg, King of the Alzheimer's doctors.

You were already thinking Alzheimer's? Of course, this is 2010. But in 1981, none of us had heard of it.

Dr. Grossberg explained everything he could to us about what they then knew about the disease. He also told us that there was nothing, literally nothing that they could offer in the way of treatment. He outlined what we should expect in the near future, and the arc that her disease would likely take. I began to wish it had been "just" a brain tumor, my previous worst-case scenario. At least there would be treatment and hope. I was so naïve then. We all were.

This was the summer of 1981, and I was days away from delivering my son, Robbie. Losing my mother, gaining my son. I'd been pregnant for nearly nine months, but hadn't expected this to result in a trade.

Dr. Grossberg was assembling a small group of people to be a support group (another term we hadn't heard before) for the family members of his growing handful of Alzheimer's patients. My father, who'd never gone to a single meeting of any organization in his life, began attending Dr. Grossberg's meetings with fervor. It was as close to organized religion as he ever got. I would go to their apartment to stay with my mother, who by this time couldn't be left alone safely. Then my father would go to the meetings where a facilitator heard their stories, offered coping strategies, and updated them on what was being learned about this dread disease. This small group meeting in a school basement was the core that developed into the Alzheimer's Association. He made some wonderful friends there; it was a godsend.

Millie continued to deteriorate, as predicted. Once when my father and I were taking her to a doctor's appointment she opened her car door as we were zipping along Lindbergh Boulevard. Abe's quick reflexes enabled him to grab it and pull it shut; I pushed down the lock button from the back seat. We were very lucky that no one was in the lane next to us at that instant.

Dad had retired as soon as he turned 62 so that he could take care of Mom full time. But her care was more than a full-time job. The repeated questions, the wandering, the undressing, the ultimate incontinence and the complications that brought were overwhelming. Then you must remember that during all this care-giving, he was face-to-face with his best friend, lover and partner of forty years, who didn't even know her own name, much less his.

We urged him to consider nursing home placement. Several of his support-group friends had already been forced to do this. He resisted. He kept her at home much longer than he likely should have. In April of 1983 he reluctantly admitted her to a residential home, where the care was less about medicine and more about oversight. She didn't need skilled nursing. Ironically, after a lifetime of high blood pressure and smoking, the history of a heart attack at age 42, and the mastectomy, her health was actually considered "good". The incongruity was staggering.

Soon after she entered the home she stopped speaking almost entirely. We were encouraged, however, by the fact that she seemed very excited to see us whenever we came to visit, so we concluded that she recognized us as her family, even though she couldn't say our names. Then one day while I was in her room with her, the custodian stopped in for her waste basket, and my mother reacted with as much animation and delight as she had when I came in. Another bubble burst. I cried all the way home.

On her 68th birthday, almost eight years to the day after her first, my mother had her second mastectomy. Some questioned why we would 'put her through' such a surgery, when her quality of life was so poor. We couldn't imagine allowing her to endure the physical pain and trauma that the unchecked tumor would have brought. And in the back of our collective minds, we held out hope for a breakthrough in Alzheimer's research—something that could bring Mom back—the Millie we knew-- from the precipice.

In February of 1987, my father died in his sleep. My five-year old son and I found him on a sunny Saturday morning when we arrived for our standing date for what we called C, C & C: coffee, cartoons, and chocolate-covered Entenman's donuts. By chance, 10-year old Rachel had slept over at a friend's the night before, and wasn't with us. Normally while I'd make the coffee, "Jeep", the nickname Rachel gave Abe for "Grand Pa" when she was four, would get down on the living room floor and watch cartoons with the kids. This always devolved into 'tickle time', and as they like to say, hilarity ensued.

Not so this week. I tried not to panic. I was torn between the need to collapse with grief and the desire to insulate my son. I worried that this would be a seminal and scarring event in his young life. In my attempt to maintain perspective, to keep from going off the deep end, I robotically called the police, then my husband, then my siblings. The police came, and so did the neighbors. It was all so surreal. The police officer was respectful and sympathetic, and went into the bedroom to verify everything I had told him: where Dad was, how I found him, no signs of foul play. I don't remember much after that, except that before we left, Robbie suggested that we should call Jeep's doctor. Perhaps I underdid the message, or overdid the downplaying.

In the following days Dad's siblings arrived with their spouses, and we buried him in one of the plots my parents had purchased years before. Before breast cancer, before heart attacks, before Alzheimer's disease. Many, many people came to Dad's funeral and *shiva*, and over and over we heard him described as 'such a *gutteh neshomeh*' –a good soul. He was well-loved. He was only sixty-six.

Strangely, Mom's old friend Katie called me repeatedly in the weeks after, telling me that my dad had willed his own death. I said that if people could do that, the nursing homes and mental institutions would be empty. Besides, Abe enjoyed his kids, grandkids and friends, and was planning to expand his volunteer work to include a literacy program. But especially, while he missed Millie being there terribly, he would never have abandoned her, even in her tragic and diminished state.

Another friend, in a misguided attempt to comfort me, said, "By all rights this should have been your mother." Really? As if there's some cosmic ledger book of *Rubin Deaths*, and the auditor accidentally debited my father's account, when he meant to do my mother's? No, 'by all rights' this should have been some child molester or murderer, who might have been stopped before he harmed anyone. But I cried and I nodded, unwilling to pursue or debate the point.

I remembered that I had long said, before my mother entered the nursing home, that if this disease killed my father before it killed her, I would never be able to forgive her. But when the time came, I realized that I'd been wrong. As strongly as I had believed that, it just didn't turn out that way. Mom, too, was a victim, I knew. She was not the cause of my father's death, and I couldn't blame her.

The following Saturday, a week after Dad passed away, my brother Michael went to see Mom. Though she was little more than a shell of her former self, with no outward signs of any cognition at all, Michael felt obligated to tell her that Dad was gone.

The next day, while Mike and I and our spouses were gathered around her bed, she began rocking herself, and making sounds that the doctors describe as 'syllabication'—repeating "Deh-deh-deh-deh-deh" over and over. Till "Deh-deh-deh-deh-dad-died" came out. We all froze. Michael and I looked at each other across her bed, our jaws dropped. I repeated,

"Dad died." I looked at my sister-in-law and at my husband, to confirm that we had all actually heard her utter her first words in so many years. Michael said, "That's what I told her yesterday, 'Dad died,' but there was no reaction." All four of us were shocked and stunned. So maybe all those times that I sat and fed her and talked to her, thinking I was doing it more for me than for her, were not really meaningless. On some level, at least some of the time, there must have been intake, and probably some degree of comprehension. That 'persistent vegetative state' in the medical parlance couldn't measure the immeasurable.

We held her hands and told her how peacefully her Abe had died, and that he'd suffered no pain. She stopped rocking, stopped the syllabicating, and her body relaxed.

For three more years, Millie was in and out of the hospital, with various infections that required IV antibiotics, serious episodes of dehydration, and a massive eye infection that nearly precipitated the enucleation of her only seeing eye. Friends said she had nine lives. She was at death's door so many times that I think the Angel of Death gave her her own parking space. She died three years and a week after Abe, her odyssey ended.

When such a protracted, long-anticipated death finally occurs, everyone thinks you should be relieved. They think you will be glad that your loved one is no longer suffering, or trapped in a body they can't use. They think you are in some way celebrating mentally. It's not so. It's the culmination of so many complex emotions, so much pain and loss. And as happens when someone walks right up to death's door repeatedly, but never crosses the threshold, you begin to think that she will go on forever, always flirting with death, teasing it, but never letting it take her. The loss, at that point, is overwhelming. Some people understand, others don't. And although it's the diametric opposite of a sudden and unexpected death, like that of my father, they are both crushing blows.

Millicent, Millie, Mom lies next to Dad now, where we can visit their graves, pour out our hearts when we feel the need, and leave pebbles on their rose-granite headstone. Her journey was not an easy one. Just as the fabled traveler Odysseus sailed treacherous waters and faced numerous dangers and losses, so Millie's travel was marked by great losses in her early years, but she experienced a classic and enduring romance with her Abe, and raised three healthy and happy children. The third phase of her journey took her down some unlit roads with hairpin curves and no shoulders. We saw her through to her destination, but we couldn't navigate for her, couldn't pave the way. Is this the lesson, then-- that we all ultimately travel alone, or to the contrary, is it possible that if we have touched the lives of others, that we will not be abandoned? If only Millicent, Millie, Mom could tell us.

Margaret R. Ruhe-Spencer
Daddy's Story

Both of my parents were Survivors of the Holocaust. Eight years after my father died my mother started writing short stories. Her stories were published in local newspapers and the *St. Louis Sagarin Review*. She achieved St. Louis celebrity status because of her charm, her elegance and her speaking and writing abilities. Marylou Ruhe gave countless hours to the St. Louis Holocaust Museum and Learning Center as a docent and speaker. My sister, Janet Ruhe Schlag, and I are proud of her accomplishments and legacy.

My father, Steven J. Ruhe died in 1983. We are also proud of his accomplishments; however Daddy never had the opportunity to create his legacy due to a pact he and my mother made many years before; more about that later.

My sister and I became aware of the brief but powerful autobiography our father had written when our mother finally showed it to us. This was fifteen years after Daddy's death and it was not in its entirety. Page one was missing. We learned later that our mother destroyed it in her desire to protect us and herself from the painful details she and Daddy never wanted to share. This was the reason for the pact.

In his own voice, written in his broken English, limited typing skill and only slightly edited for easier reading are pages two and three of my father's story. The spelling and grammar are mostly that of my father's. Italicized words are his, my interpretations are in parenthesis.

Daddy's story written circa 1949

Auschwitz-Birkenau was a Camp of concentrated Jews from all over Europe. I soon find out that the germans★ will look for men to go for work; Whoever was weak, beaten up or *unfitt* (unfit?)did not have a chance and had to die right there. That was just the way. It was better to sit quietly in the corner, hungry than stay in line for a bowl of soup. The fight for food left many beaten beyond recognition. I was in section N:26 my brother (Mietek) and father (Henry) were in different section, I do not remember the number. We talk to each other for few minutes mentioning our women★ and wondering about their situation. We had tears in our eyes. That was the first time in my life I saw my dad crying. I gave him hope and try to comfort him but inside myself I was broken up completely.

After a few days of this *I never saw my dad and brother again.* One day I was in line indicating that I will be joining a labor group. I went *thru*(through?) some kind of screening and *my left arm was tattooed with the N:B8988.* The same ink pen was used for about 100 *man* (men?) in my group. We were loaded on military trucks and shipped to Labor Camp Althammer. My arm and *so* (also?)the others was swollen and *painfull* (painful?) for several days I am sure I had some temperature, but I did not want to admit to anybody. The *scare* (fear?) to be *unfitt* to work was so great that *it is hard to believe what a person is able to do being sick as sick can be.* Some of our *man* that were not able to stay on their legs were put in a sickroom and You could find them later *rapped* (wrapped?) up in a sack with the number written on top; on the bathroom floor.

The work in this camp was *ragged* (rugged?) and hard, the winter cold did not help in being many hours outside. I was involved in carrying 100*lbs* (pounds?) bags from *fraight* (freight?) cars to *warehauses* (warehouses?) on my shoulders. I was involved in binding metal strips with wires for concrete foundations. I was occupied with preparation of hot lime to be ready for mortar. The germans★ were building *a* (an?)electric plant with *free of pay labor.* My eyes were suffering much from dust and particles. My back was hurting and my knees were swollen. After every days work by returning back to the *baracks* (barracks?)we were a target of a degenerate leader of the camp Obersturmfurhrer SS Hoffman called by the prisoners "Tom Mix". *He was a man of life and dead (death?).* Just for his personal sadistic satisfaction he would pick up any prisoner out of *appeal line* (roll call?)take him behind the hill and *shot* (shoot?) him to death, it was done to obtain more discipline, to create more *scare* (fear in?) prisoner or just a hunger to kill another Jew.

We were degraded and handled as trash. You never knew what next hour will bring. The life was so miserable that when later in season we could hear some bombardment and the *air* (raid?) alarms were sounded we were praying some time for a fast liberation and sometimes for a bomb to hit and *finish all the misery.*

With the time passing the air alarms were more frequent and the bombardment continued. The food supplies were shorter and as a result our food was very poor. We were getting thinner by the hour and weaker by the minute, while hard work continued. Many of my friends got sick and enter the sickroom. It was depressing. I never saw them again. One evening the whole Camp had to be evacuated. It was done in a hurry.

We were rushed to military trucks and sent away. We landed in place called Gleiwitz I, stay there awhile unloaded the dead ones and then to Gleiwitz II. We were pushed into barns. It was night. Soon we could hear a cannonade of guns and some machine guns. It was close, but how close I don't know. After few hours the firing stopped. We had to march in the middle of the city five in a row surrounded by heavy guards of the Luftwaffe. The civilian population passing by was looking at us with some sort of pity or *sorry* (sorrow?). It was approximately 6 o'clock in the morning. Soon after we were loaded approximately 100 *man* to a car: No food, no water, no facilities for relief. Our clothes were soaked with urine and deposits. The smell was horrible. *We were not human any more.* I was not able to think any more, I was cold, my mouth was dry, I felt I will collapse soon. I looked over the wall of the car and found some snow on an edge. I picked up and *swallow* (swallowed?). It was a relief. I continued to do this. *I was holding onto my life with the rest of my power.* The trip took approximately 3 days with stops and backing up and going forwards. On one occasion we had to get rid of the *bodys* (bodies?) of our *man* by burying them in big holes near the RR tracks. Some bread was distributed after this horrible experience to us. We stopped in a mountain type terrain in the heart of germany★ called Dora (Hartzgeburge). Dora was another concentration camp. Going thru another selection I was shipped to Komando Ellrich. The living quarters were approximately 4-5 kilometers from the working place. Under a total guard we had to march for days work in to the inner of a mountain involved in building *tunells* (tunnels?). Eight hour work (days) consisted of drilling holes with big pneumatic drills into the walls. After sufficient depth the civilian german★ workers will enter and plant dynamite and then blast. Soon after we were rushed inside while the air still thick with dust and forced to fill small cars with dynamited rocks and particles. Moisture and water constantly dripping from walls of the *tunell*(tunnel?) contributed to very unhealthy situations.

The *Capos* (Kapos?) in charge were bitter ex criminals and took every advantage to beat us and throw us down from the uneven surfaces of the place, I experienced myself several times hard blows and had been thrown down from approximately 7 feet high. I was bleeding from my nose and mouth. I begged for mercy and *promisse* (promised?) to do work for two, but to be left alone. I had a feeling that war was coming to the end and I will have the opportunity to call for justice and *I will be a man again.* In this camp the idea of the Kapos, german★ ex criminals was to kill at least one or two of us in order to gain some credits from their superiors. This was worse than hell to be in Ellrich, known as a camp of death next to Buchenwald. Our *bodys* (bodies?) were covered with swollen wounds full of *puss* (pus?). There were not facilities to clean them. The lice were all over my body. I still have some marks on my body. I believe in February 1945 the air alarms were again frequently. One night the germans★ had to evacuate us and loaded us on *fraight* (freight?) trains; *destination unknown.*

Some of the prisoners brought some news that our military guard is somewhat worried about the situation. They felt that some of the cities from where they come were heavily bombed and they have no news about their families. We did not know how to take it. In a *painfull* (painful?) voyage from Dora to Concentration Camp Bergen Belsen took approximately 2–3 days and nights. We stopped several times to re route, we met other trains with *Jewish women in shaggy clothes and no hair.* It was a shock to see this.

In Bergen Belsen we were regrouped and placed in a building where previously the german★ military were stationed. Under a penalty of death we were not allowed to leave the quarters. We were fed once or twice a day with some kind of soup and slice of bread. No work. I noticed that I was completely exhausted and so was the rest. I had a hard time to get up from my bed. I realized that my body is thin and pale. It took several days or possibly two weeks until some news got around that the german★ supervisors over the camp are wearing white bands on their uniforms. They also told us that the camp is not more a concentration camp but an internment camp. *And so it happened.* A day or so later a British tank broke the gate and enter the camp. Some were cheering and happy, some were running out some were crying, some were dying and some were just *stoned* (stunned?) and could not move. I was one of them. We were transferred to temporary hospitals for treatments and hygiene care. We were free at last but lonesome and sick. After a few weeks of treatment we were let out. With proceedings of identification and replacement of *cloth* (clothes?) we *tryed* (tried?) to regroup and find ourselves within the survivors of the same region or home town in order to find eventually some names of survivors and find families. For some it worked *it did not work for me.*

Page one is still missing. In 2008 our mother joined our father in death. We will never know the whole truth about page one. For several reasons we have surmised that our parents never wanted us to know about our father's first wife and his son, Daniel, who were murdered (not certain if by an allied bomb attack or by the Nazis in a Concentration Camp). Our mother's privacy and our father's grief were answered by their own pact of silence. May they both rest in peace and may we never forget!

*every time the word "germans" is mentioned it is not capitalized, intentionally I believe.

Amy Scharff
The Lost Spirit of Micah

If I wanted to, I could swim laps across the hot-tub in the complex where my grandparents live out the winter months. Snow blows over the Midwest while they play bridge and watch the news in their sunny Scottsdale condo. I always thought it was overkill, a tiled outdoor hot-tub big enough for thirty close friends in a climate that, at its coolest, requires a cotton sweater. But when I visit, I have no complaints. Despite the fact that all ten water jets sit at the same height on my lower back.

It was my upper back that wanted the pressure last month when I visited Gram and Grandpa at their winter home: my shoulders were carrying the balance of placating my grandfather's propensity for power trips and my own desire for a peaceful visit. So I sloped into the water and leaned on my elbow, trying to situate myself so the jet of water pummeled my thoracic vertebrae. I was glad to have the whole secluded "tub" to myself, enjoying the clear twilight and a moment alone, removed from my grandfather's passionate grasp for control: visiting them requires relinquishing my own control in order to keep peace. It's what my grandmother does every day of her life, although she has managed to retain a strength of will, perhaps passive-aggressively, that refuses to let Grandpa's orders and demands eclipse her spirit.

My moment alone, however, *was* just a moment.

A stout woman with short, bright hair appeared from around the corner. She spied me straightening and, embarrassed, squeezing the air-bubbles that had gathered at the top of my swimming suit from the water jet. She discarded her towel and took the first step into the tub. "Holy buckets!" It was hot. I said nothing, but smiled.

Soon I smelled orange, and the fruit came into view before the burly man holding it. "Oh, Hans, it's really hot in here," said the woman in a distinctively upper-midwestern accent. Hans had a large amount of thick, white hair on his head and a large amount of gut on his abdomen; and a decorative orange half-peeled in his hands. It smelled delicious. I hadn't known that decorative oranges smelled so good, or so pungent, until then. Neither had I known that they were edible.

"Oh yah?" Hans said to his companion in an accent that matched hers in dialectical roundness. The "oh" barely got through his lips, rerouted largely through his nose. He set his towel on a bench next to hers and walked off again, around the corner. Returned shortly without the orange. I could still smell it as he wiped his hands on his swimming suit and stepped into the pool. Hans' eyes flew open. "*Holy* cow, Viv, you weren't kiddin'!"

"Yah, it must be 110 in here. My spa at home, you know, we don't keep it up above 103. Orange no good?"

"No. Real sour. Tossed it." Waving his hand in her direction. "Not worth it."

I smiled again, listening to the pair. "Are you from Wisconsin?" Addressing them both.

"*I* am!" Hans' blue eyes, which looked too small for all their expression, lit again. "How'd you know?"

"I've never heard anyone say 'holy buckets' unless they came from Wisconsin." Grinning now, feeling an odd kinship with these strangers immersing themselves in the same hot water that was stewing me.

"Oh, *I'm* from South Dakota," Viv said. "He's from Wisconsin. Fact, Hans'd never heard anyone say that until he met me, right Hans?"

"No, I'd never heard anyone say it. 'Holy buckets.' Not until I met you. Say," he turned to me, "are you from Wisconsin too?"

"No, but I went to Madison. I'm very partial to that state, and live in Minneapolis now. Where do you live?"

"Oh, right out here," he said, pointing toward the sunset. "Down the street." I remembered this was a permanent residence for some, and momentarily marveled at the fact that Gram and Grandpa still lug their team of suitcases and their toy poodle out here every December from Missouri. Hans and Viv and I talked of towns in Wisconsin and South Dakota, and I listened to that endearing accent that I can still replicate like a true northerner. Something about Hans' consonants, though, told me English was not his first language.

"Yah, originally Holland," he said, a darkness suddenly in his glance.

"Y' know," said Viv, "in South Dakota I grew up on a farm, and I'm not so sure it was that different from how Hans here grew up." Viv was examining her hands, tanned and gnarled from a lifetime of work. "Y' know what happens if you wear silver jewelry in these hot-tubs, yah? I hope you don't have any silver jewelry on."

"No, I don't. I did it once. It turned black."

"Oh I swear! And y' know what's perfect for taking off the tarnish?" Viv looked up at me with a great load of suspense in her voice. Hans nodded emphatically and pointed to Viv, the obvious messenger of a powerful oracle. "*Toothpaste.*"

Hans couldn't contain himself. "Yah, you bet! Toothpaste, you know, it's a mild abrasive." Nodding. Very serious. "A mild abrasive. Take the tarnish right off."

I was soggy but appreciative. Slumped in the corner, the jet massaging my lower back still. I flung an arm onto the concrete deck to keep myself from sliding further into the water. "Well, you know your jewelry won't get cavities then."

"Cavities! Right!" A moment of joyous laughter, and then silence. I shut my eyes and leaned my head back.

When I looked up again, Hans was eyeing me tenderly. "You know, you look so much like my sister. Those eyes." He said it almost to himself, and I wasn't sure how to respond.

"Oh. Um. Well maybe I'm her! Hans! Where have you been?" The humor turned out to be much more poignant than I'd intended. They both laughed, but this time Hans' shoulders contained a gravity as they jostled.

"You're her. Huh. Yah, you could be. Your dark eyes. She left us when she was about your age."

"How old are you, hon? 25?" Viv assessing my face.

"27."

"Yah, I thought so. 'Bout right. See, my oldest is 44." I was astonished. This woman didn't look much past 55, and I told her so. She laughed, thanked me. "It's from working all my life. That, and not taking any orders from anyone else." Hans nodded his agreement again, a supportive admirer. "Nope. Not even from Hans. Right, Hans?" More silent nodding. "Yah, my husband owned a construction company. His one mistake was, whenever someone would come complainin' to him, he'd point my way and he'd say, 'She's the boss.' So I was. And when he left us, I went and got my masters and then, well, still was the boss! Just kept being what I already was." I was genuinely impressed. Women in that line of business take enough flack today, still; it must have been that much more challenging thirty or forty years ago. Back when people said things like, "That's *unheard* of!" I pictured Gram telling a story from her past, something she did once or twice that, in those days, was a little bit crazy. She definitely has some stories. I thought, they should meet these neighbors of theirs.

"But you see, I'd grown up on a farm all my life. I knew how to use my hands. And I was the oldest of three girls. Oh, I was up every day before school, slopping those pigs and up in the cow shed, making sure everything was okay for the morning milks; and that was before the crack of dawn and a five-mile walk up to the school. No, I didn't take no orders from anyone. I knew exactly what to do."

Hans and I stayed riveted on Viv, who was seeming to me like a character written into good fiction. The way she added the details to her life, tacked on the ends of her sentences: understated, leaving no room for doubt.

"Yah, I used to pull calves and castrate sheep and all of it, when I was a girl." Pull calves. I thought I knew what this meant but, feeling incredibly urban, asked anyway. "Birthed 'em. Pulled 'em right out of their mothers. You know, you just run a cow till she's tired, get her into the stanchion where she can't go anywhere, and knock her knee. Tap, tap. She'll lay right down. No place to go. And you just sit right down there at that end and pull it." My face must have given away the fact that I still couldn't quite conceive of what calf-pulling entailed.

Hans helped out. "Yah, you just reach inside, grab onto the legs." Despite my liberal upbringing and my moderate familiarity with the natural world, my eyes widened as they imagined this scene. "Tell her, Viv."

"Well, you just sit there at the end of her, reach in, grab the legs, put your feet up against her butt —" Viv demonstrated in the water, lifting both feet just above the surface and grasping an imaginary fetal cow with her hands, one over the other. "And you yank! And eventually the calf comes flying out and lands on you, and you're on your back, and you're quick sure to wipe the afterbirth off your face so you can breathe, and you clean up the calf and that's it." She made it sound so routine, like washing a car. I still hoped, although with reservations, that my grandparents might meet this couple.

"Tell her about the sheep, Viv. Tell the story." Hans was enjoying this, pointing from Viv to me in his eagerness.

"Oh, the sheep?" Viv chuckled. "Have you ever heard of Rocky Mountain oysters?" Her eyes narrowed as she looked at me. I had heard of them. "Have you ever eaten one? You know what they are? They're testicles. Have you ever eaten a testicle?" I had seen them, I told her, and I knew what they were; but I had never ventured a bite. "Well they're real delicacies. The vet would do it for free, if he was over for something else. Castrate the sheep. He'd just slit the sac and take 'em out, all careful and delicate. They're real' fragile, you know, the membrane is really thin and oh, would he be mad if he dropped one, it'd shatter all over the ground. 'Aw, shit!' he'd say, 'cause you know they was real expensive and he'd be doing it for free, for nothing for you. He was real' nice about doing it for us."

Viv paused to look at my expression and Hans jumped in again. "Go on, Viv. The Basque. Tell her about the Basque!"

"Well my husband and I, we had 150 head of sheep that needed castrating one year and we didn't want to do it ourselves. Too many. Just too much to do. So we were wondering how to go about dealing with it. Well, there was this Basque fellow in my square-dancing club. You know the Basques?" I nodded, assuming she meant did I know about who they are, not did I know each one of them. "Yah, this Basque fellow and I got to talking one night at square-dancing and he says, 'Oh, I can do them up real fast, why don't I just come over on Saturday and take care of it?' So I says yah, sure, sounds great! Well. Now this guy, he's a big, muscular guy, all dark and sexy, and he comes over that Saturday with just a big bottle of Mogen David. And I'm thinking, oh geez, he must drink on the job. What have we gotten ourselves into? But that was all he had with him. No knife, no scissors, just a bottle of Mogen David."

I was laughing silently at this point, having no premonition of what I was about to hear but loving the story anyway. I was in suspense. "150 head?" I asked, feeling very up on my farm lingo.

"Yah, 150 head. All rams. Had to be castrated. Okay. So he comes over with this bottle of Mogen David. And he says 'Just sit me down here where you want me to do it,' and we bring him the sheep and he opens the wine and —" she broke off, expecting me to guess what he did. I couldn't. "He bites off those testicles, swishes his mouth out with Mogen David, takes one guzzle for himself, and grabs the next sheep."

My jaw dropped open. This was not fiction. I could tell by the way she told the story, by the way Viv didn't ever take orders from anyone. And I could tell by the way Hans was nodding. "He castrated the sheep with his teeth?" I had to ask, put it into words, just to confirm that I understood what Viv was saying.

"Yah, with his teeth and the Mogen David. First he rinses his mouth out and then he takes a swig for himself. The sugar must've kept him going. I tell you, a hundred-fifty sheep he goes through in two hours. *Two hours.* The vet couldn't do it that fast. And he's just biting through, spitting the goods into a bucket, and rinsing with that wine. I swear, it was the darndest thing."

Granted, we were sitting in a Jacuzzi; but I got a hot-flash. "I wonder why he used Mogen David," I said, for something to say.

"Maybe he was Jewish," Hans offered.

And Viv continued, "I don't know. We used to use it at church for communion. It's real' sweet wine. But it worked for those sheep. And I swear, not one of 'em ever got infected. We'd castrate sheep, inevitably one or two of 'em would flare up. But this Basque did it and it was perfect. And every time after that, I'd see him at square-dancing, this big, sexy guy with his crazy-neat smile, and all I could see was blood all over his teeth and dripping down his chin. Oh, it was so funny."

"I guess the alcohol disinfected everything," I mused, imagining what a crazy-neat smile might look like covered in blood. And then laughed. Amazed at this woman sitting here with me.

"Look at her, Viv," Hans pointed to me, a sad but somehow enthusiastic smile on his face. "Doesn't she look like the pictures of Micah?" Viv nodded. "Oh, you could be her. Look just like how I remember her. Oh, I'm getting a little teary here."

I turned to Hans, who was wiping his eyes. "Her name was Micah?"

"Was Micah. Yes. Oldest of nine of us. You know, the oldest daughter of a mother of nine knows how to take care of kids. She was Momma's right hand. Knew how to raise us all." Hans stopped looking at me then, and looked at a woman he saw only in his mind's eye. "She studied and wanted to go work on a cruise. She went to school for it, and got a job on a cruise ship at last. Was gonna' take her around the world. She was so excited to go off on her own, working on a ship. But she knew so much about raising children that they made her work in the nursery. She'd wanted to get away from raising kids. But she knew too much, as they say. She'd wanted to work in the bar or something, you know, work around adults. But she was all cooped up with the children again. We're unsure exactly what happened. But we think that had something to do with it. Yes." Hans looked up at me once again. "And your eyes are just like hers."

"She didn't return?" I was cautious, almost afraid of his answer.

"No. She never came back from her first cruise. No one had any information." He sighed, tried to return to the present. "But you know those cruise ships. They dump their garbage right out the bottom, and there's schools of sharks just getting fat following the ships around..."

The thought was too horrific to let him keep going in that direction. Well worse than a man castrating sheep with his teeth. "How old were you at the time?"

"Oh, I was just 12 or 13. And Grandma knew. She knew everything."

Hans squinted at me, even though the sun had already set. "She was sort of clairvoyant, you know. Grandma knew things. Middle of the night one night, 'Get up, Paw. Something's wrong with the dog.' And sure enough, Paw-Paw got up, but it was too late. The dog had jumped the fence, but his collar had caught on the post. Hanged. She knew. She also knew the night Paw-Paw was hurt in the war. She woke up one night, and woke all her kids, gathered 'em around her in the middle of the night. 'Paw's hurt,' she told them. And he was. Hurt that night in France."

"Yah, your grandma was something else. I never met her," Viv said, as much to Hans as to me, "but I heard stories. There's lots of stories. Somethin' else."

"Yah, and so was Micah. Strong like you," he said affectionately to Viv. "And she had those fiery eyes, like you do," he said to me. But the difference, I hoped, was not very great. Viv's fire may not have come through her eyes, but I certainly saw it in her spirit and her storytelling and the way she laughed at her own honesty. "Not until Viv came into my life had I ever met anyone that strong." They were gazing at each other in late-life love, and I was filled with a feeling that I had happened on this story by some fortuitous fate, and not because it could happen at just any dusk in a hot-tub.

I was thoroughly shriveled and sat up so as to take good-bye slowly. Stood in the shallow water and stretched my arms, now steaming in the cornflower twilight. "Well, I'm sure glad we met," I said to Viv and Hans, leaning to grab my towel from the deck. "I'd like to talk with you again while I'm out here; maybe we'll see each other by the pool tomorrow."

They stretched and climbed from the water too, dripping into their towels and offering fond good-byes. Hans walked me to the gate. I looked into the sky and saw a full moon, low behind the hairy fronds of a palm tree. "Look," I said to Hans, and we stood a second before the gate and watched the moon. I thought of Micah watching the same full moon over some foreign sea fifty years ago. Wishing for some strength, or some freedom, or something no one will ever know. And perhaps finally settling on a choice that would grant her what she needed.

"God bless," he said to me as I walked out into the street, a block from my grandparents' place. And he looked at me as though searching for something more, something different than good-bye. I wanted to tell him one more thing before we parted, one thing perhaps about Micah; about living, now that I know, with her eyes.

I turned back to address Hans but he'd already disappeared behind the wall surrounding the pool. I wandered slowly, looking at the grass. Glancing up to cross the quiet street, I noticed ahead, shuffling toward me, the silhouette of my grandfather, apparently worried. I smiled.

"Where've you been?" he demanded. "You been in that hot-tub this whole time?" I nodded slowly, feeling full with my experience. "Listen. It's bad for you. I don't want you staying in that hot-tub for so long anymore. Don't do that again. Do you hear me?"

The things we do to create our own control.

"Yeah, Grandpa. I didn't mean to worry you."

My thoughts remained with Hans and Viv for a moment longer. Something about the spirit of Micah, the sister lost in the sea for the orders she took. Or the choices she was not allowed to make.

I turned the corner with Grandpa and we walked back home to Gram and the dinner she had made for us.

Howard Schwartz
Close Calls

I. Phoenix, 1967

I traveled by train to the west coast, taking the northern route, and I came back on the southern. On the second day I got off in Phoenix. My aunt and uncle lived there. I wanted to see the Grand Canyon. They asked, "Do you want to go by bus or plane?" "By plane." They ordered a ticket. The plane was leaving in the morning.

That night a loud voice rang out at 4 am: "Leave!" it demanded. "Leave!" But when I looked around, no one was there.

As soon as my uncle got up, I told him I had to go. "But we've already paid for your flight". "I have to leave now." He looked at me strangely and took me to the train.

Next stop, Houston, I bought a newspaper. A plane flying over the Grand Canyon crashed into it the day before. All eight passengers were killed. Almost nine.

II. Maui, 1970

Jules and I were driving on a narrow path through the forest in our rented car. In the mirror I saw a car approaching so fast there wasn't time to tell him. Suddenly it careened wildly around us, racing out of sight. Jules said, "He'll crash into the next car." He was right. We came upon the wreck a few minutes later. The man in the car he struck was dead. He was barely hurt, completely drunk.

I sometimes think about that. If that drunk hadn't swerved, I would have died in that place. No wedding. No children. No books.

III. Kirksville, 1980

The instant I stepped outside the airport door, a sparrow crashed at my feet. I boarded with trepidation, wishing I had taken the bus. I was the only passenger, my seat right behind the pilot.

As we approached St. Louis we circled the airport several times. I asked the pilot why.

"The landing gear isn't opening," he said.

I looked down and saw several fire trucks and ambulances waiting on the runway. I asked about them. He said, "If the gear doesn't go down this time, they'll coat the runway with foam so the plane can land on its belly."

We circled one last time. At last the gear opened and we landed and I got out of there.

All this happened long ago. Anyway, everyone has their own close calls.

Miriam Schwartz
An Israeli Flightmare

I.

The shuttle was supposed to arrive promptly at 4 am. Yet I didn't arrive at the curbside of that Jerusalem supermarket until 4:05 am. Just my two huge bags, and four carryon bags kept me company on that cold morning as I waited for the shuttle to the airport, praying that I hadn't already missed it.

Ten years ago exactly, there was a big bombing at this exact same SuperSol grocery store. The girl who exploded herself was the exact same age as the girl that was killed in the tragic bombing. And some say the two girls even looked alike, two beautiful young women with their whole lives ahead of them. I tried not to think too often about that tragic day, but each time I did chills ran through my body, and the hair on my arms would stand in memory of that occurrence.

I stood at that grocery store, waiting for the shuttle that was to take me out of Israel. I had been living in both Jerusalem and Be'er Sheva for nearly three years of my adult life. And now it was time for me to gather all of my things from my mother's apartment in Jerusalem, and move them to my new home in the US. I can't deny that I truly loved living in Israel. There was excitement, community, good friends, and so much good food. So many memories of travelling all over the country, camping with friends, dancing at festivals, and spending the Jewish holidays with my Israeli cousins and uncles. All of these meshed together to form so many very special memories in this incredible place. There was also an amazing peace movement that I had been involved in, and in the previous year I had attended graduate school in the desert where I had the opportunity to study Arabic, Hebrew, and conflict resolution. Yet I couldn't avoid the fact that living in Jerusalem was getting too intense for me, and that America, my other home, was calling me daily to come back.

I waited over 40 minutes for the shuttle, and desperately realized it wasn't coming. So I hopped in a taxi to the Central Bus Station, then took two different busses to get to the airport. Dragging my carryons and bags, I schlepped into the airport with just enough to check in and make my flight.

II.

"Your bags are too full young lady. You are going to have to pay an extra fee," said the travel clerk in a heavy Russian accent. Her blue eyes seemed annoyed at my tendency to over pack. "You have two options now." She said. "One is to pay $50 for an extra bag, or $80 for an overweight bag that you can create.

I thought about it. Both of my bags were overweight, one by 7 kilos! It would be quite difficult to sit and rearrange everything. But I had to do it. I chose to create a new bag. I sat on the floor of the airport, with all my belongings sprawled around me, and the guard looking at me with curiosity. This gypsy's journey in Israel had come to an end for a while.

The night before the mess at the airport, I had been in a place called Heaven. I had spent the evening in a beautiful wooden home with sprawling gardens, a spring, and a tree house/sauna, along with sweet friends and beautiful singing. Heaven welcomed me so sweetly that I didn't want to leave. Found in the outskirts of Jerusalem in a *moshav* called Ramat Raziel, it was a place of conscious living, open hearts, music, and that night we also had an incredible and powerful all women's sauna.

"So what did you decide young lady?" The blonde blue eyed clerk asked me, taking me out of my fantasies of my last night.

"I'm going to pay for an extra bag." I said not too enthusiastically.

"Fine, go pay your fine in the office. Go straight, then left, left, left, follow the hallway, and take another left. That's where you pay." With slight annoyance, I carried my black guitar bag, my remaining carry on, and the blue hiking backpack that had become my extra luggage to the next step in my journey into the hard nosed land of Israeli bureaucracy.

I arrived at a small window that didn't even have the strange Ukrainian airline listed, but I figured it was where I needed to go. I handed the woman behind the window the slip of paper saying I had an overweight bag.

"Okay, young lady, that extra bag is going to cost you 200 shekels." The woman said in a heavy Israeli accent. She had a shaved head and fake diamond earrings, and didn't even lift her eyes from the computer screen to look at me. I dug my wallet from my purse, and then I handed her my American credit card, to find her shaking her head no.

"We only take cash here at Aerosvit airlines," zhe said matter of factly.

"Okay where's the ATM, ma'am?" I said it with a shake in my voice, a note of unassuredness, realizing that perhaps I would not be making my flight to New York that day. The flight that would take me to the arms of my loving and sweet boyfriend and the Shabbat dinner that awaited me.

She directed me to go down two floors, through some hallways, and there I should find an ATM. I left that small office feeling so small, stuck in the system that wasn't planning on letting me out so easily.

On my way to the elevator I saw the wide shouldered unfriendly male plane attendant who had also assisted in dealing with my extra bag.

"Where are you going?" He inquired in Hebrew, rolling his r's in his heavy Ukrainian accent.

"I am off to get cash to pay for the extra bag."

"Well hurry it up! The plane is boarding soon. You better make this story 10 minutes, otherwise you'll miss the flight." His tough warning pushed my legs to move faster, the legs that had not yet been nourished by food or sleep that long night.

Down the elevator, to the ATM, yes! The money was out, and I made it back quickly to pay for the extra luggage. However, when I got back to the check-in counter, no representative of the airlines was there! That was when the tears began to flow. I pathetically asked for the help of the innocent female security guard. "Do you know where the airline representatives are?" I inquired, with desperation in my eyes.

"No idea" she retorted, seeming kind of afraid that I was on the edge of sobbing.

Luckily, at that moment, the airline attendant came.

"Miriam Schwartz?" she said.

"Yes, yes that's me!"

I was so happy that perhaps my day was moving towards catching my flight. "Yes Miriam, here is your boarding pass, and the receipt on the extra luggage you paid for. You must go quickly now to the gate, the flight is boarding and will be leaving very soon."

I thanked her, grabbed the boarding pass, and was on my way, on this mission to get out of that Israeli airport.

But Ben Gurion airport had other plans for me.

III.

I rolled up to the border control, grasping my Israeli passport in one hand, my American passport in the other, and my guitar bag strapped to my back, filled to the brim with books, my thesis, a purple wool sweater, and my beautiful classical guitar of course, buried beneath everything else. These two passports were more than just little books filled with papers and stamps from all over the world. They symbolized my dual identity, identities at odds with each other at times; an American identity and an

Israeli identity. Identities that made choosing where to live a very difficult decision. Identities that put me in a constant flux of hellos and goodbyes, and the movement of leaving family and friends on one side, to find more family and friends on the other side.

The woman who decided to make my life hell that day had a long pony tail of brown hair seeping over her light blue airport jacket and collared shirt. She did not seem happy with her job of sitting stuck in a small grey box all day stamping people's passports.

I handed her my American passport first, then my Israeli one. She looked them both over, her eyes deep set, her eyebrows permanently furrowed in an unhappy frown. She was deep in thought about something and this made me very worried. I shifted my weight from foot to foot; uneasy that this final step between me and the boarding gate might be the reason that I miss my flight.

"Your Israeli passport is expired." She said dryly, staring at her computer screen.

"No problem," I said. "I'll just use my American passport."

"NO! No, you will not!" She answered angrily. "You must enter and leave the country with your Israeli passport, and no other. That is the rule enforced by the Israeli Ministry of Interior."

At this point I thought perhaps she would give me my extension stamp and let me be on my way. Instead she got out of her chair, with my passport in hand.

"Follow me," She said, walking briskly ahead of me without even looking behind her.

She led me to the small airport police station and threw my passport on the cold wooden desk, telling the officer sitting there what my story was in fast Hebrew.

"Call the Ministry of Interior." she ordered the police officer. "Let them know this girl needs an extension stamp. As well, call the airline and have them send a representative to escort her to get the extension."

The passport control officer with the hard eyes and the long black pony tail left me there in the office, confused and alone. The police officer looked at me as if I was pathetic for the tears that had already started rolling uncontrollably down my face.

"Why are you crying?" said the officer roughly.

"I just… I just can't miss my flight!" I said, erupting into an even stronger volcano of tears. She looked at me inquisitively and then said dryly, "Just wait outside."

This was the beginning of my breakdown. I sat in the waiting area, my faithful guitar next to me and put my hands in my face and began to sob. My eyes were burning red, and my face began to get swollen with showers of tears streaming down my face. I was done and I knew it. I had no more energy left in me. Three hours of standing in lines, going from this counter to that counter just to get my flight had drained me. And the thought that I may miss my flight led the sobs to get harder and more intense. I hadn't slept the night before, and hadn't eaten anything the whole day. Not eating or sleeping is a catastrophic combination for me that tends to lead to at least a mild case of insanity, especially at airports. As well, I had been famous for missing tons of flights, but I really didn't have the energy to miss this one.

What to do? I was sitting there waiting, and no seemed to want to help me, or even deal with me at all. I knew the flight was supposed to take off at 8:10 am, and it was already 7:55. What I needed was a heaven sent angel to save me and get me to my flight.

I went back to the police station office, and asked the woman what was happening. She had long platinum blond hair, was short and stout, and had caked bright green eye shadow above her eyelids.

"You just need to wait. Someone from the airline is coming soon."

"I am going to miss my flight! Please do something to make it go quicker," I begged of her. When she said she couldn't I let out a loud cry like a wild boar running through the jungle, covered my face with my hands and ran back to the waiting area.

That was it; I was beginning to accept I wasn't going to New York that day. I wouldn't be there by 5 pm to be picked up by my handsome boyfriend, wouldn't be carried off with him to the Upper West Side to make a delicious Shabbat dinner. The thought made me cry harder.

Suddenly a sweet voice, like that of an angel interrupted my crying fit.

"Excuse me. Excuse me, ma'am. Are you the one who needs to extend your flight?" A beautiful young Ethiopian woman with caramel hair, dark skin, and a gentle smile stood in front of me.

I nodded pathetically to the woman, with no strength left to even use my voice.

"Okay follow me, we're going to get your extension for your passport." She said it with such assuredness in her voice that I even believed there may be hope for me to still make my flight.

We walked briskly back through security, back through the check-in counters, and down to the bottom floor. As we moved down the escalators, I told her my flight was supposed to leave at 8:10.

"I'll probably miss my flight won't I?" I said to her. She lifted her sleeve and looked at her silver watch, which said 8:15.

"I think there's a good chance you'll make it because your flight on Aerosvit is delayed for technical reasons, though I don't know how long they will keep it delayed. But we just need to work fast." We kept going down to the next floor and to the right and to where the representative for the Ministry of Interior was. I looked at the woman who was going to decide my fate that day. She had blonde hair, red rimmed glasses, and many wrinkles on her face.

"Hand me the passports." She said, and she was quickly on it.

IV.

I couldn't stop crying. The tears rolled down my face uncontrollably and I probably looked as if I had just escaped a mental institution. Somehow airports really made me crazy. The woman who worked at the Ministry of Interior and the representative from Aerosvit airlines kept looking at each other with wide open eyes, perturbed by my constant tears. Suddenly, I realized that what I needed was prayer. In these kinds of situations I turned to my Jerusalem born grandmother, Rahel. She was my mother's mother, and since she had passed away seven years before she had take on the role of my guardian angel, and who I directed my prayers towards.

"Please Savta," I prayed. "Please get me through this nightmare, onto that plane. I closed my eyes and intensely called out to her with all of my being and power.

Only a few moments later the representative of the Ministry of Interior had finally finished erratically typing and spoke to me in her heavy Israeli accent. "Hokay, zis extension on your visa vill be 800 sheckels, and zen you vill be able to pass through ze passport control."

I sheepishly handed her my Israeli debit card, not even sure if that much money was in that bank account. Suddenly the extension stamp was in my passport and I was home free! The airport representative with the compassionate eyes and I began to run up the stairs, got waved through to the front of the security line, and I ran with all four of my carryons to the gate. We ran down the moving walkways, past excited tourists who had just arrived in Israel, and past the Russian clerks at the Duty Free. Past the hip airport espresso cafes, the hummus restaurant, and shiny jewelry kiosks. With my belongings held tightly in my grip, my coat flailing in the air, and with both of us running as fast as possible, we looked like quite the scene. I tried not to get my hopes too high to avoid disappointment, but it seemed there was a chance that I may make my flight that day. We arrived at the gate, and I was greeted by two airport personnel who seemed curious to see the girl who made the plane wait.

That was me. St. Louis-born Miriam Schwartz, about to board a plane to New York City, via Kiev, Ukraine. Quickly they ran my boarding pass through the quick scan machine, and pointed me towards a hallway that would lead me to the airplane. I quickly thanked the sweet Ethiopian flight representative and ran down the hallway.

When I got out the double doors, a personal van had come to pick me up to rush me to the flight that waited for me. The driver was a middle aged Israeli man, who knew how to drive fast, much like other Israeli drivers. It seemed like he among everyone else who worked for the airline had received the protocol, "Young and irresponsible American girl is late to the flight! Get her there ASAP!"

He drove me up to the mid-sized plane and helped me unload my insane amount of carryon bags. Before me stood the giant plane glossed with the words Aerosvit in shiny royal blue lettering. Leading up to the plane was a giant staircase to board. It was obvious that everyone else had boarded the plane much before I had, and they were clearly waiting for me. But I was much too tired to be embarrassed.

I dragged my carryons along with me, up the stairs, and at the top stood the Arnold Schwarzenegger built flight attendant I unpleasantly had to deal with before. He gave me a truly evil look filled with such resentment it made my stomach flip. "I told you to hurry up for ze plane, but you didn't listen," he said with Ukrainian spit emphasizing the word listen. I walked past him, and all the other flight attendants gave me very bewildered looks, along with all the other passengers. What a surreal experience! There was one seat left in the plane, in the very last row towards the right next to the window. I quickly walked to my seat and collapsed into it, and heaved a huge sigh of relief. Somehow, my prayers had been heard and I was on my way to New York City. The end of a truly Israeli flightmare.

Bettina Schwarzman
Seders in the Basement and Story Time at the Brodsky Library

I moved to St Louis late in the summer, with two small children, Dan and Rachel, and another one on the way. Little did I know that I was about to become acquainted with a whole bunch of wonderful midwestern *neshamahs* whether they were born there or not. My first sensation upon stepping out of Lambert Field was "Ugh, it feels like walking around in a hot soup! I can't breathe!" That feeling returned every time I stepped outdoors over the next few days, and I thought that I must be extra sensitive because of being pregnant, since I usually like hot weather. As my children and I sought out the air conditioned havens around St Louis, (the Galleria, the Science Center), I came to realize that this is simply normal summer here.

Orienting myself around St Louis posed some difficulties at first for a "directions-challenged" person like me, but I simply *had* to find the supermarket. Fortunately, a nice Midwestern *neshamah* assisted me with directions. Close to tears, hot and tired, my children and I finally walked into the cool, fragrant bakery of Schnucks Ladue, only to discover, to our delight, that children under 12 could each have a free cookie, and what's more – the cookies were kosher! With Dan and Rachel nibbling contentedly on chocolate chip cookies while seated in the cart, I was able to find my way through the air conditioned aisles, perusing the blintzes.

Our first Shabbat in St Louis we walked over to Shaare Zedek Synagogue for services. At *kiddush*, while munching on lemon poppyseed cake, Rabbi Bard sauntered over to me and asked: "Are you the Schwarzmans?" It was about time we met, since we had just bought our split-level University City house from him! It came to be known as "the house that absorbed children."

The following week it was time for Dan to meet Rabbi Bard as a principal. Dan was starting first grade at Solomon Schechter Day School. Waddling up the grassy path to B'nai Amoona on the first day of school, I nearly tripped on a small girl sitting on the ground right in front of me. As I made my way around her, her mother came running up to me, apologizing for her daughter: "I'm so sorry, that's my daughter Merav!" We chatted for a while. She was Ruth Gold, married to our rabbi, as new in town as we were. It looked like I had made a friend, standing outside SSDS on that first day of school.

SSDS holds its annual dinner every fall, and this was the topic of conversation when Darien Arnstein called me a few days later, in her capacity as "parent buddy." I had never met Darien, nor had I been to a Schechter annual dinner before, and Darien started to give me advice on what to wear. I realized that Darien was trying to be helpful, but I felt my anxiety mushroom as I gazed down on my medicine ball of a belly. "Well, uhm…," I stammered, "you know, I'm pregnant…" Delighted with my great news, Darien exclaimed, "oh, then you can wear whatever you want!" I picked out what I considered to be my nicest maternity dress, pale lavender with white lace around the collar. As I walked into the grand ballroom of the Airport Mariott, I immediately realized that most everyone was wearing black, or at least dark colors. I stood out like a sore thumb! Oh well, I shrugged, I'm pregnant, I can wear whatever I want! I had a really good time that night, with all the Midwestern *neshamahs,* once I stopped worrying about my apparel.

We enrolled Rachel at the Shaare Zedek Early Childhood Center. She had suffered from separation anxiety before we came to St Louis, and I had confided in Marty, the ECC director, how worried I was about Rachel acclimating to the new school. Well, it turned out not to be a problem, and in a few days it was as if she had always been there, cheerfully singing the ABC song while she washed her hands, as the teachers had taught her in school. I was grateful to Marty for being understanding, and she and I later became "roommates," as I took over the directorship of the Religious School in the same building.

One Monday morning, after dropping Rachel off at the Shaare Zedek ECC and Dan at Schechter, my husband and I drove to St John's Mercy Hospital, where Dr Wasserman delivered baby Yael by Caesarean section. I looked at her for the first time, and thought "ooh, a dark beauty!" After surgery, I was wheeled into a room. I lay there, staring at a wall with a crucifix on it. I took it down and put it in a drawer, only to replace it before I left the hospital.

The children and I quickly found our way to the Brodsky Library. Dan and Rachel participated in the summer reading club, and fondly remember the stickers they used to receive for books they had read. Once a month, Barbara Raznick conducted a much loved story time for children. This was a delight to Dan and Rachel. Rachel, who is now 18, can still hear Barbara singing: "Run, run, as fast as you can, you can't catch me, I'm the *challah* man!" Dan is a soldier in the Israel Defense Forces now, and while I don't know that he sings this song while he pretends to conquer a hill together with his buddies, his Jewish childhood in St Louis was definitely a contributing factor to his decision to make *aliyah*.

Springtime is tornado season in St Louis, and being new in town, I suspect that we took the tornado siren more seriously than most long time locals. We'd hear it start whining, and immediately, the whole family would report to the basement. Typically, this would happen just as we were about to sit down to dinner. After a few times, we learned to keep blankets, toys, flashlights and a radio down there. The older children would play, the younger ones sometimes fell asleep, Daddy would listen to the radio for the list of counties for whom the all clear had been declared, and I would fret over the freshly cooked spaghetti that was getting cold on the dinner table downstairs.

It seemed as though the clouds not only knew when the Schwarzman family was about to sit down to dinner, they were also experts on the Jewish calendar, and not a few Shabbat dinners cooled off in the kitchen while we languished in the basement....

Come Passover of our first year in St Louis and we were standing around our table, chatting amicably with our guests, the Shilcrats and the Karabells. Karen Karabell had brought a delectable looking platter of chocolate covered strawberries, and I was just complimenting her on them when we heard that familiar whine starting up! The eight children knew the drill, and made an enthusiastic beeline for our basement. Hey, having *seder* in the basement while sitting (lying, rolling) on the floor seemed like much more fun than sitting sedately around the dinner table!

Another year, us newbies were all smarter: Our family was invited to *seder* at the Gold family's house, and we didn't even *try* for the dining room – we went straight to the basement, where we sat on the floor and discussed our ancestors' plight in Egypt. My two youngest children, Yael and Hillel, were the only ones born in St Louis, but I felt good sitting there with all my Midwestern *neshamah* friends.

Ronit Sherwin
Painted Toe Nails

"Your toes are beautiful," the nurse said, as I lay on the table with my feet in the stirrups. This would be my ninth round of donor insemination in my journey to become a single mother by choice. Unfortunately, I have become quite accustomed to the monthly routine of fertility drugs, ultrasounds, blood work and then the final procedure of the carefully and scientifically timed IUI (intrauterine insemination). In my deepest hope to bring a life into this world, this routine has become my life.

"Thank you," I said to Crystal, the nurse. I have developed a rather sacred ritual every month and that is getting a pedicure. The day before I come in for insemination, I go to get my feet pampered and my toenails painted. It's comforting to me, and now I rather look forward to it. And of course, I want the doctors and nurses to see my pretty toes during this rather sterile procedure. I share this with Crystal. As usual, I make her laugh, and she optimistically says, "And when you are pregnant, you can get a pedicure before you go into labor!" The procedure is complete, Crystal rubs my belly and gives me a smile, and I am left to myself.

My smile gives way to tears. While I have become very fond of the various doctors and nurses in this office, I am so tired of being in this place. And *in this place* I mean this physical office of "reproductive endocrinology and infertility" and this horrible place of "trying-to-get-pregnant." Ugh – I would gladly give up my monthly ritual of pedicures to be blissfully pregnant.

Some months ago, my therapist told me to do whatever I find comforting to help me get through this process. At the time, I had just lost a pregnancy and was feeling quite naturally sad, angry and anxious to start the baby-making routine again. *What do I find comforting?* I asked myself. The obvious answer for me is food, of course, in which I have easily indulged during these last months. For a person of great faith, I found it disturbing that I struggled with the question for some days. *What do I find comforting?*

The angry part of myself wanted to shout, "A baby would be comforting, duh!" There are many levels of understanding comfort. One level is the urgency of *what-gets-you-through-the-day* comfort. And sometimes it is simply the vision of ending my long day with a bowl of ice cream on the couch and a good piece of fiction. But I also began to understand that the question of "what brings you comfort" was more about what gives me meaning to live in the present and the hope to move forward into the future. While I may not have that child yet that has become my life's mission and meaning, I do have a great deal of meaning in my present life. I have fulfilling work, deep and loyal friendships and a belief in myself as a mother – one day.

Oh – and then I have my beautiful painted toenails that allow me to feel good about my body, albeit small extensions, and comfort me with the reminder that I am once again hopeful for new life to emerge.

Nathan M. Simon
Halitzah: The Unloosening

My older brother, Benjamin Morris Simon, was killed in Germany three weeks before the war ended there. He was twenty-three years old and a corporal in a heavy weapons platoon in the 272nd Infantry, 69th Division. Near a bridgehead on the Werra River, where patches of a late spring snow still lay on the ground, shrapnel from a German mortar shell wounded him. After the shell exploded, he sat up and began, in a matter-of-fact way typical of him, tying a tourniquet around his leg. He commented to a buddy he would have to be moved to the rear, then suddenly lapsed into unconsciousness and died within a few minutes.

Ben, the oldest of four children in our family, was named for my father's father, Baruch Moshe, a dealer in horses and cattle in Russia who was robbed and murdered in the Spring of 1902 on the banks of a small river in the eastern Ukraine.

My brother grew up to be a handsome dark-haired, dark-eyed young man with a square jaw, and a warm, open smile. He was bright without being brilliant (I was allegedly the brilliant one, but that, by and large, gave me little comfort). People liked him quickly and grew to like him more as they knew him better. Even as a young man he was steady, reliable and practical. He was elected to the Honor Society, a class officer, head of the high school ushers, and president of his fraternity. He had excellent grades at school and he sang beautifully. He knew what he wanted; he would practice law, marry, have a family, and join the congregation. I, of course, loved him – that was easy. And hated him and was jealous, envious and competitive. That was also easy. It was not as if I lacked friends, acknowledgement, praise, it was just that he had more. I hungered for what was his and wanted it immediately.

Despite the fact I was often the typical pain-in-the-ass little brother trying to intrude in his life, ricocheting from emulation to obstruction, we became quite close by the time I grew into adolescence. Most of the time he was forgiving, generous and tolerant, qualities in short supply in me. He loved me (Why? I often wondered.) and trusted me. He knew I would be successful and, in a way that I do not remember as condescending, let me know my brightness and accomplishments at school would some day bring me the recognition and social success I hungered for.

Ben was drafted in February of 1943. I enlisted six months later on impulse, partly out of jealousy, for I wanted to be sure I would be as big a hero as he, and partly because I saw a way that might keep me from being shot at. We both were in the infantry but our paths through the Army were different — a difference that culminated on that day in early April 1945 when it appeared that a cosmic deal, struck long before, was finally confirmed. Ben is killed in combat and I am plucked from my infantry regiment and ordered to Chinese Language School at Yale. Ben is post-humously awarded the Bronze Star for bravery and I eventually leverage a safe and soft military assignment into an Ivy League education and a career in medicine.

My brother had married eight months before he was sent to Europe. It was no surprise. Lisa Stern (not her real name) and Ben had dated for two years and had become engaged just before he reported for service. I liked her and urged him to date her. I had the "inside line" on her because I was in fevered but futile pursuit of her younger sister and spent a lot of time at the Stern's home. Ben and Lisa were a matched pair — good looking, dark hair and eyes, intellectual and low keyed. They scrambled to find a little time to love and be together. Soon after their marriage, Lisa moved to North Carolina to be near him in the months before his unit embarked for Europe. Their marriage left both sets of parents worried and unhappy. They wanted them to wait until after the war. Their reservations were muted but apparent, while everyone else in both families was enthusiastic. I was home for the wedding, the last time I saw Ben.

I did not see Lisa again until I was home on leave after Ben's death. In the four months immediately after Ben's death I was just a three hour train ride from home. When I was on weekend leave and returned to Wilmington I would frequently go out with her. I would pick her up in the same family '41 Pontiac that Ben used when they were dating. Sometimes we went to a movie, but regularly we would drive through the nearby countryside and park on a hill that overlooked the city and the Delaware River. We sat at opposite ends of the front seat squeezed against the doors as if we needed all the space possible between us. Those dark warm summer nights we talked sporadically — short sentences and often long silences.

I was discharged from the Army in the late Spring of 1946. The year that had elapsed since my brother's death had taken off only a little of the sharp edge of my parents' grief, and I returned to a sad and quiet house. By the time I came home Lisa had left her job and enrolled in a small college in Virginia. She came home frequently for weekends, but the visits to our house became noticeably less frequent as time went by. We still wrote one another but the letters were well spaced and came to be made up of the banalities resorted to by people who did not know how to be together.

I had been home for only three weeks when I received a telephone call from Lisa's father. After an unusually protracted questioning as to the state of my health and my reactions to civilian life, he finally worked around to the reason for the call.

"Ah, I....ah, I mean Lisa, she....I mean we" (more fumbling for words) "we would like you to do us a favor."

"Sure Mr. Stern, what can I do for you?"

"Lisa wants to have a *Halitzah* ceremony and she needs your help."

"A what?"

He rushed through the rest of the explanation as if he were reading a prepared apology. "It has to do with the brother of a widow's dead husband giving up his claim on her. It's a real old custom and she wants to go through with it and we need your help. Can you come up to Philly with us on Thursday so we can make arrangements with the Rabbi?" I could almost see him blushing over the phone.

"I've never heard of it," I answered, "but if she wants to do it of course I'll help." We very quickly settled on a meeting time which mercifully brought the conversation to an end.

I went into the living room to tell my parents what had happened and to see if my father could tell me anything more about *Halitzah*. Neither of them was happy about what I told them. Both of them could not see why she wanted to do it, and my father did not care to add much to what Mr. Stern had already told me about the ceremony. He knew about it and could say authoritatively (he had been actively involved in the Orthodox Jewish community since 1914 – as president of the synagogue and head of the burial society) that it had never been performed in Wilmington in the thirty-five years he had lived there. He could not see why a "modern Jewish girl, not even Orthodox," should ever want it. But that is all he would say.

I felt isolated, unable and unwilling to talk to anyone about what was happening. Somehow I found my way to Deuteronomy 25:5-10. I discovered the brother of a married man who dies childless has both a right and an obligation to marry the widow in order to have a child so "that his name may not be blotted out in Israel." *Halitzah* is the ceremony in which the brother renounces his rights to the widow and releases her to marry another.

In the days that followed my parents withdrew into a shell of silence as they tried to turn away from another proof of my brother's death. Lisa's wish for *Halitzah* had increased their mostly silent suffering. Lisa had evidently met someone at school and wanted to marry, I reasoned, and she felt compelled to cut formally and decisively some ties which ran to me directly and beyond me to my brother. Lisa had never shown interest in observing the rituals of Biblical era Judaism. She was a frequent attendee of Friday night services at a conventional Conservative congregation – services that, for adolescents, had much to do with their social life and minimally to do with religiosity or spirituality, and her family had a relaxed approach to ritual. Was her intended so ultra-orthodox as to demand *Halitzah* or had it escaped me until then how important I had become to her? What I was afraid to ask her was why she wanted to plunge us all into more pain with a ceremony.

As the date drew near, uncomfortable memories succeeded in eroding through the detached, scholarly attitude I had first adopted. It was nothing – a stupid ceremony to satisfy a mixed up, unhappy girl. But the rationale failed to immunize me against unexpected attacks of guilt, self-recrimination, and desperate struggles for solutions to unformed questions.

Lisa, her father and I drove to Philadelphia on a Thursday night. It was an uncomfortable ride for all of us, least perhaps for Mr. Stern who was partially deaf and whose concentration on driving exempted him from making and listening to conversation. The casual attitude which Lisa and I both adopted was a painfully thin veneer. I tried to show a healthy intellectual curiosity about the ceremony and she tried to explain what she knew about it in the manner of an anthropologist reporting the rituals of a distant culture.

"It has to do with a shoe," she said, "which is symbolic of our relationship. I untie the shoe and take it off of your foot and that testifies to our clean-cut separation. And then to show that I am completely free of you, I spit in your face – only you get off easy, for the way they do it now all I have to do is spit on the floor."

"That's nice," I said, forcing a smile, "the old way sounds unhygienic."

She laughed a little too loudly at the weak joke. Mr. Stern turned to us and shouted "What?" so we had to repeat the exchange again for his benefit.

Except for the pronouncing of some magic words that was the rabbi's job it seemed that was all there was to the whole business.

"Had a lot of trouble finding a rabbi who could do this ceremony," Mr. Stern shouted at us. "Looked all over Philly. Finally had to go to the Rabbinical Association. Seems that only this rabbi and one other in Philly can do this *Halitzah* thing." He pronounced it incorrectly, substituting a soft 'h' for the guttural that should have begun the word. "The other fellow was out of town, so we have to take this guy. He's a real old timer. Supposed to have been a big rabbi over in Europe some place. I guess nobody in America knows anything about it."

I agreed with a loud "yes" and he shook his head to show that he heard me and for the rest of the short ride we talked sporadically about other things.

The 'big rabbi' lived in South Philadelphia on a narrow side street in the heart of what had been the old 'ghetto'. A short, stocky, stern faced woman answered our knock.

"I'm Mr. Stern," Lisa's father said, "and I've come to see the rabbi about the *Halitzah*."

"Yeh, yeh," the old woman nodded her head in assent as she answered us in heavily accented English. "I'm the rabbi's wife." She stood aside to admit us. We came directly into a small room that was made even smaller by the heavy pieces of dining room furniture that lined all four walls and a large circular dining room table that stood in its center. A chandelier hung from the ceiling and the light bulbs threw off a tremendous amount of glaring light and heat that, added to the typically humid Philadelphia summer night, made the room a virtual steam cabinet. I began to perspire as soon as the door closed behind me.

The rabbi sat at the table facing the door through which we entered. His head was bent over a large volume that lay open on the table before him and his full gray beard seemed to touch the pages. His glasses were pushed up on his forehead and I could see his eyes moving under his heavy half closed lids as he scanned the page in front of him. He wore a heavy woolen vest over a rumpled white shirt whose sleeves were turned up to the elbows, and his short, pudgy body slumped into a high backed dining room chair. He did not look up as we came into the room.

We crowded into the room and waited while the woman pushed by us and went over to where the rabbi was sitting. "Rabbi," she said loudly.

He looked up slowly, as if he were unsticking himself from the Hebrew words printed on the page before him, and studied us with great care as his wife went on speaking rapidly to him in Yiddish.

"These are the people from Wilmington who want to see you about arranging a *Halitzah*."

"Can you speak Yiddish?" he said to us in Yiddish.

Mr. Stern quickly answered that he could.

"Wilmington," the rabbi said syllabilizing the word carefully, "is that far away?"

Mr. Stern told him that it was fairly close by, and, after a moment of silence, went on to introduce us.

"Where is the sexton?" The rabbi spoke to his wife without looking at her.

"He said he would be here," she answered.

He shook his head to show that he had heard her. It was evidently also a sign of dismissal for she retired immediately into the kitchen.

"Sit down," he said to us. We found seats around the table.

"She is the widow?" the rabbi asked pointing at Lisa.

Mr. Stern and Lisa both nodded yes.

"What is her name?"

"Lisa," Mr. Stern answered.

"No," the rabbi shook his head vigorously, "her name in Yiddish."

Mr. Stern told him and then the interrogation began in earnest.

How old is she? How long was she married? Do you have proof of the marriage? What was her husband's name? When did he die? Where did he die? How was he killed? Where is he buried? Do you have proof of his death? The rabbi spoke rapidly in a Lithuanian, accented Yiddish and nodded his head at every response Mr. Stern provided in his halting Americanized dialect.

The questioning went on into the details of my brother's death and was interrupted only by the appearance of the sexton who slipped into the room without knocking. There was another round of introductions and the sexton shook hands with us in a way that reminded me of an undertaker. After we were seated again the rabbi continued.

"Does he speak Yiddish?" The rabbi motioned toward me, but spoke to Mr. Stern, and before either of us could answer he carried on with the questioning using Mr. Stern as the interpreter.

"What is his Yiddish name?"

I answered him myself. He looked at me sharply and then turned back to Mr. Stern. I felt myself flushing and my calm detached sociological approach dissolving away in the perspiration that was trickling down my back. One of my father's favorite axioms flashed into my mind – "Conceit grows on a *Litvak* as naturally as his ears." The burst of anger I felt helped steady me. I resolved to "play dumb" for the rest of the evening.

Through Mr. Stern, whom I provided with the appropriate answers, the rabbi discovered my age, occupation and the fact that I was entering into *Halitzah* of my own free will. After the last question was answered he paused for a minute and then asked, "Is he grown up – with hair?" He made circular motions with both hands in an attempt to clarify the question.

Mr. Stern flushed through his normal florid coloring. He looked at me hopelessly and tried unsuccessfully to formulate an English translation. I cut off his stutterings.

"Tell him yes," I said testily.

The rabbi nodded sagely at the answer. There was another long pause and I could hear Mr. Stern expelling his breath through pursed lips.

"Does the boy walk first with his right or left foot?" the rabbi finally asked.

"Right, I think," I told Mr. Stern.

"So, he doesn't know," the rabbi said after my answer was translated. "Tell him to get up and take a step."

I arose from my seat and squeezed around the chairs to the only open place in the room which was near the entrance to the kitchen and close to the rabbi's chair. I stood at attention momentarily and then stepped off a short pace, beginning automatically with my left foot.

"He says right, but then he goes with his left," the rabbi said angrily, staring at me throughout his speech. "Turn around and take another step." This time he spoke directly to me.

I turned and stepped again, this time making sure to start with my right foot. This did not please the rabbi either.

"First with the left and then with the right. How am I to know which is right?" He appealed his dilemma and my unreliability to the other two men.

He pushed an empty chair away from the table. "Step up on the chair," he commanded me.

I fought down my mounting rage and did as he asked, again remembering to start with my right foot. That evidently satisfied him for he told me I could get down and then immediately took up another important matter with the sexton.

"I need five men to be judges at the *Halitzah*," he said. "Five good, pious Jews."

"Yes, Rabbi," the sexton replied. "I can get Mendel, the baker, and Chatzkel, the tailor, and….."

"They should all have beards," the rabbi broke in, "it is very important that they have beards. They must be religious Jews." He ran his right hand through his beard as he spoke.

The sexton wrinkled his brow and thought for a minute. "That will be hard, Rabbi. You know in these times…."

"If not beards then at least mustaches." The rabbi pulled at his own beard again.

"Yes, Rabbi," the sexton said, "at least mustaches. That I can do. I will get…." And he reeled off more names as the rabbi nodded in agreement.

"Tell them to be at the synagogue at 8 o'clock Sunday morning. And they shouldn't be late either."

The sexton assured him that they would be on time.

The rabbi turned to us. "You should be there at 8 o'clock too," he said, "and the girl and the boy shouldn't have anything to eat. I will tell you what else you have to do when you get there."

It was evident that the interview was over. Mr. Stern told Lisa and me to wait for him at the car. Gratefully we fled down the steps into the fresh air and, in a tense silence, waited.

In a few minutes, Mr. Stern appeared, obviously angry.

"They're all nothing but a bunch of thieves," he sputtered as he unlocked the car door. "Twenty-five dollars for a bunch of foolishness. They're nothing but thieves looking for a new angle." Then he caught himself, looked at Lisa remorsefully in an attempt to apologize and abruptly went around the car to get into the driver's seat.

On Sunday morning Mr. Stern asked me to drive. Even at 6:45 it was obvious that it was going to be a hot day. But the air was still fresh and cool and the early morning sounds seemed amplified by the relative quiet. The roads were nearly deserted and I drove fast all the way getting some satisfaction from watching the speedometer needle push up to the 70 mark. As I drove I wondered if the rabbi would call the whole thing off if he found out that I had toast and coffee. I rubbed my hand across my lips to brush away crumbs that were not there.

The chapel was a one story building next to the synagogue. Coming in from the brightness of the street it took my eyes some minutes to adjust to the darkness of the room. It was not a big room but the sparseness of its furnishings made it appear larger. There were several rows of backless wooden benches arranged in the center of the room and a few wooden folding chairs scattered along the two side walls. At the end of the room was the ark and, in front of it, a reader's table covered with a heavy embroidered velvet-like cloth. On the walls bracketing the ark were two memorial tablets with small electric light bulbs glowing dimly around their edges and in front of a few names.

The rabbi, the sexton, and the five judges were already there. Two had beards and the other three had ample mustaches. They were all short old men dressed in the Sunday clothes of workers and looked amazingly alike. They stood in a tight group near a bench that had been pulled out at right angles to the others and talked quietly among themselves.

We walked to the reader's table where the rabbi and the sexton were standing. After a brief greeting, the rabbi took a leather sandal off the table and indicated that I should follow him. At a bench near the door the rabbi told me to sit down and take off my right shoe and stocking. The judges stopped their conversation and as I bent to untie my shoe laces I was conscious of their stares.

The sandal was made of a soft beige leather. There were three short knotted leather laces over the tongue and two long white leather straps fastened to the back near the heel. I squeezed my foot into the sandal and felt my toes buckle for lack of room. After I had it on my foot the rabbi bent over me and in a low voice led me stepwise through the tying of the long leather thongs. They wrapped around my ankle and up on to my calf and I had to roll my trouser leg in order to complete the job. When I finished we walked back to the center of the room to a spot in front of the reader's table, and as if by a signal, the five 'judges' sat down beside one another on their bench. Mr. Stern and the sexton sat on opposite ends of a bench directly in front of us. The rabbi stationed me on his right and Lisa on his left.

He took a book off of the table and even before he had opened it began to recite rapidly in Hebrew. Except for the drone of his voice the room was still. Occasionally there was the intrusion of a street noise that drifted in from another century that waited outside the door.

He finally paused in his reading. "Take four steps," he said to me. I did and was grateful for the chance to move. The sandal pinched at my toes and felt heavy and hot on my foot. When I halted he motioned me back to my place.

"Repeat after me," he said to Lisa and slowly, in short phrases, led her through a sentence in Hebrew. Her responses were muted and I could barely hear the words as she said them.

The rabbi turned to me and I repeated after him the guttural sounds feeling like a blind man being led stumbling along a strange street. When I finished echoing the last phrase he spoke to Lisa again.

"Bend down and untie the strap of the shoe," he said to her, and as she knelt before me, "Hold the leg with the left hand and untie the knots and take off the shoe with your right."

I looked down at the top of her head as her fingers fumbled with the knots in the thongs. She pulled at them unsuccessfully for long, long seconds. I pushed my hands into my pockets and clenched them into fists as I struggled with her to untie them. The knots came loose and I felt the thongs fall away from my calf. She pulled the sandal off my foot and still kneeling looked up. Her forehead was beaded with sweat and her eyes were full of tears.

I became aware of my heart beating rapidly and a feeling of embittered helplessness and rage swept through me. Her open display of emotion and the strange stillness that seemed to suddenly overwhelm the room struck at me. The last vestiges of the detachment that had shielded me from immersion in the fantastic anachronism of the ceremony slipped away. I turned my eyes away from her's. I knew then that my clenched fists had been a gesture of resistance, not help. She was free now – or almost free. A month, a year, with a new name and a new lover – with the old pictures and the old letters buried safely in some attic – and the memories would melt into wisps of unreality. I was being bound to a past that I understood even less than she.

I hated her, hated her. I was flooded with hate. I tried to stop the torrent of thought by squeezing my eyes shut. The rabbi's voice forced my attention back to the ritual.

"Throw the shoe over there," the rabbi pointed to his left. The leather hitting against the floor made a loud slapping sound. She stood up.

"Now spit on the floor. There by his foot," again the rabbi pointed.

Her lips worked noiselessly and a fleck of spittle appeared, hung for a moment and then fell to the floor. I involuntarily started back from it.

The rabbi had Lisa repeat another series of phrases and then led the judges through a short chorus. He read briefly again from his book, closed it with an authoritative smack and announced that the ceremony was over.

I hopped back to the bench where I had left my shoe and stocking and quickly pulled them on. I could see Lisa and Mr. Stern standing with the rabbi and the sexton. The rabbi was smiling and talking rapidly. The sexton was shaking his head vigorously in agreement. The five judges formed a small group near them and were talking among themselves now, in loud strong tones that carried across to me. Slowly the twentieth century began to creep back into the room. I heard cars going by in the street and voices talking in English. I stood up and started to the door. One of the 'judges' detached himself from the group and hurried over to intercept me.

"It's a wonderful thing you did," he said smiling up at me from under his mustache. "It's wonderful that a modern American boy should do this. It shows that there is still Jewishness left in the modern generation. Your mother and father should be proud of you."

I could not answer him. I looked over his head through the open door to the sunlight reflecting off the cars parked outside. Oblivious to my lack of response he cheerfully congratulated me again, dropped my hand, and returned to his friends. I moved toward the door half blinded by my tears and the spears of reflected sunlight.

I have not seen Lisa again. She married shortly after the *Halitzah*. I had no contact with her until the fall of 2002. After my father's death I became caretaker of two boxes that contained my brother's letters, photos and the flag that covered his coffin when he was reburied in Wilmington in 1948. While reading and sorting the contents, I alternated between wrenching sadness, guilt and rage. I wrote Lisa to ask the question that I had answered a thousand times in my head. I began obliquely. Did she have any letters or mementos she would be willing to share? Then, directly, what had led her to request *Halitzah*? She answered in a brief note. She had no letters and wished me well.

Where am I now after all this turning over of stones of memory to expose the dark places where love, grief, guilt and anger have dominion? I am seventy-eight, not twenty as I was in 1946. I have a wife, four adult sons, and eight grandchildren. My eldest son bears my brother's name; his name has not been blotted out in Israel. I have discharged an obligation. Much mystery remains about what brought Lisa and me to *Halitzah*, but I have come to understand that in some way Lisa and I are similar. In our silences, in our failures to speak, we have been co-conspirators, each trying to shift grief and guilt to the other in a way that transforms them into anger. And I have learned that some ties can never be unloosened.

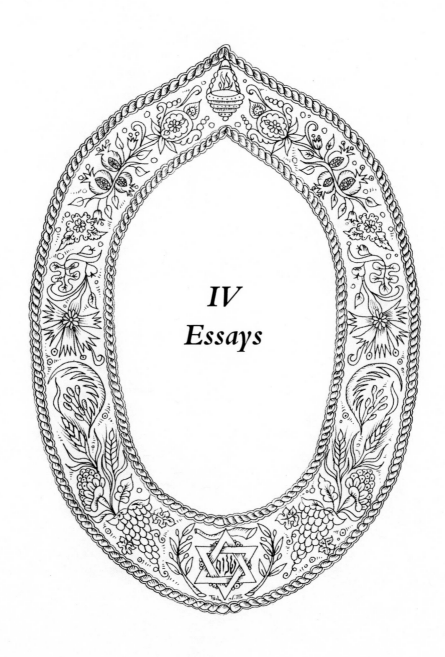

IV
Essays

Laurie Bennett
Our Daughters

I could never understand why there is a traditional Jewish preference for boy babies. I have heard that if a man has seven sons, he is guaranteed entrance into The World to Come. I am close to both my son and my daughter, but that tied-at-the-hip relationship with my son is long gone. With no credentials whatsoever, I offer the following advice on raising perfect daughters:

1) Do not torture baby girls with those elastic headbands that prove to strangers that they are, in point of fact, girls. This constriction of the brain is undoubtedly linked to the poor performance in later years of certain girls in mathematics. Leave her alone, and she will develop her own fashion sense, possibly consisting of her diaper, her father's fishing hat and your best heels. By the time she's in high school, I promise you, *you* will be taking your fashion cues from *her.*

2) On the other hand, if you dislike following fashion trends altogether, or are generally a non-conformist, do not impose your political views on your daughter. She has to survive middle school, not you. There are more favorable times in one's life to be an iconoclast.

3) Do not permit very young children to socialize at all as it is inconsistent with good nutrition. My daughter, Lissa never knew there was such a thing as white bread in the world until she had lunch at Jenny's house. That was the end of whole grains for the next 12 years. During one week of preschool, Lissa was offered five trips to McDonald's as "a special treat," by five different playmate's mothers.

4) Purchase a wedding gown costume for your four- year old daughter. She is now at the perfect level of maturity to get the white-dress-fairy-princess thing out of her system. Marriage is about building a life together, shared values, and, in many happy cases, raising children together. The wedding celebration, while joyous, has become overwrought and overblown

5) Teach your daughter to embrace failure. Straight As are wonderful, but if you never fall on your face, you're not trying hard enough. Even if it's just a recipe that turns out to be inedible, failure should

be viewed as a learning experience and not as an irreversible catastrophe. Ask any millionaire; failure is more instructive than success. Help her raise her tolerance for risk (the healthy kind, not the sort involving motorcycles).

6) Know what terrifies your girl and use it to your best advantage. Lissa was at art school in Chicago. As much as she preferred to avoid hard work of any kind, she was thankful, at least, that her curriculum did not involve much math or science. During sophomore year, she applied a lavender streak into her long, silky dark brown hair. Upon reviewing the photo she e-mailed and finding her appearance acceptable, I wrote back that I could live with it, but if she did one more artistic thing to her body, I would have her transferred to the State University as an Engineering major.

7) Lose the Cinderella Complex. She will have greater success in all her interpersonal relationships, not just those with the opposite sex, if she is a complete person, all by herself.

8) Teach your daughter that class has everything to do with how she treats others and nothing to do with one's own clothes or appearance. Parties are about the comfort and enjoyment of one's guests, and the pleasure one receives from the company of these people, notwithstanding the widely held, though erroneous, belief that one hosts parties in order to become the center of attention.

9) In a similar vein, teach your middle school aged daughter Commandment Number Eleven: The new kid is never allowed to eat lunch alone. I explained to Lissa how tough it is to come into middle school as a new kid, and that she must, upon noticing someone new in school, invite the newcomer to sit at her table at lunch.

10) Don't instill Judaism through negatives. The reality of anti-Semitism never made anybody run to be Jewish. Judaism is a lifelong study curriculum of language, history, law, tradition and ethics. The more you study, the richer the experience becomes. Continue to study yourself and become knowledgeable about Jewish traditions and values. Send your daughter to Israel on a Birthright trip. Instill Judaism through food, if necessary. Always keep it positive. We are all Jews by choice and some of us are Jews by birth, as well.

Robert A. Cohn
'Papa Portnoy' re-visited: Philip Roth as a Stepfather

Way back in September 1975, I published a lengthy article in the *St. Louis Jewish Light* headlined "Papa Portnoy: Philip Roth as a Stepfather," based on an extensive interview I had at the time with David Williams, then living in St. Louis, who had been Philip Roth's stepson when Roth was married to Williams' mother, Margaret ("Maggie") Martinson Roth. The article generated considerable "buzz" because it revealed for the first time that a number of characters in Roth's novels were based in part on Maureen Martinson Roth, especially Lucy Nelson in *When She Was Good*, and Maureen Johnson Walker in *My Life as a Man*.

I have always been a devoted fan of Philip Roth's fiction and am among those reviewers who believe that he deserves consideration for the Nobel Prize in Literature. I have continued to review Roth's books in the years since 1975, most recently *Nemesis*, a splendid short novel which vividly evokes the terrifying polio epidemic in Roth's hometown of Newark in 1944.

Back in 1988, Roth published *The Facts: A Novelist's Autobiography* in which for the first time he detailed his stormy marriage to Margaret Martinson Roth (whom he calls Josie Jensen in the book), and his relationship with her son, David, by a previous marriage, whom Roth calls "Donald" in an effort to protect his identity and to keep people from "pawing him." In *The Facts* Roth makes direct reference to my 1975 article, which he describes as a "longish piece" written by an "inquisitive journalist" from a Jewish newspaper (me). I wrote to Roth through his publisher at the time, Farrar Straus Giroux, telling him of my continued admiration for his work, updating him on David Williams, who had moved to California, and expressing regret if my article had caused him any discomfort or pain. I also enclosed my copy of *The Facts*, asking for him to sign it. I received back a very gracious typewritten note from Roth, thanking me for my letter and signing my copy of the book, which I continue to treasure.

In the weeks before the official publication of *Nemesis*, I received an inquiry from Jeffrey Posternak and Alexander Levenberg of The Wylie Agency. "We are literary agents and represent Philip Roth. I write to you on behalf of Mr. Roth with a request for assistance. Would you be able to send me a copy of an article published in the *Jewish Light* between 1969 and 1970 entitled "Portnoy's Step-son," a profile of David Williams? We'd be most grateful." Of course I was pleased, with the assistance of Mike Sherwin, Managing Editor of the *Jewish Light* who received the original request to find and forward a copy of the piece, which appeared in the Sept. 3, 1975 edition of the *Jewish Light*.

Perhaps Roth is going to publish a sequel to *The Facts* to include events beyond the period he covered in the 1988 book. In *The Facts*, Roth sets the record straight as to what the facts of his actual life really were, to quell the endless speculation triggered by the fact that many of his fictional characters, Alexander Portnoy, Nathan Zuckerman, Peter Tarnopol and David Kepesh share biographical details with their creator/author—born in suburban Newark, 1933. Going to Weequahic High School outside of Newark, a school with much in common with University City High School during the era in which it had a large number of Jewish students, who all felt very secure in its halls.

When Howard Schwartz and Barbara Raznick, editors of *New Harvest* approached me to contribute an article for the current edition, I suggested that I re-visit the "Papa Portnoy" piece, updating it and clarifying some items in it, which may not have been clear at the time of its original publication. What follows is that update, as it was written and revised with hindsight and later information.

> *"At any rate, all I can do with my story is tell it. And tell it. And tell it. And that's the truth."*
> - Philip Roth in *My Life as a Man*

David Williams is just about the last person on earth one would associate with Philip Roth, back in 1975 when I met him to the present day. What could a truck driver, of WASP stock, who lived at the time of our interview in the renascent Soulard area of South St. Louis possibly have in common with the brooding bad boy of modern Jewish writers?

The answer, which was revealed for the first time in my exclusive interview for the *St. Louis Jewish Light*, is that David Williams was the stepson of Philip Roth during the author's stormy, disastrous first marriage to the late Margaret (Maggie) Martinson Williams Roth. She is listed as Roth's first wife (he was later married to the actress Claire Bloom; they separated) in most of Roth's official biographies, but virtually nothing factual had been reported about the relationship she had with her husband since their protracted separation proceedings in 1974.

Among the fascinating insights the interviews with David Williams produced into the biography of Philip Roth as a stepfather and husband, are the strong indications that Margaret Martinson was the inspiration for Lucy Nelson, heroine of Roth's third book, *When She Was Good*, and was reproduced almost totally in the characters Lydia Jergenson Ketterer and Maureen Johnson Walker in Roth's 1974 novel "My Life as a Man."

Williams' relationship to Roth was brought to my attention following the 1975 publication of Roth's book, *Reading Myself and Others*, in which Roth discusses his own work and that of other novelists. A review of the book appeared in the *St. Louis Jewish Light*, and a reader called to request a copy of the review. She casually mentioned that Roth's stepson was then living in St. Louis. "You're putting me on," I said. "You must mean that he is somehow related to Tennessee Williams, who lived in St. Louis in his youth. To pursue the lead, I contacted David Williams, who was then living in the Soulard area, and he agreed to the interview, which was to be the first ever on his relationship with Roth.

After two exhaustive sessions with Williams, and after carefully corroborating the story, I have no doubt that Williams is indeed the former stepson of the one-time Lenny Bruce of the printed page, who published the controversial *Portnoy's Complaint*, which threw the Jewish Establishment into an apoplexy seizure in 1969, but whose books struck responsive chords with my generation.

When Williams and I sat down for our interviews, which started in his ancient refurbished three-story home on Lami Street in the Soulard area, which he shared with his then "significant other" Ellen Irons, and finished in his favorite watering hole, the Buel Street Pub on 10th and Emmett Streets, we agreed that we were not interested in producing a tabloid-style, gossipy "tell-all" story. Both Williams and I share a strong positive regard for Roth—I for his writings and Williams for his former association—and we both felt an obligation—perhaps even a duty—to provide some insights into one of the most prominent contemporary authors.

Williams, who had just turned 27 at the time of our first interview, was then employed as a truck driver and tank man for Slay Transportation Co. on 7th Street. He had his sights on anti-poverty or neighborhood work. (He later pursued those and other interests after he moved to California). Williams at the time appeared to be a kind of younger version of Eric Hoffer, a diamond in the rough, an amalgam of the working class ethic of the 1930s, the motorcycle-manliness of the 1950s and the rebellious youth of the 1960s and 1970s.

Williams has a muscular physique and grayish blond hair, which he wore, pulled back into a ponytail in the style of Thomas Jefferson or the Jefferson Airplane. A Greek fisherman's cap topped his head at all times. Beneath his delicate nose, which resembles that of his late mother, runs a helter-skelter moustache.

David Williams was one of three persons—along with his late mother and his younger sister Holly—to have had direct experience with Roth as the head of his own nuclear family. Perhaps thermo-nuclear family would be a more appropriate term, since it seems that it ended with both a bang and a whimper.

Williams told me of his relationship with his mother and Roth with a cool detachment, casually punctuating key sentences with a flick of the ash from his cigarette. He frequently exploded in a good-natured raucous laugh.

"I was born in Chicago on July 25, 1948 as David Elliot Williams, the son of Dan Dwight Williams, a commercial artist and trombone player, and the late Margaret, or Maggie Martinson Williams," David told me. He added, "I was a test baby for breast feeding."

His parents, he said, "were much too young to have had children at the time," as his mother was only 18 when he was born and his father, only 20. "My sister Holly, or 'Yana' as she calls herself (who then lived in Oakland, Calif.), was born on Sept. 22, 1950. We never had much of a home life with Maggie and Dan. They were divorced in 1955, and I was asked with which parent I wanted to live. I said 'neither' and so we were shipped down to our second cousins in San Antonio, Gilbert and Janet Berner."

According to Williams, his childhood was an ordeal by fire. "I was an out-and-out punk kid, who was into doing violent things. I was always setting off explosives, and wore dark tough guy clothes. I affected a hateful air and even wore a swastika for a brief period."

Then in 1959, Williams heard from his father, Dan back in Chicago, that he had taken a new wife, and that Maggie had a new husband, Philip Roth. They had met at the University of Chicago. Roth and Margaret Martinson Williams were married on Feb. 22, 1959. "I think— but I'm not sure—that Philip and mother were married in a temple and that mother completed a formal conversion to Judaism," Williams said. "But this did not placate Philip's parents (Herman and Bess Finkel Roth), who were very Orthodox Jews and who strongly disapproved of the marriage from the start."

Note to the reader: at the time this article was written, Philip Roth, Herman Wouk and other Jewish novelists often referred to young Gentile women as *shicksas*, a term which was originally meant humorously, but many now consider derogatory. Keep that in mind as you read on.

"I guess you could say that my mother was Philip Roth's *shicksa* goddess at first," Williams said. "Mother was a very beautiful woman before she gained weight towards the end. She was blond, shapely and sexy and even into her 30s looked like she was 17."

An examination of the faded studio photograph of Maggie Martinson, which Williams dug out of a ton of crated belongings, recalls the image Philip Roth evoked in his description of the attractiveness of young Christian women to certain kinds of Jewish men.

"I too want to be the boyfriend of Debbie Reynolds," writes Philip Roth in *Portnoy's Complaint* (1969). "It's the Eddie Fisher in me coming out, that's all, the longing in all us swarthy Jew boys for those bland, blond exotics called *shiksas*...."

In the portrait, the younger Maggie has the fresh faced look of "girl-next-door" innocence, combined with the regal elegance of a Grace Kelly, a beauty which needed no makeup to embellish or enhance it. Her soft gaze and forehead seem to be projected onto David Williams' face. There is an unmistakable family resemblance.

Roth had taken his master's degree at the University of Chicago, and returned there after serving in the Army. He became an instructor in English composition. Williams believes that Roth met Maggie either in her capacity as a staff member in one of the university departments, or perhaps as a student in one of his classes. At various intervals, from the time of the marriage in 1959 until Roth and his wife were separated in 1963, Williams and his sister Holly were together with the couple as a kind of free-form family unit.

It was a busy period for Roth. In 1959, he published *Goodbye, Columbus*, a collection of short stories and a title novella about a romance between a poor Jewish boy and rich Jewish girl, which the following year would win a National Book Award (and which was later made into a popular film starring Richard Benjamin and Ali McGraw). Roth spent most of 1960 in Rome from the proceeds of a Guggenheim Fellowship. Later that year he started teaching for two years at the State University of Iowa, and then came to Princeton as a writer-in-residence from 1962-64.

"My first real contact with Philip was a period, I believe in 1961, when I was 13 years old, at Philip and Maggie's summer cottage in East

Amagansett, Long Island. Like I said, I had become a pretty wild kid, because that's the only way I knew how to survive. I've got to say that if it were not for the positive influence Philip had on my life at that time, I might be in jail today. I was that kind of kid."

The above David Williams quote was cited in Roth's 1988 autobiographical book *The Facts*.

Williams pointed out that Roth helped arrange for him to enroll at the Morgan Park Academy, a high-income private school on Chicago's extreme South Side. Williams graduated from the school at the age of 19.

It was Winnie Theodore (Mrs. George), principal of the lower and middle schools of the academy who provided the absolute confirmation of David's relationship to Philip Roth and Maggie. "I remember David especially well, since he was close friends with my son Tom and actually lived with us off and on from the time he enrolled in the seventh grade in 1961 until he graduated in 1967," said Mrs. Theodore in a telephone interview.

"David's records here at the school list him as the son of Dan Williams and Margaret Martinson Roth. I am positive that Maggie was the wife of Philip Roth, and recall meeting her here at the school. She was a very beautiful woman, and very charming, who apparently led a very glamorous life until she died so tragically. After David graduated from here, he and my son attended East Michigan University in Ypsilante. I'm sure that David's association with Philip Roth was genuine, and you can quote me."

Mrs. Theodore described the academy as being similar to the John Burroughs and Country Day School and Mary Institute in St. Louis. It is now coeducational and goes through grade 12 with tuition (in 1975) ranging from $975 to $2,150.

"Philip just didn't throw me into the school without preparation," Williams recalled. Even though he was still working on *Letting Go* (which he dedicated to Maggie) at the time, he set aside enough time to tutor me personally in English literature. He also arranged to have me tutored in math and grammar. But Philip himself was my main tutor."

Looking a bit wistful and nostalgic for one of the few times during the interview, Williams described the way the sensitive Jewish author approached the deeply troubled non-Jewish stepson to introduce him to the world of words.

"He picked out the books and literally forced me to read them. I'll never forget that we started out with Stephen Crane's *Red Badge of Courage*. After I had finished, we'd sit down at the kitchen table over a snack and he would discuss the book with me, teaching me the basic concepts like foreshadowing, allegories and metaphors. We'd talk about it until he was satisfied that I comprehended the author's real reason for writing the book. I also remember him getting me to read *Fail-Safe*, which deals with the dangers of an accidental nuclear war."

"As a result of the preparation Philip gave me, I was much better prepared for Morgan Park Academy. Before the tutoring, I had to struggle to get through school. That first semester after the tutoring, I made the dean's list."

Williams says that "the turning point in my life was when Philip taught me to use my brains as well as my body. He opened up other options for me, and I'll always appreciate that."

Did Roth relate to Williams on a father-son basis? "No, I wasn't really into having a parent, and Philip was perceptive enough not to try to force this kind of relationship on me. He did father-daughter trips with my younger sister Holly. They were extremely close. But to me, Philip was just a good friend in those days."

Williams recalls that there were "fun times," when Philip, Maggie and he would go clam digging and swimming down by the beach.

He also talked about the manner in which the author of the scandalously (for its time) Ode to Onanism *Portnoy's Complaint*, discussed sex and masturbation with his stepson. "When Philip sat down to discuss sex with me, I was already familiar with the human reproductive cycle. But Philip was the first person to tell me that people had intercourse for fun, not just to have children. On masturbation, Philip quoted this Harvard dude who said that 98 percent of everyone masturbates and the other two percent lie."

Roth, who early in his career had often been accused by Jewish Establishment critics of being "self-hating" about his Jewishness, manifested very positive feelings about his Jewish background to Williams and his sister. "He never tried to pressure us into converting, although I recall that Holly was very interested in Judaism at the time. But he taught us that you don't have to be Jewish to feel compassion for the Jews. Among the books he asked me to read was *Exodus* by Leon Uris and we got into long and very heavy discussions about the Nuremberg War Crimes Trials. Another Jewish friend of his, Carl Zalenka, who used to write jokes for Sid Caesar, raised my consciousness about class differences in America."

He also recalls that Roth would frequently "joke and clown around, and used to sing 'The Sheik of Araby' a lot. I thought his humor was 'right on' at the time."

As to Roth's own work, Williams remembers reading "a great short story about two Jewish servicemen in a boot camp. ("Defenders of the Faith," a story in *Goodbye, Columbus*.) I remember a breakfast meeting on the naming of *Letting Go*,' and years later I saw a movie version of *Goodbye Columbus*. But the hang-ups of a 1959 Jewish kid were not where I was at by then. I'm familiar with *Portnoy's Complaint* through reviews, and also with *Our Gang* (a biting satire of the Nixon Administration), which I'm glad Philip got around to writing. I sort of lost interest after Philip and mother split."

While Philip Roth and Margaret Williams were in the midst of a protracted divorce proceedings, she was killed in a tragic car accident in Central Park. Philip Roth attended Maggie's funeral, where he sat right next to David. They were to later meet for lunch in New York.

Following his graduation from Morgan Park Academy and attendance at East Michigan University, Williams moved to St. Louis for three years to be with a friend. While here, he was involved with the antiwar movement and helped organize Acid Rescue. He also worked for a time at Pages Bar on Olive Street and as a physical therapist aide at the Jewish Hospital (now Barnes-Jewish). Williams later moved to San Francisco, where he and his sister Holly and then companion Ellen lived at Project One, a service-oriented commune.

Williams and Ellen moved back to St. Louis because he had so many friends here. Both he and Ellen, who is also a native of Chicago, were active in the Soulard Neighborhood Improvement Association, which is working to restore the once-decaying Soulard area to its former glory by restoration of its homes and places like the Buel Street Pub, a resurrected neighborhood bar where young professionals, former hippies and students sit comfortably at the same bar to bend elbows with the grizzled, blue collar natives of the area. It is the kind of place where both Archie Bunker and his "meathead" liberal son-in-law Mike Stivic would both feel comfortable. The bar was complete with witty posters and an authentic, witty FDR portrait. (After Williams later moved to California, he and Ellen, who remained in St. Louis, split amicably).

I asked Williams about the marriage of Philip and Maggie, which apparently collapsed in 1963. The end of the marriage reads like a cheap potboiler or a weary soap opera, a re-run of the classic Jewish-Gentile breakups involving such couples as Arthur Miller and Marilyn Monroe or Lenny Bruce and "Hot" Honey Harlow.

"Mother was not only a very sexy-looking woman and an intelligent person, who worked as an editor for a publishing house, she was also very destructive," Williams said. "She tried to destroy everyone in her path. The term 'castrating female' would certainly apply to her," he added. He also told me that he had never witnessed any violent domestic disagreements between Philip and Maggie and that they often seemed affectionate toward one another during their times together. "Also, Philip defended mother to me when I criticized her."

The facts of the Philip-Maggie marriage, as recorded in cryptic references in Roth's write-ups in *Current Biographies, 20ᵗʰ Century Authors* and *Who's Who in America* (and fleshed out by Roth himself in his 1988 autobiography *The Facts*) are that Roth and Margaret Martinson were married in 1959. They were legally separated on March 1, 1963. There were no children produced by their marriage (both David and Holly Williams were by Maggie's first marriage). At the time of the separation, New York State had complicated divorce proceedings, and a stormy separation proceeding received sensationalistic coverage the *New York Daily News* in 1964. Roth's current entry in Wikipedia discusses and confirms many of the facts of his marriage to Maggie, and how she is depicted in some of Roth's novels.

Williams recalled that "one of the things that mother complained about was the fact that the highly negative female protagonist of Roth's novel *When She Was Good*, Lucy Nelson, seemed to be patterned after her own life."

The book in question, *When She Was Good*, was something of an anomaly among Roth's earlier works. Departing radically from the New Jersey-based Jewish themes of *Goodbye, Columbus* and *Letting Go*" (1962), *When She Was Good* (1967) is strictly centered on small town WASP America, a book which has been praised as being in the tradition of Sherwood Anderson's *Winesburg, Ohio*, or scorned as Roth's answer to Grace Metalious' *Peyton Place*. Actually, Roth has the credentials to write credibly about small town America, having spent time teaching at Iowa State University.

Lucy Nelson, the title character in *When She Was Good*, is depicted as a strong-willed, almost compulsive woman, who lived until she was 18 with an alcoholic father, "Whitey" Nelson, and later with a Hydrox cookie-munching husband, Roy Bassart. She destroys them both in her

zeal to reform them. After a knockdown, drag-out fight with her husband
Roy, Lucy dashes off into the night, and freezes to death in the snow near
the lover's lane where her husband had first seduced her.

Glancing down the dust-jacket excerpts from various reviews and
blurbs on the book, describing Lucy Nelson as "the most venomous
heroine that literature has seen in some time," one whose "all-consuming
mission in life is the wholesale destruction of all men,"Williams chuckled
with a touch of bravado. "Yeah, that's mother all right." He added that his
mother's father, the late "Red" Martinson, had a drinking problem, and
that his mother "had to call the cops on him a few times."

In *Reading Myself and Others*, Roth's nonfiction collection of personal
essays and interviews on his work, he draws a comparison between the
protagonists of *When She Was Good* and *Portnoy's Complaint*, which is a
revealing indication of how he might compare his own background to
that of his late wife:

"Though not necessarily 'typical,' Alexander Portnoy and Lucy Nelson
seem to me, in their extreme resentment and disappointment, like the
legendary unhappy children out of two familiar American family myths.
In one book, it is the Jewish son railing against the seductive mother, in
the other the Gentile daughter railing against the alcoholic father (equally
loved, hated and feared, the most unforgettable character she had ever
met). Of course Lucy Nelson seems to destroy herself within an entirely
different fictional matrix, but that would result, among other reasons, from
the enormous difference between the two environments that inspire their
rage as well as their shared sense of loss and nostalgia."

The above is but one example of the remarkable ability of Roth to
describe the divide between the American Jewish and Gentile experiences
with insight and perception. He writes mostly about "what he knows,"
based on his direct experience, but from a fictional point of view. His
early writings about women "turned off" a generation of young feminist
critics, but in recent years some have returned to his works with great
admiration. Leah Hager Cohen, in her glowing review of *Nemesis*, Roth's
most recent novel, admits, "I wrote Roth off. Back in my early 20s, in a
fit of literary conscientiousness, I undertook to sample his work. At the
point when my nose could wrinkle no further in distaste, I was struck by
a relieving epiphany—'Oh: these are for boys'—upon which I resumed
my reading life unburdened by any expectations of venturing deeper into
Rothiana."

When Cohen was assigned to review *Nemesis* for the *Times*, she plunged into his novels to prepare for the assignment, "remediating my embarrassing literary gap, a cause to which I devoted—with a kind of mounting, marveling pleasure—much of this past summer. All of which is to say: Before you stands a convert."

According to Williams, his mother and sister used to "see themselves or their personalities projected onto several characters, but I wasn't much interested in looking for this. They said that sometimes a male character would resemble Holly or a female character would resemble me."

Of course much of Roth's work seems autobiographical, though over the years he repeatedly denied that despite the resemblances between himself and his male protagonists, his novels are fictional works in themselves. Roth says in *Reading Myself and Others*, "I have never really through my work or directly in my life, to sever all that binds me to the world I came out of."

For example, Roth, like Alexander Portnoy (and other characters), was born in 1933 in Newark, and graduated from Weequahic High School in New Jersey. Both have strong-willed mothers and fathers who worked for life-insurance companies. Roth discusses the resemblance in *Reading Myself*, but cautions that people outside of his immediate family were also the basis for some of his characters.

More recently, Roth writes affectionately about his mother, the late Bess Finkel Roth, in *The Facts*, and about his late father, Herman Roth, in the very moving *Patrimony* (1991), a non-fiction account of how Roth cared for his father after he was diagnosed with a terminal brain tumor. Yes, there are resemblances to Roth's fictional parents, but there are also important differences.

It should be added that Roth's use of autobiographical material as a basis for his work is certainly not unique to him, and all of his work deserves to be evaluated on the basis of its pure literary merit, without regard for the particular people upon whom it is based. What Jewish kid who grew up between the mid-1930s and late 1950s cannot recognize the universal stereotypes in Roth's novels?

To be sure, one must keep this caution in mind lest one exaggerate similarities between life and art. But Roth's searing novel, *My Life as a Man*, as of 1974, was his most cruelly and brutally autobiographical effort. The book invites comparison to Arthur Miller's *After the Fall*, a play in which he used a pathetic blonde woman (ironically named Maggie in the play) to depict his calamitous marriage to movie icon Marilyn Monroe. Like Roth, Miller had insisted that any resemblance between the Quentin character to himself and Maggie to Marilyn were "purely coincidental," but few critics doubted the connection between the play and Miller's real-life marriage.

So close is *My Life as a Man* to the real life of Roth, that if anyone else besides himself had written it, Roth might have sued for libel for printing the "truth with malice." One does not have to be a Ph.D. in English literature to figure out that a book entitled *My Life as a Man*, which contains a major section called "My True Story" must be at least in part "The real McCoy," as Portnoy might say.

As the protagonist of *My Life as a Man*, Roth gives us Peter Tarnopol (from the name of a town in Russia, or a word for "rooster," some say). Tarnopol is a kind of post-graduate Portnoy, who even uses the same psychiatrist, the famous Dr. Otto Spielvogel, who had said after Portnoy had poured out his soul to him for 274 pages, "Now vee may perhaps to begin. Yes?"

But Tarnopol is more than just an older version of Portnoy. In fact, the Who's Who style biography which Roth includes of Tarnopol in *My Life as a Man*, is a virtual carbon copy (satirically written, of course) of Philip Roth. Both Roth and Tarnopol attended public school in the East and graduated college *summa cum laude*. Both taught English at universities. Both wrote bestsellers on Jewish themes and won national prizes and Guggenheim Fellowships. Roth states that Tarnopol had a "nightmarish marriage to the former Maureen Johnson Tarnopol," which like Roth's marriage to Margaret Martinson Williams Roth went through a prolonged separation battle and ended with her tragic death before a divorce could be formalized.

Tarnopol's "Complaint" is diagnosed by Dr. Spielvogel as "the narcissism of the artist", and Tarnopol fires the Doctor after he published a detailed diagnosis of the problem in a psychoanalytic journal. Ironically, it is self-love and not "self-hate" which bugs our anti-hero.

In the introduction to the crucial second part of *My Life as a Man*," Roth quotes Tarnopol as stating, "Presently, Mr. Tarnopol is preparing to foresake the art of fiction for a while and embark upon an autobiographical narrative, an endeavor which he approaches warily, uncertain as to both its advisability and usefulness. Not only would the publication of such a document raise serious legal and ethical problems, but there is no reason that by keeping his imagination at bay and rigorously adhering to the facts, Mr. Tarnopol will have exorcised his obsession once and for all. It remains to be seen whether his candor, such as it is, can serve any better than his art (or Dr. Spielvogel's therapeutic devices) to demystify the past and mitigate his admittedly uncommendable sense of defeat."

I was relieved to discover this revealing paragraph, because I certainly approached this article with some of the same concerns over "serious ethical and legal problems." But Roth's having written such an explicit introduction suggests that he realized that it was inevitable that eventually someone would write this kind of article. I am also glad that it can be done in the spirit of compassion and respect for Philip Roth and my continued and increasing admiration and appreciation for his work.

In *The Facts*, Roth mimics his character Tarnopol and chronicles the first parts of his life, including his marriage to Maggie Martinson, whom he renames Josie Jensen. David Williams is re-named "Donald" in order to protect his privacy. Roth also explored issues about the similarities and differences between himself and his characters in numerous later novels, such as *The Counterlife* and *Deception*. In *Nemesis*, his protagonist is Bucky Cantor, who is 23 in 1944 during the polio epidemic. Bucky, an altruistic role model for the kids he coaches on a Newark playground that broiling summer, differs from the sex-obsessed Alexander Portnoy. Roth continues to be influenced by his own life story, but no longer seems to be obsessed with settling scores with old demons.

Back to *My Life as a Man*, it is interesting to note that none of the major reviews of the book at the time of its publication attempted to link it directly with Roth's own life, especially regarding his real-life marriage to Maggie Martinson. In contrast to the way reviewers linked Miller's *After the Fall* to his marriage to Marilyn, most reviewers ignored Roth's marriage to Maggie.

Roth's current (2010) entry in Wikipedia discusses and confirms many of the facts of his marriage to Maggie, and how she is the basis for some of the characters in Roth's novels.

The structure of *My Life as a Man* is a complex wheel-within-a-wheel-within-a-wheel. Tarnopol as the alter-ego for Roth, describes himself as being so totally obsessed with the memory of his disastrous marriage to Maureen, that he writes a story about yet another Jewish writer and Roth look-alike, Nathan Zuckerman, a University of Chicago professor who is married to another destructive blonde named Lydia Jorgenson Ketterer, who has a daughter Monica, by a previous marriage. Lydia and Maureen are depicted as demented and destructive, pill popping blonde bombshells who drive their brooding intellectual neurotic Jewish husbands up the wall and into extramarital affairs with younger women.

Roth would deploy the Nathan Zuckerman character in several later novels in the years that followed.

In the second section, "My True Story," Tarnopol tells "his own" story of his marriage to Maureen Johnson Walker, who traps him into a marriage by her seductive good looks and by faking a pregnancy test. "How could she do this? To me!" Tarnopol rages. The marriage is a total disaster, intellectually, sexually and spiritually. The psychopathic and destructive Maureen refuses to grant Peter a divorce. The marriage is terminated finally when Maureen is killed in an automobile accident.

Because Maureen continues to obsess Tarnopol even after her death, despite his brother urging him to "leave her to heaven," Tarnopol writes the Zuckerman stories to "exorcise" her from his psyche. Like some kind of Gentile *dybbuk*, the disembodied spirit of Maureen continues to haunt the author. At the end, he questions whether his gift for words alone would bring him the relief he seeks, and concludes that they cannot.

As part of the Roth continuum of the male-female characters, *My Life as a Man* fulfills the adolescent fantasies of Alexander Portnoy by giving Tarnopol his idealized "*shicksa* goddess." He breaks free from his trap of being trapped "in the middle of a Jewish joke" only to find himself in the worse prison of a silly Gentile soap opera. Alexander Portnoy could not sexually respond to a strong Israeli woman, allegedly because of his childhood castration fears over his mother Sophie and her bread knife. But alas, when Tarnopol gets his wish, he finds that the idealized "Other" woman can be castrating and also frigid. From the fear-inducing Jewish Mother to the destructive Shrewish Wife! Indeed it seems that the only sexual experience about which some Roth characters can wax ecstatic is masturbation, the works of their own hands. (More narcissism, Dr. Spielvogel?)

Williams had not read *My Life as a Man* at the time of our interviews. But after being quizzed closely about the characters and its contents, he had "no doubt" that Lydia and Maureen are based on his mother Maggie; that Tarnopol and Zuckerman are based on Roth and Monica at least in part on his sister Holly.

In the book, Tarnopol/Roth describes Maureen as having "the kind of crisp good looks that are associated with Irishmen—only a little marred in her case by a lantern jaw—a lithe, wiry little body...," a description that evokes the image of Maggie.

In the book, Maureen is described as a good writer who is at first interested in Tarnopol's work. "I would be his Muse, if he would let me," she writes in her diary. Williams recalls that his mother Maggie was a good writer who worked as an editor for a major publisher. In the novel, Tarnopol/Roth describes the separation proceedings before a Judge Milton Rosenzweig, who awarded Maureen $5,000 a year, and the sensationalist (for its day) reporting of the case by a *New York Daily News* reporter named Valducci. His story is accompanied by a photo of Maureen, "her lantern jaw slicing the offending air as she strides down the courthouse steps." In the actual case, the *New York Daily News* of April 14, 1964, a story by reporter Alfred Albelli, Margaret Martinson Roth is shown in a similar photograph. Later stories report that she was awarded $150 a week by Judge Samuel C. Coleman.

The brutal descriptions of the separation proceedings and the hardships they inflicted on Tarnopol, recalled to my mind the stern warning of Sophie Portnoy to her son Alex as he prepared to start college: "Don't run first thing to a Blondie, please! Because she will take you for all you're worth and then leave you bleeding in the gutter! A brilliant innocent baby like you, she'll eat you up alive!"

There are numerous other examples which could be provided to link the characters in *My Life as a Man,* but I have already belabored the point. Suffice to say the similarities between the Roth characters and those in his own life are seemingly greater than between the Mark Zuckerberg character in *The Social Network* movie to the real-life founder of Facebook. It appears that any resemblances between Roth and Maggie and Tarnopol and Zuckerman and Maggie and Lydia/Maureen are more than "coincidental."

Any doubts about the completeness of the basis of Maureen to Maggie were put aside in Williams' mind, when we discussed the fact that in the book Maureen is killed instantly when the car in which she is a passenger crashes into a tree.

The book describes how stunned and shaken, but ashamedly "relieved" Tarnopol is on receiving the news parallels fact as well. Tarnopol discusses plans for Maggie's funeral with Maureen's mother and then with his parents who advise him to put on a dark suit and make an appearance at the funeral ("Don't be a *pisher*! Go!"). He seems puzzled when he tells his parents that Maureen's remains are to be cremated, a practice which was frowned upon by Orthodox Jews.

Roth's real-life reactions to Maggie's death are described in an article by Lenny Bruce biographer Albert Goldman in the Feb. 7, 1969 issue of *Life* magazine. According to Goldman, 1968 had been an exceptionally traumatic year for Philip Roth. He had undergone serious surgery which nearly cost him his life, He was in Florida recovering from the surgery and finishing writing *Portnoy's Complaint*. He went back to his New York apartment when "one morning the phone rings and he hears his step-daughter (Holly) saying "Mother has been killed." Goldman adds, "Philip is stunned. He goes through the funeral arrangements in a trance."

In the pleasant ambience of the Buel Street Pub, I finished the interview with David Williams as he sipped a Tequilla Sunrise and I drank a draft beer.

"Is that the way your mother died? I asked.

"Yes, I was working for Braniff Airlines, when on May 19, 1968 my sister called to tell me that mother had been killed in a car crash in Central Park. She was with this black dude, and I understand that they were stoned, and she was killed when he crashed his XKE into a tree at 4:30 a.m. Dan and I went to New York for the funeral."

In my original story on my interview with Williams, I misunderstood his ambiguous answer to my question about whether Roth was at the funeral. In *The Facts*, Roth recalls that not only was he there, but he sat right next to Williams.

Somewhat ashamed of myself for doing a final bit of fact checking, I asked Williams if his mother's remains were cremated. He took a long, thoughtful gulp of his drink and gazed at his reflection in the mirror in back of the long row of bottles across the bar.

"Yeah."

Thus ended my "gonzo" and super-long interview with David Williams, the stepson of Philip Roth, which I have now revised and updated. Williams would eventually move from St. Louis back to California, where he reportedly joined a motorcycle club and is pursuing other interests. Philip Roth has continued his prolific literary output, working mostly in seclusion in his quiet Connecticut home, which has received acclaim. His books have twice received the National Book Award, the National Book Critics Circle Award, and three times the PEN/Faulkner Award. He has also received the National Jewish Book Award in Fiction. He received a Pulitzer Prize for his 1997 novel *American Pastoral*, which featured the Nathan Zuckerman character he introduced in *My Life as a Man*. He is described as having a "supple, ingenious style" that is often compared to Henry James, and he has been promoted by his admirers (including me) for the Nobel Prize in Literature.

In 1990, Roth married his long-time companion, the British actress

Claire Bloom. In 1994 they separated, and in 1996, Bloom published a memoir, *Leaving a Doll's House*, which described their marriage in detail, somewhat turning the tables on Roth for his descriptions of his first marriage. In more recent novels, including *The Human Stain, The Dying Animal, Exit Ghost, Everyman* and *The Humbling*, Roth has wrestled with issues around mortality, fear of death and desperate sexual escapades designed to deaden the pain. In *Indignation* and *Nemesis*, Roth reaches beyond his personal concern to put forward the thought, "There but for the grace of God go I." The young, rebellious and sex-obsessed Alexander Portnoy or Nathan Zuckerman in a different time could have been the Anne Frank of *The Ghost Writer*, or Marcus Messner, the Jewish kid in 1951 who is killed in the Korean War, or Buddy Cantor, whose poor vision keeps him in Newark as his buddies go off to fight the Nazis in Europe.

So perhaps, Doctor Otto Spielvogel might say, "Now vee have really begun. Yes?"

Marty Ehrlich
Words on Music

It has been said that the only home we ever have is in a song. A song in which you are most solitary while feeling closely connected. Or is it the other way around. Where the singer owns nothing, "neither map nor discipline," while carrying the thoughts of a culture like a sack. A sojourn through a place to which there is an open return.

from *Sojourn* (1999)

Open Air. Under the Sun. Waiting to perform the concert you hear on this disk, outdoors on an August afternoon, fortuitous with pleasant weather, I thought back to playing music outside in St. Louis, circa 1970. Weather permitting, we'd meet in the park. Might be three saxes, two drummers, and a poet. Filling the space with sound, under the sun. Music growing unabashed and seemingly unbound. At that time a great door opened for me.

from *The Open Air Meeting* (1997)

The concept of this recording came to fruition with the composition of the three pieces entitled "*Scroll*". They were the last music I wrote, and they share an image and a function. The image is that of the moment in the synagogue service where the Torah is opened, its parchment now in the light and air, and then when it is tightly closed, the text rolled further on into the life of the telling. The function is that of a musical procession, moving into and away from the diverse "fables" that are the other pieces… It is my hope that this music moves for you from the particular to the universal in a way that parallels your work in the world.

from *Fables* (2010)

My compulsion is to give expression to the place where beauties that should not be forgotten and beauties that have yet to be imagined collide, coexist, and transform. It is in this place that my artistic heart resides.

from *The Long View* (2002)

What is the news on the rail? There is so much beauty in the world…so you start somewhere, here perhaps, and you see where it goes. Finding one's voice is an ongoing and open-ended endeavor. The ongoing work of hearing how we hear. The resonance may change over time, but the work of going back and forth from the music to our life experiences is continuous. I hold on to the belief that music, with or without words, speaks in the world, not above it.

from *News on the Rail* (2005)

Sounds startle the air. On this night, birds call across as if the light won't come. There is no silent center to start from. For generations we've opened a door. A burning patience, waiting to hear what hasn't been said. Just before, they say the darkest hour is just before. "All right now...Later... Easy now." These sounds will find a center or the center will change. "I think that music as we know it is autobiographical," Hemphill said. Just friends, metal hued breath across strings, entering open, way above, only to slide into the song, leaving still. Birds in the darkness, waiting for no one. Open the door, wake these sounds. Just before the dawn.

from *Just Before the Dawn* (1995)

Shelly R. Fredman
With a Prayer

My mother is one of those twice a year Jews, but for some strange reason during a brief segment of my childhood, my sister and I went to bed each night with a prayer. A lavender elephant and a yellow giraffe that my mom and her best friend had painted on our bedroom walls floated above our heads as my sister and I chanted, "Now I lay me down to sleep, I pray the Lord my soul to keep, if I should die before I wake, I pray the Lord my soul to take."

The singsong rhythm of it, my sister's voice riding mine, the fact that it came every single night—no matter what--were a balm to me, until the day we lost it—through apathy, or the hectic first weeks of my brother's life—a token of childhood, gone.

I still have the phrase, though, unuttered, some fifty years later, and I carry it, I think, as a vestige of a time when I dared to speak, one on one, with God. This was, once, how it may have been for all of us. Laden with the thousand year old heft and weight of the Rabbinic take on prayer, the *siddur*, we tend to forget that prayer, originally, biblically, was about an impromptu moment of encounter with God.

Think of Jacob fleeing Esau in the dark desert night and pausing to build an altar of stone. Think of Sarah, when God's messenger told her, after some ninety years, that she was to give birth to a child. Her laughter. Not a simple yelp of glee, Sarah's was a sound rich with emotion.

Between Sarah and ourselves lies the liturgical history of the Jewish people, a legacy that attempts to put us in touch with our highest selves, and is potentially redemptive, and yet for many of us the liturgy often feels to be a burden.

Enter Rabbi Nahman of Bratslav. Born on the Sabbath into the family of the Ba'al Shem Tov, the young Nahman was dissatisfied with the prescribed prayers of the liturgy and so, alone in the attic of his parent's house, he composed his own prayers, in the Yiddish that he spoke, pleading with God to draw him closer.

This lone outpouring of the soul before God, a surging emotionalism that Nahman experienced in his prayer life, is one I've touched upon only rarely, and not unsurprisingly, in my darkest hours. Falling airplanes and hospital rooms tend to bring out our most prayerful moments. Yet most of us show up in that room at a disadvantage—we arrive at the place where reason fails us as novices. Nahman's brand of engagement with

God is one he suggests we attempt, at least, regularly. At the heart of it lies discipline—a willingness to enter into Divine relationship.

In the early days of my own spiritual quest, I lived for a time within the Orthodox community of St. Louis. Yom Kippur at the Young Israel synagogue on Groby was a place Nahman might have felt at home in. At the *Neilah* service, in a basement *shul* the founders hadn't quite raised the funds to complete, as the last ribbons of light streaked the sky outside, over on the men's side—and yes—this only happened on the men's side, as the *Hazzan* called out, "*Adonai HuhaElohim*," one man at a time gave a *g'shrai*, a cry, a shriek, "*Adonai HuhaElohim*."

I, too, had been fasting for an impossible 26 hours and in that vacuous, drifting emptiness that was my body and mind at the tail end of this prayer marathon—a sea of black and white *tallit* swaying, rocking, stamping their feet before me—all the voices now, rising, it seemed the *shul* itself hovered just a few inches above the earth.

I could hear in these prayers the broken hearts we all carry, piercing the surface, finally, of our intensely secular lives. But what the Orthodox Jews really taught me, and any musician or ballet dancer worth her toe shoes knows, is that prayer, no matter how expansively I want to define it, that is, some act of relinquishing yourself to a higher Source of Mystery, whether that's Heschel praying with his feet in Selma or a poet with her pen in Cape Cod, has to occur every single day.

Nahman seems to know there is a purer distillation of who we are waiting at the still, broken center of each of us. This is a God I have known only in my most radiant, faith-driven moments, and I've only had glimpses. I came to know Her in my body—lying in savasana—corpse pose—at the end of a yoga class. That sense of peace and wholeness and pure exhaustion the best of yoga teachers can give you. What's left when you let go completely of everything you don't need.

Or in the hospital room of a dying friend—her husband's book of Psalms, only half read—open on the hospital cart before me. Or in the marshes of Wellfleet in Massachusetts, with the poet and priestess Mary Oliver as my guide, feeling in the slow, patient filling in of silver green grasses and dark muddy earth, the returning tide waters, a hint of Godness, a realm beyond reason, a place where faith is not so foreign. At moments like these, if we've been paying attention, the prayer will come.

I like to think I've been transformed by these impromptu prayerful moments. And I think, perhaps, there is some tie back to Sarah, Nahman, even my childhood self, in that room with the lavender elephants hoping for a connection, long-distance, even, a glimpse, at least, of Home.

Daniel Kohn
The Times—They Have a' Changed!
Thoughts on the Relationship between
Diaspora Jewry and the State of Israel

In case you haven't noticed it, the times have changed regarding the relationship between Diaspora Jewry—Jews who live all over the world— and their general thoughts, attitudes, emotions and feelings of connection to the State of Israel. Actually, they began to change in 1982, the year of Israel's military operation called *Shalom HaGalil*, or Peace for the Galilee, more commonly referred to as the invasion of Lebanon, but it wasn't immediately apparent just how much changed back then.

For years, it has become obvious that there is a split between the older and younger Jewish generations regarding how they view the State of Israel. Earlier, older generations of Jews learned about and experienced what I call the heroic, or romantic vision of the State of Israel. Perhaps they even remember a time before Israel existed in which Israel's very existence was seen as an unbelievable miracle against all odds.

To most of them and a few immediate generations following— including mine—Israel was the little country that could. It was a miracle that it ever even came into existence through a tenuous international coalition that in 1947 voted on the Palestine Partition Plan in the United Nations General Assembly and formally approved the establishment of the country. And it was even more of a miracle that Israel, after announcing independence, managed to survive the onslaught and invasion of five of its hostile, neighboring countries that sought to destroy it at birth. And to this generation, not only was it a miracle that Israel survived but that it managed to emerge from this conflict with slightly more territory than allotted to it under the U.N. Partition plan.

Despite tough economic times, Israel astonished the world with its ingenuity in making "the deserts bloom," pioneering drip-agriculture in its desert-like lands and replanting the forests of antiquity. It even managed to more than double its population, taking in literally millions of Jewish refugees from around the world, especially the Arab countries that persecuted their Jewish populations upon Israel's establishment and had expelled them with no compensation for the loss of property and assets these Jewish communities had built over centuries of living in relative peace with their Arab neighbors. Israel was also a pioneering society populating its landscape with communal agriculture settlements,

Kibbutzim and *Moshavim.* And even after its establishment, it managed to withstand the vicious attacks of the Palestine Liberation Organization's army that launched brutal terrorist attacks against Israeli civilians.

When it appeared in 1967 that Israel stood on a terrifying precipice—even another potential Holocaust—when Egypt, Syria and Jordan announced their intentions to attack and drive the Jews into the sea—many people, Jews and gentiles alike, saw Israel's massive victory over her foes in just six days as evidence of divine intervention. Despite the fact that the earliest Israeli settlements began to be established in the occupied territories of the Sinai desert, Gaza Strip, West Bank and Golan Heights, hardly anyone noticed or blamed Israel for finally expanding a little beyond its narrow geographical confines. And when the P.L.O. kidnapped and murdered many on the Israeli athletic team during the Munich Olympics in 1972, who could help but not sympathize with Israel, the eternal victim?

In 1973, Israel was once again the heroic, romantic "good guys" when the "bad guys," namely Egypt and Syria, launched a sneak attack against Israel on the holiest day of the Jewish calendar, Yom Kippur. But in dramatic and daring military operations, Israel managed to turn the situation around soundly defeating both countries and even laying down the groundwork for future peace. For just a few years later, Anwar Sadat, the president of Egypt, traveled to Jerusalem and became the first Arab country to establish peace with Israel. During this same time, the heroic, romantic vision of Israel was again burnished when Israeli commandos staged a daring and stunning military rescue of foreign and Israeli Jews who had been kidnapped by P.L.O. terrorists and their supporters in Entebbe, Uganda.

This is a very short, highly condensed version of some of the highlights of what I call this heroic, romantic vision of Israel. It was an era of "miracles," when Israel could do no wrong. It was a time when Israel was the darling and leader of the emerging third world countries. Israel's technical expertise in agriculture, science, medicine and valiant struggles against overwhelming and hostile foes made them appear to Diaspora Jews around the world like a dream come true, the fulfillment of Theodore Herzl's Zionist dreams and even the visions of the biblical prophets who declared that the people of Israel should serve as a "light unto the nations" (Isaiah 60:2-3).

This is the story of Israel that I grew up with. But I am the "cusp" generation. I bridge this generation and all those that follow. Israel was a heroic and romantic place even for me, the last of the baby boomers and beginning of generation X. I grew up living the Mid-West American Jewish dream in St. Louis, Missouri. As a child, my family spent a couple of months in Israel in 1972. It was a magical place for a 9 year-old boy, where I could go down to the local street corner kiosk by myself and ask to buy Bazooka bubble gum in my fragmentary Hebrew, cavort on the hulks of burned out Syrian tanks on the Golan heights left over from the Six Day War, and play soldier with my fellow childhood Israeli friend.

Like the immediate generation before me, I grew up with Israel as a potential, last-ditch place of refuge from Anti-Semitism. Growing up in an affluent and comfortable suburb of St. Louis, I was surrounded by fellow Jews yet I still had to deal with the occasional Anti-Semitic joke and comment. I never experienced anything truly violent or virulent, but it was sufficiently ever-present that even as a teenager, I was aware of the pervasiveness of Jew-hatred and prejudice. Therefore, it was only a mild shock to me that once, my mother said that I should never let my passport expire for God-forbid that we might one day have to flee America for a safer haven, namely, Israel. I grew up with strangely similar experiences as the generation of my parents and grandparents, with this older, heroic, romantic vision of Israel as a mighty David battling against the Goliaths of hostile Arab countries that had to be kept safe and secure lest one day it might even have to become my own home!

But everything changed in 1982. I didn't know it then and I don't think anyone else really did either. After all, how can you tell the moment when the tide changes from going out to coming back in, or vice versa? In retrospect, I suppose we can all point to specific events that presaged the beginning of the end of this heroic, romantic image of Israel amongst Diaspora Jewry. It was the invasion of Lebanon and the massacre of defenseless Palestinian old men, women and children in the refugee camps of Sabra and Shatilla.

It was the summer after my first year of college and I clearly remember a cover of *Time Magazine* with a photograph of a heavily armored Israeli tank racing through the Lebanese countryside with the cover story caption screaming out, "Israel's Blitz" or something along those lines. Did I realize that *Time Magazine* was being historically ironic, even critical of Israel's invasion of Lebanon by calling its military operation by the same German word that became synonymous with Nazi Germany's lightning warfare of World War II? I doubt it. All I really remember is that my young Israeli playmate from 1972 with whom I used to play soldier, was right now a real Israeli soldier who, I later learned, had faked his medical records to obscure some minor health impediment in order to join his unit in battle in Lebanon. If I were in Israel now, I contemplated back then during that indolent summer of partying with friends and chasing girls, I could be in Lebanon with my friend, dealing with life-and-death situations. But from my perspective, it all seemed very far away to me and even romantic in the way young men dream of military service and daring deeds of bravery.

Israel was still far away to me when I learned that Israel, which had launched this invasion of Lebanon to prevent the P.L.O. from firing Katyusha rockets indiscriminately into Northern Israel, had proven to be complicit in allowing their Christian Lebanese military allies to enter the undefended Palestinian refugee camps of Sabra and Shatilla on the outskirts of Beirut and kill anyone they found there. I read with vague interest of the world's condemnation of Israel and of the massive internal protests of Israelis against their own government and military for allowing this to happen. What had happened to the heroic, romantic Israel that I had grown up with? These newspaper articles just didn't jibe with my feelings of how Israel "really" was supposed to be in my own mind.

But I was determined not to let it slip away just yet. As a young rabbinical student, I enjoyed a two-week tour of Israel with fellow young adults sponsored by Hillel, the Jewish college student organization, which later morphed into the Israel Birthright trip for contemporary young adults. I plunged into the heroic, romantic Israel of my childhood and imagination. Like most, if not all Jewish young adult trips to Israel, the touring experience of Israel was enhanced by the intense social and sexually charged environment provided by the fellow participants on the trip itself. I had a wonderful time on the trip and Israel was redeemed in my eyes as a heroic and very romantic place.

Studying to be a rabbi, I learned Hebrew, Jewish history, and traditional Jewish texts and excitedly looked forward to my year of study in Israel, a much-anticipated standard component of my rabbinical program. While in Israel, I immersed myself in the Israeli experience. I arrived months early and participated in a military program designed to attract foreign Jews to make *aliyah*, that is, move to Israel and become citizens. I finally got to fulfill my Israeli military fantasy by receiving military training, wearing an army uniform, carrying a weapon and touring the country, north to south, from the mud I crawled in to the mountains we hiked in.

After this three month program ended, I volunteered on a *kibbutz*, waking up at 4 am to work in the fields, and doing my time in the communal kitchen cooking meals and washing dishes for the community. I even met and dated an Israeli woman that year, hanging out with her friends, improving my Hebrew and exploring my fantasy of "what if"— what would it be like to really live in Israel and be an Israeli? I continued my rabbinical studies in the fall taking classes at Hebrew University in Jerusalem and struggling to read lengthy, technical academic articles in Hebrew. I participated in regular hikes and overnights with the Society for the Protection of Nature in Israel, recapitulating the experiences of the first Zionist pioneers who hiked the land with a copy of the Hebrew Bible in their packs, reading passages describing the landscapes I was seeing right in front of me. The earlier portents of the invasion of Lebanon, Sabra and Shatilla, and even the Israeli security zone in Lebanon, a 10 to 15 mile swath of Lebanese territory controlled and patrolled by the Israeli army to prevent the newly emerged Hizbollah from attacking Israel, were somewhere in the back of the mind. But the tide was slowly changing.

In 1987, the first Intifada broke out while I was still living and studying in Israel. Suddenly, neighborhoods and streets that I used to pass through become dangerous, subject to sudden rock throwing attacks. Buses that traveled through the West Bank and Arab neighborhoods of Jerusalem were fitted with thick protective mesh fencing around the windows to minimize shattered glass when they would be attacked by rock throwing Palestinian protesters. My school field trip buses were accompanied in certain areas of the West Bank with army jeeps filled with soldiers to prevent such attacks. The nightly news was filled with video footage of rock throwing Palestinian crowds, Israeli soldiers firing tear gas canisters and beating protesters, cars in flames from Molotov cocktails, and ambulances carrying away the injured on both sides. My parents and friends called and wrote me worrying about my safety. I assured them I was safe, and for the most part, I was. Perhaps my life became a little more inconvenient but that was about it. But psychologically, emotionally, I was in turmoil. What was happening to my heroic, romantic vision of Israel? It was time to see Israel from a new perspective, one I had never experienced before.

A fellow left-leaning rabbinical student organized an informal trip to the West Bank through a contact with the American Friends Service Committee, better known as the Quakers. We set off in a mini-van with a young Palestinian woman as an interpreter and went to visit a Palestinian refugee camp and the city of Ramallah. We were stoned by Palestinian children in the refugee camp and were warned against taking pictures as the Palestinians would think we were collaborating with the Israeli security forces, and the Israeli soldiers who watched us from the nearby hills might confiscate our cameras, perhaps believing we were agitators supporting the Palestinians. At Israeli checkpoints, we agreed to refrain from speaking Hebrew or using our Israeli student I.D.'s and to play "dumb" so as to experience no favorable treatment. It was uncomfortable and intimidating to be detained for hours and listen to the Israeli soldiers belittle us in Hebrew not knowing we understood every word they said. My heroic, romantic vision of Israel was drifting further away from me, carried away on a tide of disbelief, incomprehension and even disgust.

A second year of studying in Jerusalem only increased my disappointment in Israel and served to dispel my heroic, romantic vision of Israel. My honeymoon with Israel gave way to daily disappointment, frustration and anger. The news from and about Israel went from bad to worse as both Palestinians and Israeli soldiers resorted to ever more violent tactics short of outright combat. Israel suffered increasing casualties in Lebanon to attacks by Hizbollah. A distant friend and former Jewish camp counselor of mine was killed in Lebanon. I read a lengthy article about his life in the weekend magazine of the *Jerusalem Post* without recognizing his name, thinking to myself that his story was fairly close to mine—an American, enamored of Israel, made *aliyah*, joined the army, become an officer, and while on patrol with his unit in the security zone on the slopes of Mt. Hermon in Lebanon, was ambushed by Hizbollah and when rushing to the aid of a wounded soldier was himself killed. The army subsequently mounted a massive airborne assault in order to rescue the embattled soldiers of the stranded army unit. I didn't even know that I knew this young man until I finally looked at the photographs accompanying the story and my heart sank and my stomach clinched in on itself as I recognized my friend from years ago.

By the time I left Israel in 1989, soldiers had been given orders to break the bones of Palestinians to keep them off of the streets. Thousands were arrested and placed in administrative detention—held for months and even years without charges. I concluded my studies in Israel and returned to complete my rabbinical program in New York with a far better understanding of the ancient sources of Judaism but with a growing incomprehension of the modern incarnation of Jewish statehood. I finally spoke Hebrew fluently but never had I felt more disinclined to speak it with Israelis I met.

Back home in the United States, when I tried to speak about my strong but ambivalent feelings about Israel in synagogues and with friends, I was criticized and felt hostility from the older generations that didn't understand that the heroic, romantic vision they had of Israel was changing underneath them and was not necessarily being passed on to a new generation. The tide was changing—and this time I knew it. But few others did—not yet.

To further telescope and condense my perception of the changing face of Israel, hope sprang anew when the Palestinians and Israelis signed the Oslo Peace Accords in 1993, recognizing one another and pledging to work together to bring the State of Palestine into existence, living together side-by-side in peace. Briefly—all-too-briefly—my exuberance and euphoria began to fade as the reactionary, rejectionist elements in both Israel and among the Palestinians began to lash out against this vision of peaceful co-existence. Prime Minister Yitzchak Rabin was assassinated by a Jew opposed to the peace process. The second, or Al Aqsa Intifada, broke out, this time characterized by direct, deadly combat between Palestinians and Israelis. Hamas, an Islamic rejectionist Palestinian military organization, sent waves of suicide bombers into Israeli civilian population centers. In response, Israel began to destroy the economic infrastructure of Palestinian areas in Gaza and the West Bank and demolish the homes of the families of suicide bombers in retaliation. Israel withdrew from the Gaza Strip and the Palestinians began to fight among themselves engaging in a brief, bloody civil war resulting in the two major regions of a future Palestinian state governed by two different, antagonistic forces. And wave upon wave of rockets began to fly out of Gaza to land in the nearby Israeli towns. Hamas captured and to this day still holds an Israeli soldier, Gilad Shalit, who has spent the last four years in captivity. When Israel invaded Gaza to secure his release in 2006, Hizbollah in Lebanon also captured and kidnapped several Israeli soldiers in solidarity, sparking a second war in Lebanon. Only this time, for the first time ever, Israel lost this war. The heroic, romantic vision of Israel was slowly disappearing on the tides of change.

Israel's second, punishing, destructive invasion of Lebanon in the summer of 2006 perhaps persuaded Hizbollah to restrain its military offensive capabilities in the future but the rain of over 4,000 missiles that fell on northern Israel profoundly affected Israel's sense of its own vulnerability and limitations in its military prowess. The fact that Israel failed to secure the release of its captured soldiers or militarily defeat

Hizbollah in direct combat deeply eroded Israel's heroic, romantic self-narrative. But this was just part of the story. This was also a failure to live up to its heroic, seemingly miraculous romantic military exploits of the past.

And finally, Israel's deadly mishandling of the Gaza flotilla in May of 2010 proved to be a far more decisive demarcation between Israel's heroic, romantic past and it's current image now held by younger generations of Diaspora Jews. In an effort to prevent Hamas, Gaza's militant Islamic regime that explicitly calls for the destruction of Israel, to manufacture weapons or build military defensive structures, Israel prevented the importation of all but the most basic humanitarian supplies for years. Given the flood of propaganda on both sides, it was not entirely clear what happened or why Israel's attempt to commandeer the largest vessel in the Gaza flotilla bringing supplies to the beleaguered Palestinians resulted in the death of nine protesters. But what is clear is that the tide has completely changed now—and it's been nearly 30 years in the making.

The heroic, romantic vision of Israel is gone from the majority of the young Jews of the Diaspora. It only continues to exist in the desperate hopes and determined, fevered imaginations of those unwilling to recognize the tidal changes that have shaped and changed Israel from its earliest years. This perception has yielded to an ambivalent or even negative view of Israel. There is no longer a widely shared sense that Israelis are the "good guys" and that the Arabs or Palestinians are the "bad guys." In fact, it may well be that the opposite is true. Perhaps this was never a healthy image in the first place.

Israel has become associated with many deplorable practices towards the Palestinians and sadly, this negative image is not limited to Israel's treatment of Palestinians but extends to the sphere of internal religious politics as well. Israel must now contend with the increasing cultural and religious tension between extremist Orthodox Jews and their growing violent intolerant behavior towards liberal or even secular fellow Jews. Israel has enough challenges to deal with regarding its international image regarding the Palestinians without adding in the numerous reports of liberal Israeli synagogues vandalized by intolerant Ultra-Orthodox Jews, or images of Hasidic Jews throwing chairs, punching and spitting at religious Jewish women who have dared to take on more egalitarian Jewish practices, or the numerous attempts by prejudiced, bigoted Israeli lawmakers to limit or eliminate the legitimacy of all other forms of Jewish religious expression other than their own. Because of all of this, there is no longer a "gut" connection between most young Jews of the Diaspora and the State of Israel.

As a rabbi in the Diaspora, as a Jewish educator and teacher of young Jews in California, I am in a quandary. In addition to teaching my students about the Torah, Jewish holidays, *Shabbat* (the Sabbath), keeping Kosher and other aspects of living a Jewish religious life, I also teach about Jewish history, Theodore Herzl, Zionism and the State of Israel. But I struggle with the message that I should be sharing with my students about Israel: Is there still an expectation that devolves upon me to teach about Israel as a heroic, romantic state? And if I do so, am I teaching them about a state that no longer exists? As my students grow ever more aware of the political reality of Israel and the Middle East, am I actually distancing my students from establishing an emotional connection to Israel? There is an increasing and profound disconnect between this historically archaic vision of the heroic, romantic Israel of its immediate past and the contemporary reality of Israel that is no further away than the daily headlines of major newspapers or instantly accessible Internet videos. The vision of Israel that I grew up with and even experienced as a child and young adult is no longer an authentic message in the ears and eyes of my students nowadays. I have no idea how to teach my students about Israel anymore. The experience and education that I received about Israel no longer holds true in the real world. The reality that I grew up with no longer exists and I am left struggling with what to do now.

As difficult as this may be for some to read, everything that I have learned in my Jewish and rabbinical studies, experienced in my own life, and understood about history and the Jewish tradition, informs me that the land of Israel and the State of Israel is not just another piece of real estate on this planet to me or the rest of the Jewish people. It is more than the current barely functioning democracy its government is right now or a Jewish-majority society struggling to define its own identity. As uncomfortable as it may be, the Jewish tradition compels the Jewish people to wrestle with this connection between *Am Yisrael* and *Eretz Yisrael*, the bond between the people of Israel and the land of Israel. A personal or national Jewish identity that somehow does not acknowledge or struggle with this deep historical and contemporary connection to the land and country of Israel is not authentic or complete. A Jew can love Israel or hate Israel, but a Jew who takes his or her Jewish identity seriously cannot ignore Israel.

I have many questions and few answers, but am okay with that. The

Israelite patriarch, Jacob, according to the stories in the Torah, was renamed
Israel when he struggled in combat with an angel (Genesis 32). He was
given the new name, *Yisrael*, which is Hebrew for, "he who struggles with
God." Historically, the Jewish people are used to struggling with God and
with our religious identity. So if we throw in a new conflict, struggling
with our relationship to the land and state of Israel, this is just another,
familiar complication.

No matter what answers we may generate regarding how to resolve
our relationship with Israel, the results of this struggle are not the purpose
for our wrestling. Rather, it is the struggle itself which is ennobling and
holy. And I conclude like a typical rabbi: may this struggle we face, whether
with God or with Israel, the people or the land, yield more light than
heat, more knowledge than propaganda, more insight than blinders, and
more love instead of hate among all of the residents of the biblical Holy
Land, her neighbors, and all of us—gentile or Jew, the distant relatives of
its once native people.

Robert E. Kohn
The Jewess in Kate Chopin's *The Awakening*

*In a book centered on characters [, …] Mlle. Reisz is the most eccentric
of all and, from many critical perspectives, the most mysterious. Her
harsh Germanic surname and its incongruity with the euphonious
French 'Mademoiselle' establish her from the start as an unbeautiful
cultural misfit; her lack of forename, which is unique among the
novel's featured characters, signals that she cannot be intimately
known. (166).*

So writes Mary Biggs in her superb essay on Kate Chopin's *The
Awakening*. Although no critic has, to my knowledge, suggested that Mlle.
Reisz is Jewish, it is a reasonable assumption, given: that Reisz is a fairly
common German Jewish name; that German Jews immigrated to New
Orleans throughout the 19th century; and that the Touro Synagogue
was founded in that city in 1828 by German, Spanish and Portuguese
families.* While Anti-Semitism was less of a problem in Louisiana than
in other southern states, there was still a concern on the part of Jews that
"we not stand out." It was perhaps for that reason that Chopin depicted
Mlle. Reisz as a person who chose not to be intimately known and who
"compressed all of her emotions, warmth, kindness, and sensuality into
her music" (Biggs 167). There is a strong hint of Anti-Semitism in the
novel, when the proprietor of a grocery store where Mademoiselle had
shopped, tells Edna Pontellier, who is looking for her new address, that

> He knew Mademoiselle Reisz a good deal better than he
> wanted to know her, […] In truth, he did not want to know
> her at all, or anything concerning her--the most disagreeable
> and unpopular woman who ever lived in Bienville Street.
> He thanked heaven she had left the neighborhood, and was
> equally thankful that he did not know where she had gone.
> (Chopin 98-99)

Likewise, the wealthy Alcée Arobin says of Reisz , "I've heard that
she's partially demented," […] extremely disagreeable and unpleasant"
and he rebukes Edna for wanting to talk about "her at a moment when I
desired to talk of you" (Chopin 138).

Born in St. Louis in 1851, Kate O'Flaherty's "father was a successful

St. Louis merchant who had married into an aristocratic family of French origin. [She] attended the best school available to young women in the city" and after graduating, "spent two years busy with the social activities appropriate to a person of her class; in 1870 she married Oscar Chopin, of a prominent Louisiana Creole family, and moved with him to New Orleans" (Margaret Culley vii). When I began to suspect that Mlle. Reisz was Jewish, I worried whether the patrician Kate Chopin might herself have been Anti-Semitic. Too often have I had to wrestle with issues of Anti-Semitism involving authors I admire, such as Henry Adams (Kohn, *Corrupt Edition*) and Martin Heidegger (Kohn, *Romantic Realism's*), though I finally made my peace with them as I had with the German composer Richard Wagner. I was prepared to do the same with Chopin (Kohn *Edna. Pontellier*), except that the matter turned out happily

I discovered an article by Michael Tritt which revealed that Chopin's earlier story, "Cavanelle," was first published in April of 1895 in "the inaugural issue of *The American Jewess*, self-described as 'The Only Publication in the World Devoted to the Interests of Jewish Women'" (543). Although "Chopin's tale (the sole contribution by a non-Jewish author) has nothing to do with Jews," it has been presumed "that the editor of the magazine, Rosa Sonneschein, who lived in St. Louis for a time and was likely an acquaintance of Kate Chopin, included the story in her magazine in order to capitalize on Chopin's renown" (543). Tritt himself argued that

> Sonneschein included the piece not only to increase circulation but because 'Cavanelle' artfully dramatizes--and to a degree ironically challenges and complicates as well--beliefs expressed in *The American Jewess*. Furthermore, by examining Chopin's story in the context of the magazine, one can particularly appreciate the way 'Cavanelle' undermines popularly held stereotypes of men and women. (543)

So Mlle. Reisz's detractors were playing out the kind of stereotypes that Chopin wanted to discredit.

I am uncomfortable using the word "Jewess" in the title of this essay, but I am using it because it is uncomfortable. What kind of stereotypes are operating in me that make me cringe? What kind of stereotypes were operating in 1895 that may have motivated its use by Sonneschein? I also wonder if the fact that Chopin published her story in a prominent Jewish magazine four years before she wrote *The Awakening* gave her the idea to include a Jewish character? What gives me the most satisfaction, as a Jew, is that it was the "very first chords which Mademoiselle Reisz struck upon the piano," when she played for the guests at Grand Isle, that sent the "keen tremor down Mrs. Pontellier's spinal column" and instigated the awakening that would orchestrate this great American novel (Chopin 44).

---

* A Boolean search for < Reisz and German and Jewish > on Google yields close to 5,000 results. The JewishGen website lists 138 Jewish burials to date, under the surname Reisz, for the State of Louisiana alone.

Works Cited

Biggs, Mary. "*'Si tu savais'*: The Gay/Transgendered Sensibility of Kate Chopin's *The Awakening.*" *Women's Studies* 33 (2004): 145-181.

Chopin, Kate. *The Awakening.* 1899. New York: HarperCollins, 1972.

Culley, Margaret. *Kate Chopin,* The Awakening: *An Authoritative Text, Contexts, Criticism.* New York: W.W. Norton, 1976.

Kohn, Robert E. "The Corrupt Edition of *The Courier's Tragedy* in Thomas Pynchon's *The Crying of Lot 49.*" *Notes & Queries* 253.1 (March 2008): 82-86.

_____. "Romantic Realism's Last Charge." *Interdisciplinary Literary Studies: A Journal of Criticism and Theory.* 10.1 (Fall 2008): 71-83.

_____. "Edna Pontellier Floats into the Twenty-First Century." *Journal of Popular Culture* 43.1 (February 2010): 137-155.

Tritt, Michael. "Kate Chopin's 'Cavanelle' and *The American Jewess*: An Impressive Synergy." *Mississippi Quarterly: The Journal of Southern Cultures* 59.3-4 (Fall 2006); 543-557.

Pier Marton
Beyond Belief

...the thrall in which an ideology holds a people is best measured by their collective inability to
imagine alternatives... — Tony Judt

> *Everything exerts itself to have you believe that culture is great, that it's cool, that movies are life, that poetry loves you, theatre awaits you, and that painting concerns you... They say, 'Believe, we'll do the rest.'* — Philippe Muray

If you can't say something good, don't say anything at all. — Bambi

NOT IN
... we are where we always were? Alan Watts.

To think in a loud and busy environment is extremely hard, yet our buzz of activity assumes there is no such place as solitude.

At all costs, shuffled away and perpetually distracted, we do away with boredom, loneliness, death... and thinking. The media, in its endless formats, refines itself over the years: "Make it more and more real, we need three dimensional interactivity *now!*"

But we were never present. There has never been a "now." From the start, we had always intended to get *away*.

NOT THE PRESENT
"Ecology," another word for "survival," is applicable to a great variety of domains. A year and a half ago, I spoke at a Saint Louis University *Media Ecology* conference.

Now needing to go further, I bring up Arne Naess's "Deep Ecology" (more on this Wiki).

I will simplify one of its principles: when a harbor needs to be cleaned because the pollution has been noticed, it is already too late to accomplish anything serious (or "deep") about it.

The trouble started much earlier. Our faulty interactions with ourselves, each other and our surroundings had prevented us from hearing the ringing alarm. In other words, the "canary in the coal mine" had been dead for a long time.

We must be invested in *the source* of our troubles, and not the symptoms. More importantly, *when it is news, it is too late.*

I SEE WHAT YOU MEAN

To make matters worse, we live in a visual culture, which may mean that we
live shallow lives. St. Exupéry puts it this way: *What the eye can perceive isn't worth
seeing.*

But we should not be surprised: the subject of ethics - can one visualize that? -
is hardly the topic of news. Anything of importance will often be a subtle and
complex substance, almost a private issue, and most often, a lonely endeavor.

My late friend and former teacher, Jean Baudrillard, dotted the i's this way: *Even
though the images show everything, nevertheless there is nothing to see.*

"Seeing is believing"; yes, believe and *then* you will see. As has been said before,
life is elsewhere. Our eyes may be the actual source for our blindness.

I KNOW BECAUSE I WISH (TO ESCAPE)

We assume we will know more if we turn towards "brightness and
light," but apart from math, physics and chemistry, most theories and
religions are based on mesmerizing forms of wishful thinking. Against
the strongest evidence, we relentlessly hope our assumptions for a master
plan are on target: some still attempt to turn around the killing of tens
of millions during WWII into the undeniable proof that a god must
exist.

Nasrudin, the wise fool of Sufi tales, tells this story:

> In a small village, late one evening, a man found his neighbor Nasrudin
> on all fours by a streetlamp, apparently looking for something. He asked
> him "What are you looking for?"
>
> "My keys." answered Nasrudin. After a half-hour of scrounging
> together on the ground, the man turned to Nasrudin to ask "Are you
> sure this is where you lost them?"
>
> To which, Nasrudin answered: "No, I lost them by my house."
>
> The man jumped up and asked "So why are we looking for them
> here?"
>
> Nasrudin's answer: "Because that's where there is light."

PROJECT EMPTINESS

As the classic German film *Schatten (Warning Shadows)* makes clear, we
are always projecting ourselves and believing our images. The screening
process has not taken place properly. Cocteau demands more: *Mirrors
should do a little bit of reflection before giving us our images back.*

We *actually seek* to become images, as wedding photographers will attest
to with their collections of so-called "picture perfect moments."

NON THINKING – A SERVICE INDUSTRY

When facing the hardship of life, entertainment and the arts provide a greatly needed sigh of relief. An entire industry, now with a global reach, delivers its captive audience its pre-digested movies. Television dispenses a daily dosage of non-thinking in the form of groupthink. News often only offers a gloss on reality: show a bit of the good side, a bit of the bad, and the lure of objectivity is achieved: the voice of god itself! All the thinking has now been done *for* you.

There are no dangerous thoughts; thinking itself is dangerous
     — Hannah Arendt.

Even multiple points of views, like the number of cereals in a supermarket, become a neutralizing factor. Dissent is co-opted, even welcomed, the more *not* to think.

Ignorance is bliss, but so are knowledge, discussions, panels... the same contented vacuum reigns everywhere. Debate, discuss, keep us looking elsewhere, or maybe just *looking*.

Institutions, media and books make it official: we *don't need to think,* all we need is to agree or, as the expression goes, to agree to disagree. It is even possible to discuss or teach ethics without being implicated.

Thinking isn't to agree or disagree, that's voting. Robert Frost.

WE ARE!

Patriotism is the last refuge of a scoundrel. Samuel Johnson.

For the sake of feeling that we belong somewhere, we have become aggregates of fear, huddled together by nation, religion, gene or history, illustrating the etymology of "consensus": we make sense because we consent (and vice-versa). Our lives are tautologies (a rose is a rose) and reflect our well-rehearsed dictionaries.

Containment is one of the functions of language: by using the currency of language, schooling, degrees and the workplace, our membership is sanctioned. Culture has become the railing for handling life, our great pacifier.

AN AESTHETIC OF BLIND SPOTS

We are amused by the fact that cats are caught up by any dangling piece of string. Yet we fail to acknowledge that our eyes and minds will do just the same with any moving object or any bright or colorful spot on a screen. The natives are still fascinated by the beads, the fireworks and the glitter. From bling to diamonds, our poverty at least sparkles.

After the striking branding campaign done by the Nazis, with their high-impact red, black and white colors, the prospect of aestheticizing and packaging reality should make all designers and artists highly wary. Yes, we can be manipulated, but what is the cost of learning and re-learning all of these lessons?

The blue-eyed blond heroes of our fairy tales may not hold a candle to the limping, onetoothed stinking hunchback who knows how to care and be respectful.

The refuge of beauty...

Those in power may display arrogance, but what I call "the arrogance of normalcy" could be even more nefarious. By ignoring and segregating those whose handicap we can clearly see, we have cornered ourselves: actually *we* are the ones who are acutely handicapped. The so-called horror films and its witches and monsters, more than anything else, publicize and reinforce our fears of ourselves.

(YOU WILL) KNOW WHAT YOU KNOW

In the dictionary, everything is defined by everything; a tautological closed system where you don't have to be a linguist to sense that you don't actually learn anything. At times, our vocabulary goes on a rampage: "roadkill," "collateral damage," "trash," "(human) refuse," "bums." We learn to become comfortable with our blindness.

Language, as Barthes has said, is tyranny, but it is also criminal containment, segregation and avoidance.

STASIS OF STATUS QUO

What is presented as communication consists generally, to use Jakobson's coined function, of just a phatic mode of interacting: nothing more than saying "here I am, too."

We imagine eternity as the extension of a status quo *against* change. "Freeze!" as the police would say.

MESSAGE AS MASSAGE

As U.G., the Indian-born teacher hinted at, we are all sensory addicts, with art being the greatest piece of evidence in that constant search for sensual stimulation.

We need very cold showers, not just coming to our senses, but coming to *beyond* our senses.

DIFFERENT LIES

So... I beg to differ. Or shall I have to shout to differ? Silence is often criminal collusion.

Power reigns much more easily through silence: Karadzic's 200,000 victims were greeted by silence. The Holocaust, Rwanda, Bosnia, Congo, and on and on... the pattern is clear.

I probably have said too much and used too many words. As I finally veer towards another type of silence, it is appropriate I remember Umberto Eco's words: *A sign is anything that can be used to tell a lie.*

Howard Schwartz
Gathering the Sparks
The Forgotten Meaning of Tikkun Olam

For many modern Jews the term *"tikkun olam"* has become a code-phrase synonymous with social action. It is linked to a call for healing the ills of the world. Indeed, *tikkun olam*, literally meaning "repairing the world," has become the defining purpose of much of modern Jewish life. What many of those who use this term do not know is that this idea is rooted in the last great myth infused into Jewish tradition, a cosmological myth created in the 16th century by the great Jewish mystic, Rabbi Isaac Luria of Safed, known as the Ari (1534-1572). Here the term "myth" refers to a people's sacred stories about origins, deities, ancestors and heroes.

How is it that a concept rooted in medieval Jewish mysticism has so endeared itself to contemporary Jews? In order to understand this unlikely development, let us first consider the myth itself, known as "The Shattering of the Vessels" (*shevirat ha-kelim*):

> At the beginning of time, God's presence filled the universe. When God decided to bring this world into being, to make room for creation, He first drew in His breath, contracting Himself. From that contraction darkness was created. And when God said, *Let there be light* (Gen. 1:3), the light that came into being filled the darkness, and ten holy vessels came forth, each filled with primordial light.
>
> In this way God sent forth those ten vessels, like a fleet of ships, each carrying its cargo of light. Had they all arrived intact, the world would have been perfect. But the vessels were too fragile to contain such a powerful, divine light. They broke open, split asunder, and all the holy sparks were scattered, like sand, like seeds, like stars. Those sparks fell everywhere, but more fell on the Holy Land than anywhere else.
>
> That is why we were created—to gather the sparks, no matter where they are hidden. God created the world so that Israel could raise up the holy sparks. That is why there have been so many exiles—to release the holy sparks from the servitude of captivity. In this way the people of Israel will sift all the holy sparks from the four corners of the earth.
>
> And when enough holy sparks have been gathered, the

broken vessels will be restored, and *tikkun olam*, the repair of
the world, awaited so long, will finally take place. Therefore
it should be the aim of everyone to raise these sparks from
wherever they are imprisoned and to elevate them to holiness
by the power of their soul.

In most religious traditions, myths were created anonymously in
ancient times. By the time that Homer wrote *The Iliad* and *The Odyssey*
3000 years ago, most Greeks had already ceased to believe in the pantheon
of Greek gods, and they merely existed to serve as a literary backdrop to
Homer's narrative. But not only did mythic development continue in
Judaism until the late middle ages, we even know the name and teachings
of the creator of a myth that has become central to modern Jewish life.
How did the Ari arrive at this myth, which is at the core of his teachings? A
closer examination of it will reveal that it is both a remarkable example of
the synthesis of existing Jewish traditions and an act of creative genius.

While the Ari did not invent the term *tikkun olam*, he transformed
its meaning, and created the underlying myth that defines it. The term
is first found in the Mishnah, dating from the 2nd century CE, where it
means "guarding the established order." The term is also found in the
third section of the *Aleinu* prayer, dating from the talmudic era, where
it means "perfecting the world under the rule of God." Maimonides in
the 12th century expanded its meaning. He defined it as an approach to
the rulings and customs of the rabbis that is intended "to strengthen the
religion and order the world." The Ari's myth changed the meaning of the
term for good, so that it now refers to his all-inclusive myth, which begins
with the creation of the world and ends with the messianic era, known as
"the End of Days."

There are three stages of the Ari's myth and all three stages find likely
sources in the Bible. So too did the he draw on many other existing
myths, scattered throughout the Bible, rabbinic texts and kabbalistic
teachings The first stage, that of the contraction of God, describes how, at
the beginning of time, God's presence filled the universe. Therefore there
was no room for creation, and God had to contract Himself (a process
known as *tzimtzum*) in order to create a space for creation. Why did the
Ari assume that God's presence took space? This is revealed in the biblical
episode in which God tells Moses to build a tent of meeting. But when
Moses attempts to enter it, he is unable to do so: *A cloud covered the tent
of meeting, and the presence of God filled the Tabernacle, and Moses was not*

able to enter into the tent of meeting (Exod. 40:34–35). Implicit in the Ari's understanding of *tzimtzum* is a covenant between God and the future creations he made possible by contracting Himself.

The second stage, that of the shattering of the vessels, may have been inspired by the biblical account of Moses throwing down and breaking the first tablets of the law (Exod. 32:19). which, like the holy vessels, were crafted by God on high. So too is there a biblical passage about scattered sparks, found in Ezekiel 10:2, where fiery coals from the Temple altar are scattered by some angelic figures over the city of Jerusalem: *Fill your hands with glowing coals from among the cherubs, and scatter them over the city.* This passage manages to work in the scattering, the sparks, the concentration of sparks on the Holy Land (especially Jerusalem), and the holiness of the sparks, since they come from the altar.

The shattering of the vessels also strongly echoes a well-known midrash about prior worlds that God is said to have brought into being and then destroyed. This myth is based on a verse from Isaiah, *"For, behold! I am creating a new heaven and a new earth"*(Isa. 65:17). It states that God created and destroyed many worlds before this one, until God created this world and declared, "This one pleases me, those did not." The 20th century rabbi, Kalonymus Kalman Shapira, who died in the Warsaw ghetto, directly links the Ari's myth to the prior worlds: "At the time of creation, God created worlds and destroyed them. The worlds that were created and those that were destroyed were the shattered vessels that God had sent forth. Out of those broken vessels God created the present universe."

Although the myth of prior worlds strongly influenced the Ari's myth, the greatest influence derives from kabbalistic teachings about the ten sefirot. According to this alternate creation myth, God is said to have brought the world into being in a series of ten emanations, making it possible for God, a purely spiritual being, to manifest the world we inhabit. Rabbi Kalonymus Kalman Shapira said of this process of emanation, "In his wondrous hidden way, God contracted His light again and again until physical bodies were created. Thus the world is but an emanation of His light." Rabbi Abraham Joshua Heschel described this process of emanation as "the inner life of God."

The light inside the vessels that shattered has a whole rabbinic history in itself.

It finds its source in a beautiful midrash about the light created on the first day. Here the ancient rabbis noticed an apparent contradiction between Genesis 1:3, where God says, *"Let there be light"* and the fourth day of creation, when God created the sun, the moon and the stars (Gen. 1:16-18). If God did not create the sun until the fourth day, they asked, what was the light of the first day? The rabbis identified it as a primordial light, and there is much rabbinic speculation about where it came from. Some describe it as the light of paradise, while others say it was created when God wrapped Himself in a garment of light, as found in Psalms 104:2.

What happened to this light? God withdrew it from the world, and it became known as *ha-or ha-ganuz*, the hidden light. Some say it was taken back into paradise when Adam and Eve ate the forbidden fruit. The *Zohar*, the central text of Jewish mysticism, dating from the 13th century, says that this light was hidden in the Torah, and that whenever anyone studies the Torah with great concentration, a ray of the primordial light will come forth and illumine them. In another beautiful myth, God is said to have put a bit of the primordial light into a glowing stone, and given it as a gift to Adam and Eve when they were expelled from Eden, as a reminder of all they had lost. This initiates a series of tales about how this glowing jewel was passed down, reaching Noah and later Abraham, among others.

The third and final stage of the Ari's myth, that of gathering the sparks, may have been inspired by the biblical account of the Israelites gathering the manna that fell from heaven: *The Israelites did so, some gathering much, some little* (Exod. 16:17). Just as the manna fell from heaven to nourish the people's bodies, so the holy sparks are intended to nourish their souls. But how are these mysterious, elusive sparks gathered? The Ari explained that whenever the Torah was studied or one of the commandments of the law was fulfilled, some of the holy sparks were raised up. Here, too, the Ari's explanation is revolutionary. Until the time of the Ari, the meaning of God's commandments was never to be questioned. If a student asked, "How do we know this?" the standard rabbinic reply was "We know this from Moses at Mount Sinai." Now, for the first time, the Ari proposed that there was a purpose to the law, beyond serving God's will. Studying the Torah, observing the law, healing the ills of the world, or performing good deeds all made it possible to gather the sparks, and thus fulfill the great mitzvah of *tikkun olam*. As Rabbi Hayim Tirer of Chernovitz put it, "The Jewish people must make a mighty effort to return these sparks to the Creator."

There are profound theological implications to the Ari's myth. It implies that a cosmic error, the shattering of the vessels, took place long before the creation of humans. Thus it shifts responsibility for the fallen state of existence from Adam and Eve to God. This development underscores the daring of the Ari's myth, as does his teaching that God created the people of Israel in order to repair the worlds above and below.

However, while most traditional commentaries on Lurianic kabbalah regard the shattering of the vessels as a cosmic catastrophe, some modern commentators, especially women, note that the sefirotic process of contraction resembles birth pangs, and that, from another perspective, the breaking of the vessels can be viewed as a birth process of the universe, not unlike the Big Bang. Rabbi Zalman Schachter-Shalomi, whose teachings draw on those of the Ari, regards this as a legitimate interpretation, appropriate to our own age.

A close examination of this new myth reveals that it is bookmarked by two major mythic traditions in Judaism—creation and the messianic era. Just as the shattering of the vessels is a new creation myth, describing how God made space for creation and then brought this world into being, so too does the method for repairing the world require each individual to gather the scattered sparks in order to repair the world. The resulting transformation of the world is identical to what is expected to take place in the messianic era, when the world will be restored to its original state.

However, it is important to note that the Ari's teachings make a significant change in the messianic myth. Traditionally, the arrival of the messianic era will not take place until God decides that the time is right. According to the Ari's myth, however, this depends on the progress made in gathering the sparks, an undertaking that individuals can accomplish on their own. Thus each generation has the challenge and opportunity to repair the world sufficiently to restore it to its original glory. And this repair includes the worlds both above and below, which, the *Zohar* says, are equally in need of repair.

The startling notion that there is a rent in heaven finds its source in a myth found in the *Zohar*. Here it is said that when God permitted the Temple in Jerusalem to be destroyed, God's Bride, known as the *Shekhinah*, confronted God, and declared that she was leaving Him until the Temple, her home in this world, was rebuilt. Until then, the *Shekhinah* chose to go into exile with her children, the children of Israel. So it is that one of the most important purposes of gathering the sparks is, amazingly, to heal heaven and restore God's bride to Him.

The Ari's teachings, known as Lurianic kabbalah, became the leading school of kabbalah, deeply influencing Sephardic and Hasidic kabbalists.

In their commentaries, they sometimes embellished the Ari's myth. The Hasidic master, Rabbi Menachem Mendel of Rimanov, for example, stated that "When the task of gathering the sparks nears completion, God will hasten the arrival of the final redemption by Himself collecting what remains of the holy sparks that went astray." These additions to the Ari's myth are evidence of the continued myth-making process in Judaism.

It is important to recognize the historical context of the Ari's myth. He lived in the 16th century, not long after the Spanish expulsion of the Jews in 1492. The Jews of Spain were forced to find new lands, and they settled throughout the world, especially in the Balkans and the Middle East. Jews who had been part of an advanced culture, that of Spain, now had to find a way to survive under far more difficult conditions. Until they learned of the Ari's myth, these exiles found themselves isolated and unhappy in far-flung places. The myth changed this by offering an explanation about why God had sent them there—it was their destiny to do holy work, to raise up the holy sparks that had fallen on these distant lands. Suddenly they found that they had a purpose, where before they had an exile. Thus the myth of the Ari transformed their perception of their fate. Is it any wonder that within a year it had spread throughout the Jewish world?

As for the Jews who lived in the land of Israel, especially in Jerusalem, they were regarded as abundantly blessed, since more of the holy sparks were said to have fallen there than anywhere else, and all those sparks made the holy land holy. Note that the myth of the scattered sparks provides an intrinsic reason for the holiness of the land of Israel, independent of the chronicles and covenants of Genesis.

Although most modern Jews are unaware of the mythic context out of which *tikkun olam* emerged, the concept itself continues to enchant and energize us. We look at the world around us and see that it is deeply in need of repair, and we are still able to hear the ancient calling that tells us that we must take responsibility for it ourselves, that each of us must do our own part in our own time.

Just as it is possible to draw a line directly from the biblical injunction, *Justice, justice shall you pursue* (Deut. 16:20) to Jeffersonian democracy, so too can a direct line be drawn from *tikkun olam* to the modern social action and environmental movements. Together, justice and repairing the world are the watchwords for the present generation.

The rabbis inhabited a world that defined itself as the people of Israel, no matter where they were scattered. Because of the many covenants of

God with Israel, especially the giving of the Torah, it was natural for the Ari to view Israel as having a singular destiny. But in our own time we should be able to read this myth in a more universal sense, about God having created all of humanity to gather the sparks. The goal, to restore the world, is obviously critical for future survival. It can only be fulfilled if all of humanity collaborates on this endeavor. Just as the Ari's myth still resonates in our own time, his message also has universal meaning. We can only conclude that the Ari was a rare genius who understood the need for a guiding myth for the Jewish people, and created it out of pieces of other Jewish myths, which he fit together into a single, seamless, unifying myth.

Indeed, it may be best for us to think of the Ari's myth as a conceptual system

like Einstein's theory of relativity. Einstein expresses his "myth" in equations and the Ari through Torah exegesis, reading the myth into the text. Just as we really can't visualize what Einstein puts in his equations, so we really can't visualize *tzimtzum* or emanation or *sefirot*, but we can recognize the comprehensive intentions of the Ari to unify all of Jewish teachings into one all-inclusive myth.

There is a famous Hasidic tale, "Lighting a Fire," about a ritual the Baal Shem Tov performed out in a forest, lighting a fire and reciting a prayer he created for that occasion, which saved the people in a time of great danger. Subsequent generations lost the details of that ritual and the place it had been performed and the words of the prayer, but they still had the story, and that was enough. Most of us are only dimly aware of the arcane kabbalistic meaning of the Ari's cosmology, of the theory that both heaven and earth are in need of repair, and that we must seek out and raise up the holy sparks that will make it possible for us to restore the worlds above and below. But we have retained the knowledge that it is incumbent on us to take responsibility for the world we inhabit, and that we must do all that we can to repair it, for ourselves and our children and future generations. And, like the Hasidic tale of the lost ritual, what we have retained of the meaning of *tikkun olam* is enough.

Susan Talve
Synagogue: Breaking the Color Barrier

Ask any person in the St. Louis area what our greatest challenge is and the answer you'll get is racism. As is true of many Midwestern cities, racism is the poison at the root of our devastating disparities in health care, education, housing, transportation, employment, and poverty. Racism also leaves many of our institutions, places of worship, and neighborhoods segregated, allowing fear and ignorance to grow in hearts and minds.

Twenty-five years ago, a group of 30 Jews decided to start a new community, and I was the lucky one chosen to guide the group. We located Central Reform Congregation (CRC) within the city limits—a direct response to the urban sprawl (read: white flight) that, with the last Jewish congregation leaving for the suburbs, was further segregating the people of St. Louis.

As the only rabbi in the city, I participated in vigils against racism-induced violence as well as Dr. Martin Luther King birthday celebrations. CRC also developed a relationship with Cote Brilliante, a black church: Our two institutions began mentoring 87 first-grade students, following them until they graduated from high school, inspiring the city-wide Mentor St. Louis initiative.

Jews of color were starting to find their way into our sanctuary.

Some of these Jews attended services at various area congregations. A few attended Orthodox congregations and day schools where, by their own accounts, they felt marginalized. Another two Jews of color had grown up in white Jewish homes before CRC was founded. In third grade they'd noticed they were different. By junior high they felt they had to make a choice between being black and being Jewish; there were no role models for being both. They couldn't choose not to be black, so they stopped identifying as Jews.

1997 was a transformative year in our congregation: The beautiful Josephine was born to a white Jewish mother and a non-Jewish African American father. There was no question that her parents would raise her to be a Jew. And when I held her at her naming ceremony, I promised her: By the time you begin to notice how you fit into your surroundings, we will have a community that includes others who look like you. You will see yourself reflected in the diversity of our temple. Your parents' good intentions [to stay active in the synagogue] and our own [to treat you with respect] are not enough.

As a first step in fulfilling my promise, we invited as a speaker and teacher Julius Lester, a black Jew, professor of Judaic Studies and history at the University of Massachusetts, Amherst. He is also author of *Love Song*, an autobiography reflecting on his Jewish journey, from learning that his maternal great-grandfather was a German Jew to converting to Judaism as an adult. Julius taught us that for him becoming Jewish was less a choice and more a naming of who he really was. While he had found a niche in the Jewish community, I sensed he didn't hold out much hope that CRC would ever become an integrated, safe, and welcoming place for Jews of color. As an African American, he resonated with the sounds, rhythms, and stories of black America. That wasn't our culture at CRC, not then.

I began to understand that to authentically embrace black culture, I'd need the help of black Jews, but this would not be easy in St. Louis, where separation and segregation run deep. I worried about my promise to Josephine.

It became clear that the first work we needed to do was internal. In that way the process was similar to what we'd learned in reaching out to gay, lesbian, bisexual, and transgender Jews. At first we had made a commitment to welcome the GLBT community, but we soon learned that welcoming wasn't enough; we had to listen and respond. We couldn't expect them to sign on as other members did. In the 1980s many didn't feel safe being "out" in our presence. They could suffer discrimination, perhaps lose their jobs, even their children. So rather than just talk about being inclusive, we decided to support and staff a gay and lesbian *havurah* outside the synagogue, to consider gay and lesbian households family units, and to invite same-gendered couples to participate together on the *bimah*. We also made sure that gay members taught in our religious school—an especially important and controversial choice in the early '80s during the HIV-AIDS scare. In addition, we instituted the practice of inviting prospective members to brunch so we could tell them, among other things, that if they were uncomfortable with same-gendered couples showing affection and participating in the same manner as heterosexual couples, this was probably not the congregation for them. We engaged in advocacy for GLBT rights, too. But the most important thing we did—all of us, even the GLBT members—was to face our own inner homophobia. We put it out in the open and worked to dismantle it.

Perhaps, I reasoned, this same model would work to tear down the barriers keeping us from racially integrating the synagogue. I prayed for help.

Help came in 2000 in an unexpected way, after we did something we said we'd never do: build a building. Although we'd never wanted to put more money or resources into bricks than into people, we'd long outgrown the church that had hosted us for 16 years and it was time to move on. Our first funeral in the new building was for an African American Muslim woman who had been raised Baptist. Her family wanted a welcoming and inclusive place for her service. She had many friends in our community, and I was honored to participate with the imam. At the end of the service, a lovely African American woman asked me if we were going to say Kaddish, the mourner's prayer, for our friend. This is how I met Yavilah McCoy, the founder of the Ayecha Resource Organization, dedicated to raising awareness of Jewish diversity and supporting Jews of color in the United States. I could hardly believe that a fourth-generation African American Orthodox Jewish woman devoted to assisting Jewish organizations to become more inclusive lived in St. Louis and was sitting in our sanctuary.

Still, it took us a few years to commit to seriously integrating our community. Finally, in 2003, with the help of Betsy Goldberg Zangara (an intern from the George Warren Brown School of Social Work), Linda Holtzman (a member experienced in dismantling internalized racism and anti-Semitism), and CRC's co-rabbi Randy Fleisher, we launched a two-year congregational engagement program to help us achieve our goal of building a truly diverse community.

Our next step was to participate in a retreat for change agents facilitated by Yavilah and Linda. We practiced listening without excuses. We tried to stop patting ourselves on the back for "marching in the '60s" and focused on the challenges facing us today. Just about everyone cried at some point. By the fourth day, we began to embrace privilege, not as a source of embarrassment, but as a tool we could use to be effective allies.

As part of the larger congregational engagement program, we asked every adult member of the congregation to read *Uprooting Racism* by Paul Kivel, a supportive how-to book designed to help white people understand the dynamics of racism and act on the belief that it is wrong. Over the course of a year, every group within the congregation, including the board, spent at least one meeting in a directed discussion of the book. We also participated in a series of listening programs which were often painful to hear. The Jews of color and their families spoke about being shunned, ignored, even feared. Many related how no one would sit next to them at services. At one retreat, in which white board members, religious school teachers, and the rabbis surrounded a group of Jews of color in a "fishbowl," we heard reflections such as, "White Jews think we're usurpers and ask questions like, 'Are you Ethiopian?'" "I walk into CRC and many people assume I'm visiting—and it's my temple!" "Some Jews think that for black Jews it's just about religion, but for white Jews it's a way of life." "I miss the songs of my African American heritage. Do you have to lose one culture when you enter another?" "People look at converts as being different from being really Jewish, but I know my soul has been Jewish forever."

At the end of one "fishbowl" session Yavilah broke into a stirring gospel rendition of *Adon Olam*, a standard at her family's Shabbat table. We were all drawn in by the deep gospel sounds with Hebrew words. I could not control my tears, and I was not alone. And there was revelation for each person within the circle, too, coming out of exile into the embrace of a Jewish community that recognized and valued their whole, black and Jewish selves. They no longer had to choose.

We also ran programs to expand our cultural experiences. Dr. Ephraim Isaac, a leader in both the Ethiopian and Jewish Yemenite communities, spoke of our shared Semitic origins and chanted "Song at the Sea" from the Torah in Yemenite trope, captivating especially the children of color, who saw a black rabbi in African robes teaching Torah on their *bimah*. Rabbi Capers Funnye of Chicago (Michelle Obama's cousin) modeled how the sounds and rhythms of black culture are a garment for a soulful Judaism— how seamless the merging of the worlds can be. Joshua Nelson, a black Jew known as the king of kosher gospel, performed in our sanctuary. In addition, we framed multiple copies of the Multiracial Jewish Network's "Because Jews Come in Many Colors" poster and displayed one in every classroom and in our gathering areas, hoping that the many different faces would relay the message that we can only be our best within a culturally and ethnically diverse community. And a Jews of color *havurah* emerged that gave our families a chance to participate socially together around Jewish themes.

During this period we also nurtured a relationship with the St. Louis branch of the African Hebrew Israelite community, which has close ties to its sister community in Dimona, Israel. Though many of their members are not Jewish, we share the rhythm of the holidays, the Hebrew language, and a love of Israel. We've enjoyed many shared meals and programs, among them the annual co-developed Jewish Diversity Seder. For the past five years we—as many black Jews as white—gather to tell the story of American slavery using the liberation theology of the Exodus. The *haggadah* takes the same form, but rather than wine, we sip from the life-giving water that wet the dry lips of the slaves in the fields, and we've added a dandelion to the seder plate to remember this food staple of slaves. Each year our longtime member Janet Ward tells how her great-grandfather attained his freedom and bought her great-grandmother from slave owners. She reads the African American poet Paul Lawrence Dunbar's stirring "An Ante-Bellum Sermon," written in the voice of slaves, and we can all imagine our ancestors walking with Moses toward the dream of something better:

> *Now ole Pher'oh, down in Egypt*
> *Was de wuss man evah bo'n,*
> *An' he had de Hebrew chillun*
> *Down dah wukin' in his co'n;*
> *'T well de Lawd got tiahed o' his foolin',*
> *An' sez he: "I'll let him know—*
> *Look hyeah, Moses, go tell Pher'oh*
> *Fu' to let dem chillun go."*

We've made significant strides since Josephine's baby naming. I see the changes reflected in the collaged photographs on seven large picture boards that chronologically depict the story of our congregation. The last two collages look a lot like the "Because Jews Come in Many Colors" poster: About 20 of our active adult members are black and many of them have children. On some Friday evenings, African drumming and dance are part of our Shabbat service, and a growing number of African Americans worship with us. I've even officiated at a marriage of a biracial couple who decided to raise their kids to be Jewish because of us, because they have a place to do this.

Still, I know that we have a long way to go to keep my promise to Josephine, who will celebrate her bat mitzvah next year. But for this congregation, situated in the city just a few miles from the Old Court House where the slave Dred Scott lost his case for freedom, I have hope that we are chipping away at the racism that plagues us.

In our prayers for Shabbat we read:

> *To pray for a Sukkat Shalom is to pray for a full house; a shelter that reflects creation in its glorious diversity. As we continue the holy work of uprooting the scourge of racism from this and all communities, we look*

forward to the time when our Jewish family will embrace Jews of all colors. Then, our Sukkat Shalom will become truly multi-racial as it was always intended to be.

May it come soon.

Randy Zimring
If I Close My Eyes

If I close my eyes and "feel," I can imagine my modern self, and indeed all of us on a pilgrimage to the Holy Temple in ancient times. We are holding *lulavs* and chickens, first fruits, or our best goats for sacrifice. I wave and wave my sheaf hoping for God to see me, and give me favor. I don't even notice the others asking for the same. It's just my Creator and Me. I stand in front of the Holy of Holys. Can I get any closer? I have journeyed so far. I hope and plead for answers to my prayers. Health and Wealth, and good matches for my Children. I sway and sway and beseech my maker that "I believe with perfect faith." I more vigorously now wave my *lulav* and beg to get attention from what I think of as a God, who has the attributes of half male and half female. I'm no expert, there are no shortages there. I could be wrong, but it "feels" right and I hope it's true. The Female side of God shows mercy to me and the Male side of God fiercely protects me from natural and human dangers. Wasn't that his promise to my forefathers? Or was it? It was so long ago before we gave our best to build this edifice, the Temple and home for our God. Why did we do it? Because it "felt" right. All we have is our Torah and ages of father to son, and mother to daughter stories that have come down to us. But, if I close my eyes, the temple transforms for me into the altar of Abraham. My very same Creator directs Abraham, whose heart is torn to flaming pieces, to kill his son. Isaac stretches his neck and says to his father "here I am" just as Abraham stretches his neck to his maker and says "here I am." I "feel" as if I'm standing there on a long pilgrimage of time. I wave and sway to get the almighty's attention yet one last time. It was so very long ago.

Notes
on the
Contributors

Notes on the Contributors

Elaine Alexander is the second child of Max (Mordekhai Pesakh) and Paula Zysling Kempinski who survived the Shoah, because they were sent to Auschwitz, whereas the rest of their immediate families perished at Chelmno. Elaine has taught reading remediation and is currently a free lance writer whose work, to date, has been most widely published in the Sears, Roebuck catalogues. She is the mother of two.

Beth Arky, who grew up in West County, graduated from Horton Watkins (Ladue) High School in 1978. Since graduating from Northwestern University's Medill School of Journalism in 1982, Arky's career has taken her from copy editing at a small-town Colorado paper to editing at national publications including *Entertainment Weekly* and *TV Guide*. Most recently, she has contributed to *People, USA Weekend*, the *New York Daily News* and *iVillage*, and now blogs for Seventh Generation, the cleaning and paper products company, about the many small steps she's taking to "green" her family. She lives in Park Slope, Brooklyn, with her husband, Alan, and their 7-year-old son, Matthew.

Gloria Attoun has been expressing herself through writing, music and performance for over 30 years. Predominantly a songwriter/singer and musician, she performs regularly with the band *Augusta Bottoms Consort*. Gloria also performs solo in the area as well as other parts of the country and has produced four music CDs. She graduated from University City High School's "High School of the Arts" program and from the University of Missouri at Kansas City.

Abby Bader is a former St. Louisan who currently lives in Colorado.

Debra Solomon Baker is a graduate of University of Michigan and Harvard Graduate School of Education and has been a Language Arts teacher at Wydown Middle School in Clayton, MO for more than a decade. Her own children, Max, age 10, and Sarah, age 8, are among the best teachers she knows. They remind her to laugh, to imagine, and to never lose hope. Debra blogs about her experiences as a teacher and as a parent at http://msbaker.edublogs.org.

Diann Joy Bank is a professional storyteller/educator known as "The Joy of Storytelling." She shares her Jewish folklore through her performances and story writing workshops. Diann is the published author of "Grandma Annie's Gourmet Delights," in the book, *First Harvest: Jewish Writing in*

St. Louis, 1991-1997. She has produced her audio cassette tape, "*Stories to Grow On*" and her CD, *The Joy of Jewish Tales*," stories of her Jewish heritage.

Lane Barnholtz was born, raised, and bar mitzvahed in St. Louis. He has worked as a journalist, writer, and editor for a dozen years and currently teaches at St. Louis Community College. "Pavel Spits on Stalin" is an excerpt from a novel he is working on.

Laurie Bennett has been writing short, humorous essays for *Suburban Journals* since April of 2004 under the Opinion Shapers column. She is a practicing Attorney specializing in Probate Law. Laurie appears at the Family Court of St. Louis County to donate time as a Guardian Ad Litem for the Domestic Violence Docket of St. Louis County.

Henry Berger taught history at the University of Vermont before accepting an appointment in the Department of History at Washington University in 1970 where for 35 years he taught the history of United States Foreign Relations and American cultural and political history. He served as Chair of the Jewish, Near Eastern and Islamic Studies Program from 1981 until 1990. He is a regular contributor to *Belles Lettres*, a quarterly publication of the Center for the Humanities at Washington University and is completing a book, *St. Louis Abroad: The Foreign Relations of an American City, 1764-1910*.

Saramina Berman is a retired, licensed clinical social worker, docent at the St. Louis Holocaust Museum & Learning Center, past interviewer for the Shoah Foundation, former 6th grade teacher, widow, proud mother of 3, and devoted grandmother of 5. She was born in Chicago in 1926, went to New York as a bride in 1946, where her children were born, and lived in Santa Monica, Marina del Rey, and Palm Springs, California before coming to live in St. Louis in 1977. Her claim to fame is having earned her Bachelor's degree and Teaching Credential at the University of California at Riverside, a commute of 55 miles in each direction, when she was 50 years old.

Leah Silberman Bernstein, a self-described Meta-Denominational Jew, is a graduate of Columbia University and the Jewish Theological Seminary's Joint Master Social Work/Jewish Studies program. A St. Louis native, Leah writes in her spare time from parenting her children, Abigail and Gabriel, wifing Steven and serving as the Development Director of Provident, Inc., a St. Louis-based 150 year old, non-sectarian social service agency.

Denise Bogard is founder and coordinator of the St. Louis Writers Workshop. Denise has been a professional award-winning writer for 33 years and has been published in many journals including *Oklahoma Literary Review, St. Louis Magazine, St. Louis Post-Dispatch* and the anthology, *Are We Feeling Better Yet? Women's Encounters with Health Care in America*. She coordinates the writing program and teaches writing at Lift for Life Charter Middle and High School and conducts teacher workshops on how to teach writing. Denise's first novel is in the hands of her New York agent, and she is completing her second novel.

Louis Daniel Brodsky, born in 1941, has written sixty-five volumes of poetry, including the five-volume *Shadow War: A Poetic Chronicle of September 11 and Beyond. You Can't Go Back, Exactly* won the Center for Great Lakes Culture's (Michigan State University) 2004 best book of poetry award. He has also authored fourteen volumes of fiction and coauthored eight books on William Faulkner.

Jan Garden Castro wrote *The Last Frontier* (poetry), *The Art & Life of Georgia O'Keeffe*, and other books. Castro was a finalist for the 2007 Fulton Fiction Prize from *Adirondack Review* & received the CCLM Editor's Award for *River Styx* Magazine. Castro is Contributing Editor for *Sculpture* and publishes frequently. Her poems have appeared in *New Letters, Exquisite Corps, Roof, Chronogram,* and *clwn wr 09h*.

Michael Castro is a poet and translator with twelve books to his credit. He is co-founder of the literary organization and magazine, *River Styx* and teaches at Lindenwood University. The poems in this anthology are from an as yet unpublished collection, *Sepharad*.

Jack Cohen moved to St. Louis in 1974 and married Laura in 1975. Their first child, Alison, was born in 1976, and their next child, Norma Jean, was born in 1978. Jack and Laura were two of the founders of B'nai Torah in St. Peters in 1984, and have been actively involved since then. Jack is currently the President.

Robert A. Cohn is Editor-in-Chief Emeritus of the *St. Louis Jewish Light*. He has published articles in every edition of *The Sagarin Review*, *First Harvest* and *New Harvest*, and has won numerous national awards for his writing

Allison Creighton completed her MFA at the University of Missouri, St. Louis, where she received the Graduate Prize in Poetry for 2002, and was nominated for an AWP Intro Journals Award. Her work has appeared in *Natural Bridge, New Harvest: Jewish Writing in St. Louis, 1998-2005, The Mochila Review* and *The Potomac Review*. Allison received first prize in the 2010 Wednesday Club of St. Louis's poetry contest, which was judged by Kim Addonizio. She currently teaches at Fontbonne University.

Marty Ehrlich's roots in St. Louis go back to performances with the Human Arts Ensemble and the River Styx Poets in the early 1970's. After getting a degree from the New England conservatory, Ehrlich moved to New York City in 1978, where he has been based since, working with a who's who of contemporary jazz and classical music in America and Europe, and releasing more than 25 ensemble recordings of his compositions. His recent CD releases include "Fables" on *Tzadik*, "Things Have Got To Change" on *Clean Feed*, and "Hear You Say" on *Intuition*. He is a Guggenheim Fellow in Composition, and currently an Associate Professor of Music at Hampshire College.

Helen Eisen, a long-time St. Louis resident, was born in a Displaced Persons (DP) camp in 1946. She is the daughter of Polish Jews who survived the Shoah and in 1950 landed in New York. This experience informs many of her poems. Some of them, written during a three-month residency at Hedgebrook, are included in her first chapbook published by Cherry Pie Press, *The Permeability of Memory*; others appear in *The Original Coming Out Stories, 2nd Edition, Natural Bridge, Drash,* and *Breathing Out: Poems by Loosely Identified.*

Edward Farber, a retired former commercial artist, writer and advertising executive in St. Louis, is now concentrating on the writing of fiction and fine art, both lifelong pursuits. His stories have appeared in literary magazines including *Artisan, Ascent Aspirations, Cricket Magazine, EWG Presents, The Shine Journal* and *Pine Tree Mysteries*. Some of his paintings can be seen online at www.FineArtAmerica.com/profiles/Edward-Farber

and his own website, www.Farberart.com.

Merle Fischlowitz was born and grew up in St. Louis. During his career as educator and psychologist he lived in Missouri, Maryland and Hawaii. He also lived six months in Haifa, Israel, 1971-1972. The poem "Megiddo" was written when visiting that ancient archaeological site during Chanukah, 1971. Merle has written poetry since high school and enjoys using words to express his deep feelings about people and the world around him. He and his wife Teresa live in San Diego and share six grown children and four grandchildren.

Ben Fixman is a legendary businessman in St. Louis whose life story is both inspirational and unique. A native St. Louisan, Ben fought his way through a challenging family situation in his childhood, poverty and the Depression to build one of the most successful companies this area has ever seen. At the age of 86, he is most proud of his accomplishments as a husband and father of three wonderful daughters.

Harris Frank is an 85-year-old lifetime resident of St. Louis. He is a graduate of St. Louis Country Day School (now MICDS) and the University of Southern California. He served in the Navy during World War II in the Pacific Theatre; and for the past 45 years has been associated with Solon Gershman, Inc., commercial realtors. The father of two and grandfather of four, Frank, a recent widower, has also devoted a large portion of the last three decades in doing pro bono work for a wide range of non-profit organizations.

Ronnie Fredman was raised in St. Louis and is 54 years old. He lives in University City.

Shelly R. Fredman teaches at Barnard College, at the Writer's *Beit Midrash* at the Skirball Center for Adult Jewish Learning in New York City, and she leads seminars that explore "writing into sacred texts." Her work has been published in *Best Jewish Writing, Women and Judaism*, the *Chicago Tribune Magazine, Tikkun,* and in a number of anthologies and magazines. Although she now lives in New York City, she treasures her St. Louis roots.

Jeff Friedman teaches at Keene State College in New Hampshire and is a contributing editor to *Natural Bridge*. His fifth collection of poetry,

Working in Flour, was published by Carnegie Mellon University Press in 2011. Friedman's poems, mini stories, and translations have appeared in many literary magazines, including *American Poetry Review, Poetry, 5 AM, Agni Online, Poetry International, Prairie Schooner, Antioch Review, Quick Fiction, Nighttrain, The 2River View, North American Review, Boulevard,* and *The New Republic.*

Michael Getty is a freelance writer and a member of Central Reform Congregation in St. Louis. He is a Jew-by-Choice, volunteers as a Jewish educator, and maintains a blog at www.almostjewish.wordpress.com.

Rabbi Yonason Goldson has been teaching for 14 years at Block Yeshiva High School. After graduating from the University of California, Davis, with a degree in English, he hitchhiked across the country and backpacked across Europe before arriving in Israel, where he discovered his Jewish roots, became Torah observant and met his wife. After nine years in Israel, Rabbi Goldson taught for a year in Budapest, Hungary, moved to Atlanta and later to St. Louis. He wrote a regular op-ed column for the *St. Louis Post-Dispatch*, and his writings have appeared in a few small magazines. He currently writes Torah articles online for his website http://torahideals.com and recently published his first book, *Dawn to Destiny: Exploring Jewish History and its Hidden Wisdom.*

Rabbi James Stone Goodman serves Neve Shalom Congregation and the Central Reform Congregation. He is also a writer and a musician who has produced five CDs to date, the most recent *The Book of Splendor.* He integrates story, poetry, and music in a performance art form. Rabbi Goodman recently finished an M.F.A. in poetry writing at UMSL. He plays guitar, oud, and percussion and his work is available on two websites: www.stonegoodman.com and www.neveshalom.org.

Felicia Graber, a retired teacher from the Parkway School District, is a docent and speaker at the St. Louis Holocaust Museum and Learning Center. She also talks about her own experiences as well as about those of Child Survivors of the Holocaust in area colleges, schools, and community agencies. She is the founder and co-chair of the St. Louis Holocaust Survivors and Descendants. Felicia's writings have been published in magazines and newsletters nation-wide including *The Sagarin Review, First Harvest* and *New Harvest.* She is a contributor to the anthology about child survivors, *And Life is Changed Forever,* published by Wayne University Press, 2006. Her book, *Amazing Journey, Metamorphosis of a Hidden Child* has been published in the spring of 2010. She lives in St. Louis with her husband, Rabbi Howard Graber.

Suzanne Greenwald is a psychotherapist in private practice and a local actress. She has three children and eight grandchildren, and currently lives in University City with her new husband.

Maurice (Bud) Hirsch is a native of St. Louis, went to St. Louis Country Day School, has a Ph.D. in Accounting from Washington University, taught accounting at Southern Illinois University Edwardsville. He is a community volunteer, serves as business manager of Chesterfield Arts. A horseman and photographer besides poet, Hirsch has published three collections of his poetry. Hirsch and his wife live on a horse farm in Chesterfield and their children and grandchildren all live nearby.

Rita Horwitz is a retired Registered Nurse. She has published in nursing and medical journals, and contributed the "Pediatric Surgery" chapter in *Alexander's Care of the Patient in Surgery.* Rita was recognized in *Who's Who in American Nursing.*

Jane Ellen Ibur received a Visionary Award from Grand Center for Outstanding Arts Educator in 2008 as well as the Hank's Award from the St. Louis Poetry Center. Her poem "All Soul's Day" was a finalist for the Orlando Prize from AROHO in 2010. Recent poems appear in *Folio, Sou'wester, River Styx, Natural Bridge, Lilith, Boulevard, MARGIE.* She has co-hosted "Literature for the Halibut" on KDHX radio for 18 years. She continues to teach every age everywhere and co-directs the Gifted Writers Project with her brother Edward for middle and high school writers at www.giftedwriters.org.

Andrea Jackson has lived in St. Louis for over 40 years and has an M.F.A. in Creative Writing from the University of Missouri – St. Louis. Her fiction and poetry have appeared in various journals, in print and online, as well as in *New Harvest: Jewish Writing in St. Louis, 1998-2005.*

Natasha Kaminsky was raised in Sarasota, FL before her family relocated to St. Louis in 2009. She received her BA in Creative Writing and Religion from Florida State University in 2010. Natasha is currently working on her MA in Near Eastern and Judaic Studies at Brandeis University's Graduate School.

Bob Karsh is a semi-retired internist and rheumatologist who now harbors a delusion that he is a writer. Please humor him.

Sharon Katz-Weintraub is a recently retired special educator who has taught children at every level, as well as college students, in a long and varied career. Professional writing has always been a part of her life, but she especially enjoys creative writing. She is most interested in writing life stories with themes that might touch others' lives.

Rabbi Daniel Kohn originally from Clayton, Missouri, earned a degree in English Literature from Washington University and was ordained by the Jewish Theological Seminary in 1991. He has served as a spiritual leader of several congregations on both the east and west coasts and is a professional Jewish educator. He is the Rabbi-in-Residence of the Contra Costa Jewish Day School in Lafayette, California, a Master-Teacher for Lehrhaus Judaica, an adult education consortium for Jewish Studies in the San Francisco Bay Area, and the guest rabbi of Congregation Gan HaLev in Marin County. He has published hundreds of articles and is the author of several books, *Jewish FAQs*. Rabbi Kohn lives in Mill Valley, California with his wife and three children,

Robert Kohn is Professor Emeritus of Economics at Southern Illinois University Edwardsville. He has been publishing essays in literary and art criticism since 2000. These include "Spinozan Judaism" in the 2005 issue of the *Harvest: Jewish Writing in St. Louis* series, an essay on Jonathan Safran Foer's novel *Everything is Illuminated* in the Summer 2007 issue of *The Explicator*, and "Unwitting Witness for Postmodernism" in the November 2009 issue of the *Journal of Modern Jewish Studies*. The latter essay is based on a 1975 sermon of Rabbi Harold Saperstein that was included in a volume of his sermons posthumously published by his son Marc Saperstein, formerly the Gloria M. Goldstein Professor of Jewish History and Thought at Washington University.

Susan Koppelman, PhD., has edited nine thematic collections of U.S. women's short stories, one collection of stories by St. Louis writer Fannie Hurst, and co-edited two more books. A feminist literary historian who has specialized in recovering the history of U.S. women's stories, she is now writing stories. After 22 years in St. Louis (1974-1996) Koppelman and her husband moved to Tucson, but travel back often to visit family.

Cissy Lacks is a well known teacher, photographer and writer. She has a PhD in American Studies and a master's degree in Broadcast and Film. She is a recipient of the PEN/Newman 1st Amendment Award for a person who defended the 1st amendment at some risk to herself. Presently, she is Editor of *QUEST*, a publication of the Urological Research Foundation.

Lynn Levin is a poet, writer, and literary translator. She is the author of three collections of poems: *Fair Creatures of an Hour*, a 2010 Next Generation Indie Book Award finalist in poetry; *Imaginarium*, a finalist for *ForeWord Magazine*'s 2005 Book of the Year Award; and *A Few Questions about Paradise*. Her poems have appeared in *Ploughshares, Boulevard, Kerem, The Torah: A Women's Commentary*, and many other publications. A St. Louis native, she now lives near Philadelphia and teaches at the University of Pennsylvania and Drexel University.

Robert M. Levin, a St. Louis native known as "Bob" to his friends, earned his B.A. and M.S.W. from Washington University. While a post-grad student, he came perilously close to earning an M.F.A. in Creative Writing having studied with Stanley Elkin, Howard Nemerov, Jarvis Thurston and the Distinguished Letters Gang. He has published a few magazine and newspaper articles. *A Brief History of Howard* is his first novel. After a two-year stint in Los Angeles, he relocated to Atlanta where he now lives with his wife and children.

Stacey Levine was born and grew up in St. Louis and was a recipient of the PEN/West Award for Fiction, several writing grants and fellowships. Her collection *The Girl with Brown Fur* will be published in April 2011 by Starcherone/Dzanc Press (Buffalo, NY).

Morton Levy is a retired Hematologist-Oncologist whose non-medical publications have appeared in *Moment, Ft. Myers* magazine, and numerous anthologies. His work has been selected to be read at the Big Read on Sanibel Island each of the past three years. He is a member of the St. Louis Writers Guild, the San-Cap Writers on Sanibel Island and the Missouri Poetry Society and served as a panel discussant on Critiquing at the 2010 Annual Meeting.

Bobbi Linkemer is a ghostwriter, editor, and the author of 16 books under her own name. She has been a professional writer for 40 years, a magazine editor and journalist, and a book-writing teacher. Her most recent books are *Words to Live By: Reflections on the Writing Life from a 40-Year Veteran* and *How to Write a Nonfiction Book: From Concept to Completion in 6 Months.*

Liz Lippa was born in Vienna, Austria, raised in three continents, and has lived in many cities in the U.S. As a Holocaust survivor, her outlook on life is unique. She started her college education after raising 6 children and being an active community leader. Liz has developed videos and hosted a TV interview program addressing issues of education and human development and is a part of ETC Senior Theatre Group, a professional storyteller and a member of the Holocaust Survivor Memoir Writing group.

Gerry Mandel, a graduate of Washington University in St. Louis, spent 30 years with St. Louis ad agencies as a writer/producer/creative director. He presently writes short stories, essays, plays, a novel, and produces video biographies of WWII veterans. His plays have been produced by St. Louis area theater companies, and a documentary he wrote and directed about the Lewis and Clark sculpture on the riverfront won an international award. He lives in Kirkwood, Missouri, with his wife Mary Lee and two golden retrievers.

Marvin Marcus taught Japanese at Washington University for twenty-five years with a specialization in modern literature — especially, 'personal narratives' such as essay, diary, memoir, and reminiscence. He has written poetry over the years, much of it 'found poetry'— versified reworkings of academic talks and presentations that interested him in terms of language and image that led to the publication of a book of such poetry, *Orientations: The Found Poetry of Scholarly Discourse on Asia* (Mellen Poetry Press, 2004).

Pier Marton, a videomaker/new media artist and writer, has taught video production at Washington University for the past 13 years. Issues of ethnicity, spirituality, audience passivity, and violence have been recurring themes in his video works. His exhibits include the Museum of Modern Art, the Whitney, the Jewish Museum in N.Y.C., the Beaubourg Museum in Paris, and a variety of other international venues like the Berlin

Film Festival and French Television. His works are in the collections of the M.o.M.A. in New York, the Carnegie Museum in Pittsburgh, the Beaubourg in Paris, the National Gallery of Canada, and the Japan Victor Corporation Archives in Japan. His website is: http://piermarton.info

Maryellen McSweeney, a native San Franciscan, has lived in St. Louis for more than thirty years. She is a retired faculty member from both the University of Missouri-St. Louis and St. Louis University.She is an active member of B'nai El Congregation

Charlotte Mielziner resides in St. Charles, Missouri and is wife to her best friend, Jim and mother to Valerie. She is a freelance writer and member of St. Louis Independent Publishers Association. She loves to cook, garden and competes in obedience and agility with her dogs.

Miriam Friedman Morris is the only child of Holocaust survivors Hildegard Taussig Friedman and the artist, David Friedman. She studied art and design at the University of Cincinnati, Ohio, and the Fashion Institute of Technology, New York, and received a Bachelor of Arts degree from Empire State College, New York. Miriam is devoted to her father's legacy remembering his dedication to speak for the victims through his postwar art series, *Because They Were Jews!*

Rabbi Steven Moskowitz is the rabbi of the Jewish Congregation of Brookville. He blogs at www.rabbimoskowitz.com.

Barry Nove grew up in Creve Coeur and Chesterfield, Missouri. He recently published a short story,"Good Breeding," in *Spectacular Speculations* (August 2010), an online magazine. Barry is a member of the Jewish Genealogy Society of Greater Washington, DC, and speaks nationally on the Ellis Island Experience. Barry has dedicated *Isaac in a Bind, Again* to his grandfather Irving Rosenfield, *z"l*.

Nikki Nymark is a retired journalist and psychiatric social worker. She has published three books of poetry, is active in the St. Louis Writers Guild and the St. Louis Poetry Society. She is currently working on a fourth book.

Jordan Oakes is a St. Louis journalist and part-time writing teacher. His work has appeared in various local and national publications, including *St.*

Louis magazine, the *Christian Science Monitor*, and books such as Rolling Stone's *Alt-Rock-a-Rama*. He embraces his Judaism without squeezing the life out of it.

Gerald Perkoff is Curators Professor Emeritus of Family and Community Medicine at the University of Missouri – Columbia School of Medicine, Columbia, MO. He has published three books of poetry and is the editor of *Voices of the Lady - Collected Poems of Stuart Z. Perkoff* and of *My Mother's Maiden Name* by Roslyn Singer, a memoir. He and his wife Marion have three children and five grandchildren and they live in Columbia, MO.

Nancy Powers Pritchard's poems have appeared in *Mankato Poetry Review, Natural Bridge, PMS (PoemMemoirStory), Melic Review, Main Channel Voices, Poetry Southeast, Fugue, Re)verb,* and others. She received an MFA at University of Missouri–St. Louis and a B.A. from Webster University. She teaches poetry to middle school students in the St. Louis Public Schools for Springboard and is marketing and communications director at Moneta Group in Clayton, and is a proud member of The Salon.

Marilyn Probe's work is published in journals such as the *Big Muddy, Journal of the Mississippi River Valley, Kerf, CAJE,* and *OASIS,* and the "Flood Stage" Anthology. She is a recent *Poetry Society in America Arts in Transit* winner. Her city roots go back to her grandfather Nathan Harris, pioneer union leader and unofficial mayor of St. Louis' Orthodox Jews in early 1900's.

Miriam Spiegel Raskin is a St. Louis area writer and doer who is actively involved at Central Reform Congregation. Her writings often reflect her childhood experiences as a German refugee and her subsequent reflections on the Holocaust. She has published a book of such writings under the title, *Remembering and Forgetting: A Memoir and Other Pieces of My Life.* In it, she describes the family's lucky departure from Germany in March 1939 and their subsequent adaptation to life in the United States. Her works have been published in *Marking Humanity: Stories, Poems, Essays by Holocaust Survivors,* compiled by Shlomit Kriger, and in various local and national literary magazines.

Barbara Raznick has been the director of the Saul Brodsky Jewish Community Library for more than 25 years. She is a storyteller, appearing at many venues in St. Louis, as well as nationally. She co-edited all of the issues of the *Sagarin Review: the St. Louis Jewish Literary Journal* and edited *First Harvest* and *New Harvest* with Howard Schwartz.

Carol Rose, writer, educator and spiritual counselor, lives in Winnipeg and St. Louis with her husband, Rabbi Neal Rose. Her book of poetry, *Behind the Blue Gate,* was published in 1997 and she is the co-editor of the anthology, *Spider Woman: a Tapestry of Creativity and Healing.* Her awards include the Jewish Book Award, Harry Fuerstenberg Award for Poetry in 1998 and 2nd prize for the Stephen Leacock International Award for Poetry in 1994.

Ann Leslie Rosen received her MFA in Creative Writing from the University of Missouri-St. Louis in 2006. A native of St. Louis, her work has appeared in *The Cape Rock, Sambatyon, Animus,* and *New Harvest: Jewish Writing in St. Louis, 1998-2005.* Aside from being a writer and editor, she happily spends most of her time being mom to her three young children.

Warren Rosenblum is associate professor of history at Webster University, St. Louis. His publications include *Beyond the Prison Gates: Punishment and Welfare in Germany, 1850-1933* and a number of articles for scholarly and popular publications. He lives in St. Louis City with his wife and two girls.

Leah Rubin is a St. Louis-based blogger and freelance writer. Retired from a career in healthcare management, she enjoys a variety of volunteer roles in the community, and is an avid reader. Rubin won the 2008 Erma Bombeck Writing Competition for her humorous essay "Legacy." She blogs at www.funnyisthenewyoung.com.

Margaret R. Ruhe-Spencer is employed by Lutheran Senior Services. She facilitates financial and estate planning for senior residents in West St. Louis County and St. Charles. She has one daughter. Margaret received her B.A. from Washington University and an MBA from Webster University. A lifelong resident of St. Louis, Margaret is an avid reader and writes human interest stories about her "older" friends.

Jane Schapiro is the author of the nonfiction book, *Inside a Class Action: The Holocaust and the Swiss Banks* (University of Wisconsin) and a volume of poetry, *Tapping This Stone,* (Washington Writers' Publishing House). Her poems have appeared in journals such as *The Southern Review, Prairie*

Schooner and *Southern Humanities Review.* Her essay "My Friend and Bruce Springsteen" appeared in *The Sun.*

Amy Scharff has been writing down her thoughts and experiences since she was a child, and became a professional business writer as an adult. Eventually she left business to teach high school in St. Louis, her hometown; and then she went and had a child. With what remains of her discretionary time, she is now a Writing Specialist at Webster University's Writing Center, where she continues to work with words and inspire other people to do the same

Jackie Schechter is 16 years old and a junior at MICDS. She has been writing poetry and short fiction for five years and attended Interlochen Center for the Arts for three years. Her poem "Wendy" was awarded the Silver Key in the 2010 Scholastic Writing awards contest and it was published in *Missouri Youth Write* online magazine.

Lon Schneider grew up in St. Louis and began writing poetry, short fiction and essays in the late nineties. His works have appeared in *Israel Horizons, Rashi, Sierra Nevada College Review, West Wind Review and Roque Dalton Redux.*

Steven Schreiner teaches at the University of Missouri-St Louis. His recent poems have appeared in *Gulf Coast, Margie, Tar River Poetry, Stosvet: Cardinal Points,* and elsewhere. He is the founding editor of *Natural Bridge,* a journal of contemporary literature, and the author of *Too Soon to Leave,* a book of poetry, and *Imposing Presence,* a chapbook.

Henry I. Schvey has taught in the Performing Arts Department at Washington University since 1987. He is a scholar, director and playwright. The poem "Sleepaway Camp" included in this anthology reflects his abiding interest in the Holocaust. It was inspired by a visit to the Treblinka Extermination Camp in 2010.

Howard Schwartz is Professor of English Emeritus at the University of Missouri-St. Louis. He has published four books of poetry, most recently *Breathing in the Dark,* and several books of fiction, including *The Four Who Entered Paradise* and *Adam's Soul..* He has also edited a four-volume set of Jewish folktales, which includes *Elijah's Violin & Other Jewish Fairy Tales, Miriam's Tambourine: Jewish Folktales from Around the World, Lilith's*

Cave: Jewish Tales of the Supernatural and *Gabriel's Palace: Jewish Mystical Tales.* He has also edited three major anthologies. *Reimagining the Bible: The Storytelling of the Rabbis,* was a finalist for the National Jewish Book Award for 1999. In addition, Schwartz has also published twelve children's books. His latest children's book, *Gathering Sparks,* won the 2011 Sydney Taylor Book Award. His book *Tree of Souls: The Mythology of Judaism,* won the National Jewish Book Award in 2005. His most recent book is *Leaves from the Garden of Eden: One Hundred Classic Jewish Tales.*

Joe Schwartz is a published writer with one book to his credit. *Joe's Black T-Shirt: Short Stories About St. Louis* was published in August of 2009. Since then he has been reviewed by the *Riverfront Times,* interviewed on KDHX radio, and had a one-man book signing at the Mad Art Gallery. His entire book is available for free on www.Scribd.com.   Since December 2009, the book has been visited over four thousand times.

Miriam Schwartz has studied at Hebrew University in Jerusalem, New College in Sarasota, Florida and Ben Gurion University of the Negev in Beersheva, Israel, focusing on Middle Eastern Studies and Conflict Resolution. After living in Israel for two years, she recently returned to the States.

Rachel Schwartz is a Professor in the School of Public Health at Saint Louis University. A dual citizen of the United States and Israel, she lived, studied, and worked in Israel for 14 years where much of her family still resides. She completed graduate studies at Washington University (including an MFA in Creative Writing and a doctorate) and worked there, and then received an additional degree in Biosecurity and Disaster preparedness from Saint Louis University. She is married to Greg Evans, and has a daughter, Maayan.

Shira Schwartz is a graduate of Ladue Horton Watkins High School, Class of 1997, and a graduate of Oberlin College, Class of 2001. She received her bachelor's degree in both Jewish Studies and Women's Studies, with a minor in Religion. Her poetry has appeared in *Crescendo, Oberlin Alumni Magazine, First Harvest, New Harvest* and *The St. Louis Jewish Light.*

Tsila Schwartz is a native of Jerusalem who makes her home in St. Louis. She is a folk artist who specializes in *Ketubot* (Jewish Wedding Contracts) and other Jewish texts. She has also illustrated the book *Rooms of the Soul,* and her calligraphy appears in the books *Elijah's Violin* and *Leaves from the*

Garden of Eden.

Bettina Schwarzman lived in St Louis from 1995 to 2003. She now lives in Bangor, Maine, where she is working on a book about how to raise Jewish children in a not very Jewish environment. She lives with her husband who is a congregational rabbi, and those children who are still at home. The whole family remembers their stay in St Louis very fondly.

Ronit Sherwin is the founding Executive Director of Nishmah: The St. Louis Jewish Women's Project and has worked as a Jewish educator in the St. Louis community for ten years, teaching families, teens and adults of all ages. As native of Cleveland, Ohio, Ronit completed a Bachelor of Science in Education from the Ohio State University and Master's degree in Theological Studies from Harvard University. Ronit is also the glowing mother of boy-girl twins, Natan and Batya.

Nathan Simon came to St. Louis in 1951 to attend Washington University Medical School and has lived here since. He is a psychoanalyst in private practice and a Clinical Professor of Psychiatry at St. Louis University. Among his scientific publications are articles on abortion, adoption, medical care delivery, heart disease and (a book) on ICU stress. His poetry has been published in *New Millenium Writings, Journal of Acadia Friends*, and *TAP*. A memoir appeared in *CCAR Journal* in 2006.

Pat Lorraine Simons and her husband, Dr. Paul Simons, have two sons, Daniel and David, and four grandchildren. A number of Pat's stories and poems have been published in literary journals, as well as in magazines and anthologies for children.

Pamela Singer has lived in the St. Louis area for a quarter-century, after studying writing at the Iowa Writers Workshop and at Trinity College in Wales. She currently works for the federal government and will receive a Master's in Public Policy from the University of Missouri-St. Louis in May, 2011.

Jason Sommer is author of three poetry collections: *Lifting the Stone*, from Forest Books, London, and from University of Chicago Press, *Other People's Troubles* and *The Man Who Sleeps in My Office*. Sommer has won an Anna Davidson Rosenberg Award for poems on the Jewish Experience and read his work at the National Holocaust Museum. He has held fellowships in poetry at Stanford University, at the Bread Loaf and

Sewanee writer's conferences, as well as a Whiting Foundation Writer's Award. He teaches literature and writing at Fontbonne University in St. Louis.

Judith Stix is the author of *Woman/Years* (collected poems 1956-2007). She has written essays, reviews, and contributions to Jewish history and genealogy and two full-length biographies, *Bessie Lowenhaupt from Life*, about the St. Louis Jewish painter (1881-1968); and *Naturalist in Mexico: Thomas Baillie MacDougall, Twentieth Century Romantic.*

Maria Szapszewicz is a Holocaust survivor born in Poland who came to the US in 1959. She survived ghettos, slave labor camps and two concentration camps. Maria is a docent and speaker at the Holocaust Museum and Learning Center and a speaker at universities, schools and churches. She has published a CD, *Memories and Dreams* and a book, *For the People I Loved and Can't Forget.* She was honored as a Women of Distinction by the Girl Scouts in 2010.

Rabbi Susan Talve is the founding rabbi of Central Reform Congregation in the City of St. Louis, Missouri.

Jane O. Wayne's fourth poetry collection, *The Other Place You Live* (Mayapple Press) was published in 2010. Her work has appeared in magazines such as *Poetry, Ploughshares, Iowa Review, The Massachusetts Review* and *The American Scholar.*

Sharon Weissman writes poetry as tributes/memorials and as a method of coping with the illnesses and deaths she has experienced in her previous work as an oncology social worker and in her current job as a hospice chaplain. She is married to Alan and has two sons and one grandson. She is an active member of Congregation Shaare Emeth

Renee Winter is a native St. Louisan, who lived in St. Louis until 2004, when her husband (Paul Roth) accepted a position at University of California Santa Cruz. She has been practicing law for over 30 years and loves to write. She is the mother of two daughters and has two granddaughters.

Randy Zimring lives in Chesterfield with his wife, Muriel Goldenhersh Zimring. He is the father of Megan and Joe and his hobby is fly fishing.